M000228932

Rimsky-Korsakov
LETTERS TO HIS FAMILY AND FRIENDS

Rimsky-Korsakov
LETTERS TO HIS FAMILY AND FRIENDS

Tatiana Rimsky-Korsakov

TRANSLATED FROM THE RUSSIAN BY
Lilia Timofeeva

EDITED BY
Malcolm J. Crocker
AND
Margarita Maksotskaya

AMADEUS
PRESS
An Imprint of Hal Leonard Corporation

Copyright © 2016 by Malcolm Crocker and Margarita Maksotskaya

All rights reserved. No part of this book may be reproduced in any form, without written permission, except by a newspaper or magazine reviewer who wishes to quote brief passages in connection with a review.

Published in 2016 by Amadeus Press
An Imprint of Hal Leonard Corporation
7777 West Bluemound Road
Milwaukee, WI 53213

Trade Book Division Editorial Offices
33 Plymouth St., Montclair, NJ 07042

All photographs are from the Rimsky-Korsakov family archive and appear courtesy of the Rimsky-Korsakov family.

Printed in the United States of America

Book design by Lynn Bergesen

Library of Congress Cataloging-in-Publication Data

Rimskaia-Korsakova, T. V. (Tat'iana Vladimirovna), author.
  Rimsky-Korsakov : letters to his family and friends / Tatiana Rimsky-Korsakov ; translated from the Russian by Lilia Timofeeva ; edited by Malcolm J. Crocker and Margarita Maksotskaya.
      pages cm
  "This book is a combined translation of the two following books in Russian, both by Tatiana Rimsky-Korsakov: "N. A. Rimsky-Korsakov v semie (iz semeynoy perepiski)" – St. Petersburg: Kompozitor, 1999; and "Detstvo i unost' N. A. Rimskogo-Korsakova (iz semeynoy perepiski)" – St. Petersburg: Kompozitor, 1995"—Supplied by publisher.
  Includes index.
  ISBN 978-1-57467-454-5
  1. Rimsky-Korsakov, Nikolay, 1844-1908. 2. Rimsky-Korsakov, Nikolay, 1844-1908—Family. 3. Rimsky-Korsakov, Nikolay, 1844-1908—Friends and associates. 4. Composers—Russia—Biography. 5. Rimsky-Korsakov, Nikolay, 1844-1908—Correspondence. I. Timofeeva, Lilia, translator. II. Crocker, Malcolm J., editor. III. Maksotskaya, Margarita, editor. IV. Rimsky-Korsakov, Tatiana, 1915-2006. N.A. Rimskii-Korsakov v sem'e. Translation of (work): V. Rimsky-Korsakov, Tatiana, 1915-2006. Detstvo i iunost N.A. Rimskogo-Korsakova. Translation of (work): VI. Title.
  ML410.R52R473 2015
  780.92—dc23
  [B]
                        2015016228

www.amadeuspress.com

Contents

Editor's Note

I first made contact with the Rimsky-Korsakov family through meetings with Andrey Vladimirovich Rimsky-Korsakov, grandson of the composer Nikolay, in 1977 in Madrid and again in 1991 in Moscow. He introduced me to his sister Tatiana Vladimirovna Rimsky-Korsakov (1912–2006), who lived in St. Petersburg. In the 1990s and 2000s I made several visits to that city for an ongoing collaboration with scientific colleagues. I would normally meet her each time, and we occasionally went to hear one of her grandfather's operas or a performance of his music at his St. Petersburg apartment, which she had carefully restored as a museum.

Tatiana Rimsky-Korsakov was a strong advocate of her grandfather's music and had also restored his summer home (dacha) in Loubensk, to which I went twice at her invitation. During my St. Petersburg visits, I learned she had written a book titled *Rimsky-Korsakov's Childhood and Youth*, published in Russian in 1995, covering the composer's life up to age twenty-one (1844–1865). A second book, *Rimsky-Korsakov in His Family*, covering the rest of his life until his death in 1908, remained unpublished, since with the Soviet Union's collapse, the publisher faced financial difficulties. I was pleased to help get this book published in Russian in 1999.

Publication of this new book in English was only achieved with Tatiana Rimsky-Korsakov's kind cooperation and the dedicated work of our translator, Lilia Timofeeva. Tatiana condensed her entire first book to form the first two chapters; her second book, with minimal abridgments, forms the rest of the current book.

I have worked extensively with Tatiana Rimsky-Korsakov, Lilia Timofeeva, and linguist Margarita Maksotskaya to improve the text and bring this book into publishable form. Ms. Maksotskaya has helped immensely in improving the translation and adding notes to explain biographical and other details.

The main contribution of this book is the large number of previously unpublished letters lodged in the Russian Institute of Art History in St. Petersburg. Many letters are between the composer and his wife. Others are to or from his mother, his children, his confidants Belsky and Kruglikov, and other friends and colleagues, including Balakirev, Borodin, Cui, Lyadov, Musorgsky, Stravinsky, and Tchaikovsky.

When Rimsky-Korsakov began writing his autobiography, *My Musical Life*, at age fifty, he admitted he had already forgotten many early details. Nevertheless, his wife edited and published the memoir in 1909, a year after his death. Vasily Yastrebtsev's *Reminiscences of Rimsky-Korsakov* (published in English in 1985) adds many details, but it only begins in 1891 when Yastrebtsev became a frequent visitor to the composer and his circle.

The present book is a window into the life of a cultured Russian family when Imperial Russia was at its zenith, and it fills in much about the composer's career missing from his autobiography and Yastrebtsev's reminiscences. We learn here about Rimsky-Korsakov's passionate early interest in music, especially that of Glinka, and his youthful attempts at composition. There are stories from the musical soirées at the Purgold home, where Rimsky-Korsakov, Musorgsky, and others developed their musical talents and tried out their own works, and where Nikolay met his wife-to-be, Nadezhda Purgold, herself an accomplished pianist and composer.

We learn first-hand about Rimsky-Korsakov's troubles with official censors and his difficult relations with Balakirev. We see how he was both criticized and praised for editing and producing versions of operas by Borodin, Dargomizhsky, and Musorgsky. We read of his involvement with student protests after the 1905 revolution, and his fall from official favor. Due to his outspoken advocacy for political reform, his most famous opera, *The Golden Cockerel*, was never performed during his lifetime.

Margarita Maksotskaya and I are greatly indebted to Robert W. Oldani of Arizona State University, Philip Ross Bullock of Oxford University, and James Krukones of John Carroll University, who made many valuable comments and corrections. Merton Shatzkin, Vlad Morosan, and Paul Serotsky provided valuable assistance with historical, cultural, and religious matters. To Ruth C. Crocker we express profound thanks for her considerable support in reviewing the manuscript, creating epigraphs and titles, and helping with the index and stylistic matters. We are also in great debt to our editors, Barbara Norton and Jessica Burr, without whose skilled work this book would not have been possible.

Malcolm J. Crocker
12 May 2015

Preface

This book is based on the correspondence housed in the Rimsky-Korsakov family archive of letters. The main part of the Rimsky-Korsakov family archive can be found in the collections of the Russian Institute of the History of Art in St. Petersburg, Russia. The first chapter of the book covers the history of the Rimsky-Korsakov family and the composer's early years in his hometown of Tikhvin as well as his years at the Naval College in St. Petersburg. The rest of it describes the period of Rimsky-Korsakov's life between the performance of his First Symphony in December 1865, when he was twenty-two years old, and his death in March 1908. The book also sheds new light on the composer's wife, Nadezhda Purgold, and her family.

The Rimsky-Korsakov family was exceptionally loving, based on mutual respect and love and the parents' anxiety for all their children's well-being. In his letters to his wife, Nadezhda, the composer always asks about their children. In the book you will also find the correspondence between Rimsky-Korsakov and his mother, Sophia Vasilyevna. From his childhood, the composer was surrounded by his mother's love, and he savored all the love and affection they shared in their letters to each other.

After the Second World War, Vladimir Nikolayevich Rimsky-Korsakov (1882–1970), the youngest son of Nikolay Rimsky-Korsakov, worked on publishing the correspondence between Nikolay and his wife, Nadezhda. He also left detailed comments about his efforts on his unfinished book about his father.

Vladimir Nikolayevich Rimsky-Korsakov began to write *Reminiscences* to tell the story of his family and its head, Nikolay Rimsky-Korsakov. Vladimir collected many materials and started to write some chapters of *Reminiscences*. However, fate did not let him fulfill his goal. He was working hard on his book *Reminiscences* during the last years of his life; but when he was eighty-eight years old, he was killed in an accident on a street in St. Petersburg. Fortunately, Vladimir's work was not lost. Some of his material is used in this book, which is dedicated to his memory by the author, Tatiana Rimsky-Korsakov.

This book includes excerpts from 516 letters from the correspondence between Nikolay and Nadezhda Rimsky-Korsakov. Only a few selected letters from this group have been published previously, in the journal *Musical Heritage*, vol. 2 (1954). These letters were the ones that have the most value for the history of Russian music. More than a hundred additional letters included in the present book involve the correspondence between the Rimsky-Korsakov parents and their children, and with their relatives and friends. Semyon Kruglikov was the composer's closest friend.

Tatiana Rimsky-Korsakov

1
Beginnings

Operas make me love music so much that it is impossible for me to love it more than I do.

—Rimsky-Korsakov (age fourteen) to his parents, 4 May 1858

Origins of the Rimsky-Korsakov Family

The roots of the modest Rimsky-Korsakov family, into which Nikolay Rimsky-Korsakov was born in Tikhvin,[1] can be traced back to the late fourteenth century. The first recorded event occurs on 9 January 1390,[2] when Ventseslav Korsak, a son of Zhigmont Korsak, arrived in Moscow from Lithuania. He came to serve the Grand Prince of Moscow, Vasily Dmitrievich, as a member of his retinue and was accompanied by his fiancée, Sophia, a daughter of the Lithuanian Prince Vitautas. Soon after Korsak's arrival, he and his descendants became known as Korsakovs. By the middle of the seventeenth century, the first ten generations of the family tree consisted of several branches. The family members were granted estates in Novgorod, Kaluga, Smolensk, and other regions of Russia for various services. The family members had spread outside the province of Moscow. Many of them were rewarded for bravery and courage in wars.

Three hundred years after Ventseslav Korsak came to Moscow, the Korsakov family had grown, and several members of the family claimed that there were some Korsakovs who did not possess the right to bear the family name. In order to maintain the purity of the line, the three brothers of the oldest branch—Gregory, Fyodor, and Voin—pleaded with Tsar Fyodor Alekseyevich to grant them and fifteen other family members the favor of being named Rimsky-Korsakovs. They wished to be distinct from the other Korsakovs, since they believed they were descendants of Roman subjects. This petition was granted by an order of the tsar on 15 May 1677. Only six of these petitioners continued this family line, which has been preserved to the present day. Nikita Guriyevich, father of the fourth branch of the family, to which the Tikhvin family of Rimsky-Korsakov belonged, was directly descended from Ventseslav Korsak via nine generations. Unfortunately, there is little information about them. Jakov Nikitich (1679–1734), a representative of the tenth generation, first served in the Novgorod regiment. In the time of Peter the Great he was appointed mayor of Koporie and subsequently promoted to a judgeship. Later, in 1711, he was designated vice governor of the In-German territory, later named as the Petersburg province.

Voin (1702–1757), the eldest son of Jakov Nikitich, became the first member of the Rimsky-Korsakov family to serve in the Russian navy. In the times of the Empress Elisabeth, Voin, one of the empress's favorites, was put in command of the entire Kronstadt squadron.[3] At the end of his days, he held the rank of vice admiral in the Russian navy. Voin had three sons. However, Pyotr (17??–1815) was the only one who continued the line. In contrast to his father, Pyotr did not distinguish himself in government service. He lived on his Nikolskoe estate in the Tikhvin district of Novgorod province. Andrey, the first son of Pyotr, was born in Nikolskoe. A small notebook belonging to Pyotr has survived, and on the first page it contains the following record made in the owner's hand: "This year 1784 on 7 August, God's servant Andrey, the son of Pyotr Rimsky-Korsakov, was born." Nikolay Rimsky-Korsakov (1793–1848), Pyotr's other son, followed the example of his grandfather and spent his entire life in naval service. He circumnavigated the globe from 1823 to 1826 on board the sloop *Predpriatie* (*Enterprise*) under the command of O. E. Kotseby. During the journey, the Russian sailors discovered a group of islands and atolls in the Pacific Ocean now known as the Marshall Islands. They named one of the atolls Rongelap Rimsky-Korsakov in honor of Nikolay Rimsky-Korsakov. In 1842 Nikolay Rimsky-Korsakov was appointed to the position of assistant to the director of the Petersburg Naval College; a year later he became the head of this educational establishment. Nikolay Rimsky-Korsakov did much to improve the training and education of future naval officers.

Andrey and Sophia Rimsky-Korsakov; Voin

Today little would be known about Andrey Rimsky-Korsakov, who, in the course of time, became the head of the Tikhvin line of the Rimsky-Korsakov family, if copies of his letters, which he collected and made into a book titled *Book of Correspondence or Friends' Letters*, had not survived. There he made extracts, sometimes rather lengthy, of his own letters as well as those of his correspondents. The most valuable is a copy of Andrey Rimsky-Korsakov's letter to his friend A. D. Komovsky. It was written in 1848, in Andrey's old age, and it includes his detailed autobiography. Andrey began his government service when he was seventeen years old in the office of the Foreign Ministry and gradually made this into his career. At the beginning of 1821, Andrey Rimsky-Korsakov arrived in the province of Orel, where he became engaged to Sophia, a daughter of Vasily Skaryatin, a rich landlord and one of his servants. Sophia Skaryatina was born on 15 September 1802. She was brought up in the family of her father and received an excellent education. She studied French from her early years and could speak it fluently and write it well. She was taught to play the piano, to sing, and do needlework.

Vasily Skaryatin seemed to consider Andrey Rimsky-Korsakov, whose social status was not very high and whose income was rather small, a bad match for his daughter. Therefore, Andrey had to elope with his fiancée to St. Petersburg, where they were married. His unlawful marriage was an obstacle to further government service, and Andrey was obliged to go on indefinite leave. Soon after their wedding the newlyweds left for Tikhvin and took accommodations in a house built at the beginning of the nineteenth century, while Pyotr was still alive. Their first son was born on 14 July 1822 and was named Voin, after Pyotr's great-grandfather. At the end of 1827 Andrey resumed his government service and was appointed vice governor of Novgorod province and promoted to the rank of active state secretary. He only stayed in this office for a year. After leaving the service in Novgorod, Andrey settled in St. Petersburg, and in 1829 he became the director of the Commerce Bank, where he worked for two years. At that time Voin was sent to the naval school of the Alexander Corps, located in Tsarskoye Selo (not far from St. Petersburg). After studying there for three years he entered the Petersburg Naval College and hence continued to live apart from his parents.

In 1831 Andrey received a new appointment to the post of governor of Volyn, and he and his wife went to Zhitomir. It was an especially hard period of his life. The administrative work was complicated because the governor had to deal with the Polish nobility, who were in disgrace after the recent Polish uprising.[4] Andrey's tactfulness, kindness, tenderness, and liberal attitude toward the rebellious Polish people caused him to be reported to the tsar as a weak governor. On these grounds, he was completely dismissed from the position in 1835 without being given a new appointment. After his dismissal, Andrey and Sophia Rimsky-Korsakov came back to Tikhvin. The house, a little piece of land, and a very modest pension constituted the family's total wealth. They had a few serfs, but Andrey liberated them one by one, and the family hired some of the former serfs as servants. Although Sophia was a daughter of a wealthy property owner, no dowry was provided for her marriage. This might be because Sophia was an illegitimate child or because she had run away from home and had married against her father's will.

At Tikhvin

After Andrey settled in Tikhvin, he strove to find himself. Masonic ideas appealed strongly to him. He considered self-edification a "perpetual learning process in which everyone acts as his own teacher." Andrey started to write a book titled *Pieces of Advice for Healing My Scarcity of Moral Education*, in which he wrote various ideas, citations, and poems along with his own ideas in Russian and French. The table of contents of this book, which contains 152 sections, includes the subtitles *To Carry Out My Own Lawful Duties Zealously*, *Love Not to Possess Anything Excessively*, and *Without Distinction*. In addition to this book, he always kept a separate notebook within easy reach titled *Selected Poems of A. S. Pushkin*.

Sophia Rimsky-Korsakov devoted herself completely to her husband and family. Yet she did not avoid simple Tikhvin entertainments such as local concerts, plays, and balls. Sophia was an inquisitive woman who was eager for everything that made life beautiful and who strove for plenty within the limits of their way of life. Her favorite reading consisted of novels and poetry. Her albums are full of poems copied down from various sources. She was fond of animals, so there were always several dogs in the Tikhvin house, some canaries flying around in the rooms, and a big parrot as well. She paid special attention to her flowers, which she took care of either in the house or in the garden by herself. She was often busy with her favorite activity—fine needlework.

The marriage of Andrey Rimsky-Korsakov and Sophia was happy. Although she was eighteen years younger than her husband, she did not let the difference in their ages interfere with her happiness. As one of the Tikhvin inhabitants remembered, Sophia was certainly a pretty woman and undoubtedly very intelligent, educated, and tactful. Andrey was always courteous and neatly dressed, and he had perfect manners. He was considered to be a liberal. He avoided close communication with the local nobility and lived unpretentiously. Tikhvin society respected him, and he acted as a justice of the peace in settling the issues of those who came to seek his advice.

After finishing his studies at the Naval College in 1836, the couple's elder son, Voin, devoted himself completely to naval service. He was frequently away at sea for extended periods and could visit his parents only from time to time. Sophia was over forty and Andrey almost sixty when all of a sudden a significant event took place in their life: it turned out that Sophia had become pregnant again. It troubled her very much to have another baby at that age, and after a twenty-two-year interval. However, she regained her spirits after she had a striking dream in which an angel descended from heaven and extended a brightly lit candle to her. It made such an impression on the deeply religious Sophia that she interpreted it as a sign from heaven bidding her to give birth to a new boy. She told some of her friends about her dream and illustrated it in her album.

Voin learned about the coming event from his father's letter about five months before Nikolay's birth. He responded immediately:

> Your letter struck me. I am so astonished that I cannot collect my thoughts to express the feelings it has aroused [in me]. I think now that a new, unknown to me, feeling has been growing inside me. It seems to be not a brother's love but a much more tender feeling, which is more affectionate, and resembles the love of a parent. My dear Mama and Papa, I will do my part to bring up the baby with all my heart as if it were my son.

Nikolay Rimsky-Korsakov, 6 March 1844

The birth of Nika (as the newborn Nikolay was called) caused his parents, who after such a long time were unaccustomed to looking after a baby, to experience very tender feelings for the new member of the family. In March 1844 Andrey Rimsky-Korsakov made the first entry in his diary: "Nika was born on 6 March at 4:53 p.m." A further entry reads: "Mama breastfed him for nine days. But on the eve of 15 March, due to her inability to carry on, she trusted this to Fedosia, a wet nurse." Three weeks later Nika was baptized. Voin came to Tikhvin to participate. In the same diary Andrey Rimsky-Korsakov made the following entry: "On 27 March at 7 p.m. he was christened. Voin was his godfather."

Nika was a healthy and lively child. Voin was afraid that the boy's playfulness might disturb his parents and wrote in one of his letters to them: "Tell Nika that if he doesn't stop producing so much noise, I will send you some trash to stuff in his mouth." When Nika was three years old he received a toy drum as a present. It certainly added more noise to the Tikhvin house. However, the toy was beneficial for the boy, since he developed a sense of rhythm with it. While Andrey was playing the piano, Nika would take his toy and beat the drum, keeping time with the music and following all the changes in time and measure that his father created on purpose.

Influenced by the hardship of naval service, Voin believed that his brother should become accustomed to working hard. He wrote to his parents: "Make some kind of work clothes for him and let him play in the garden. Let him dig earth and become messy, he can easily be washed clean at any moment, and our Nika will be as neat in the evening as he was muddy in the morning. I think the boy should not be afraid of getting dirty." When this letter was written, dated April 1848, Nika was just four years old. The boy's games and surroundings were not those of an urban child. The Rimsky-Korsakovs' house was located on a high bank of the Tikhvinka River. The Great Monastery of the Assumption was located across the river opposite the house, and behind it was a large garden. Next to the house, up the Tikhvinka, which was navigable at that time, there was a sluice through which waters rushed, creating a great noise. There was a high hill covered with woods nearby. The house where Nika grew up was a one-story wooden building with an attic and several rooms facing the river and the monastery. This house did not look like those owned by the bourgeoisie or by merchants, of which there were many in Tikhvin. It was different and was even called a "manor house" by the locals. The house had a nice garden, and beyond it there were fields and a primeval forest with the picturesque Tsarina Lake. People said that one of the wives of Tsar Ivan the Terrible who was imprisoned in the Tikhvin Convent by his order had been hidden from the Swedes on the bank of the lake.

Sophia adored nature and inculcated in her son a taste for beauty from his early years. The child listened with delight to birdsong and liked copying it. He learned the names of many plants and observed butterflies, dragonflies, and insects. He romped around as much as any healthy child. The boy also became interested in building model ships, in which he was undoubtedly influenced by his elder brother's occupation and his life near the river. In his turn, Voin advised his parents to accustom his brother to bathe in the river and to start teaching him how to swim. "You should make use of the benefits of the summer to make Nika strong. Could you please give him as much exercise as possible to develop his physical strength and power? Can he walk for a long time?" the elder son asked his parents.

Andrey wrote about their life in Tikhvin to one of his friends: "The husband lives in harmony with his wife in the family. They take comfort in their elder son's intelligence, conduct and behavior; they are very pleased with his state of health and intelligence of the youngster." Indeed, Nika made them proud. He started learning French words when he was five and a half; at the same time he started reading in Russian, and by six he could read in French as well.

Early Education

After considerable deliberation, his parents decided on their son's future. He was to enter the Naval College and become a naval officer like his brother, uncle, and great-grandfather before him. First the parents educated Nika themselves. This duty fell mainly to Sophia. She taught him how to read and write, and it was from her that he received his earliest music education. The family atmosphere was suited to it. Andrey Rimsky-Korsakov often sat at the piano playing without any music. He liked to play various pieces from operas of the times by Méhul, Rossini, Mozart, Cherubini, Verstovsky, and Glinka.[5] Sophia Rimsky-Korsakov sang romances as well as Russian and Polish folk songs that she had heard in Zhitomir.[6] She also sang lullabies to her son Nika when he was very little, songs he remembered years later. Nika was able to remember melodies when he was just two years old. He turned out to have perfect pitch and joined in singing with his father when Andrey played the piano. By the age of six Nika was able to play melodies and pieces harmoniously from his father's repertoire. He had learned the names of the notes and was able to identify all of the notes played on the piano correctly from another room. Ekaterina Unkovskaia, a neighbor, was hired to teach the six-year-old Nika to play the piano. The usual lessons included scales, exercises, and simple pieces, which the little pupil did not seem to like very much. To entertain himself he accompanied his mother's parrot, which had been taught to sing a simple tune.

At the end of 1850 Voin arrived in Tikhvin, where he spent more than a month with his parents and his little brother. He learned about Nika's progress in his studies and also about his behavior, and after returning to Kronstadt he wrote: "I think you should remind my brother Nika that he is grown-up enough and should take care of himself and that he should start to behave as follows: try to refrain from crying. I am sure he will not cry at all this year, otherwise Mama would certainly agree to keep records of such occasions in her book and report the total monthly figure to me."

When Voin visited Tikhvin, little Nika rained down millions of questions on him about ships and naval terms, leading the elder brother to call the younger a "question mark." Voin advised his parents in his letters: "You could give commissions to him like going to buy some small things at *gostiny dvor* or at the market.[7] Believe me, the child will appreciate it instinctively, and it will naturally develop in him a sense of self-esteem and sense of duty—true essentials in a man's life—without the need for tiresome and dry lessons." In Voin's opinion, the sense of duty, the sense of responsibility, and the feeling of self-esteem were essential for the life and activity of all men at that time.

His parents taught Nika not only the Russian language but also arithmetic, history, and drawing. Voin approved of all of these studies. He also encouraged his brother's piano lessons. At that time, in addition to an old instrument, a new piano was bought for the Tikhvin house, and Voin wrote from Kronstadt: "I am very glad about the fact that you have purchased a new instrument. It should allow Nika to develop a new talent that will not be in vain." When Nikolay was about eight years old he was given a new music teacher. They studied transcriptions of Italian operas for the piano as well as Meyerbeer's *Le prophète* and also played a Beethoven sonata for four hands. These music lessons began to have a beneficial effect on Nika's musical development.

Suddenly Voin's life took a new turn. He wrote to his parents: "I am designated to take part in an expedition heading to the Amur and Japan.[8] I am appointed as the captain of a schooner that will be bought in England for that purpose." The English schooner *Fearless* was purchased and, renamed the *East*, set off on a voyage to the Far East under the command of Voin Rimsky-Korsakov. The objectives of the expedition were both scientific and diplomatic. The voyage lasted almost five years. During it Voin visited the eastern parts of Russia, Japan, and China. He sent letters to Tikhvin from all the ports of call describing his experience and impressions in detail. They were read aloud, and one can imagine the considerable effect they had on little Nika.

When Nika was ten years old he developed a keen interest in astronomy. His mother had long before pointed out to him the beauty of the sky. It was a pleasure for him to look at the sky during the August nights. When he was eleven Nika studied the popular astronomy lectures of S. I. Zelueni, a lieutenant commander. Now it was Nika who taught his mother when and where they could observe this or that star, planet, or constellation in the sky.

Later Olga Fel, who was a wonderful pianist, was appointed as Nika's music teacher. She took note of the boy's talent and suggested that she teach the boy herself. Although she was not a teacher by profession, their lessons were successful. Later on Olga reminisced that during his lessons, while he was playing the pieces of music, the boy sometimes added some notes himself or did not finish the piece as written, saying that it was prettier like this or that something in the piece was superficial. Even if she agreed with his opinion in her mind, she used to tell him, in order to keep discipline, that he could not do so: "You are not better than the composer, so kindly, please be good enough to play it as it is written."

Olga insisted that the boy be taught music seriously. By that time he had developed a considerable repertoire. The boy played music for four hands and took part in domestic musical parties. Nika found the printed music of *The Songs of an Orphan* from Glinka's opera *A Life for the Tsar*. He enjoyed that music very much. Nikolay studied this music all by himself. Without the knowledge of the adults, Nika wrote a duet for voice and piano for the children's poem *The Butterfly*. Then he undertook composing an overture for four hands to be played on the piano. Even if his parents noticed Nika's efforts to compose, they did not pay much attention to them. He himself thought of his compositions as a game. The impressions on him of his brother's letters about his naval service overshadowed everything else.

The day for Nika's departure from his parents was approaching. He tore up his early musical compositions one day on a whim. His future naval profession, the ocean, which he knew only from books and his brother's letters, occupied his dreams. Music no longer interested him much. Andrey Rimsky-Korsakov could not even imagine that his son would become a musician one day.

On 26 July 1856 Nika's father brought him to Petersburg. By 20 August 1856 all of his entrance examinations were over, and the following record was made in the Register Book of the Naval College enrollees: "accepted." Nikolay's examination records contain the following assessments of his knowledge: "Russian: reading—very good; writing—good; Russian grammar—good enough; Arithmetic: program for his age—very good, knows more than required; Geography—very good; French: reading—very good; translation—can speak fluently." The results of his medical examination state briefly: "Generally healthy."

Naval College, St. Petersburg, 1856–1861

On 24 August 1856 Nikolay Rimsky-Korsakov entered the Naval College at the age of twelve and stayed there to live and study for five and a half years. The same day, Andrey Rimsky-Korsakov went back to Tikhvin. Accustomed to the coziness of his Tikhvin home and his parents' love, Nikolay found the official atmosphere of the Naval College cold and unwelcoming. On 28 August 1856 Nikolay wrote his first letter home:

> My dear Mama and Papa,
>
> By this time Papa will have arrived home and everything will have become as it was before. I am getting used to my new life in the college. We get up at 5:30 a.m.; around 6 we have tea; at 7 we do our homework; at 8 lessons begin; at 11 they are finished; at 1 we have lunch; after lunch if the weather is fine we go for a walk on Vasilyevsky Island;[9] at 3 we have classes again; at 8 we have dinner; and at 9 we go to bed. This order is repeated every day. I have not been beaten yet. One cadet tried to beat me but he failed; the others do not beat me, just push or pinch or pick on me from time to time, but I do not care.
>
> Good-bye, my Mama and Papa. Give me your blessings.
>
> Loving you,
>
> Your son Nika

This letter started the correspondence between Nika and his parents. They carefully preserved all of their younger son's letters, which allow us to follow the major episodes in his life at that time.

All the naval cadets were assessed weekly in every subject using a twelve-point scale. Nikolay wrote home on 9 September 1856: "For the time being my studies are going rather well. This week I got, in arithmetic—11, algebra—11,

French—10, geography—10, Russian—8.[…] We have begun to learn English. I already know a few words and can make sentences. So far I think English is very simple."

In addition to his regular studies, Nikolay took piano lessons from one Ulikh, a violoncellist, hired by his brother, who considered piano lessons necessary for the general education of his younger brother. Unfortunately, Ulikh turned out to be a second-rate pianist and tutor. In September Nikolay wrote home: "Today we were taken into the grand hall where we were formed up into two ranks: one for good pupils for the week and the other for lazy ones. The head and Zeleny thanked and praised the diligent students and reprimanded the slothful ones. So far this week I have been working hard in three subjects: history, French and Russian; my average grade was 10, and my name was listed once on the 'praise' board."

On 11 November 1856 Nika wrote: "Upon waking up at night and looking through the window, I saw to my pleasure stars and constellations, in particular: Orion, Betelgeuse, Rigel, Sirius, Procyon, Castor, Jacob's Belt, Pollux, and all those stars I admired with you, Mama, in Tikhvin last winter when we were looking through the window of the living room." Another letter of his, dated 2 January 1857, says: "At about 4 p.m. I saw Venus; it was to the right of Jupiter, but much further to the south than it had been. Venus seemed to be twice as big. I also saw Orion, Sirius, Aldebaran, the Pleiades, Canis Minor, and some others. I hope you still remember these constellations."

When spring came Nikolay became homesick and yearned for his favorite places in Tikhvin. On 28 April 1857 he sent the following letter home:

May will start soon. The weather is perfect. The first grass has appeared in the garden of the Marine Nikola Church. I suppose so far there will have been buds on the currant bushes and the violets will be blooming in Tikhvin. And I think tulips and daffodils will be in blossom soon. I wish I could go for a walk far beyond that "red" meadow. It would be so nice and pleasant. I imagine that the next time I come to Tikhvin, my first pleasure, walks…I can imagine the wild strawberries, raspberries, mushrooms; you, Mama, cooking jelly in the garden or watering flowers in the evenings; the bathhouse and my bath there with Papa; I recall the large garden: the fir tree, birches, strawberries, currants, raspberries, rowans, willows, acacias, flower and potato beds, cabbages, potatoes, beets, fennel, rutabagas, turnips, carrots, and everything that I liked so much. I recollect the

Ivan-grass growing behind the kitchen garden, and lilacs, tulips, daffodils, violets, carnations, dahlias, and other flowers; butterflies, insects, bees, flies, gadflies, mosquitoes, bumblebees, dragonflies, grasshoppers, etc. I imagine all this as if I were in Tikhvin. I wish I could be there sooner. I do not know if I will manage to hear the nightingale that sings behind the hospital. Could you write to me, please, if the bird-cherry trees, birches, aspens, oaks, elders, maples, lindens, acacias, currant bushes, and other plants are flowering? I think in the evenings you may hear the singing of martins, robins, larks, and other birds. I hope to see all of these and listen to them as soon as I arrive in Tikhvin. But seeing you is the most important thing for me, for sure. Good-bye, my dear Mama and Papa. I'm asking for your blessings.

Loving you,
Your son…

His dream came true. Nikolay left for Tikhvin to spend the summer there with his parents. He enjoyed the warm atmosphere of his parents' home again and his life in the midst of nature. It was very hard for him to part with all of his favorite things again in the middle of August when the time came to go back to the College. At that time the railroad did not yet reach Tikhvin, so they had to ride to Chudovo,[10] where they boarded a train, which arrived in St. Petersburg the following day. Nika described his journey to his parents as follows: "We arrived in Chudovo at 3 at night. We got on the train at 4:30, and we reached Petersburg at 8. I saw so many stars on my way: Ursa, Arcturus, Capella, the Pole Star, Altair, Vega, Deneb, Hydrus, Ophiuchus, Scorpius, Gemini, Jupiter, and Venus; the last two were shining very brightly. While watching them I remembered you, Mama and Papa."

Parting from his parents sowed some sad thoughts in Nikolay's mind about the necessity of living away from his family home and natural surroundings, and he could not get rid of these thoughts. The boy wrote again to Tikhvin:

These thoughts are as annoying as gnats, and require a net to be fixed as if against mosquitoes, like a net for my other thoughts, which could be placed in my head instead of it being like an open window. [...] Mama, I wish you could look at the stars more often so you will remember me. And you, Papa, I suppose you have stopped playing the piano, but I would prefer it if you didn't. I would listen to it every day. Would I be so lucky to hear it from here? Do you remember how we used to sing together? Could you write to me more often? Good-bye, my dearest Mama and Papa. I'm begging for your blessings. I remain loving you heartily,

Yours affectionately,

Your son, Nika Rimsky-Korsakov,

S. Petersburg, 15 Aug. 1857

The New World of Music

Nikolay's studies proceeded smoothly; he received high grades, and the piano lessons with Ulikh recommenced. The boy did not seem to be fond of those lessons. Yet a significant event took place in Nikolay's life that revealed the new world of music to him. Pavel Golovin, one of Voin's friends, a naval officer, took him to the theatre to see an opera. Nikolay described this event in a letter: "I have a lot to tell you about. Golovin afforded me the pleasurable experience of seeing the Russian opera at the theatre-circus.[11] They performed *Indra* in three acts with dances. It was translated from the German language, the music was written by von Flotow."[12]

One day later, he again went to see an opera with Golovin. This time they were in the Bolshoi Theatre. Before his visit, he wrote home to Tikhvin: "Can you imagine how happy I am about my going to the theatre today? *Lucia di Lammermoor* in three acts composed by Donizetti will be performed there. I will hear the huge orchestra and a tam-tam. And I will see the conductor waving his baton. The orchestra has twelve violins, eight violas, six violoncellos, six double basses, three flutes, eight clarinets, six French horns, and so on." The Italian music impressed him much more than Flotow's. His next letter said: "The decorations were beautiful, and the music was even better. I liked the tenor—Mangini, a baritone—Bartolini, and all the other voices were also very good. But what I liked most of all was the music. (It was composed by Donizetti.) It has beautiful tunes. I enjoyed the harp solo performed by Schultz. It goes without saying that I liked the orchestra very much. It was just perfect!" It happened to be *Lucia* by Donizetti that first brought operatic music into Rimsky-Korsakov's life. At that point music took over his heart forever.

Sometime later Nikolay wrote another letter to his parents:

While I am sitting at the bureau writing a letter to you, the hand organ in the street is playing the duet from *Lucia*, which I would play on the piano with great pleasure if I had the printed music. Generally speaking, if I had money I would buy the printed music for that opera in a shop, the orchestration of which I liked so much. I do not know why, but some of the tunes seemed so familiar to me, as if I had played them before.

Voin returned from his long voyage in the middle of September 1857. The next day after his arrival, he spent about twenty minutes visiting Nika and then left for Kronstadt again. Voin, being a very strict teacher of his godson, began assessing his younger brother's knowledge as soon as they met. Voin and Nikolay wrote together to their parents: "He examined me a little in geometry, algebra, and arithmetic, and made me read in French and English." Voin Rimsky-Korsakov added in his turn: "At last you have an opportunity to read letters written by both brothers on one and the same sheet of paper. [...] Yesterday and today I spent time with Nikolay and in the first meeting I was very pleased with him."

In the same letter, Nikolay told his parents about his visit to Pavel Golovin's sister, Praskovia Novikova, and how he took with him the printed music of some operas for them to study together. He said: "I am going to play them; among all those printed music sheets (that is about ten operas) I like *Norma* and *Lucia* the best. I am now learning the duet, the sextet, and the aria of the madwoman from *Lucia* by heart, so that if with God's help I come home for Christmas, You will have the opportunity to listen to them, and I'd like Papa to learn to play them."[13] In his next letter, dated 19 October 1857, he said:

> I am keeping on studying the printed music of operas such as *Robert le diable*, *Moïse*, *Puritani*, *Norma*, and others.[14] I wish I could study *Lucia di Lammermoor*, but I cannot find it anywhere; only yesterday in a pile of music I found a little fantasy from *Lucia*, from which I have already become familiar with a part of the duet, the finale, the chorus of soldiers, and the aria of the madwoman. I wish you could listen to the opera, its tunes are constantly sounding in my head.

Sophia Rimsky-Korsakov managed to find the printed music of *Lucia* arranged for piano and sent it to her son immediately. His letter home read:

> Thank you very much for the sheet music. I appreciated it greatly. I know the tune, which Mama indicated on page 12. That is the very tune that a hand

organ plays every Sunday. I also like the sextet on page 8, but it is varied too much there; in addition it has five flats and so it is very difficult. But if it is played as I do with one sharp and without variations, it is far more tuneful and easier to play.

During his visit, Voin gave Nika money to buy two tickets for the Russian Opera. Nika then wrote home to Tikhvin: "There were *Martha* of Flotow, from which I play the overture, and *Moskal Charivnyk*, a Ukrainian opera [based on a play] by Ivan Petrovich Kotlyarevsky. You can imagine how happy I am. They say the music of *Martha* is charming, and I think so too, judging by the overture."

He was becoming more and more involved in music, and it was starting to become a rival to his naval studies, although Nikolay himself probably did not realize it. Voin, who was concerned about his younger brother's future occupation, did not show any signs of anxiety. On the contrary, he still considered it a necessity to give his brother some musical education. At the same time, Nikolay wrote to Tikhvin: "I should say that the more I listen to operas, the more I like them. So, that pleasure is beneficial for me. It is very pleasant to listen to music such as *The Barber of Seville*, *William Tell*, *Lucrezia Borgia*, *La sonnambula*, and so on."[15] In other letters, he wrote: "I beg Papa to allow me to spend 15 kopeks for some musical note paper. Then, Mama, we could copy something together from *Der Freischütz*. I would like to rewrite the overture from it, but I am afraid it is too long, yet it is so beautiful. The overture is one of the best in the world, similar to *Don Juan*, *La vestale*, *The Magic Flute*, etc., if it is not even better.[16] I wish Papa could listen to it performed by the orchestra!"

At the end of December 1857 Nikolay arrived in Tikhvin to spend the Christmas vacation there, and then he returned to the Naval College on 6 January 1858. He again suffered from the separation from his parents. The boy wrote home: "I have some tightness in my chest. Whatever I think of or do, that feeling of uneasiness gnaws at my heart as if it were a worm, constantly making me think: yesterday you were at home with your Mama and Papa, and now you are in the College among strangers." Yet Nikolay had the opportunity to make his life more pleasant at the College by visiting the opera. His letter continued: "Could you imagine they will perform *Robert [le diable]* in Russian tonight? I am going to hear it and have already bought a ticket for the third circle of the gallery." Nikolay described his impressions in his letter to his father: "Oh, I liked it very much! It is the best among those I have seen before. What beautiful music! The accompaniment is particularly perfect; all the instruments are amazingly suited to each other."

After seeing the opera *William Tell* by Rossini at the Bolshoi Theatre, he wrote home to Tikhvin: "The overture is one of the most beautiful and it represents gradually the following: the sunrise, a storm, a shepherd who is tending his sheep; and it finishes with a wonderful *galop*. This had to be performed twice after loud applause. I liked the whole opera very much, but especially I enjoyed the overture and the trio. All this I have seen with the money given to me by Voin for that very purpose." On his birthday, Nikolay sent the following letter home: "I have turned 14 years old. But it seems that just recently I was a little child running around in our garden, playing 'horses,' and going to gather mushrooms with our late nanny."

Andrey Rimsky-Korsakov sent some parental advice on his son's birthday: "May God bless you and give you strength not to do again what you have confessed to previously. And the most important thing is that you have to control your shortness of temper, which cannot bear any contradiction or criticism, as well as your impatience and depression in case of failure."

The Easter vacations were approaching, and Nikolay anticipated his visits to the opera:

> I still have two rubles given to me by Voin and it is enough for me to go to the opera four times. I will try to listen to *Fenella, or The Mute Girl of Portici*, which is good, especially its choruses, then *A Life for the Tsar*, which is performed perfectly as a Russian folk opera, also *Askold's Tomb* or the *Mermaid*, or any other good opera. Do not think that if I am enjoying myself at operas I will forget about my studies. I certainly will not.[17]

The time came for Nikolay to take his examinations. Although he was very busy cramming for them, he went to see the ballet *Le corsaire*.[18] He evaluated it as follows: "I did not like the ballet itself; it was much worse than an opera." The Russian Opera performed *A Life for the Tsar* conducted by K. N. Lyadov—the first time that Nikolay had heard it in the theatre. He was very impressed by Glinka's music and shared his opinion with his mother: "The whole opera is breathtaking."

In his letter to his parents on 4 May 1858 Rimsky-Korsakov confessed: "Operas make me love music so much that it is impossible for me to love it more than I do." Nikolay was so delighted with the orchestration of *A Life for the Tsar* that he decided to try to reconstruct the orchestral score using the piano arrangement he had, where there were orchestral instruments indicated. The task was too ambitious for him. Nikolay went to a music store in order to look through the score of the opera, which was too expensive for him to buy for himself. He tried to remember, as much as possible, the way it had been orchestrated by the composer. Try as he might, he failed in his orchestration project.

The Naval College cadets were to have practical training after their third year of study. However, Voin obtained permission for his brother to take part in a voyage on his ship *Prokhor* a year before the training. Nikolay wrote to his parents on 12 May 1858: "So, I am going to sail. I am very glad. We are going to Revel [now Tallinn, Estonia]. It is very joyful and beneficial to sail, isn't it? I will not be afraid of tossing in the future. And it will be very useful for me because I will learn all of the equipment on the ship and I will know it as well as if I had already passed my practical studies at the College."

The *Prokhor* set off from Kronstadt on 2 June 1858. On the eve of its departure, Nikolay wrote to his parents:

> My dear Mama and Papa, it is about a week already since I have been on the ship. I like it very much. I keep watch. The watch commander sends me to report to my brother, the senior officer, about vessels we have seen, of added sails, and so on. In the morning, I am sent to supervise the cleaning of the deck and to check ship signals. In my turn, I keep records in the ship's log where I write down the wind, the course, the leeway, the speed and various events. I was designated to serve at the cannon with the other cadets. I will be happy if they send me to one of the topsails. I have learned to row a boat with other cadets, and I have got many blisters and scratches.

At the very beginning of the voyage, a dramatic event took place that almost cost Nikolay his life. Voin informed their parents:

> There was an accident that I hope will help him to outgrow his absent-mindedness. He was sent along with other cadets to climb up to the topsail. He was leaning

on the shrouds and was dreaming to such an extent that he did not hold onto them. At that very moment one of the nearby ropes tore, the shrouds were shaken because of the movement of the mast, and he fell into the water. It is just a miracle that he did not hit anything while falling down. So he is lucky to just have a bruise, which he might have got from hitting the water, and some scratches on his body from rolling over the shrouds.

Sometime later, Nikolay also described the occurrence in detail in a letter home to Tikhvin:

I was leaning on the shrouds of the mizzen-mast. At that moment the cadets began pulling on them. Because the shrouds were poor, they broke. While I was standing on them, I was not holding on but merely resting with my stomach on the shrouds. The shrouds shook and I fell downward, counting all the ratlines (on the rope ladders) with my head and my feet. After I had turned over about three times, I slipped between the shrouds. I hit my side on the mainyard and fell into the water. I went down deep; my boots became heavy with water, and it seemed as if I had had weights hanging on my legs so that I came up just two feet above the surface and could not move up. At this moment, the boat reached me and the boathooks caught me. Nevertheless, I managed to climb up the ship's ladder by myself to the deck and entered my cabin, and lay down on the bed. They just applied some Goulard water to my body.[19] The next day I was already on my feet; the following day I was able to go out. In addition, I have even already climbed up again to the topsail. Well, really, falling down from the topsail is even more than from a seven-story building.

"He Is So Gifted"

Voin did not see any danger in his brother's great interest in music that might prevent him from training properly to become a naval officer. On the contrary, he was certain that Nikolay's musical education ought to be encouraged. Therefore, when the *Prokhor* docked at Revel, Voin rented a room with a piano and sent his brother there to practice. Voin wrote to his father: "I don't know how much he is inclined to music, but I think that he is so gifted that I would sin against the Lord to neglect it, and merely bury the talent granted by Him. You should be certain that he will not be deprived of anything special if he spends all of his free evenings in music." However, Nikolay was also successful in his "major" studies (as Voin considered them). His letter continued: "I don't miss any opportunity to examine his knowledge when I have a chance. I should say with delight that he is studying well. He is much smarter than many of his comrades and continual practice has begun to develop him. The most beneficial thing is that he has no time to be absentminded."

At the end of July 1858 Andrey Rimsky-Korsakov suddenly became seriously ill. As soon as Voin found out, Nikolay was sent to Tikhvin. The days Voin and Nikolay spent with their parents flew by. Upon arrival back at the College, Nikolay sent a letter home immediately: "It does not seem to be very pleasant here. But what can be done? I cannot spend all my life in Tikhvin. I lived some time in Tikhvin. Now I should spend some time in Petersburg. I should not just have fun walking around in the forest and so on. I should study, and the latter is much more useful than the former."

Nikolay was still interested in astronomy. That autumn he had the opportunity to observe a comet, which had a bright tail. Nikolay wrote to his parents: "We look at the comet every night; it is situated a bit lower than Ursa Major next to the constellation Leo. Can you see this beautiful comet? What a tail! How perfectly it curves its tail! How bright it is!"

Nikolay went to the opera as often as he could. He saw *Askold's Tomb* by Verstovsky and said later: "I bought a ticket to watch and listen to Russian music, which I have not heard since I saw *A Life for the Tsar*. And Russian music is very pleasant." After going to see a ballet, the boy complained to his parents that "ballet itself is very boring; the dances are all the same, so that you soon become very tired. On the other hand, I like dances in an opera very much. It is very pleasant to see them since they make changes in the plot and the music in operas for them is a thousand times better than the music by Pugni for dances in a ballet."[20]

On 30 November 1858 Nikolay wrote home:

I am absolutely happy today. Imagine, Glinka's *A Life for the Tsar* will be performed and I am going to see it. I will say that it is a classical opera, which is perfect, not just lovely. I know this music, so it is even more pleasant for me to listen to it performed by good singers and by the orchestra, but not played on the piano and sounding absolutely monotonous. Moreover, it is nice to see the Krakovienne and Mazurka danced by Polish performers.[21] Even their music is not the same as that for ballroom dancing; it is quite different from useless ballroom dance music.

A week later Nikolay added in his next letter: "Even now, as soon as I go deep into thought, the Polish mazurka—the best in the world—comes into my mind." In February 1859 he reported to his parents his marks for the past week: "My marks this week have been as follows: French—10, English—10, Russian—10, Geography—11. I'd like to say that the more I study, the more interesting it seems." The boy bought *Kamarinskaya* by Glinka, and his opinion of it was: "This simple Russian folk song is arranged for orchestra in such a way that it is worth listening to. Glinka has managed to make such a fugue from the stupidest and the most monotonous tune that it will glorify the famous composer forever. If I come home at Christmastime I will play it for you. I am sure you will like it very much."[22]

Nikolay got a chance to attend a symphony concert for the first time in his life in the spring of 1859. He wrote to his parents: "There is a great concert in the Bolshoi Theatre. There are 150 musicians and 180 choristers participating. They are going to perform the *Pastoral* Symphony by Beethoven, *A Midsummer Night's Dream* by Mendelssohn, the *Leonora* Overture by Beethoven and some other things. I am so eager to listen to symphonies at least once." Later he wrote home to Tikhvin about the concert: "Most of all I liked the overture. It is so lovely, and it was played perfectly. The music of Beethoven's symphony is more serious, therefore I did not grasp it very much."

Nikolay learned to play and perform a sonata for violoncello and piano together with Ulikh. Their performance took place on 4 April 1859 at Golovin's home. The following day Nikolay wrote to his parents:

> My concert yesterday was performed successfully according to the opinion of the listeners. So I was very pleased. Thank you ever so much for your present—six silver rubles, which I plan to spend on notes,[23] and not on entertainments. I am thinking of doing so. Entertainments finish leaving some pleasant impressions for some period of time, whereas music notes will be useful for the rest of my life. Although they are not a pleasure in their essence, yet they can be used to produce this whenever I want.

He was growing fonder of the music of Beethoven. He played Beethoven's *Pastoral* Symphony for four hands, that very music I have heard in the concert. I think there is no better symphony than this one. Beethoven even managed to place the singing of a nightingale, a quail, and a cuckoo in his Andante at one and the same time, so that the first is performed by the flute, the second by the oboe, and the last by the clarinet. Thus, they produce the complete effect of a roll-call of nightingale, quail, and cuckoo in the Andante of the symphony.

In the spring of 1859 Ulikh felt that his pupil's piano playing was better than his own. He thought that for Nikolay to improve further in playing the piano, he would need a professional teacher-pianist. Therefore he advised Voin to look for another music teacher.

At the beginning of June 1859 Nikolay went on a second training voyage on the same ship as before again under the command of his brother. The *Prokhor* was kept berthed at Kronstadt for a considerable period of time. The lack of any possibility to play the piano made Nikolay depressed, and he wrote to his parents:

My dear Mama and Papa, we are still here at Kronstadt, and I do not know when we will head to Revel. It is so boring for me to wait. On Sunday, I went to Petersburg and spent the whole day there playing the piano. I am longing to go to Revel not only because it will be more interesting there but also because there will be regular piano lessons in Revel. By that time, I will have collected a considerable amount of printed music. So far I have bought a great deal this year. *A Life for the Tsar* cost 10 rubles, the opera *Ruslan and Lyudmila* cost the same. There are many pieces for four hands: the *Kamarinskaya*, the overture to *A Life for the Tsar*, Polish krakovienne, the *mazurka*, *interludes*, and the *Midsummer Night's Dream* of Mendelssohn, which with the *Pastoral* Symphony charmed me at the concert. Well, while listing my music, I have forgotten that it is time to go on duty. I have to finish. Goodbye, my dear Papa and Mama. Give me your blessings. Your loving son, Nika R.-Korsakov.

In August 1859, while the *Prokhor* was moored at Revel, there was an organized trip to Lake Timer. Voin, Nikolay, and some local young ladies took part in it. After the journey, Voin wrote to his parents: "My darling brother, under the influence of the ladies, has been growing into a real gentleman. Our last trip showed that the real reason for his gallantry is the effect of his passion, which he, as a youth, cannot hide. I am sure there can't be anything serious in such childish love."

Nikolay was growing up, and his parents worried that his son might acquire bad habits. They asked their son whether he had begun smoking. Nikolay answered: "To be honest with you, I have tried it, but I didn't like it at all." His parents were also anxious about their young son's love life. Voin comforted them:

> The fact is that Nika's passion is a true youthful passion, exactly as it is supposed to be, I can certify that. But I beg you not to panic and make a mountain out of a molehill, and it is most important not to interfere with it. Believe me, no studying would be more beneficial to him than this. On my part, I am just happy that it happened like this. Neither did I try to dissuade him; on the contrary, I used this chance to remind him that he had to be neat, dandified, and smart to be liked by young ladies. Under the influence of this passion he began to look after his nails, take care of his hairstyle, of his shirt so as not to show it under his uniform, and he has even changed his awkward manners. Think: can anyone be worried that such a boy as Nika should have feelings of passion?

A New Music Teacher

A new academic year began. That coincided with another significant event that had an important effect on Nikolay's life. A new music teacher was hired for him—Fyodor Kanille. The boy told his parents about their first meeting: "He listened to my playing and praised me. Then he himself played perfectly." Just two weeks after their first meeting, regular music lessons began. Nikolay wrote home:

> I liked him very much. He managed to make his lessons into something pleasant instead of being dry. He assigned me to study a polonaise by Weber, a very good piece; he played it with me for four hands and explained it. We talked a lot about Glinka. We played his *Spanish Overture* and the overture from *Prince Kholmsky*, then *Iphigenia in Aulis* by Gluck and some other pieces.[24] We studied the scores and did many other things. In general I will go to his lessons with great pleasure.

Nikolay was very glad to find a person who shared his views on music and who also considered Glinka a great genius. In his turn, Kanille immediately discovered and appreciated the talent of his pupil, so he liked giving lessons to Nikolay and did not worry about the length of time they took.

Nikolay wrote home about his next visit: "I visited my tutor. I spent two hours discussing music with him. He gave me a sonata by Beethoven to arrange for four hands." Soon the pupil boasted to his parents in his letter that Kanille approved of his arrangement of Beethoven's sonata.

> He praised me and said that I should go on doing this and that it was very useful. You asked about his origin. He is purely Russian, although his surname is Italian. I am eager to buy *A Life for the Tsar*—the full version. It costs ten silver rubles. I have this sum, but I decided to ask for your permission in any case. I would like to collect all of those works since they are of the same quality as Beethoven's and Mozart's; they will be immortal forever. There is not any weak place in them, the weakest ones are a thousand times better than the best parts of Donizetti and Verdi, whose operas are so praised by the uncomprehending public. Whose opera is the best in the world?—Glinka's *Ruslan and Lyudmila*. Who else composed so many wonderful romances, such as the Scherzo, *Kamarinskaya*, and the Waltz-Fantasia? Who else has written such overtures as those two Spanish ones by Glinka? It's a pity he is appreciated so little and they remember only some of his romances and *A Life for the Tsar*. It is true he can't be compared to Beethoven and Mozart because their music is in an absolutely different spirit; it's abstract and dry. But Glinka is a lyrical composer, who has combined in his music both abstract nature and talent. Wait a little, I will play it for you and you'll see.

Considering his new student's attitude to music and how well he coped with arrangement, Kanille decided to investigate Nikolay's talent for composition. The boy was happy about it. He wrote home on 1 November 1859: "My music lessons are proceeding well. The teacher gave me a chorale to write. I should select the bass and other accompaniments for four voices for it. He told me the rules for how to do this, and he ordered me to compose it without the help of the piano. We'll see whether he will be pleased with me." Nikolay coped with the task successfully. Kanille encouraged his gifted student to compose further and directed him to write exclusively by ear, without using instruments. The boy wrote home again to his parents:

S. Petersburg, 26 November 1859.

My dear Mama and Papa, it will be December soon, hence Christmas and my vacations. I'm longing to see you, and my brother has promised me so, but I'd prefer you met me without reproaching me for [the fact] that I've had poor marks or that I have misbehaved. [...] You are likely to ask what exactly I did wrong. I'm confessing to you heartily that I have played pranks, and I tried to smoke several times. I was caught once. Later, when my brother was at the College, my company commander reported this to him. He certainly told me off and forced me to give my word that I will never smoke in the College. Certainly I gave it up after this lecture. Please do not be angry with me. My pranks in the College never were as bad as those of most of my comrades.

Kanille introduced Nikolay to the works of different composers: Bach, Beethoven, Schumann, and Balakirev. His teacher invited the student to a concert in which he himself participated. Nikolay wrote home: "I attended the University concert and listened to the Second Symphony of Beethoven [D major] and was much delighted. It was so wonderful! I have this symphony for four hands, and I know it almost by heart by now; when I heard it played by the orchestra, I can't even compare the effect it had with the effect when it is played on the piano. My teacher performed a polonaise by Chopin."

Since Nikolay obtained bad marks in his naval studies, his brother not only forbade him to play piano for four hands during the week but also made him report every weekend about his behavior and progress at the Naval College. Voin informed his parents: "Thus, we began our communication in writing." Nikolay obeyed his brother completely.

At last the dreams of his parents came true: Voin announced his engagement. His fiancée was Maria Bauer, a daughter of Narzissa and Fyodor Bauer. Nikolay visited Bauer's home with his brother. The younger brother wrote home to Tikhvin on 10 December 1859: "My dear Mama and Papa, I can imagine how happy you are to learn about Voin's engagement. Yesterday, we had dinner at his fiancée's house with all of her relatives. We spent the whole evening there having fun and singing till about 3 a.m." Nikolay looked forward to his trip home at Christmas. He wrote in a letter:

My tutor is giving me a task to compose two marches while in Tikhvin in the style of Beethoven's. In addition, he wants me to learn two waltzes by Chopin at Christmas. They are not the kind of waltz for dancing, but piano pieces similar to concert ones. And I'm determined to study them for two hours every morning. Besides, I'm going to compose something, as my teacher has ordered. In a word, I will have enough music to deal with. Good-bye, my dear Mama and Papa. I am asking for your blessings. P.S. My brother allowed me to smoke in his presence, but he forbade me to do it in secret. He said I should do it openly.

Another important event occurred in Voin's life in addition to his forthcoming marriage: he was promoted to the rank of head of the Kronstadt port headquarters. The wedding was scheduled for 18 January 1860. Nikolay arrived at Kronstadt on the eve of the ceremony and spent two days there. He described the event in a letter to his parents: "The wedding was performed in the Church of the Navigator College, and then we headed to the Catholic church, where the second part of the ceremony took place. Then we went to the house of the newlyweds. There we celebrated with champagne so that by the time of my departure I had become a little tipsy. During the wedding I often thought of you, imagining that you were happy and praying for Voin's happiness."

Before going to Kronstadt Nikolay had his lesson at Kanille's house and showed him the pieces he had composed in Tikhvin. "Hurray! The sonata is appreciated!" he jotted down in the margin of the letter. In his next letter Nikolay wrote:

This time he told me to make variations on [the folk song] "In Flat Dales."[25] By today I have made some variations. He approved of one and said that the other one should be improved. Shrovetide has come. Today I have already had some blini with fresh caviar. In the morning I visited Kanille. He assigned me to study one of Chopin's nocturnes and he looked through my variations on "In Flat Dales," which he liked a lot. If you remember, while in Tikhvin I composed some variations on the lullaby. When I showed them to him, he commented that it was not bad for the first time. Nevertheless, this time he praised me greatly, and after playing my first variation (perfectly as usual) he beat "Bravo" on the keys. He told me to do two more variations, and later, when I become good enough at counterpoint, he will assign me to compose something in that style.

A week later, Nikolay wrote again:

> I visit my teacher every day and play for two hours. I have not gone to the theatre since they perform operas such as *Il trovatore* and *Traviata* by Verdi, and my musical ear does not like such dramas. I like Glinka, Mendelssohn, Beethoven, Chopin, Meyerbeer, and Rossini. Oh, I forgot to mention Franz Schubert, who is also a classical composer. During Maslenitsa,[26] I studied an ecossaise of Chopin and wrote an andante and scherzo in the style of Beethoven; my teacher liked them very much. Now I'm certainly a real composer.

Thus, having recognized the true talent of his pupil, Kanille helped him to reveal his abilities and to develop his talent for independent composition. Nikolay spent all of his money to buy staff paper. He wrote in one letter home: "I'd rather walk than ride in a carriage. For I will never find such beautiful things in the future; they are not sold anywhere else, and I am unlikely to have another chance like this to write them out." Then, on 6 March 1860, he wrote the following letter to his parents:

> My dear Mama and Papa, Today is my birthday. I will to try to be diligent in studying and to behave myself in the seventeenth year of my life. It seems that my sixteenth year was successful for me, and I cannot complain about my laziness or misbehavior. I am praying to the Lord asking for this year to be no worse than the past one, and in my turn, I will do my best to make this new year even much better. Since it's my birthday, I'm going to a concert tonight.

The concert was quite good. They performed compositions by Beethoven, Mozart, Wagner, and Liszt. Surprisingly, Nikolay wrote even before attending the concert: "It will be interesting to listen to everything except for the symphonic poem of Liszt, since it is nothing more than sheer nonsense, for Liszt…never has possessed any talent for composition. I'm curious to hear Wagner's music; they say it is something new and original." He began attending symphony concerts more frequently and rapturously described to his parents what he managed to see. His lessons with Kanille brought him at least the same pleasure as the concerts. His tutor was becoming more to him than just a teacher—Kanille grew into his close friend. Nikolay assured his parents: "It is unlikely for me to find a better teacher than Kanille. He is invaluable to me. You can see for yourselves: instead of spending an hour for the lesson, he deals with me for two or three, teaches me how to compose, and begs me to come practice any time I like."

During the Easter vacation Nikolay had the good luck to go to Kronstadt again. Voin and his wife had moved into a new, larger apartment. Voin, bachelor until the age of thirty-seven, was happy to experience the comforts of family life. He wrote to his parents on the day of his brother's arrival: "I managed to get Nikolay released from the College for our housewarming party and he is going to stay with us for the holidays. I hope he will not be bored, since Marie's piano, presented to her by her mother, was brought to this new apartment and at this very moment Nika and Marie are playing a Beethoven symphony for four hands." Nikolay also sent a letter from Kronstadt: "My dear Mama and Papa, I'm in Kronstadt now. Voin's new apartment is nice; it is spacious and comfortable. Here I am determined to occupy myself with composing a nocturne and a march and prepare thoroughly the tasks assigned to me by my teacher. There is a perfect piano here; it is a pleasure to play on it. And I can play as long as I wish, either with Mashenka for four hands or all by myself."

The Easter holidays came to an end. Nikolay began cramming for his examinations, but even during this period, he did not miss his music lessons. He reported to his parents:

> My nocturne is ready. My teacher liked it. You ask me to send you one of my pieces, but it will be distributed to everyone in the town. Nobody will play it as I (the composer) would like it to be performed; hence, none will like it. I know that the public is affected not by the music but by the name of its composer. I once played my own scherzo and gave it out to be Beethoven's, and everyone admired it. I left them in blissful ignorance of this fact.

Before the examinations came to the end, the cadets were offered to choose a ship for practicing sailing. Nikolay wrote to Tikhvin on 5 May 1860:

> I am designated to the ship *Vola*. There are going to be twenty-five cadets, all of them are my friends, and the company is supposed to be good. We could have chosen the *Eagle*, *Prokhor*, or *Vola*, and I chose the last because there is nothing interesting for me to sail on the *Prokhor*, and there will be bad company on the

Eagle, so I am not eager to be there. There will be only hard drinking, as there was last year.

Upon noticing that Nikolay was becoming completely absorbed by music, with what passion he devoted every single spare minute to it, Voin became seriously alarmed. Now he noticed that his music was becoming a very dangerous rival to his naval studies, which Voin considered to be the most important thing for his brother. The elder son wrote to Tikhvin: "What shall I do about Nika? I have decided to send him to sea. By the way, there is a Machiavellian goal to draw him away from music, to which I'm afraid he devotes too much time at the expense of his major studies."

On 4 June 1860 the *Vola* weighed anchor. For his period on board, Nikolay was assessed by the captain "in behavior and knowledge of the service—very good." Nikolay looked forward to his next meeting with Kanille, but he had to face a gross disappointment. Rimsky-Korsakov wrote to Tikhvin:

> I should tell you some very important news about my music lessons: I will not take lessons anymore. My brother says they distract me, although I have the opposite opinion. I do not play in the College, and on Sunday, I do not sit at the table the whole day preparing weekly lessons because I have enough time for this at the College. However, I will not argue about it, and I even will not mention it since the money is not mine. I have never been in the habit of asking him for money. Well, I have to study by myself. Therefore, I will try, if not to go ahead, then at least not to forget what I have learned. I took what he had said in my stride. In his turn, Kanille takes it the opposite way. He immediately suggested that he should teach me free of charge, but I rejected the offer on the spot, knowing it would upset my brother. Then Kanille urged me to visit him each Sunday; I had to refuse again, saying that even though it had been very pleasant for me, it would appear like lessons to others. We agreed on my occasional visits for playing for four hands. I hope my brother will not forbid this.

Nikolay's composure only seemed restrained. Since his early years he had hidden his innermost feelings from the world. He kept this habit throughout his whole life, and because of this, many people, not knowing the composer well, confused it with coldness and even severity. His parents considered Voin's decision to cancel the music lessons with Kanille to be too cruel a measure for their younger son. At the same time, they found it necessary to express their worries that the music might actually interfere with his studies at the College. Nikolay responded: "I beg you not to reproach me about music. Believe me, it is very offensive for me to hear that music, which I like very much, has become a subject for reproaches and very unfair ones."

His brother held his ground and informed his parents that he would allow Nikolay to recommence his music lessons only when he was able to translate from French fluently and not to make mistakes in Russian. Pretty soon the elder brother tempered justice with mercy, and Nikolay wrote to Tikhvin on 20 October 1860: "Yesterday Voin visited me and asked me to come to Kronstadt on Saturday. He said he would not forbid me to visit my teacher any time I'd like and that he even would be glad." This permission brought Nikolay back to life, since he seemed to have been very depressed. After the ban on music was lifted, Rimsky-Korsakov recommenced composing his own pieces and told his mother, "As concerns music, I have written a Scherzo and a Rondo."

In the autumn of 1860 the new opera house opened. It had been rebuilt from the old Theatre-Circus by the architect A. Kavos (1801–1862) and named the Mariinsky.[27] On opening night they performed *A Life for the Tsar*. On 15 November 1860 Nikolay attended the concert and wrote a letter home later:

> I was at the concert at the Mariinsky Theatre. I listened to Beethoven's *Eroica* Symphony, Glinka's *Kamarinskaya*, the final chorus from *A Life for the Tsar*, different choruses from Wagner's *Tannhäuser*, and some other works. I was especially impressed by the *Kamarinskaya*. It was clear that everybody enjoyed listening to it. They applauded with great enthusiasm; it can't even be compared with the other pieces in the concert.

As was customary, Nikolay spent his Christmas vacations in Tikhvin with his parents. He returned to St. Petersburg on 8 January 1861. Soon after his arrival Rimsky-Korsakov went to the Mariinsky, where they performed Rossini's opera *William Tell*. The next week he at last managed to hear, for the first time in his life, his favorite opera: Glinka's *Ruslan and Lyudmila*. Nikolay was delighted with the music itself but disappointed with the "poor performance." In a letter dated 9 February 1861 he informed his parents that "the day before I received a message about the birth of my nephew—Peter. I'm absolutely happy about this growth in the Rimsky-Korsakov family."

Nikolay became fond of a new activity at the Naval College that he liked very much, and he wrote to his parents about it: "Almost every night a big company gathers for singing, so that we have a chorus made up of eighteen tenors and basses. We sang the chorus from *A Life for the Tsar*, the chorus of the fishermen from *Askold's Tomb*, and many other pieces. There is only one bad thing; the authorities did not like it." Voin considered that this new hobby of his younger brother—conducting the choruses—would interfere with Nikolay's studies and that it had to stop. "On the advice of my brother I had to turn down the offer to become a chorus director even before the voyage began. My friends were very sorry but what I could do?" he wrote to his parents from Revel.

By 1 June all the cadets were sent to Kronstadt and assigned to ships. Nikolay had to undertake this last sailing practice before graduating from the College in the summer of 1861. The *Vola*, to which Nikolay was again assigned, went to Revel and Helsingborg,[28] changing its location frequently, and from time to time it was on the high seas for long periods. Try as he might, Voin failed to distract his brother from music or to suppress Nikolay's inclination to compose music. The only thing he achieved was for his brother to start keeping his composition attempts secret. During his last cruise Nikolay did not have any opportunity to go ashore and play the piano, unlike on his previous voyages. Nevertheless, he composed in his mind. "I should try to write a sonata for four hands," he wrote to Tikhvin. "I've drawn up a plan already, now I should brace myself and start writing."

In September 1861 all the cadets returned to their classes. Andrey Rimsky-Korsakov sent an admonishing letter to his younger son: "I am aware now that it is your last year of study and that next year you will be designated as a reefer. We are hoping very much to see you decorated with an aiguillette.[29] You should continue your last year of training in the College with proper zeal and diligence in order to be honored by being named among the first ten best students." Voin was expected to become the director of the Naval College on 1 January 1862. However, anticipating the event, Andrey Rimsky-Korsakov added some more authoritative words in his letter: "It is necessary for the sake of your brother Voin to maintain his good name. Try to behave yourself in your relations with your comrades; do not show any kind of superiority in your words or manners, so that nothing could make them think of your relying on your brother's protection. Your modesty, calm, and helpfulness will bring about your comrades' liking."

Nikolay wrote to his mother: "I am glad that I seem to pay more attention to classes in the College than I did last year. It should please you. I hope to pass my examinations with rather good marks." Andrey Rimsky-Korsakov wrote another didactic letter to the youngster:

> Do not become friends with those who are inclined to drinking and gambling. The former is harmful for one's health and mind, and the latter ruins one's pockets and steals time. If you set a firm rule for all your life never to gamble, you will keep your head, since gambling makes a man anxious, which leads him to passion for envy, anger, and greed or gives cause for quarrels and enmity. Here are some more words of advice: do not gossip with your comrades about the deeds of the unbridled and prodigal [students]. Do not speak of them pretending as though you did not see or know anything. Even if somebody tempted you to speak about him or her, you should be silent and not talk about anyone in public. Thus, you will preserve respect for yourself which you can earn in your early years.

In October 1861 Andrey Rimsky-Korsakov suffered his first heart attack. As soon as they received the news, the alarmed sons rushed to Tikhvin, where they stayed for three days until their father was out of danger.

Meeting Mily Balakirev, 1861

Ever since Voin had opposed his brother's music lessons, Nikolay had avoided this topic in his letters home. However, he did not mean to abandon his passion. On the contrary, since he was now permitted to do so, he visited Kanille on Sundays; the latter encouraged his pupil's composition efforts and directed his musical creative work. Although Nikolay studied hard at the College, he found time for writing pieces of music, an increasing number of which captivated him more and more. He did not show his work to anybody except his teacher, and he did not discuss his compositions with anyone. Kanille observed his student's talent for composition despite some technical imperfections. The teacher himself was not able to impart sufficient musical knowledge to the young composer, so he decided to introduce Nikolay to Mily Balakirev, an acquaintance of his, for the latter to give his opinion about the young man's creative work. This meeting took place on 16 November 1861, and Nikolay could not help telling his parents about it. He wrote home: "Last Sunday, Kanille introduced me to M. A. Balakirev, a famous musician and composer, and to [César] Cui, the composer of the opera *The Prisoner of the Caucasus*, which is to be performed on the stage rather soon, and some parts of which have already been very successfully performed in the concerts of the Russian Musical Society. Thus, I am very pleased with this meeting and it may be very beneficial for my music."

The discreet tone of the information he sent home about his becoming acquainted with Balakirev did not reflect Nikolay's high spirits after such a significant meeting with a truly well-known composer whose talents had already become widely admired. He was not only happy to make such an acquaintance, but also inspired by the approval that Balakirev expressed for his own compositions, which he had showed to him on the advice of Kanille. These were his Scherzo and Nocturne and some parts of his symphony. Balakirev was quick to recognize that the young man was gifted and insisted on his continuing to work on his symphony. Nikolay took up the challenge without delay. He did not write to his parents at all about his musical undertakings. Nonetheless, he worked hard on his symphony, to the extent his studies allowed him to do so, following his first meeting with Balakirev. Every Saturday night he went to Balakirev, showed him the pieces he had composed, and then improved them following his advice. At Balakirev's home he also became acquainted with Musorgsky and Stasov.[30] Thus, Rimsky-Korsakov joined Balakirev's musical group. Upon visiting Tikhvin the next Christmas, he went on composing and finished the first part of his symphony there.

Voin, together with his family, moved into an apartment on the premises of the Naval College.[31] Nikolay wrote his next letter home from his brother's new home: "S. Petersburg. 23 January 1862. My dear Mama and Papa, there is little time left before the examinations, just about a month. I spent this Saturday at my brother's. They have almost settled down, and there is a spare room for me." The same letter also described his visits to a concert of the Russian Musical Society, where he listened to a Schumann Symphony, the overture to *The Magic Flute* and the quartet from the same opera, and a Beethoven concerto performed by a sixteen-year-old pianist. In his next letter, dated 4 February, Nikolay told his parents that he attended another concert and had heard Bach's Orchestral Suite, *The Triumph of Bacchus* by

Dargomizhsky, the concerto for harp by Parish Alvars,[32] and some other pieces. "Yesterday I was at Balakirev's as usual," he continued. "I have such a wonderful time there that I don't know how I can thank Kanille for such a wonderful introduction."

On 5 February Nikolay reported to Tikhvin: "The examinations are to begin on 5 March. At present we are having measurements taken for our dress clothes; our underwear is being ordered and so on." Concerning the fitting out of the graduates with uniforms, Nikolay's brother Voin wrote to his parents:

> In my opinion, all of the graduates are comrades and they shall all be fitted out with uniforms in a manner that the poorest of them can afford, so that nobody shows off his superiority to the others, and secondly, so that they do not have cause to compete with each other in foppishness, which results either in taking additional money from their relatives or, what is even worse, getting into debt. I demanded that Nika should set an example for the others this year.

The approaching examinations at the Naval College were very serious, and, considering his parents' wishes, Nikolay wrote to them:

> My dear Mama and Papa, let me tell you that the task you gave to me to be in the first ten is very challenging. I am not alone among those who will do their utmost to be there. In any case, you should not worry about my efforts, I will make them, but then we will see what God has in store for us. Mama, you wrote very much that music should not interfere with my passing my examinations successfully. Do you really think that I am so weak-willed that I cannot allocate my time so that one thing does not interfere with another?

In order to set his mother's mind at rest that music did not prevent him cramming for the examinations, Nikolay wrote nothing about the fact that he was continuing to compose and to work on the Scherzo of his symphony. In a letter dated 9 March 1862 he thanked his parents for their birthday present to him and reported the results of his first tests: "I'm happy that the week passed well and today I at last have had a good sleep. The examinations were: Astronomy—11, Physical Geography—12, Mechanics—10, Religion—12, hence everything is going on all right."

Death of Nikolay's Father, Andrey Rimsky-Korsakov

In the middle of March Nikolay received alarming news about his father's serious illness. He and Voin left for Tikhvin immediately. They arrived on 19 March 1862, but it was too late. Before they got there, Andrey died after a second, more serious stroke. He was buried two days later in the major apse of the Cathedral of Assumption of the Tikhvin Monastery. The following day Voin took his mother with him to St. Petersburg. Nikolay left Tikhvin a day later with his uncle, never to return during his lifetime.

2

The Sailor

Despite all the disgusting things surrounding me I am going on composing.

—Rimsky-Korsakov to Mily Balakirev from Kiel, 1862

Return to the Naval College

After returning to the College, Nikolay Rimsky-Korsakov passed all of the rest of his examinations successfully. He fulfilled the dream of his parents—he was named among the top ten best students. On 31 March 1862 he was recommended to be designated as a reefer.

The final examination in the presence of admirals and naval authorities was held on 28 March 1862. Two weeks later eighteen-year-old Nikolay was promoted to the rank of reefer and assigned to make an overseas voyage on the clipper ship *Almaz*.[1] After his appointment to the *Almaz* Nikolay was given a short leave, which he spent with his mother in his brother's apartment in St. Petersburg. When the leave was over he went to Kronstadt, since the clipper had been berthed there preparing for the voyage; his mother moved to Sonion-Sary, Finland, where Voin had rented a country house for his family for the summer. The younger son sent a letter to his mother, Sophia, from Kronstadt dated 14 June 1862: "My dear Mama, how have you settled down there in Sonion-Sary, and how do you like the place? The *Almaz* left the dock and came to anchor in the harbor but too far away. Now the real work will start. I am looking forward to receiving a letter from you. You should write to me about your life there, about your visit to the place."

His mother responded some days later:

> I hope, my dear, you will discharge your obligations in good faith so that your commander will be able to recommend you fairly as a young man who does his duty bona fide. Thus, you will make your Mama very happy since I wish heartily for my younger son to be as a good a citizen as my elder son. We have been

having a nice time here. I think that I will enjoy my stay here until my departure. The place is beautiful; the sea is just a few *sazhens* away from the house.[2] Nature is wild here, with cliffs and woods. Goodbye, my dear. God bless you. I embrace you. Your Mama.

Nikolay had a chance to visit his mother again for a while. Later he again wrote to her from Kronstadt:

> I am living a routine life: I get up at 6:30 and go to work; at 12:30 I come back; then at two I go to work again, and at 6:30 I return. So far this week I have read three plays of Shakespeare and almost finished the second volume of Gogol. I would like to know what you have been doing since my departure. Write to me about everything. Do you walk to the cliff where we sat together? I have also read the *Parisina* by Byron. This is a wonderful poem, and *Woe from Wit* by Griboedov, which you might know. Why does one feel so well while reading such things? Why is the finale of my symphony developing so well? I have read *The Roman Women*; it is a historical novel, extremely interesting, based on the chronicles of Tacitus, a Roman historian. After *The Roman Women*, I began reading Pushkin's *Mermaid*, *A Feast in the Time of Plague*, and *Mozart and Salieri*; now I am stuffing myself with *Eugene Onegin*. I'm reading it and recalling a lot of pieces I heard in my childhood where father read it in the evenings…

The younger son's affection for his mother was undiminished. That was understandable. He was an affectionate child. Nobody managed to replace her warmheartedness and her care for him either at the College or, especially, when he was at Kronstadt.

Trip Abroad on the *Almaz*: Kiel, London, New York, Brazil

At the beginning of October 1862, P. A. Selene, captain of the *Almaz*, was ordered to set off for the American coast to watch "naval military operations taking place there." Nikolay was ordered to sail with the *Almaz* on its long voyage. Nikolay said good-bye to St. Petersburg on 19 October. Balakirev, Cui, Kanille, and of course Sophia saw him off at the pier. Two days later the *Almaz* left Kronstadt and began its journey via the Kiel Canal and the North

Sea to England. Sophia was the first to send a letter to her son, even before receiving a message from him:

> S. Petersburg. 24 October 1862. My dear Nika, today is the fourth day since you left and the fifth since we parted. I see you in my mind staying on board and keeping the portrait.[3] Certainly, I have been crying a lot so that I got a bad headache. I was even unable to have dinner. I applied a mustard plaster and stayed in bed until 8 o'clock. I hope this time while you are away will pass quickly, but I am afraid it will drag on as slowly as it has been doing since your Papa left. It does not matter how busy I keep myself, I cannot force time to pass more quickly. Good-bye, my dear. God bless you and all of you on the *Almaz*.

Five days passed after the departure of the *Almaz* from Kronstadt until it reached Kiel. Nikolay wrote from there to his mother:

> My dear Mama, on 21 October at 9 o'clock in the morning we weighed anchor. The next day the wind got stronger and rocked us pretty fiercely. So strong was the tossing that we could not set anything on the table in our cabin. Everything fell off and we had to eat from a common pot because everything would spill from the plates and the plates themselves would be broken. Our cabin was in a complete mess. Half of my comrades became seasick; everything fell off the table—a chest, suitcases—and everything that was under the table was rolling along the deck. It was impossible to do anything, as one risked falling down any minute. During the whole passage, two reefers as well as I had to be on duty as navigators. Today we have cast anchor in Kiel Bay, not far from the coast. I am writing a short message this time since I do not have much to tell you. My next letter will be longer. So good-bye, my dear Mama. I ask for your blessings. Your son.

That was the beginning of the extensive correspondence between Nikolay and Sophia, which continued throughout his long voyage. Its rhythm was disturbed only by the clipper's lengthy ocean passages. At that time Nikolay did not have anybody closer to him than his mother, so it was natural that she would become his regular correspondent when he left his homeland for long periods. Although he could not be truthful to her about everything, yet, he trusted her with many of his thoughts, sometimes sad ones. He was also the only one with whom she shared her innermost thoughts. Their correspondence went on for more than two and a half years; within this period, Nikolay wrote seventy-five letters to her, and she more than thirty to him. He also sent letters to his Petersburg friends, namely Balakirev and Cui. Though the correspondence was not so intensive, Rimsky-Korsakov wrote six letters to Cui and received the same number of responses. However, Balakirev stopped answering him after the eighth one. Nonetheless, Nikolay kept on writing to him for some time. Overall, he sent twenty-three letters to Balakirev; however, during his last five months at sea he did not send any more.

The clipper's anchorage at Kiel came to an end. The *Almaz* weighed anchor and sailed for England. It headed to Gravesend, a little town on the left bank of the Thames that today lies opposite the port of Tilbury.[4] Sophia, like any mother, was worried about the possible influence on her younger son of people who were, in her opinion, unreliable, people who could lead him down the wrong path. She agreed on the long separation from her son partly due to the desire to protect him against the bad influence of Balakirev's group. But she was afraid that there would be another danger waiting for her son abroad: that he might absorb wrong political ideas, as she considered them, and most of all from Alexander Ivanovich Herzen,[5] who had been to London. Sophia hurried to warn her Nikolay: "My dear, I hope you will not try to meet the editor of the *Bell*, even out of curiosity, while you are in London. Do you know how many young people were ruined by this bell ringer?! Beware of his pernicious ideas!" Nikolay avoided the topic in his letters. He did not meet Herzen (although one of his friends wanted to arrange such a meeting), but not because of following his mother's advice. He considered her views to be out of date. Nikolay himself was not active in politics in those days: he knew little about politics and was not well versed in the political ideas of the times.

Sophia went to Tikhvin and described her visit to Nikolay:

> My dear friend, I should tell you that I was in my house and I did not feel any regret that it would be sold to strangers. While I was inside I did not remember our happy days, I only thought of your father lying on the table. All the things that were there have been packed; the firewood has been sold, the buyer will get only the walls. Good-bye, my dear. God bless you and have mercy upon you and your comrades. I am embracing you. Your Mama, Sophia R.-Korsakov.

The *Almaz* needed reequipping, so it remained in England for the whole winter. It was not difficult to go from Gravesend to London, twenty-five miles away. One had to cross the Thames by boat and then take a train to the Fenchurch Street Station, near the Tower of London. The train trip took about forty minutes. The reefers were allowed to go in turn to London in groups. In early December 1862 Nikolay's chance came, and he spent four days in London with two of his friends. Soon after his return to the clipper, he described his impressions in a letter to his mother. He wrote about his visits to the Crystal Palace,[6] the zoo, Madame Tussaud's, the British Museum, Westminster Abbey, and the Covent Garden Theatre, where he heard a new English opera, *The Triumph of Love* (about which he wrote to Sophia, "It was pretty bad. The singing was also not very good"). His letter to his mother continued:

> On the fourth day we went to the Tower. We looked at the knights' armor, wax figures of English kings and commanders in full armor, prisons, instruments of torture, and at last jewelry: crowns, scepters, and so on. From there we went home; on our way we visited St. Paul's Cathedral, then had dinner and returned to the clipper. Now we are staying in Greenwich because it is much quieter here, fewer vessels. It is about four miles from Gravesend. I think we will be here for a long time, probably even until February.

In December 1862 Rimsky-Korsakov completed the Andante of his symphony. The manuscript of this Andante (orchestrated later, now held by the St. Petersburg Conservatory) is inscribed by the author: "Composed in England in the winter of 1863." Despite utterly unsuitable conditions, Nikolay continued composing music and managed to do so without a piano. (There were no musical instruments on the clipper.) He sent his Andante to Balakirev as a "present" for his Christmas tree and hoped to hear some criticism from him. Nikolay was sure that his composition had a lot of rough places, and Balakirev would be able to notice all of them and point them out. He sent another letter to his mother, Sophia: "My dear Mama, Happy New Year to you, my brother, Mary, and all of you there in Peter. I do not know where and how you will celebrate it; I will certainly be on board as I am every day. It was Christmas Day yesterday, and it did not differ from any other day, only the sailors sang songs and each drank two glasses of vodka."

Rimsky-Korsakov found his isolation from his Petersburg friends to be hard. The musical circle of composers, with its creative atmosphere, was broken. He needed the inspiration provided by the circle to maintain his own creativity. At the beginning of January he wrote to Balakirev: "The New Year celebration was a dull one. We drank champagne, yet I was extremely bored. What will I do in the coming year of 1863? Will I compose much music, and well?"

On the first day of the New Year Sophia wrote to her son:

> 1 January 1863. My dear, yesterday I received your letter dated 26 December. Happy New Year to you and bless you with prayers; let God guide you. This time you get the blessings only from me, it is very sad to think about it. At midnight, I cried about you, the one who is temporarily absent, and about the one who has left us forever. My dear, you are the first one to whom I have written this year. I almost forgot to tell you that your letters are so badly written that it is nearly impossible to make them out; also the last one had a lot of grammatical mistakes.

Nikolay had decided to go to sea hoping that on board he would have time to compose. At first he did. Earlier he had written to Balakirev from Kiel: "I have a very strange kind of character or is it strength, I don't know for sure, but despite all the disgusting things surrounding me I am going on composing. I've contrived the middle part of my Andante on a Russian theme." He told Balakirev that he had in his mind two new themes for a new symphony and that he wished to compose a chorus on a poem by Pushkin or Lermontov or a fantasy chorus, for example, on mermaids.

Rimsky-Korsakov's wish to go to London again was fulfilled, although with some delay. He managed to set off on 9 January 1863, this time with another friend. A letter to his mother says that he again visited the Crystal Palace, and then "after lunch I went to a bathhouse since we don't have a decent one in Greenwich.[...] Since you can't visit any places of interest in the evenings, I went to the Covent Garden Theatre. I listened to some 'Nonsense opera'—*Ruy Blas*."[7] Nikolay described this opera in a letter to Balakirev: "I thought that it would be something by Mendelssohn. I wanted to listen to at least some good orchestration, but it turned out to be an opera by some Howard Glover. What the hell!!! So disgusting!!!"

On the second day he sailed on a boat along the Thames and saw the Victoria dock, which impressed him greatly. On the third day the young fellows visited Parliament; they looked around at everything. They even attended an English trial. Then they headed to the National Gallery.

Sophia was depressed. She wrote to her son:

> My dear friend, I should tell you that when the wind is very strong, I am sick at heart. I remember urging my little boy to go to foreign countries. And that his care would comfort me! How often I do need that care and how long I must wait for his return! I'd like to know whether you have got used to the idea of your voyage for about two more years. What about your compositions? Are they proceeding well? Do you have any chance to play the piano?

Sophia's distress was due in part to the rumor that the design of the clipper *Almaz* made it utterly unsafe. However, the worries about its seaworthiness were unjustified. In the four months that passed from the day that the *Almaz* put out to sea from Kronstadt, Nikolay's hope that he could continue to compose while serving on board was fading. He wrote to his mother on 12 February 1863:

> There is a rather bad piano in the hotel in Greenwich. I play there sometimes. My compositions are not developing. Only now do I understand perfectly well what Kanille meant when he said that a composer must be in a musical atmosphere. But I don't have it here. Moreover, it is very difficult to keep in touch with Balakirev, which is absolutely necessary for me. If I ask him something, I must wait for an answer for two weeks. [...] I have told you about the unmusical atmosphere that surrounds me. Indeed, when I play, my companions are bored; when they sing, they are even worse than bitter radish to me. Never was I as happy as I was last winter! And I composed such good things at that time about which I now just remember with sadness. [...] I don't know what to expect in the future. Englishmen do not possess a musical ear at all; their romances and songs are so disgusting, even worse than Italian, French, or German ones. Italian songs are as cloying as oversugared raspberry jelly; French—vulgar, light, and pointless; German—a bit "Zirlich—Manirlich"; and English—too dry and dispassionate. For sure, the most musical nations are the Hungarian, Spanish, Russian, and also Persian along with other oriental nations in general.

He complained about his idleness in the field of music to Balakirev as well:

Nothing comes to my mind, nothing is being created; I can't undertake anything; I dislike everything somehow. Some pieces cross my mind from time to time, but who knows whether they are good for anything. Three months have passed already and I still have not composed anything. [...] The society on our clipper is just awful. I am sick and tired of it. I think everything is proceeding so badly because I have fallen into such company. Some drink and talk smut; the others are mere clerks; the third ones are simply stupid; the fourth ones have bad characters. [...] but the most important thing is that I do not have a friend with an interest in music. I have absolutely nobody to share it with.

Sophia Rimsky-Korsakov wrote back to Nikolay objecting to his strong criticism of the musical abilities of some nations:

I am afraid you are not right. I think, my dear, you have not lived long enough yet to arrive at such set opinions. You should wait for a while. I am afraid you will be in a huff with me for those words. One friend of ours told me that you have a habit of becoming sulky. I do not even want to think that you will be upset after reading my letter. I am embracing you, my sweet, God bless you and let Him guide you and all of your companions. Your mother, S. R.-K.

Nikolay explained in his next letter: "Speaking about the talents of nations, I mean their natural abilities. And to get an idea about this one does not need to live for a long time; one just needs samples of songs, dances, and any other national melodies. Only they represent the melodiousness of any nation."

Suddenly the *Almaz* received orders to make for Libava (now Liepāja, Latvia) on the Baltic Sea to intercept British ships, which were thought to be providing Polish insurgents with arms and volunteers. Before their departure Nikolay managed to send a brief letter to his mother, dated 14 March 1863:

Dear Mama, can you imagine? We are leaving for Libava the day after tomorrow. [...] I do not have the faintest idea how long we are going to be there. Where we are to go from there, I also do not know. Next to Libava, we are going to carry out. [...] I am writing just a note since I do not have any time. Good-bye now. I'm asking for your blessings. Your son N. R.-Korsakov. Bow to everyone.— Well, I'm going back to Russia again.

On the third day after his arrival in Libava, Rimsky-Korsakov described the passage from England to Russia in the letter to his mother:

Libava. 26 March 1863

My dear Mama, we left Greenwich on 16 March. The storm caught us in the North Sea; it lasted for a day and a half and the ship was tossed about significantly. Both the lifeboats were damaged by the water. But we did not sustain any other damage. It was not very pleasant to be in the cabin because the deck became wet due to the tossing about, and the water came into the cabins. We reached Libava in the evening of 23 March and on the 24th we put to sea again. We rolled about the whole day under tri-sails and in the morning of 25 March we anchored in Polangen [now Palanga, Latvia], a frontier post. Yesterday at 12, we left Polangen and returned to Libava at 5. I do not know how long we are going to stay or toss in the Baltic Sea, maybe a month or a month and a half. [...] Now you should address your letters to Libava.

The future depressed him. At the end of his letter, he sounded sad:

Soon it will be a year since my graduation. Soon it will be a year since I completed my Scherzo (a good Scherzo). Soon it will be a year since that happy time when I lived after my graduation with you and I was not either a reefer or a cadet or a midshipman or a general, but just a burdensome musician—a sponger, who did not cause any harm to anybody, and who was able to visit Balakirev and other dear people. Now I'm in service, I'm of use; I seize smuggled goods and do many, many things....And many do not despise me, as they would do if I were a useless musician; they even consider me to be a good boy. I'm sending my Andante to Balakirev from here. I hope now it will reach him. [Balakirev never received the Andante Rimsky-Korsakov had sent him from England.]

Later the *Almaz* received orders to resume its journey to North America.

The atmosphere on the clipper did not encourage composition. Rimsky-Korsakov described it in a letter to Cui sent earlier from Greenwich:

Perhaps I will compose something under the influence of the poetic sultriness in the cabin, the whistle of wind in the sails and the round oaths used by the naval officers every second. At sea, it is good to compose only music like "The Ocean" of

Rubinstein or the storm in the *William Tell* overture.[8] And how glorious, grateful, pleasant, and noble is naval service! Imagine you were going to the North Sea: the sky is of a dull, dirty-gray color; the wind is moaning; the tossing is so hard that you can hardly keep on your feet; you are constantly being sprinkled with cold foam all over the deck; and sometimes you are sluiced over from top to toe. It is cold. You feel like vomiting a little....How would you like it?

At the same time, Voin Rimsky-Korsakov received some positive reports about his younger brother and sent the following letter to him:

> I was very happy to hear that my brother is a brave reefer. This gives me a hope that you have reconciled yourself to naval service or at least you do not give it up, like so many young people. The sea will form your character; make it stronger and more definite than music would do. If your musical inclinations disappear then they are not worth caring about, because their very instability will show that they have simply been illusions but not something essential for you. If in two or three years of sailing your inclinations are still preserved, it will show that they are not artificial but real ones, buried in your heart and body. Then, well, why not, you can develop your musical skills further?

Their trip on the clipper ship *Almaz* to New York lasted more than two months. Rimsky-Korsakov started to write a letter to his mother while he was aboard: "26 September 1863. Sixty-three days at sea and still 420 miles from New York. How do you like that? It is a long voyage, isn't it?" On the next day, 27 September, he continued the letter, in which he described the storm and the ocean in more detail at his mother's request.

It had been nine months from the time Rimsky-Korsakov finished the Andante for his symphony that he had composed during his stay in England. Fully sixty-five days of this period were spent at sea. The composer had not written anything for a long time. In his letter to his mother, Nikolay confessed that if he stayed more than five years abroad he would not be able to compose anything. That was still his mood when the *Almaz* finally reached New York.

Without waiting for another letter from his mother, Rimsky-Korsakov started writing a new letter in which he shared his impression about a trip to Niagara Falls. He was impressed with the American vessels, saying that they were "highly comfortable: they are equipped even with a barber's shop." He continued in another letter: "On the next day (28 October 1863) we went to see the falls and we took a photograph. Then we went to an Indian village that was located nine miles from Niagara Falls." At the end of that letter to his mother, Rimsky-Korsakov told her about his musical experience in New York City: "I have been to the opera in New York twice. The first time, I heard the opera *Rigoletto*, but I had to leave, because they sang horribly. The second time it was Mozart's *Don Giovanni*. They sang exceptionally horribly, but at least I was not bored. Goodbye, my dear mother—I am asking for your blessings. Your son N. R.-Korsakov."

At the beginning of December the composer spent two days in Washington, D.C., and on his return to the *Almaz* he wrote a letter with details about his trip to the capital of the United States: "Washington, as you can see, is still a young city; the streets are incredibly wide; the whole city is spread all over the hills; most of the streets are very dirty, and in some places the city looks like a village."

Rimsky-Korsakov was not in the mood for composing music during his stay in the United States. In a letter to Cui in early December 1863 he wrote: "I have not written anything, I have not orchestrated anything, and I have not shown my face in the field of music at all: why—I do not know; and only bad things were coming to my head. Only I know that I have not written anything, not because of my laziness, but because of something else of which I am unaware." His letters to Balakirev were full of the despair he felt about not composing anything. Balakirev responded to him: "From your letters I can see that the trip abroad was very useful for you. Unhappiness has developed you, and in your letters I have started to see not a nice young child anymore, but an honorable young man."

During the whole of March 1864 the *Almaz* stayed in the United States, going from one place to another. There were rumors on the ship about its making a long trip abroad after North America, but nothing was definite. Finally, after one month's stay in New York, the fate of the *Almaz* was decided. It was to go on a long voyage to South America. In his last short note to his mother from New York, Rimsky-Korsakov wrote: "New York, 25 April 1864. I think we are leaving in about an hour. A priest is coming to give a special service; there were many guests from other ships that came to say good-byes. The weather is so nice here that probably we will be going well by the trade winds. So, good-bye. I am asking for your blessing. N. R.-Korsakov."

It took two months for the *Almaz* to reach Brazil. The composer had just turned twenty. He continued to share his concerns about not being able to compose anything in his letters to his mother. In these letters he also asked his mother not to share his thoughts and feelings with his brother. In one of his letters to his mother, written the day before the ship reached Rio de Janeiro, Nikolay wrote:

> Dear mother, I am sorry that I have not written to you for a long time. And today I would like to fill this void. I am telling you that the weather has been clear and warm, but the wind was not very favorable. We expect to reach Rio tomorrow morning. We will have to say good-bye to the warm weather, since the Tropic of Capricorn is approaching and there will be cold, snowy winds, rain, fog, and other nasty weather. The ocean is quite boring, I cannot say too much about it: just water, flying fish, the moon, stars, again water, and that's it. Please remember that I am writing all of this only to you and kindly ask you not to share my thoughts with anybody. What shall I write? About the clipper?—I am already used to it. About the captain?—I do not want to write about him. About myself?—Nothing exciting. I am healthy, do my service, eat, drink, smoke, sleep, read, I have drawn a map of the southern sky, have found all of the constellations according to the French astronomer Arago; I have read a few books by Byron, and finally I sit in my cabin and I am silent as usual, and, of course, I have not written any music. It seems to me that I am becoming more and more indifferent to it: you can easily get used to anything, you can easily teach yourself to sleep more or less, you can teach yourself to sleep either seven or thirteen hours a day, to keep your service for six hours and not get tired, not to see land for sixty days and consequently not being able to compose for over a year.

The composer had finished writing this letter when the *Almaz* docked on 26 June at Rio, where it stayed for two weeks. Brazil left many impressions on the composer, and he shared them with his mother in his letters. The letters were usually long, with lots of details. While in Brazil Rimsky-Korsakov visited the Tijuca waterfall, which he liked a lot and described in one of his letters to his mother:

> You cannot even imagine, my dear mother, what a pleasure I had experienced walking in the Tijuca Forest. But how tastes can be different! I am writing to

you this letter and there is our doctor sitting next to me and complaining about our trip. He says that nothing could be worse than going up and down in the mountains, walking along the forest among marshes and snakes, and how he would be happy being back in the city.

After Rio, it was decided to go to Montevideo. However, the ship could not reach the city and had to return to Rio because on the way to Montevideo a terrible storm damaged the hull and it started to leak. After this the captain was very concerned that the ship would not be able to continue its long voyage. It was decided to stay in Rio for three months in order to repair the hull. While they were docked in Rio, the emperor of Brazil visited the ship. The composer continued writing letters to his mother in which he told her about all of the constellations he had seen. He also shared his worries regarding music:

> During my two-year voyage, I have not written anything. I have become musically stupefied. As for the rest, I have moved forward, but in the activity I have chosen for myself, I have completely moved back. On returning to Russia, I will have to bid farewell to music, because I see it clearly that I am unable to do anything with music. Meanwhile, I have to admit that I am becoming more and more thrilled about our voyage. I want to see as much as I can of the world.

Finally, on 24 October 1864, the *Almaz* started its voyage back to Europe. It took about two months. On 16 November the *Almaz* left the southern hemisphere and passed the St. Peter and St. Paul Archipelago. By New Year's Eve the ship had arrived at Villa Franca near Nice, France, where it stayed for three months. During his stay in Nice, Rimsky-Korsakov took many long walks. In his letters to his mother, the composer continued to share his impressions about what he had seen. Finally, on 21 May 1865, the *Almaz* reached Kronstadt. Later, in his memoirs, Rimsky-Korsakov wrote: "My trip abroad has come to an end. Many unforgettable memories about beautiful weather of foreign countries and the ocean; I have suffered many rude and unpleasant impressions about naval service during my voyage, which lasted two years and eight months. What can I say about music? Music has been forgotten and my enthusiasm for creative activity has been suffocated."

By the end of 1865 Nikolay was already a mature young man with rather extensive life experience. By this time his joyful childhood with his parents in

Tikhvin had become a thing of the past. His "green years" of study at the St. Petersburg Naval Academy, during which he had become acquainted with the musical society of St. Petersburg, were finished. He had just begun to compose a symphony under the guidance of Balakirev and other musical friends when he had to go on a long sea voyage, which was compulsory for graduates who wished to attain the rank of a naval officer. The voyage had separated him from music for almost three years, and during this time he had given up composition, leaving the symphony unfinished.

Return to the Musical Circle of Balakirev

Now, on his return from his voyage, he resumed his participation in the musical circle headed by Balakirev. He renewed his meetings with Musorgsky and Cui, as well as with the critic Stasov, all members of the circle. Among his new acquaintances were Borodin and Lodyzhensky,[9] who had also joined Balakirev's circle. Under their influence he completed the symphony he had begun before his voyage. It was performed with some success in December 1865 at a concert conducted by Balakirev at the Free Music School.[10]

Despite his successful debut in the world of music, Rimsky-Korsakov could not leave the naval service because of the financial advantages that position offered. Fortunately, he was assigned to service ashore in St. Petersburg, and his duties did not demand much of his time. He rented furnished rooms on Vasilyevsky Island, and his office was at the harbor on the island. He usually spent two or three hours each morning at his desk preparing various documents such as reports and requisitions. After this he was usually free and went for lunch at the house of his brother. Voin, twenty-two years Nikolay's senior, was now a rear admiral. Since Voin was the director of the Naval Academy, he lived in an apartment in one of the buildings of the Academy. These were both located on Vasilyevsky Island, on an embankment of the Neva River. In the evenings Rimsky-Korsakov could participate in the musical meetings held either at Cui's or Balakirev's home. Balakirev lived on Nevsky Prospect at that time, and Rimsky-Korsakov often paid him friendly visits, sometimes even spending the night.

He looked up to Balakirev, considering him to be the highest authority on musical issues. Musorgsky and Borodin became his closest friends. The latter lived on the campus of the Academy of Medical Surgery where he, being a chemical scientist, had his own laboratory, so their meetings and conversations about music often took place there. Being devoted to chemistry no less than to music, Borodin would interrupt their discussions about music and rush to attend to his flasks and test tubes at the laboratory to make sure "nothing boiled over," as Rimsky-Korsakov used to say. One day Borodin also paid a visit to Nikolay's apartment. He wrote to his wife, Ekaterina, after this visit:

> He was indescribably glad to see me. He immediately ordered the samovar and began drinking tea in an extremely amusing manner; being tall, wearing a civilian jacket, moving clumsily and beaming with joy, he sawed the air, vociferated, made tea, stoked the samovar, and then finally poured tea. So funny! […] We set ourselves to playing […]. I played him pieces of my new symphonic work in progress. Korsinka stormed about and shouted that this was the best of all my compositions.[11] He clamored and gestured so much! He stuck out his lower lip, blinked his eyes, and accompanied sometimes in bass and sometimes in treble. Then I heard a clock chime and counted: one, two, three, and four. And I had come there at half past nine in the evening! And in the intervals between playing we did not forget to drink tea; indeed we drank up two whole samovars! I haven't played music so much to my heart's content and had so much tea for ages!

Rimsky-Korsakov's circle of acquaintances in the field of music expanded over time. He was introduced to Lyudmila Ivanovna Shestakova, a sister of Glinka, at Stasov's birthday party on 2 January 1866. After this he was a frequent guest in her house with the other members of the Balakirev circle, and Dargomizhsky also often paid visits to those parties. But Rimsky-Korsakov's acquaintances were not limited to those musical interests. He was often also at his brother's home, where a completely different group of people gathered. According to his own words, he was treated differently in those two opposite "worlds." In Balakirev's circle he was considered to be a talented composer, an indifferent pianist, and a nice but none too clever officer. Among Voin's friends and relatives he was primarily a naval officer, and then an expert on serious music and an amateur musician who played the piano brilliantly and at odd moments composed some music. At the parties held by his brother or his friends, Nikolay used to play piano music for four hands, perform his own arrangements of works by Liszt and Glinka, and play quadrilles from

Offenbach's *La belle Hélène* for the younger partygoers to dance to. But he kept this entirely secret from Balakirev.

Meanwhile Rimsky-Korsakov went on composing. By the middle of 1867 he had already published twelve romances and completed his *Overture on Three Russian Themes* and his *Fantasy on Serbian Themes*, composed especially for a concert of Slavonic music. "Everyone liked the *Serbian Fantasy*," Cui wrote in his review of that concert, "and it was played again at the request of the audience. Korsakov is certainly becoming its favorite."

About the same time, Nikolay was again almost transferred away from St. Petersburg to the nearby city of Kronstadt. But again his old friends intervened, and he was sent instead to the Eighth Naval Depot, housed on the Kryukov Canal in St. Petersburg itself. He sometimes served as the officer of the day there, while at other times he was on duty in one of the workshops that belonged to the naval office in New Holland (one of Petersburg's districts), and on still other occasions he was assigned to guard duty at the prison. Later he moved into another furnished apartment, but still on Vasilyevsky Island.

Rimsky-Korsakov spent the summer of 1867 at his brother's country house in Tervajoki (in Finland, forty miles from Helsinki). His mother, Sophia, was also there. After the death of her husband in 1862, Sophia left Tikhvin and lived with her elder son's family. Nikolay Rimsky-Korsakov began composing his first program music for symphony orchestra—a descriptive orchestral piece called *Sadko*—at Tervajoki.[12] Stasov at first had offered this project to Musorgsky, but later he suggested to Rimsky-Korsakov to take it up: "Compose *Sadko*, dear Korsinka. It's very intriguing for me to see what will be the result. I wouldn't tease you to pick up the idea if I were not sure you would do it successfully." His next letter read: "It's your first really Russian composition. It belongs only to you and not to anybody else. [All his previous compositions were written under the considerable influence of Balakirev.] They say you must spoil before you spin, but you have managed not to."

Sadko was performed at the end of 1867 at a concert of the Russian Musical Society conducted by Balakirev. It enjoyed considerable success. The composer and critic Alexander Serov[13] wrote in his review: "The music introduced by the author is sparkling, rich, original, and distinctive. *Sadko* belongs to a person of considerable talent, who can draw paintings with the help of music." However, there were less flattering reviews, such as, for example, one in the newspaper *Golos* (*The Voice*) written by one Famintsin: "The author is undoubtedly talented, but he is under the influence of plebeians to too great an extent."

Nevertheless, Rimsky-Korsakov's talent was unmistakably recognized, as Musorgsky said in a letter to his friend: "You, Korsinka, have revealed your sweet nature in the Andante portion of your symphony. You have claimed 'only God is sinless' in your *Russian Overture*. You have proved in the *Serbian Fantasy* that it's possible to compose quickly and nicely at the same time. And your *Sadko* will certainly establish you as an Artist." Musorgsky wrote this after looking through the manuscript of *Sadko*, before it was performed in the concert hall. Rimsky-Korsakov responded: "I'm so grateful to you, Modest, for that idea you have given me at Cui's. Do you remember? […] Now I'm going to rest a little, as my pate has become rather exhausted from thinking too much. I will rest a little, be idle for a while, compose some romances, and what I will do later on I don't know yet."

But soon he started working on a new symphony, making some drafts and showing them to his friends. Neither Balakirev nor any of the others approved of them. According to Rimsky-Korsakov, Balakirev, when he criticized something, used culinary terms instead of musical terms, many of which he didn't know. For example, he could say, "This composition has both sauce and pepper but doesn't have roast beef." It was impossible for Rimsky-Korsakov to understand from such remarks what was wrong with his composition. Disappointed, he put off the composition of his Second Symphony indefinitely.

At that time musical evenings began to be held at the household of Vladimir Purgold. Vladimir was the brother of Nikolay Purgold, the father of Nadezhda Purgold. Nikolay and Vladimir came from a cultured family originally from Germany. After Nikolay's death in 1861, Vladimir took responsibility along with Nikolay's wife, Anna, to look after the orphaned family. Vladimir was known to Nikolay Purgold's children as Uncle "Oh!" Purgold had been a distinguished member and sponsor of the Free Music School from the time it was established. He became acquainted with Balakirev and a group of young composers through his membership in the Free Music School. The musical evenings at his home included the Purgold sisters ("musical lasses," as Stasov called them). Such gatherings allowed the young composers from Balakirev's circle, as well as Stasov and Lyudmila Shestakova, to become frequent guests at the Purgold household, which at that time consisted of Vladimir; Nikolay Purgold's wife, Anna; and Anna's three daughters: Sophia, Alexandra, and

Nadezhda (Rimsky-Korsakov's future wife). The other daughters were married and lived separately; the Purgold sons also lived by themselves.

On one notable evening, when the Purgold sisters met the young composers for the first time, they performed romances and played a piano arrangement of *Sadko* for four hands. Rimsky-Korsakov, the youngest among the group, considered it an honor to be introduced to Dargomizhsky. For his part, Dargomizhsky could hardly help noticing the young composer and even went so far as to declare: "He is very talented and should be taken care of in order to allow his talent to flourish."

Although Rimsky-Korsakov was officially engaged in his naval duties, once he came back into the world of music he stayed there. In 1868, during his summer holidays, he began working on the program for a Third Symphony without completing his postponed Second Symphony. He had been invited by Lodyzhensky to stay at his estate in the village of Makovnytsy (not far from Tver).[14] He left for Makovnytsy at the end of June and spent about three weeks there together with Borodin and his wife. He wrote to Musorgsky: "I spent my days pleasantly, riding horses in the company of Borodin, eating berries with cream and taking long walks." From Makovnytsy he paid a visit to his relatives in Finland. During this time his Third Symphony, *Antar* (as he named it), became his second one to be published.

At the end of the year Rimsky-Korsakov attempted to take another step forward in his musical development: he asked his naval superiors to permit him to conduct concerts held by the Imperial Russian Musical Society, at the Society's request. However, the secretary of the navy, Nikolay Krabbe, an admiral, vetoed the request: "His Majesty, the Tsar, does not welcome efforts by his officers to become participants in public performances either in concerts or in theatres." For this reason his career as a conductor was delayed.

Musical Evenings with the Purgolds

In the mid-1860s both of the younger Purgold sisters, Nadezhda and Alexandra, began taking part in musical evenings held at Dargomizhsky's home. Nadezhda accompanied the singers on the piano; Alexandra possessed a brilliant soprano voice, and her performances were always full of spirit. Dargomizhsky had been working on his opera *Kammeny Gost* (*The Stone Guest*), and Alexandra sang the parts of Laura and Donna Anna at these musical parties. Nadezhda was charming. At one such party, Dargomizhsky, watching her playing the piano, turned to his neighbor, Yuliya Platonova, an artist, and said, "Look at this perfect Greek profile. Her face looks so virginal and pure. The girl is so charming and so gifted. I like her very much."

The young composers improved the musical level of the Purgold soirées greatly. In its turn, the creative atmosphere of the Purgold household encouraged the young composers to develop their talents. However, the pair of charming and gifted sisters certainly provided the greatest attraction. Musorgsky composed a group of songs called *Detskaya* (*The Nursery*) especially for Alexandra. In his turn, Borodin dedicated a comic piece to Nadezhda called *Serenada chetyrekh kavalerov* (*The Serenade of Four Admirers*), which was sung by an ad hoc quartet of Borodin, Musorgsky, Rimsky-Korsakov, and Stasov. The young composers gave the sisters nicknames invented by Musorgsky. Nadezhda was called "our charming orchestra" for her readiness to accompany them on the piano at any time and for the outstanding quality of her performance. Stasov remarked: "It's really quite odd that a fragile little woman [like] Nadezhda is able to play such sophisticated and monumental compositions." Alexandra was called "Donna Anna-Laura" for her brilliant portrayal of those two female parts in the opera *The Stone Guest*.

The musical evenings at Vladimir Purgold's home were always lively. General Veliaminov, an amateur singer, usually took part in the performances. Sometimes he was rather amusing. Rimsky-Korsakov remembered one incident:

> The general stood placing his left hand on the chair of an accompanist and holding a key in his right hand (it's strange, but for some reason he always held a key in his hand during his performances), with his leg to one side. He tried to sing *Svetik Savishna* [*Darling Savishna*] by Musorgsky. Being short of breath, he urged the accompanist at the end of almost every five-beat measure to let him breathe. Having made his request, he went on singing until he suddenly cried out, "Let me gasp!"…and so on and so forth.

Large musical gatherings at the Purgold home usually ended in dinners with toasts to musical good fortune, to the composers' success, and so on. Sometimes they organized dances, and on those occasions Musorgsky or Lodyzhensky would play the piano so the others could dance. After one such evening at the Purgolds', Lyudmila Shestakova wrote to the "musical lasses":

"As soon as I woke up today I had the desire to write to you, my dear Alexandra and Nadezhda, to tell you what a nice evening I had yesterday at your place. I don't remember when I enjoyed an evening so much as I did yesterday. Everything was so lovely, especially the singing."

The closing party for the 1869–1870 season was particularly well attended and unusually lively. The spring "white nights" had begun in St. Petersburg, and although it was well past midnight, all the guests, as well as the hosts, went out to see Lyudmila Shestakova off. She lived not far from the Purgold family, on Gagarin Street. Lyudmila told her friend later, "There were about twenty people. And those who lived nearby might have heard our voices and laughter."

The musical evenings at the Purgold family home continued to play an important role in the development of the talents of the young composers. Many of their compositions, a number of them stimulated by the challenge of testing the talents of Nadezhda and Alexandra, were performed for the first time at such evenings. Indeed, the composition of the group remained nearly the same whether they gathered for such evenings at the homes of the Purgold family or at the homes of Balakirev, Cui, or Stasov. Shestakova too was always ready to receive the young visitors. On occasion they might even come around in advance during the day to show Lyudmila something new about their compositions.

Rimsky-Korsakov's development was particularly marked. He usually spent a part of each summer in the country house of his brother in Tervajoki. His mother was always very glad when he could spend some time there with her. He lived in Tervajoki in the summer of 1870 while the Purgold sisters were abroad in Germany, where, among other things, they arranged for the publication of Musorgsky's *Seminarist* (*Seminarian*), which had been banned in Russia. Dargomizhsky had died on 5 January 1869, and pursuant to the terms of his will, Rimsky-Korsakov began working on the orchestration of Dargomizhsky's unfinished opera, *The Stone Guest*, in Tervajoki. Feeling that his end was approaching and that he might not complete his opera, Dargomizhsky had specified that Cui was to complete the composition and Rimsky-Korsakov was to orchestrate it.

Stasov wrote to Rimsky-Korsakov:

> When I woke up, I felt that I should tell You immediately that I see You developing more and more, getting more serious and deeper. Do You know that among all your

company You are the most thoughtful? [...] None is more devoted to his work than You, none is spending more time studying than You. Do You know what is the only thing You are lacking in my opinion? It is passion. But I'm sure it will come with time. [...] This must happen all at once and in the way of a conflagration.

Soon after receiving this letter, Rimsky-Korsakov composed a romance he called *To My Song*, to words by the German poet Heinrich Heine, and it was sung at a party held by Shestakova. Stasov wrote to Nadezhda Purgold about this romance: "He has never composed anything like this before. Although all his romances were beautiful, they were all rather calm, even a little cold. Now he has entered a new phase."

Romantic Stirrings, 1870

A romance seemed to be in the offing. Around this time Rimsky-Korsakov was working on his first opera, entitled *Pskovityanka* (*The Maid of Pskov*). He had begun composing it at the end of the summer of 1868. In the autumn of the same year, Alexander Borodin wrote to his wife, "Korsinka has played some pieces from his opera *The Maid of Pskov*. . . . It has such a sweet scent of freshness, youth, and beauty that I simply became limp with excitement. What a huge talent this man possesses!" Nadezhda Purgold was very interested in the development of this opera, and Rimsky-Korsakov, appreciating her musical talents and feeling her sympathy, showed her each new piece he composed; sometimes he even came round simply to play a duet with her, and of course he continued to attend the musical evenings. His visits to the Purgold family became more frequent. They played various compositions for four hands and spoke about music and his new opera. Rimsky-Korsakov was extremely interested in her opinion about *The Maid of Pskov*. He paid great attention to her judgment, which he considered far from superficial.

After the three musicians, among them Rimsky-Korsakov, visited Pargolovo,[15] Nadezhda Purgold wrote in her diary:

30 August 1870. (About two a.m.) How unexpected and, one may say, romantic our meeting was! The moon, a balcony, a lovely night. It's so funny! No sooner had I hummed "Come to the kingdom of roses and wine, come, I'm waiting,"

singing this, I thought, it's very annoying that he hasn't visited us for ages, when I heard familiar voices and at last saw his white service cap. I thought they were coming toward me. No, they were passing by. I was at a loss. At last Sincerity seemed to notice that somebody had been on the balcony; then I asked them to come in.[…]Sincerity has enlivened me, and I hope tomorrow he will revitalize me even more. It's so nice that we are meeting tomorrow. Today was like a dream, it was so unexpectedly soon.

By the pet name "Sincerity," of course, Nadezhda meant none other than Rimsky-Korsakov himself. It was a nickname given to him by the sisters. All the other friends also had nicknames generously handed round by the "musical lasses." All of them together were called "Brigands" for their courage in opposing routine in the world of music. Another nickname for Rimsky-Korsakov was "Pirate"; Cui was called "Causticity" for his frequent cutting remarks; Musorgsky was "Cruel Tiger" or "Humor"; Balakirev was "Power"; Stasov was "Bach." Nikolay Lodyzhensky took part in the meetings of Balakirev's group somewhat rarely and accordingly received the nickname "Fim," or Mif (Myth) spelled backward. He was a talented composer of romances but composed very little. Later he would become a diplomat. Stasov called the group of young composers "the Gang."

Three days later Rimsky-Korsakov and Musorgsky again visited the Purgold family. Alexandra Purgold sang the romance *Pesnya zolotoi rybky* (*The Song of the Golden Fish*) by Balakirev and *Ya veru, ya lubim* (*I Believe I Am Loved*) by Rimsky-Korsakov. The accompanist was Nadezhda Purgold, who described this evening in her diary:

What should I write about today's evening? It was so good, so perfectly good, as rarely happens.[…]Nothing prevented me from abandoning myself to the inspiration and enjoyment of music that Sincerity inspires in me. I'm becoming sure that his music is far closer to my soul and me than the music of Humor. There is some irresistible attractiveness, sympathy, warmth, and immensity of the highest degree. Today I don't feel any dissatisfaction. I felt rather good, rather joyful. When I listen to some of my favorite pieces by Korsinka, then so great an inner delight arises that I can't control myself and show it with some gesture, movement or word.[…]Everyone blessed by God with such a gift of talent should feel just this sort of happiness.[…]It occurs very rarely when you feel so free, easy, and comfortable in the presence of somebody else, as happens when one is next to Sincerity. His presence does not disturb you at all, and on the contrary, it even encourages you a little. It has been a long time since I felt the music I played to such an extent as I did today. After playing *The Fish* and *I Believe I Am Loved* I was trembling. It took me some time to calm down and regain my senses. You might think it strange that I can feel so much when I merely accompany. But it happens to me and in such moments I feel so wonderful. Is it possible to express in words how wonderful you feel?

For his part, Nikolay Rimsky-Korsakov began to call Nadezhda "Golden Fish."

The next entry in Nadezhda's diary was made after she returned to St. Petersburg:

What makes me happy is that our relations now, after being resumed, are even better than before. We are very good friends now. Recently, analyzing my behavior and myself, I found another shortcoming, which I'm suffering from. But it seems that I'm already recovering because of the very reason that I became aware of it. This shortcoming is that I have a habit of too openly displaying my feelings not only before others but also before myself. Strange as it might seem, it is true. I notice this drawback particularly when I am evaluating my relations with other people. It is very tempting for a person to pretend to be in love and even to show it off before the others. In fact, though, this never should occur. You should always examine your attitude to others as deeply as possible. And even more important is to be careful not to show your feelings in front of others, whether they are true or not. I'm lucky that Korsinka is such a rare person that whatever you tell him, any kind of nonsense, and no matter how poorly you behave, nothing bad will ever happen. I would bet my life that he would never let the matter go further, or even tease you. In a word, he will behave as a very generous and intelligent person. But not everyone is like him. And I might even say no one is like him. Indeed, there is no one else like him, nobody else, yes, nobody!

But meetings were not the only things. In those days one could exchange written messages throughout the day with the help of a courier boy, who could be found easily on the street. The following brief exchange, from 5

December 1870, between the budding couple marked the beginning of their regular correspondence: Nadezhda Purgold wrote, "I'm waiting for you, Korsinka, tomorrow at 6." And she received the answer, "Without fail."

In the middle of December the Purgold family held a party at which fifty-seven people were present. Following a banquet, Dargomizhsky's *The Stone Guest* was performed, with the participation of the "musical lasses." But two weeks after that dinner, at the end of 1870, the girls' mother died, and Nadezhda and Alexandra, of course, discontinued their participation in the musical evenings for a while. But fairly quickly Lyudmila Shestakova began to lead them back onto their familiar track and organized a dinner to which she invited the sisters, Rimsky-Korsakov, and Musorgsky. Then she held a musical evening at which all the members of Balakirev's circle were present. The previous musical life of the Purgold sisters gradually resumed.

3

Falling in Love

I love you so much, more than anyone else, my darling Golden Fish.
—Rimsky-Korsakov to Nadezhda Purgold, 1871

Romance Blossoms

The more frequent the meetings between Rimsky-Korsakov and Nadezhda became, the more often they sent written messages to each other. Rimsky-Korsakov wrote to Nadezhda on 17 April 1871: "I'm free on Monday evening, since Mily wrote that I shouldn't come [to see him]. So, if Golden Fish would like, we could play in the evening instead of the morning." The next day he received an answer: "I'm very glad that you're free on Monday, but we won't be able to play in the evening. The reason is that we've booked a box for tomorrow's performance of *Ruslan*. So come in the morning as we arranged. But in the evening, if a 'bad' man likes, we will listen to *Ruslan* together. We have one vacant place in our box for this 'bad' man. Is it convenient for You? I'll be waiting for You after 1 p.m. tomorrow. N. Purgold."

Another message from Nadezhda later showed her happiness that an event had been unexpectedly canceled. She was supposed to go to the theatre to hear the opera *Rogneda* by Serov, and this would have prevented her from meeting Rimsky-Korsakov. She notified him: "We are not going to *Rogneda*. Thank God! I'd rather play good music in the evening. Do come as early as possible, please."

On another occasion, when for some reason Rimsky-Korsakov decided to change the date of their meeting, he wrote to her: "Golden Fish! I think it would be better if I don't come to You. As I told You it might happen that I would be late, and in the evening I think it is better not to come this time. Could You please arrange another day? Could it be Monday, for example? Whenever You like and at your convenience." He received a response the same day,

Why should we, Korsinka, postpone the meeting for such a long time, till Monday? If it's not possible on Friday […], then come the next day, that is, on

Saturday. But the evening is still preferable. But could You come a little earlier, then we will finish playing earlier. Although it's very difficult to organize, we should try. There is only one bad thing, You've promised Saturdays to one of Your friends. But this once, You might cheat. […] I hope You'll bring the episode concerning Matuta with You.[1] I shake Your hand firmly. N. Purgold.

Nadezhda Purgold

Nadezhda tried to persuade Nikolay that she had innumerable shortcomings, that she was not as talented as he thought. On 30 April 1871 she wrote in her diary, after discussing such issues with him:

I can't read today. I'm constantly thinking of yesterday's conversation with him. It's awful that he is so dazzled, that he doesn't want to see my pettiness. Doesn't he believe that what I said yesterday, I said sincerely? However, I was not completely sincere. I didn't tell him everything that might be said against me. And even more important, I used general phrases and didn't name some rather convincing facts. They are so evident, but it's so awful to admit them even before myself that I still haven't done it yet. He is so flawless, pure, and sinless, and that is why he can't see sins in others. He illuminates me with his own light, and he doesn't notice that he is admiring the reflection of his own light. It's the same as if the sun would admire the moon, that is, its own reflected light. This very comparison came to my mind in the morning. It's a pity I didn't think of this illustration yesterday. I would have told him. It's a very good illustration. I would have mentioned exactly this comparison when we discussed my critical thinking and my general musical development.

He said that I had advanced very much in music, that he could always ask me about anything and consider my opinion. But he doesn't notice or he just forgets where I got all of my knowledge. I have learned all this from that very musical circle or, even more precisely, particularly from him. As I'm much closer to him than with anyone else in the circle, therefore he influences me much more. Consequently, there is just the reflection of light, so familiar to him. So I don't bring into the circle anything new, fresh, of my own, and hence, I can't have that high moral influence that he is talking about. How confused he is! How clear all this is to me, and how I should have proved this to him! I'm certain that he will understand this sooner or later, but the sooner the better. I hope I will be strong enough to take it in my stride in any case. However, he is absolutely right about everything concerning Alexandra Purgold. He has showed his brilliant mind, his keen observation, and his wittiness in judging people in defining her role in the circle. He described her role in the circle very correctly, and he sounded so persuasive. On comparing me to her, much of what he said was true. But it's awful, as doing this he again illuminated me with his own kind, bright, and warm light, and therefore he exaggerated and lost the right direction. But this just proved how poor and illusory are my role in the circle and my influence on it. Moreover, try as he might, he still failed to define it exactly. It's something like ethical influence. It's certainly very pleasant, but meaningless. I'll give an example that shows it clearly.

Imagine that I had left the circle, that I had died or something of the kind. It would not be noticed. It wouldn't influence things in any way. Everything would be the same as usual. The musical evenings would be exactly the same as before; they would play all the same [music]. They could carry on perfectly well without me. Certainly, I know that if I died it could temporarily put a damper on things. Maybe they would become upset a little due to our personal, but not musical, relations. Especially Korsinka would be upset, as we are very close friends, and I think he considers me even more than just a friend. But as for the music itself, it would not be noticed, and [my absence] would not influence it in any way.

Now let's consider Alexandra. What if she were to leave the circle? On the contrary, it would have a big influence. The musical evenings would be spoiled since nothing could be sung. And they would compose less for that very reason, as one has a much greater desire to compose when one thinks of a brilliant performance by a particular person, and when you don't have such a person, consequently, you would compose less. In fact, I'm absolutely sure that some of Musorgsky's works wouldn't have been composed at all if it hadn't been for Alexandra. Without even thinking of it, he composed his "Children" because of her and for her, as he knew perfectly well that nobody else but she could sing them as he wished.[2] She inspired others with her singing. Finally, she is very open, merry, and sociable, and with her brilliant character, she can make everyone feel good. She is certainly the life of the party. What concerns me in particular is that I do not possess such character traits and I do not make the party more enjoyable or something of that kind....

And Korsinka is such a wonderful, pure, bright, and wholehearted personality. I will probably never ever meet anybody else like him for the rest of my life. And our meeting will remain a bright spot for me forever.

Summer arrived. The Purgold family moved to Pargolovo, and Nadezhda wrote from there to Rimsky-Korsakov, "Come to us tomorrow, Pirate. We have settled down completely and everything goes on as usual. It's very nice here in Pargolovo." He responded, "I'll come tomorrow or in the nearest future. And when we meet, Golden Fish should tell me off, and for what, I'll tell you later."

Nadezhda made no further diary entries concerning the reason, according to Rimsky-Korsakov, she was supposed to tell him off. Her next entry continued along the earlier line of thought:

How disgusting I seem to be to myself! How miserable I can be in my own eyes! The only thing I know for sure is that I'm far, far worse than him, that he is much, much above me, and even my eyes are not able to reach that height. I'm not worthy of even his single glance, his single bright, warm, open, magnificent smile! His smile reverberates around him; I have never met anyone with such a smile as his. For only this lovely smile I'm ready for…I don't know myself what I'm ready for.

Rimsky-Korsakov sent a brief note to her after a conversation that seemed by then to have been ridiculous. "Oh, I'm so vexed at myself, Golden Fish, vexed and, because of this, sad." She responded immediately, "If you might be vexed at somebody, then it must be me, not You. As everything I said and did yesterday was absolutely contrary to what I should have said and done. I beg Your pardon if yesterday my awful temper caused you to feel sad or even a shadow of it."

Nadezhda followed the development of *The Maid of Pskov* with the keenest interest, mixed up with thrilling private feelings. The postscript had the same message: "Could You bring the last piece of Olga's part with You on Saturday? Although it seems You don't believe I like it, I will tell you again, little do I like something to such an extent as this part. If it is possible, could you come as early as possible?" By this she meant a piece from Olga's part in *The Maid of Pskov*, composed by Rimsky-Korsakov shortly before.

Rimsky-Korsakov often visited the Purgold family along with Musorgsky. On 23 June 1871 he wrote to Nadezhda: "Let's change our plans for Friday, Golden Fish. Cruel Tiger has asked to come with me, but not until 5:30 p.m.

So I suggest that you don't expect me at noon; we are to be at Your place at 6 p.m. We will be unlikely to have a long walk, as Tiger is bringing various promising compositions with him and I am bringing 'bad' ones Olga and Nanny with me.[3] Do you approve?"

An Offer from the St. Petersburg Conservatory

At the beginning of July 1871 the Purgold sisters traveled north to spend several days in Vyborg while Rimsky-Korsakov was visiting his mother Sophia in Tervajoki;[4] his brother had rented a country house there for his family. Soon after returning to St. Petersburg, Rimsky-Korsakov received a letter from Mikhail Azanchevsky, president of the St. Petersburg Conservatory, offering him a professorship to teach the theory of composition and orchestration and to become the conductor of the student orchestra as well, with a stated income of 1,000 rubles per academic year, a considerable sum in those days. Rimsky-Korsakov had become well-known in musical society by that time, and indeed his reputation was quite exalted, as evidenced by the offer of this prestigious position. His compositions were being performed in various concert halls with considerable success.

The offer to take up the post was very important for him. Nikolay wrote about this to Sophia, who was in Tervajoki:

> Thinking it over, I came to the conclusion that the offer is very beneficial for me in many ways: firstly, in monetary terms; secondly, I'll be doing work I like very much and which I'm good at; thirdly, it will be good practice for me, especially in conducting; and lastly, it will give me the opportunity to gain a foothold in the sphere of music and apart from the naval service; for remaining there under my present circumstances I would consider unfair and improper. Taking into consideration all this I accepted the offer.

The composer was just twenty-seven years old. He, who had never taken a single systematic academic course in music theory, ventured now to teach students. Later on he described the boldness of this undertaking honestly: "I was an amateur, I didn't know anything [...] and I frankly admit this before all of you. I was young and presumptuous, and my presumption was encouraged, and I took the position. [...] I had to appear to possess all of the necessary knowledge, but sometimes I had to pick up some things from my students." The newspaper *Golos* commented about his appointment:

> The board was certainly right to invite a young talented Russian man. [...] There is only one thing that disturbs us. This is the age of Rimsky-Korsakov. [...] Don't take it as a reproach, but for a professor to have some gray hair is the proof of his being an experienced teacher. Many are likely to be surprised that the teaching of music theory in the Conservatory is trusted nowadays to a person who has recently belonged to a circle that rejected the advantages of classical music completely.

The byline of the article listed "Rostislav" as its author, which was a pen name of Pheophil Tolstoy,[5] a music critic. The same author wrote in the *Journal de St.-Pétersbourg* a little later: "On one lovely day the musical world found out with great surprise that in the heart of it, namely at the Conservatory—Holy of Holies of musical classicism—there is a representative of a circle of innovators, and in the very position of professor in musical theory and orchestration." Thus, the basis of concern in the world of music was not Rimsky-Korsakov's lack of theoretical background (nobody, after listening to his compositions, could raise the objection that he might lack some theoretical knowledge), but rather the fact that the Conservatory had hired an advocate of innovative trends in music, which in its turn might lead to a disregard for the Western classical school of music. However, Borodin wrote to Rimsky-Korsakov: "I'm sincerely happy for you. You couldn't be in a more proper place. You are certain to be of benefit to musical business and students." With the autumn term beginning and eager to complete his own musical education, the composer attended the lectures of the other professors along with the students and undertook the writing of countless musical exercises.

Nadezhda admired the music of *The Maid of Pskov* as well as its composer, and this inspired her to take a most active part in the creation of this opera. In addition to playing over all of the completed parts of the opera, she wrote out fair copies of some parts, made vocal and piano arrangements, and even took part in the orchestration of the opera. In a letter to his wife, Borodin praised Nadezhda highly: "And how do you like Nadezhda Purgold! To think, that after Korsinka played an interlude from his *The Maid of Pskov* to her, she wrote it down from memory! Could you imagine, not just simply for piano, but for orchestra. [...] What a fine girl she is! Really, what a girl!"

Despite the fact that Nadezhda tried to downplay her musical achievements, Rimsky-Korsakov thought highly of her abilities and entrusted her with the orchestration of parts of the opera. After one of his visits, while he was traveling by train back home from Pargolovo, some ideas came to his mind concerning changes to the orchestration of his Interlude. He wrote a letter describing them to Nadezhda and suggested that she make all the changes he had outlined. At the end of his letter he wrote, "I'm expressing my confidence so that the 'bad person' will take it into consideration, and I'd like to look at her completed work on Friday. And this 'bad person' should take action bravely. Somebody else might be a coward but not she, as she is very clever!"

Too soon the time was approaching for them to move back to the city. On Thursday, 16 September, Rimsky-Korsakov sent a message to Nadezhda Purgold at her new city address: "Golden Fish, have you moved in, and if so when might I see You?" Nadezhda was in St. Petersburg already and answered: "There is such a fuss and mess in our apartment that we won't invite anyone before Saturday. But I wish I could see You earlier. By returning to the city I returned to tedium. My arm is still hurting me and I can't play at all. I would like a 'bad man' to cure me." It was more convenient for Rimsky-Korsakov to visit Nadezhda now, as he had moved into another apartment in the middle of August. Now he was renting an apartment with Musorgsky on Panteleimonovskaya Street, not far from the Phurstatskaya Street apartment into which Nadezhda had recently moved.

At the end of October 1871 the first preview of almost the entire Rimsky-Korsakov opera *The Maid of Pskov* (only the overture was not yet ready) was given at the Purgold family apartment. There were many people there. Beside the "customers"—the group of young composers—there were Shestakova, Stasov, Azanchevsky, and many others. The opera was played on two pianos: Nadezhda played one piano, and Rimsky-Korsakov accompanied her in difficult places on the other one. The singers were Musorgsky, Alexandra Purgold, and Vasilyev. The arrangement of the opera for voices and piano had been made by Nadezhda. As Rimsky-Korsakov reminisced, the performance was "beautiful, passionate, and stylish."

A Brother's Death, November 1871

Nadezhda and Nikolay's feelings for each other were reaching their climax when all of a sudden, exactly at the same time, two dramatic events befell

Rimsky-Korsakov, events that served as a test of their feelings for each other. The day of 6 November began with the pleasant news that the Theatre Committee had approved *The Maid of Pskov*, which had been submitted by the composer to the board of the Imperial Theatres, and had been approved for staging at the famous Mariinsky Theatre. Later that day he attended a musical evening at the Purgold family apartment. But that same evening he received the news that his brother, Voin, had died two days earlier in Pisa, where he had been seeking medical treatment for a stress-related illness. Voin had undermined his health by working too hard. For the last ten years he had been the principal of the St. Petersburg Naval Academy and had taken too much responsibility upon himself. He was a self-sacrificing sort and had devoted himself completely to his service duties. The authorities at the Naval Office permitted Rimsky-Korsakov to go to Pisa and transport his brother's remains to St. Petersburg. Before taking his leave, Rimsky-Korsakov visited Nadezhda, and they apparently had a heart-to-heart conversation. After returning home he sent her a message:

> My dear, nice girl, I don't know myself why I'm writing to You now, when I've just said good-bye. But I'm in such a mood that I'd like to talk to You some more. Although I don't know exactly what I'm talking about; but You're so wonderful that I feel you understand in any case. You should be strong now, because if I know that You are all right I will feel good as well. It's annoying that You won't be able to write to me because I might miss Your answer. You know that I will be constantly thinking of You; so I need to be sure that You are safe and sound and for this You are to be like this.
>
> Good-bye, see You soon, for sure.
>
> Your N. Rimsky-Korsakov.
>
> If You receive this letter early, then drop me some lines for the journey. I'll be in till 11.30 a.m. Good-bye.

The next day, the day of his departure, she sent a letter to him at Pisa:

> Despite the fact that You, Korsinka, told me that it would be impossible to write to you, I'm writing in any case. Certainly You didn't think that I would be so strange as to write to You at your destination on the same day You left for it. Before receiving Your letter this morning, I was eager to scribble some words to You, but I was shy

about sending it. And when I got Your message I became sad and annoyed that I didn't do it, but it was too late. Instead of that, I'm talking to You now. On Your instructions, Fim [Lodyzhensky] visited us after dinner and told us about his seeing You off. He calmed me down greatly when he said that You looked healthy and were of good cheer. You were so nervous yesterday that I was just worried about You. On fulfilling Your request and Your wish, I'm trying to behave myself. I have forced myself to study [Musorgsky's opera] *Boris* [*Godunov*]. For Modest's sake I'd like to play much better on Friday than I did on Saturday. I will try to see that such a bad thing won't happen again. And when you come back, then we will have a real performance of *Boris*, repeat our dear "Pskovie girl" [*The Maid of Pskov*] and many, many other good things. Only come back as soon as you can. But remember, please, my request: take care of yourself. You'd better stay somewhere for an additional day to have a rest rather than become very tired. It's so strange to think that You will read my letter somewhere far away from here, in some absolutely different environment. Maybe my letter will transport You to another, better place.

Good-bye, Korsinka. I shake Your hand firmly.

Could you write to me when you're planning to start your journey back and what date you might be here?

Rimsky-Korsakov arrived in Pisa on 12 November, and the next day he wrote to Nadezhda:

I arrived late at night yesterday, extremely exhausted, and I put off my promise to write to You, my dear, till today. I've sent a telegram to Modest today. I was thinking of You all the time during the trip. I was wondering whether You behaved as You had promised. If I happened to see something lovely on my way I always had a great desire to look at it together with you. My letter is very brief, but it is because I cannot write much. And I just tell You that I'm not longing for anything else but coming back to St. Petersburg as soon as possible.

Your N. Rimsky-Korsakov

P.S. As soon as I see you, I will play You a new composition which came to my mind during the journey. If I have to stay here for a little longer, I will write to You then.

Two days after his arrival in Pisa, the composer received the letter from Nadezhda. He responded the next day:

It was very good and not strange of You to write to me on Monday. I received your letter yesterday and it made me feel merry. Thank You, my dear good girl, for it. We all are leaving tomorrow. We have settled all of our business here. But I can't tell exactly the date when we shall arrive in St. Petersburg, as I don't know how many times we will have to stop on the way. I think probably somewhere between Tuesday and Thursday next week. I know that I will still have to deal with a lot of sad things, but I also know for sure that when I see You all those sad things will go to hell. So, see You soon; thanks again for writing to me.

After Nikolay arrived in St. Petersburg, Voin's remains were delivered to the church of the Naval Academy on Vasilyevsky Island, where a funeral service was performed on 30 November 1871. The burial took place on the same day at Smolensky Cemetery, not far from the local church. A little while later a cross made of black marble was erected at the tomb.

On 11 December 1871 the Purgold family hosted a musical evening at which *The Maid of Pskov* was performed for the second time, followed of course by a special dinner with many toasts to "the success of our dear operas." In addition to *The Maid of Pskov* this meant Musorgsky's *Boris Godunov* as well as *The Stone Guest*, which by then had been completed by Cui and Rimsky-Korsakov and had been approved by the Theatre Committee. The composer's mother, Sophia, was introduced to the Purgold family and all of their guests during the evening.

Rimsky-Korsakov and his musical activities began to occupy all of Nadezhda Purgold's thoughts. She wrote to him on 20 December:

What a strange boy You are, insisting on my writing to You today. In any case, I indeed would like to know how You are. I was perfectly all right yesterday, and You were unwell, and I'm worried about how You feel today. Well, let's change the subject, in any case, I'm eager myself to talk to You. I've read another tale of Gogol—*Sorochinskaya yarmarka* [*Sorochintsy Fair*].[6] It's also good and I think it might be even a good plot for an opera, but not one in Your style. And it can't even be compared with *Maiskaya noch* [*May Night*]. What can I do? I have become obsessed with *May Night* and can't get rid of it from my thoughts. [...] But certainly, the main thing is that You should listen to Your inner self. You should compose according to a story of your own choosing. There are many interesting stories available. We can read many together. I'm still thinking of Your mother.

She is very nice, and I'm so glad she liked me. Till morrow, dear Korsinka. Take care, and I order Your eye not to hurt.

The same day Rimsky-Korsakov responded:

Tell Nadenka, "a bad" girl, not to worry about me. I'm absolutely well today, although yesterday I felt so-so till I went to bed. [...] Balakirev is keen on playing the overture in the fifth concert and asks me to visit him today in the evening. So, I'm going to visit him with that "bad" overture and I hope that Golden Fish will hear it played by the orchestra later on. I wish I could manage to compose that overture perfectly well. Because it should be like that. Because that overture from the first to the last note belongs to this "bad" girl, whom I love very much.

(The composer was referring to the overture to *The Maid of Pskov*, which he had not yet completed.)

At the end of December 1871 Rimsky-Korsakov and Nadezhda Purgold officially announced their engagement. Rimsky-Korsakov was the first who exchanged an "indifferent You for a *loving* you" writing:

My dear, I'm so annoyed and vexed that I had to waste this evening instead of spending it with you, my sweet girl. I spent half of an hour at Fim's, then I was at Borodin's till 11 p.m. Well, this visit might be excused as I dealt with my business to some extent, namely I looked through the overture and discussed some issues concerning its orchestration. But it soon became so boring that I left for home. Now I will sit down to work on the overture, but I think I won't deal with it for long. Although I'm in very good spirits, I feel a little exhausted. Well, I'm certainly a minion of Fortune, but do I deserve it? I will certainly come to you on Saturday, but just for a while. And let Nadenka send me away after a short time, as we have arranged.

Thursday. 12 a.m. at night

The next morning Nadezhda responded to his letter:

My dear, it's so terrible that I won't see You today. [...] And I'm writing to tell You, that it would be much better if tomorrow You manage to come after 12 p.m. but not after dinner. I don't think we will have any additional guests in the morning, but after dinner we are receiving a group of our relatives, and You know how they can disturb us. Just as I was finishing my message I got Yours, my dearest. Thank You for it. But how did You dare to say "if I deserve this"? No, my bright light should never speak like this. Yesterday, I felt uneasy. I felt stuck and couldn't keep up a conversation of any kind with anybody. I was lucky enough that I was able to leave for home early. At home I sat sewing and thinking of ...—a little Nick knows of whom and of what. I wish this disgusting day could finish sooner.

The loving couple kept writing sweet messages like this to each other till their wedding. "Little, 'bad' Nika," Nadezhda wrote, "you're bound to come for dinner today. Otherwise, Sonechka will be angry with you.[7] And I will be upset because at night you'll be busy. As far as I remember you have to go to listen to that stupid quartet at night. After dinner we'll begin playing immediately." And on another occasion: "How is Nika behaving? What about his eyes? Let him come back early from his relatives, then we could see each other for a while. Nadya." He responded, "I'm behaving properly. My eyes are more or less well. I'll try to come as soon as possible. Your N."

Finally, after some misunderstanding, Rimsky-Korsakov wrote:

> My darling, please, forgive me for those stupid things I've done. Please, forgive me and forget about this. After leaving you, I didn't know what to do with myself. I was so mad at myself, my dear. And now, while I'm writing this letter, I'm at a loss and don't know what to say. There is only one thing I want, that you would forgive me for my stupidity and triteness. I promise I will do my best [to make sure] that this will never happen again. What the devil! I love you so much, more than anyone else, my darling Golden Fish.

Soon Nadezhda responded:

> My darling, my joy, I can't understand why you haven't come today. Just because I didn't answer your letter? Do you think I'm angry with you? Do you? There is nothing I should forgive you for, as you've done nothing wrong. And you should have scolded me for my telling you such nonsense when we were saying good-bye. I haven't answered your letter as I thought you would come early today, earlier than my letter would have reached you, and I would tell you everything I had wanted to tell you. And because you did not come for such a long time I became

absolutely unbearable. Then at last, Cui made me feel better since he praised my compositions very much—in particular two of my compositions. I'm so sad, my dear Nika, that you haven't come today. N. Purgold.

Early in the summer of 1872, Rimsky-Korsakov rented an apartment in Pargolovo to be closer to his fiancée. The Purgold family rented a summer house there as well. By this time *The Maid of Pskov* had been accepted for performance at the Mariinsky Theatre. Despite the fact that depictions of the tsar's family were prohibited on the stage, Rimsky-Korsakov was permitted to use the character of Tsar Ivan the Terrible by special dispensation. Krabbe, the chief of the Naval Office and a connoisseur of music and the theatre, was very influential in getting this permission. The court may have decided that the time of Ivan the Terrible was a long time ago, and so the libretto was approved under the condition that the scene with the Vetche be slightly modified.[8]

A Wedding, 30 June 1872

The wedding of Nikolay Rimsky-Korsakov and Nadezhda Purgold took place at noon on 30 June 1872. The ceremony was performed in the Church of Sts. Peter and Paul, which was situated in Shuvalov Park, not far from Pargolovo. The church itself is worthy of note: its construction was ordered by Countess Varvara Petrovna (Shuvalova) Poliet in 1831, and it was designed by A. P. Bryuloff in the Gothic style. It was erected on the top of a hill, its steeple beautifully reflected in the water of the lake nearby. The following note was made in the church register of births, marriages, and deaths:

The Groom—Nikolay Andreyev Rimsky-Korsakov,[9] assigned to the Office of the Department of the Navy.
The Bride—Nadezhda Nikolayeva Purgold, a daughter of deceased Nikolay Fyodorov Purgold, a former active state secretary.
The Witnesses were:
For the side of the groom: Ilia Semeyonov Bizheich,
    Modest Petrov Musorgsky, a public officer
For the side of the bride: Vladimir Fyodorov Purgold, an active secret state secretary
    Semeyon Dmitriyev Akhsharumov,[10] an assistant of the secretary

From the church they went to Pargolovo, where the reception was held at the Purgolds' country house.

Following the custom at that time, the newlyweds planned to go abroad for their honeymoon, and it had fallen to Nadezhda Purgold's brother Fyodr to plan their journey. Before the wedding, the composer's mother had written from Tervajoki on 8 June: "My dear Nika, I received your letter on 6 June, and I'm very pleased that your wish to go abroad will be fulfilled. However, I doubt that you will be able to get paid leave.[…] I can't tell you anything good about myself. I'm still sick, I can't get rid of my cough and sometimes I run a fever.[…] Hug our dear Nadya for me, and tell her I'm waiting for her promised letter."

After the reception the newlyweds were seen off at the Warsaw railway station in St. Petersburg, from which they began their honeymoon journey. They went to Switzerland via Warsaw and Vienna and visited several places of interest. In Switzerland they took a hiking tour to the Riga massif, visited the Rhine and Rosenlöwe glaciers, and toured the Chamonix Valley. Unfortunately, the sky was overcast on that day and the clouds covered the peaks of the mountains. Nadezhda wrote in her letter to her elder sister: "It's awful even to say that we were in Chamonix but didn't see Mont Blanc." From there they went on to Italy, where the beauty of Lakes Maggiore, Lugano,[11] and Como captivated them. Then they visited Milan and Venice, after which they retraced their route back to St. Petersburg, through Warsaw and Vienna. They spent the rest of the summer at Pargolovo.

In the autumn the young couple moved into a house on Shpalernaya Street in St. Petersburg. César Cui became their neighbor, and later on Musorgsky rented an apartment in the same building as well. Nadezhda reminisced later, "We used to hear him playing the piano when the windows were open."

Just four months after Nadezhda's wedding, her sister Alexandra was married as well. Her husband was Nikolay Molas, an amateur artist.[12] Later on he became the head of the publishing house of the Department for Independent Principalities of the Ministry of the Court. Stasov commented on this event in a letter to Medvedeva, a friend of his: "You see, how expertly and friskily both the sisters arranged their affairs of heart."

Now their family friends visited the Rimsky-Korsakovs' new apartment. The hostess of the house was very charming. Nadezhda had refined features, with fine arched eyebrows and lovely eyes. Two heavy braids crowned her head. Her beautiful face always reflected even the slightest change in emotion. She never used anything like face powder or lipstick to beautify herself. She was quite tall, but next to Rimsky-Korsakov, who was much taller, she looked like a little girl.

Once the Rimsky-Korsakov house received an honored guest, Pyotr Tchaikovsky, who visited St. Petersburg fairly often. He came to one of their musical evenings and played the finale of his Second Symphony on the piano, which delighted everyone in the house. Tchaikovsky described this evening in a letter to his brother Modest: "The company was so excited that they nearly tore me to pieces, and Mme. Korsakova begged me to arrange the music for four hands."[13] After his visit to Rimsky-Korsakov, Tchaikovsky composed a song, *Kolybelnaya* (*Lullaby*), to words by Apollon Maikov, and a romance, *Pogodi* (*Wait a Little*), to words by N. Grekov. He dedicated the lullaby to Nadezhda and the romance accordingly to Rimsky-Korsakov. It is strange that Rimsky-Korsakov should have learned about these dedications only many years later, after Tchaikovsky had died.

Rimsky-Korsakov was occupied now with composing his Third Symphony and the rehearsals for his opera *The Maid of Pskov*, which were to be held in the Mariinsky Theatre. Later he would reminisce:

> The artists [at the Mariinsky] worked honestly and they all were very polite. Only O. A. Petrov was not very pleased.[15] He complained that the opera had too many tedious passages and minor staging mistakes, which he found difficult to improve through acting. He was right about many things. However, I was young and showed my temper quite easily. I didn't want to concede this to him. I didn't allow any significant modifications. I think he was annoyed about this, and Napravnik was too.[16] Napravnik conducted pretty well. He even helped catch mistakes made by copyists as well as my own slips of the pen. […] It was only much later I understood that he (Napravnik) had been right.

The Maid of Pskov

The opening night of *The Maid of Pskov* took place on 1 January 1873. The audience was delighted and demanded ten curtain calls from Rimsky-Korsakov. However, those who opposed the new Russian musical school, to which Rimsky-Korsakov belonged, criticized the opera severely in their reviews. An anonymous critic wrote in the *St. Petersburg Leaflet*:

Rimsky-Korsakov is certainly talented, but being carried away with high ideals concerning music drama, about which he has only dark, hazy notions, he ran to extremes of eccentricity, to its outrageously perverted apex. [...] In order to address the greatest challenges of modern music, it is not enough just to be talented. As expected, *The Maid of Pskov* is a clear evangelistic message of the musical religion, which he propagates, and apparently it reveals all of the possible extremes of this "religion." But this has at least one beneficial effect: the opera provides further proof that the way chosen by the composer is false and cannot lead to the creation of a musical ideal. [...] The fundamental shortcomings of his composition are its monotony and dull colors, the monotony of structure, dryness, and insipidity. [...] Despite the fact that the author and the performers were called before the curtain several times, I am sure the opera will not enjoy a long life. It will not remain in the repertoire for long, as this composition is nothing more than a mediocrity. On the other hand, I should admit there are many particular places where his talent is in evidence.

Another music critic, G. A. Laroche,[17] criticized the opera in an article published in the *Moscow Bulletin*. At the end of his review he wrote: "In general, the whole opera of Mr. Rimsky-Korsakov, and his symphonies as well, display not only the poor and false direction chosen by the composer, but also his bright talent. I venture to say that the relationship between this talented composer and this poorly chosen direction is merely odd and superficial. I think one day some fortunate conditions might help to sever this."

Although Cui made a number of mild criticisms about the opera, his main opinion was a contrary one. "*The Maid of Pskov* is a most enjoyable phenomenon in our art. This profound and talented composition has enriched our repertoire. This provides new, convincing evidence that the direction chosen is serious, and it shows that a new Russian operatic school will play a significant role in the future."

The Maid of Pskov was performed successfully ten times within a forty-five-day period and always played to a full house; it was certainly a very important event in Rimsky-Korsakov's life. But another event had at least equal significance. In January 1873 the Department of the Navy created a new position, Inspector of Military Bands. Rimsky-Korsakov was appointed to the new post on 14 May. Since the position was for a civilian, it meant that he had to leave military service after eight years in the navy. The military rank of a lieutenant was exchanged for that of a "public officer," and, from this moment on, Rimsky-Korsakov was able to devote himself completely to his new "service," that of music. Because the position had just been created, Rimsky-Korsakov was trusted with defining its duties himself. He set them forth in a memorandum entitled "Duties of the Military Bands Inspector." They included review of the military band repertoire, the appointment and supervision of bandmasters, and the control of the quality of musical instruments.

Rimsky-Korsakov also promoted the opening of a new specialized course at the St. Petersburg Conservatory for training future naval bandmasters under the sponsorship of the Department of the Navy. He composed the curriculum himself for this new specialty. At the same time he established a new musical school, under the aegis of the Eighth Naval Depot, for training future members of the bands. The future musicians not only studied but also lived there. Rimsky-Korsakov would write later: "It was at this time that I became a musician officially and undeniably. I was excited. All my friends congratulated me." Being accustomed to carrying out his duties conscientiously, he began to study wind instruments. Nadezhda wrote about this to her elder sister from Pargolovo, where they spent the summer of 1873:

> Nika is very busy. He often goes to St. Petersburg and has visited Kronstadt twice already. He was officially introduced to the authorities there, and observed the military bands and so forth. You've asked what musical instrument he is playing now. It's better to ask how many. At present we have a trombone, a tuba, a trumpet, a French horn, a flute, and two fifes in the house. He pays much more attention to the trombone, as he likes it most of all. He does exercises with it a lot and plays different tunes on it. But he has to do his exercises in the suitcase in order not to disturb others.

By "suitcase" she meant a small room in the attic reserved for this purpose and so called by the family.

The First Child

Before long the Rimsky-Korsakovs were expecting their first child, and so, at the end of the summer, they moved to another apartment in a house on Furstatskaya Street. Another young couple, Nadezhda's sister Alexandra and

Alexandra's husband, Nikolay Molas, lived next door. The new apartment was quite good except that it didn't have running water. Long before the baby's birth, they put an old wooden rocking cradle in the child's future bedroom for the happy event. This cradle had served as a bed for little Nika himself. On 20 August their first child was born in that very apartment. The boy was named Mikhail, after the character Mikhail Tucha from *The Maid of Pskov*.[18] Rimsky-Korsakov was completely happy about having a son. He wrote to his mother:

> Mishka is three days old already. He cries noisily in a loud voice. There is one trouble, he doesn't know how to eat, but I think he will gain this wisdom in a day or two. Nadushonok remembers you often. She is sorry about your absence and that you can't brush her hair, which is in a mess. She failed to braid her hair properly before Mishkin's birth. There was a lack of time since the delivery began very quickly. [...] We apologize for our Misha not yet being able to bow to you. Since he can't even eat properly, there is no question of that.[19]

Rimsky-Korsakov's study of wind instruments stimulated Alexander Borodin's interest as well, and the collection of instruments was loaned to him. When Misha was just two months old, Borodin wrote the following letter to the child:

> Dear Mr. Rimsky-Korsakov,
>
>   Sir, Your father has given me a toy trumpet to practice with, but not to keep. Now I find myself in serious difficulty. Your father asked me to return it as soon as possible, but Your mother, who does not like noisy toys in general, asked me to keep it as long as possible. On finding it difficult to fulfill both wishes at the same time, I decided to ask You to help me with this difficult matter. I am accordingly forwarding the toy to You and authorizing You to deal with it in the exercise of Your best judgment.
>
>   Sincerely yours,
>   A. P. Borodin

The next day Borodin received "Misha's" response:

> Dear Mr. Borodin,
>
>   [...] Sir, I have done my best to carry out the honorable duty you have laid before me. I gave the toy to my father. In order not to disturb Mother, who

doesn't like the noisy toys my father is so fond of, Father sent it to the toy shop from which it had been originally procured.

Your humble servant,

M. N. Rimsky-Korsakov

Rimsky-Korsakov became more and more involved in family and public duties. It is noteworthy that he attended faithfully to the former throughout his life, even as his musical career took flight. In early 1874, for example, in addition to his being an inspector and professor, he became the conductor of a symphony orchestra. His first public appearance as a professional conductor took place at a concert sponsored by the St. Petersburg Committee of Assistance. (The Committee helped those who had suffered the consequences of a bad harvest in the Samara region.) Before this concert Stasov wrote to Nadezhda: "Your Honor Madam Admiral![20] I would like to congratulate the Admiral himself and You on the occasion of his performing as a bandmaster. [...] Hurray! At last!!!"

The concert took place in the Great Hall of the Assembly of the Nobility.[21] Rimsky-Korsakov included his Third Symphony, which had been completed only a short time beforehand, and a number of compositions by other Russian composers. He managed to overcome the excitement that he had experienced during the final rehearsal, and the concert went off smoothly, although he himself was not completely satisfied. When he shared his memoirs about this concert, he would say that they had not managed to feed the hungry population of Samara, as only a few people had turned out for the concert and they had had barely enough money to pay the members of the orchestra. Little wonder. The "new" Russian music had only just begun its journey toward acceptance, and the even newer conductor Rimsky-Korsakov was yet almost entirely unknown.

The Free Music School

Rimsky-Korsakov took on another responsibility that spring. This time it was a voluntary one. At the request of the faculty of the Free Music School, he became the director of the school, replacing Balakirev. G. Y. Lomakin, a choirmaster, and Balakirev had established the school in March 1862. The first director was Lomakin, and then Balakirev replaced him in 1870. After four years of work, Balakirev left the position and the world of music as well. For some time he had been suffering from deep emotional stress caused by the failure of the concerts held by the Free Music School and the failure of his own piano recital in Nizhny Novgorod, where the public simply did not show up. He had hoped to improve his financial situation with that concert because he was grievously insolvent, but his hopes were not fulfilled and he became bankrupt.

According to Rimsky-Korsakov's account, Balakirev experienced a dramatic change in character about that time. From previously being a radical liberal and an atheist who mocked religion, he turned into something of an ardent religious fanatic, a mystic, even a chanting hypocrite. Rimsky-Korsakov wrote in his memoirs:

> When I visited him, I noticed many new things he would not have had before. There were icons in each corner of every room with lighted icon lamps before them. His bedroom was closed tightly. If he had to enter it in someone's presence, he hurried to close the door behind him, but you still could see through a crack in the door a room swathed in a mysterious darkness, broken by tiny flashes of an icon lamp. […] He gave up smoking and eating meat. He still ate fish, but only fish that had died a natural death. He did not have fur clothing. When it was freezing cold, he wore a light coat and covered his beard completely with a woolen scarf. […] His love and mercy toward animals ran to extremes. If he happened to find even a repulsive sort of insect in the room, for example, he would catch it carefully and let it go out through the window, saying, "Go, dear, go, God bless you!" […] He was still intolerant of other people who did not agree with him on something or who thought or acted independently; opposite to his own way of thinking. The epithet "scoundrel" was always on the tip of his tongue, and he loosed it on nearly every person he met. He struck everyone who saw him at that time with this mixture of Christian meekness and backbiting, his love for animals and hatred for people, and his continuing interest in art with a triteness characteristic of someone living a solitary existence.

Having left the world of music, Balakirev went on to work in the luggage department of the Warsaw railway station and disappeared completely from musical circles.

4

A Busy Musical Life, 1874–1881

Sometimes it's just impossible to get down to work. But I have a lucky trait of character: I think no one else is able to forget all about cares, trouble, and worries as quickly as I am and to turn to music.

—Rimsky-Korsakov to his student Ilia Tyumenev

The Navy Bands

In the summer of 1874, the Navy Department sent Rimsky-Korsakov to the city of Nikolayev to carry out an inspection of the local navy band. The Rimsky-Korsakov family, including nine-month-old Misha and his nanny, left for Nikolayev with him. They were accommodated in an outbuilding of what the locals referred to as "the palace"—the house of the commander-in-chief of the Black Sea Fleet. At that time the house was the largest and the most beautiful building in the city and possessed a large acreage with many accompanying buildings.

The composer's wife wrote to her sister Sophia from Nikolayev: "Nika started his work the day after our arrival. He is very pleased with the local bandmaster and with the band itself." Everything would have gone along swimmingly but for an unpleasant and unexpected domestic problem. They had to discharge the baby's nanny after she was caught putting little Misha into the stove! Rimsky-Korsakov broke the news to his mother, Sophia: "The nanny has turned out to have such outrageous behavior and to be so dishonest that I lack words to describe it. We simply can't bear her any longer. Today is the third day that Nadya and I have been taking care of Misha day and night by ourselves. We don't permit the nanny even to come near him." It took some time to find another nanny to relieve them of this burden.

Meanwhile Rimsky-Korsakov went on working with the navy band and considered that they were making progress. Nadezhda wrote to her sister: "The citizens of Nikolayev are looking forward to hearing the navy band playing on the local boulevard. But Nika will force them to train much more before they play in public." Rimsky-Korsakov himself shared his opinion with Stasov: "Every day I train the military band for two or two and a half hours, and I'm very pleased. I'm gaining a brilliant experience, which I couldn't even have dreamed of. I orchestrate a good deal of music for the band, and I hear my own compositions played immediately."

In Crimea: The Intriguing Tatars

The composer had a ten-day break from training the band, and he and his wife used this opportunity for a vacation in the Crimea. They sailed to Sevastopol, and from there to Bakhchysarai. There were no hotels in the town at that time, so they stayed at the house of a mullah located in front of the Khan Palace, with its famous Fountain of Tears. They very much liked the long street near the mullah's house, with its different cafés and small shops from which one could hear oriental music and the cries of vendors. They could hear the singing of muezzins from the minarets, and they found the services in the mosque very interesting. There was music in the streets day and night and always singing and musicians playing in front of every cafe. It was an absolutely new and exciting experience for them. They went from Bakhchysarai to Yalta through the Baidarsky Gate, traveled along the southern seashore of the Crimea, and then went back to Nikolayev. Rimsky-Korsakov returned to training the band. He went to the Crimea once more during his stay in Nikolayev, but the second time he went alone to "observe more and probably pick up some Tatarian peculiarities," as he wrote later to Stasov about his trip. In the middle of August the family returned to St. Petersburg and spent a while in Pargolovo with Vladimir Purgold at the "red country house."

Kronstadt

In St. Petersburg Rimsky-Korsakov returned to his busy musical life. He had to spend a whole week in Kronstadt to prepare a concert of the united military and navy bands from Kronstadt and St. Petersburg. He conducted rehearsals indefatigably day and night. His wife wrote to him: "My dear, we are all well. There is no news, so I have nothing to write to you. Good-bye. Try not to shout at the instrumentalists too much. I am worried about your voice. You might lose your voice. I'm very bored without you." On the eve of the concert, Rimsky-Korsakov sent a note to his wife:

My darling, honey, Golden Fish! I cannot come home before the concert, as there is a rehearsal in the evening. I hope it will go well. They do not want to change the time of the concert, so it is to start at 3 p.m. I think that we will not be able to come back the same day. [...] If Mother and Marie are not coming here, then you should come. I will be able to meet you at the ship docks. You could come at 11:30 on Sunday and the next morning we will go home. [...] Come, my darling. The ship departs from Nikolayev Bridge. Can you respond to me?

The concert took place at the headquarters of the Kronstadt Riding School on 27 October 1874. Six united orchestras totaling about three hundred musicians took part in the concert. The program included compositions of Glinka, Meyerbeer, Beethoven, Schubert, Wagner, and Chopin. They played twelve arrangements for brass band, of which eleven were by Rimsky-Korsakov. The concert was repeated the next day. Nadezhda and Cui came from St. Petersburg to attend the concerts. Both were very successful. The *Kronstadt Bulletin* published an article signed by one "N. R." that remarked: "The concert could not have been performed better. It provided great enjoyment for the packed audience. [...] It has shown what extraordinary results can be achieved by a person who is completely and sincerely devoted to music."

Bessel wrote in his review of the concert published in the *Musical Leaflet*:[1] "Rimsky-Korsakov was appointed as inspector only about two years ago. Almost all the performers are soldiers of low ranks. These 'musicians' had played only marches and dance music before, and they did it rather badly. [...] This interesting concert enjoyed great success. [...] Rimsky-Korsakov has established de facto that his activities as the inspector of military bands have been very fruitful."

The same autumn Rimsky-Korsakov began to carry out the duties of the director of the Free Music School. In the spring of the following year, 1875, he conducted the first concert of the school since Balakirev's departure. The program of the concert came as a great surprise to everyone. It was expected that they would play compositions of some Russian composers who had been promoted by Balakirev. On the contrary, Rimsky-Korsakov chose the music of Handel, Haydn, Bach, Allegri, and Palestrina.[2] Cui commented: "The concert was unbearable to listen to. The music had a deadly monotonous, depressing effect on the listener." Supposedly with great satisfaction, Famitsin wrote a review published in the newspaper *Pchela* (*The Bee*):

> By this concert Rimsky-Korsakov has made a frank confession to the public. To some extent he has renounced the narrow view of his art which is expressed by that group of young Russian composers and performers who cannot appreciate, or just do not want to appreciate, the significance of music composed in the pre-Beethoven age, and who had considered Mr. Rimsky-Korsakov their adherent. Mr. Rimsky-Korsakov certainly gave an unpleasant surprise to the people loyal to that group.

Among all the composers belonging to the group of Balakirev, Borodin was the only one who supported the composer. He believed that even if Rimsky-Korsakov had become interested in studying "old" classical music, it was natural for him since he knew little about it. The composer wrote in his memoirs many years later that when he had indulged in studying the compositions of Bach, Palestrina, and many others, "it seemed to me then as if the formidable figures of these geniuses were superior to our own innovative obscurantism."

A Growing Family: A Daughter, Sophia

In October 1875 another child was born to the Rimsky-Korsakov family. The baby girl was named Sophia, after the composer's mother and Nadezhda's elder sister. After Sonya's birth, Nadezhda was ill for a long time (several months, according to Rimsky-Korsakov's memoirs).[3]

Rimsky-Korsakov conducted a second concert at the Free Music School a year after the first. The concert took place in February 1876 and again consisted of Western European classics. As before, Rimsky-Korsakov's musical friends were displeased. Cui wrote in his review: "The concert gave birth to the concept of super-boredom." Soon after that a third concert at the Free Musical School was performed, in which Rimsky-Korsakov presented only Russian compositions, including those by Borodin, Cui, Dargomizhsky,

Musorgsky, Balakirev, and himself. His friends rejoiced. Stasov spoke with admiration: "What a concert! [...] It was the day of triumph for the Russian School. [...] There was not one weak or uninteresting composition! We stayed at the Molases' till 1 a.m. celebrating, remembering, criticizing, reminiscing again, and triumphing again and again!" Now the tone of Cui's review was quite different: "Judging by the program and the performance, it has been the best and the loveliest concert of the season!"

Rimsky-Korsakov paid much attention to the Free Music School, but he also taught students in the Conservatory, and simultaneously he himself studied. He completed innumerable exercises in counterpoint, even sending them to Pyotr Tchaikovsky for his review: "I'd like to show You my work. I would appreciate Your opinion about it." After looking through the exercises, Tchaikovsky responded:

> I am struck dumb with reverence, bowing before Your noble artistic modesty and amazingly strong character! [...] It is such a heroic deed for a person who composed [the symphonic poem] *Sadko* eight years ago that I would like to trumpet it to the whole world. [...] I'm absolutely certain that with Your tremendous talent and that perfect conscientiousness You possess You are bound to create such great compositions that they will surpass everything that has been composed in Russia before.

Rimsky-Korsakov did not compose any significant chamber music until 1876. Then he wrote two works, the String Sextet in A Major and the Quintet for Piano and Winds in B-flat Major, for a competition held by the Russian Musical Society that year. He began work on his String Quartet in F major in 1875, although it was not published until 1878. Between 1874 and 1878 he composed a considerable number of choruses. In addition, in 1879 he published collections of Russian folk songs.

One such collection consisted of forty Russian folk songs taken down from those sung to him by T. I. Philipov.[4] The other contained one hundred folk songs, including those the composer had heard in his childhood in Tikhvin from his mother and his uncle Pyotr. These songs were sung to him by Anna Engelgardt, Musorgsky, Ekaterina Borodina, Dunyasha Vinogradova (a servant of the Borodin household), and Kruglikov, who was a colleague at the Free Musical School at that time.

Boyarkinya Vera Scheloga (*Vera Scheloga, the Boyar's Wife*)

Rimsky-Korsakov's family spent the summertime in Pargolovo at "the red country house" with Uncle "Oh!"[5] There the composer started to work on a revision of *The Maid of Pskov* and composed some pages of music for a prologue to the opera. The prologue carried its own name *Boyarkinya Vera Scheloga* (*Vera Scheloga, the Boyar's Wife*). Impulsively, perhaps playfully, Nadezhda expressed reservations about the draft; but so upset did Rimsky-Korsakov become that he threw the draft over the fence with the words: "If that's the case, then there is no need!" His wife rushed in horror to gather up the pages and save them.

Anatoly Lyadov

Rimsky-Korsakov had been teaching a student named Anatoly Lyadov since 1873. Lyadov was a rather talented student, but lazy. Rimsky-Korsakov wrote about this student at the end of an academic year: "Very gifted. At the beginning of the semester he was conscientious, but during the second part he worked little. I can't judge if he has made any progress." Another pupil, Gergy Dyutch, was equally lazy. At the beginning of 1876 both of them were expelled from the Conservatory because of absenteeism. They came to Rimsky-Korsakov to ask him to intercede for them to be reinstated, but he refused. The composer reminisced about this: "I was firm and refused point-blank. I wonder how I managed to become such an impassive bureaucrat at that moment." And yet, sometime after this, they were in fact reinstated and, surprisingly, relations between the rigorous teacher and the slothful Lyadov soon became friendly again. He graduated with high honors.

Now, at the end of the summer, Rimsky-Korsakov, along with Lyadov and Balakirev, who had returned to musical life, began to work on editing the compositions of Mikhail Glinka for publication. Lyudmila Shestakova suggested that they undertake this work together. The composer wrote in his memoirs many years later: "I infinitely admired and worshipped this man of genius. I assimilated his techniques greedily. [...] That was very beneficial schooling for me."

At the end of 1877 Rimsky-Korsakov left for Kronstadt to preside over a charity concert given for wounded soldiers by the navy band. Misha was four and Sonya only two years old at that time. Nadezhda wrote to him there, pleading:

My darling, it's so sad that you will stay there for a long time. And if you are not coming on Friday too, I'll be just desperate. It will be too long. And you know we should prepare for Christmas. We have to choose a good tree and I wish we could do it together. I am afraid I will not manage to do it alone. Dr. Serdechny came yesterday. He examined Misha as carefully as he did the first time and came to the conclusion that there is nothing seriously wrong with him. [...] Sonka is well. [...][6] If there should be a repeat of the concert, why don't you instruct one of local bandmasters to oversee it in your place and come back home? Never before have you been away for such a long time. I am worried you will become exhausted after so many days. Do not work too much. I am kissing you, my darling, on the forehead, on the eyes, on the cheeks, and on the lips.

Your N. R.-Korsakova

P.S. Misha and Sonya said they were bowing to you.

By the beginning of January 1878 the composer had completed a revised version of *The Maid of Pskov* with a prologue. The prologue, *Vera Scheloga, the Boyar's Wife*, was considered to be an independent one-act opera. It was performed at the Rimsky-Korsakovs' home during the same month, with Nadezhda accompanying the singers on the piano. Alexandra Molas sang the part of Vera, O. Veselovskaya took the part of Nadezhda, and Musorgsky was given the part of Boyar Scheloga.

On 16 March 1878 there was another concert performed by the navy band. Rimsky-Korsakov arrived at Kronstadt three days beforehand and began rehearsals immediately. He wrote to his wife:

I've started writing my letter, but it will be very brief, as I'm extremely tired and exhausted. [...] The trip was very good, the road was wonderful. What have you been doing and how have you been behaving? What about Mishuk and Sophia?[7] Kiss them for me. I hope to receive a letter from you tomorrow. I am likely to write to you on Wednesday. Embrace you, Nadyushart[8]—"my heart."

Your N. R.-Korsakov. Monday, 9 p.m.

Rimsky-Korsakov sent home three more short letters:

My darling Nadyushonok, my sweet, my honey! I can't come as rehearsals are proceeding badly and tomorrow morning I have to conduct a rehearsal myself, as

I can't rely on anybody else. [...] What about Mishuk and Sonka? How are they? [...] If you don't have enough money you should ask Sonechka. It means nothing to borrow just for three days. I'm afraid the repeat of the concert is scheduled for Friday. Drop me some lines with this messenger boy. If there should be any emergency, send me a telegram. Kiss Mishuk and Sonya for me. Goodbye, see you later, my dear good girl.

And the next day:

My darling,

I'd begun to worry as I hadn't received a letter from you for a long time. Your last one arrived only today in the morning. Now you've comforted me with the news that you're calm and in good spirits. You see, Rauchfuss found that Misha is well.[9] And what did I say? Tell Misha that he is my dear lad, and Sonka that she is a silly little Sonka, Sophia Nikolayevna and cute little rascal, and you're Nadyushart—my heart. I'm behaving well: I'm not changing my clothes while the windows are open and I'm not going out without a jacket and high boots, and so on and so forth. But I become rather tired from rehearsals, although I'm in a good mood, as they are going well enough. The managers of the concert manage so "well" that the posters have been stuck up only today and they have just started selling tickets. Subsequently, there are likely to be vacant seats. But I don't care; I only hope the concert will be good. I'd like to tell you off for having written me too much when you were tired. That's because of your being a silly goose, but a sweet one. Kiss our little rascals for me. I hope they still remember me. Bye-bye, hugs.

Your N. R.-Korsakov.

Wednesday, 4 p.m.

P.S. And yet I'm kissing you for your having written a long letter.

On the day of the concert he managed to send a short message: "The concert is not going to be repeated tomorrow. So I'm arriving home tomorrow about 11 a.m. I might stop to pick up my salary on the way. Till tomorrow, my dear. I'm kissing you and our children."

In the mid-1870s Borodin composed a polka on a simple repeated tune that was considered a joke. Stasov called the tune "Tati-Tati." It could be played with one finger even by a person who did not have the least idea

Top: Andrey Petrovich Rimsky-Korsakov, the composer's father, in a sketch from 15 April 1828.

Right: Sophia Vasilyevna Rimskaya-Korsakova, the composer's mother, beginning of the 1860s.

Left: Voin Andreyevich Rimsky-Korsakov, the composer's older brother, beginning of the 1860s.

Bottom: Nikolay Rimsky-Korsakov on the clipper *Almaz (Diamond),* seated in the second row on the right, sometime between 1862 and 1864.

Top left: Nikolay Fedorovich Purgold, father of Nadezhda (the composer's wife).

Top right: Vladimir Fedorovich Purgold, known as Uncle "Oh!", who looked after his deceased brother Nikolay's family (including daughter Nadezhda Purgold).

Right: Nadezhda Purgold, beginning of the 1860s.

Nadezhda and her brother Fedor Purgold, beginning of the 1860s.

Alexandra Purgold, the composer's sister-in-law, 1870.

The Purgold family at their red country house at Pargolovo (near St. Petersburg), early 1870s.

Nikolay Andreyevich Rimsky-Korsakov, around 1872.

Nadezhda Purgold, around 1872.

The Church of Sts. Peter and Paul, in Shuvalov Park, where Nikolay and Nadezhda Rimsky-Korsakov's wedding took place on 30 June 1872.

Nadezhda Rimskaya-
Korsakova (née Purgold),
1882.

Nikolay Andreyevich Rimsky-
Korsakov, 1882.

Nikolay and Nadezhda Rimsky-Korsakov's children *(clockwise from top left)*: 1) Misha and Sonya; 2) Andryusha; 3) Misha and Nadya; 4) Volodya and Nadya.

1884 г.

Въ залѣ квартиры Римскихъ-Корсаковыхъ
(Уг. Владимірской и Колокольной; д. № кв. 5)
Данъ будетъ спектакль любителей
Программа:

«Зомби»

историческая комедія въ 2 дѣйствіяхъ

Дѣйствующія лица:

Мурильо, маэстро.	Н. Н. Римскій-Корсако.
Истуріусъ ⎤	Б. О. Таденгаузенъ
Фернандесъ ⎟ его молодые	Е. И. Фриденъ
Карлосъ ⎟ ученики.	С. Н. Римская-Корсако.
Гонзало ⎦	А. Н. Римскій-Корсако.
Себастіанъ, нищій шутъ пропавшій изъ пр.	О. И. Фриденъ

Дѣйствіе происходитъ въ Севильѣ.

«Двѣ Саши»

или
«1е Апрѣля.»

Комедія-шутка въ 1 дѣйствіи

Саша Полская	Н. Н. Римскій-Корсако.
Лина ⎤ ея сестры.	О. И. Фриденъ
Надя ⎦	В. Н. Фриденъ
Ѳедя, ея братъ.	А. Н. Римскій-Корсаковъ.
Гувернантка въ домѣ Полскихъ.	Б. О. Таденгаузенъ
Саша Липака	С. Н. Римская-Корсако.

Дѣйствіе происходитъ въ деревнѣ, въ домѣ Полскихъ.

Начало ровно въ 7 часовъ.

Порядокъ спектакля: 1) Двѣ Саши, 2) Зомби.

The program of two plays—*Two Sashas, or The First of April* and *Zombie*—written by Nikolay Rimsky-Korsakov and performed by his children at their home, January 1884.

how to play the piano. However, to accompany it you needed a professional pianist. Rimsky-Korsakov came up with the idea of composing some pieces containing variations on Borodin's original piece of music, and a group of four composers—Borodin, Cui, Rimsky-Korsakov, and Lyadov—became engrossed in the task. The variations were titled *Paraphrases* and were published by the firm of A. Bittner. Franz Liszt happened to see this publication. The variations made him so excited that he wrote to the authors: "Dear gentlemen, you have created a composition that seems like a joke but is actually of great interest. [...] Nothing could have been wittier than your twenty-four variations and fourteen pieces." Liszt even added one more variation himself.

La nuit de mai (*May Night*)

While they were engaged, Nikolay and Nadezhda had read Gogol's "One Night in May" together. Later Nadezhda had suggested to her husband that he should use this story as the basis for an opera. At the end of the summer of 1877 Rimsky-Korsakov recalled the story, and it began to occupy his thoughts. From February 1878 he became completely absorbed in the task of creating *La nuit de mai* (*May Night*); it soon became his only creative pursuit. He spent the summer of 1878 with his family in Ligovo, not far from St. Petersburg. They rented a country house there with the Akhsharumovs. The work on the opera went very quickly. By October *May Night* was completed. Rimsky-Korsakov dedicated it to his wife.

A Growing Family: A Son, Andrey

In October 1878 Nadezhda gave birth to another baby boy; he was named Andrey, after the composer's father. However, the birth of another son greatly increased the housework needed, on top of which, one by one, the children began to fall ill. To cap it all, Nadezhda herself contracted diphtheria. Rimsky-Korsakov wrote to his student Ilia Tyumenev:[10] "Sometimes it's just impossible to get down to work. But I have a lucky trait of character: I think no one else is able to forget about all cares, trouble, and worries as quickly as I am and to turn to music." Most of the time the composer was very busy with his occupation and did not have the opportunity to devote much time to his family, but when family emergencies arose he put everything aside and came to his wife's aid. But this time it was especially difficult because Nadezhda did not escape the round of family illnesses herself.

Rimsky-Korsakov's children knew he was very fond of them and were happiest when he had time to play with them. Their favorite thing was to climb onto his lap and listen to him sing to them. Certainly the children had their own favorite song, a Russian folk tune, which they asked him to sing again and again. Being very little, they couldn't understand the words completely and called it "Kazhenushka" ("Wifelet," their amusing mispronunciation, meaning "my wife, let's"). His eldest daughter, Sophia, shared her reminiscences many years later. She remembered her father teaching them how to use watercolors, gilding Christmas pine cones and nuts with them, and coloring Easter eggs with thread. He himself used to take the boys to the barber shop, since ladies were not allowed to come inside.

Rimsky-Korsakov continued to conduct concerts at the Free Music School. In March 1879 he went to Kronstadt again to conduct the next concert of the united navy bands. He had expected to have enough time to visit his family before the concert, but circumstances prevented it. He sent a letter Nadezhda by special delivery:

> Dear Nadya,
>
> There's no possibility for me to come since the rehearsal can't be carried out without my guidance. I'm sending you my traveling bag. You should pack two clean shirts for me (one with a high collar and the other with a starched one), and also a tailcoat, a waistcoat, a pair of black trousers, and a white necktie. [...] Can you drop me some lines [about] how you all are and about your own shoulder blade? How are Mishuk, Sonka, and Andrey? Kiss them all for me. I'm very bored here. The rehearsals are full of miscues. And I dislike them. [...] Write me about everything and send it back with this deliveryman.
>
> Goodbye, darling Nadyusha, my dearest, best, and sweet Nadya. I kiss you and the children.
>
> Your N. R.-Korsakov. Tuesday, 4 p.m.

On the day of the concert, Rimsky-Korsakov had to send an urgent message in the morning:

Dear Nadya,

You've sent me the wrong waistcoat, so I'm in difficulty. Send me another one with this soldier. I need the black waistcoat that has an open front with three buttons. I hope to receive it just before the concert. If you are at home when the soldier comes, then drop me some lines about all of you. Tell Misha to look at the thermometer so that you can write me what the temperature is outside. Tousle Sonka's hair properly and kiss Andryushka.[11] Tell Misha that there are about two hundred instrumentalists there, three small drums and two big ones. I'm about to go to the rehearsal. I'm so tired from all this and feel exhausted.[…] I kiss you and the children, my dear, nice Nadya, my heart. See you soon. I'm waiting for your letter.

The necessary waistcoat was found and sent with a note:

It's so annoying, my dear Nika, that it turned out to have been the wrong waistcoat. Annushka is to blame. I packed everything myself except the tailcoat set. I charged Annushka to pack it. Thank God, we all are well. Misha looked at the thermometer and said that it was +5° C [41° F], but he was not quite right. It is +6.5° C [44° F].[…] Lyadov came yesterday. We played a lot of music and had a pleasant time. He's been missing you a lot at the Conservatory and hasn't even gone for coffee without you. Good-bye, my dear. I'm kissing you. Misha said he bowed to you.

Rimsky-Korsakov conducted two concerts in Kronstadt on 22 and 23 March. The *Kronstadt Bulletin* published a review signed "B. F. R.": "The concerts have shown that our navy band conducted by a talented and experienced professor has made great progress recently and reached the same level as our best Royal Guards bands in terms of music.[…] At the end of both of the concerts the audience thanked Professor Rimsky-Korsakov for the aesthetic pleasure they had received."

After returning from the concerts, the composer spent only a few days in St. Petersburg and then left for Moscow. Lyadov, Borodin, and Nadezhda saw him off. He had been invited to conduct a concert at the Bolshoi Theatre. It had been organized by Pyotr Shostakovsky, a pianist, conductor, and manager of the symphony concerts held by the Moscow Philharmonic Society. Rimsky-Korsakov stayed in the hotel Slavyansky Bazar (Slavic Fair) and spent ten days in Moscow. On his arrival he sent a letter home saying that he had arrived in Moscow safe and sound. But his wife had written to him before she received his letter.

After seeing you off yesterday I walked home. Borodin and Lyadov accompanied me. On coming home I found a letter from your mother. She is sorry that I will spend the holidays alone and she will even come for two days. How kind she is! I and our children are well, only Sonya still has a runny nose and a light cough. [...] Uncle "Oh!" and Sonechka paid us a visit after dinner. The children were happy and because of this very naughty. At night I stayed home, and, as I was very bored, I allowed Misha to go to bed a little later so that he could be with me at evening tea. He became extremely interested in the samovar. He asked a lot of questions about it, watched as it was fizzing and embers of coal were dying slowly. It's a pity that you're so far away in Moscow. The rehearsal has finished by this time and I still don't know anything. What about the orchestra? Are you pleased with it? I'm dying to know everything as soon as possible. Bless you for having a successful concert. I'm embracing you and kissing you affectionately, my darling.

The first Moscow concert was held that same evening, 3 April. The next day Nadezhda received a telegram with the signatures of Shostakovsky and Daria Leyonova, a singer who took part in the concert. "Tremendous success. The Moscow audience has met the most talented creator of *The Maid of Pskov*, *Sadko*, and dear Russian music very enthusiastically. The scenes from *A Life for the Tsar*, the romances of Glinka, the overture to *Khovanschina*, and the *Fantasy* delighted the packed audience.[12] Tell this to Shestakova, Stasov, Musorgsky, Borodin, and all our dear friends." Upon receiving this telegram Nadezhda sent a letter to Moscow immediately:

My dear Nika,

At night I received a telegram that made me excited. Mother also read it. (She has come today and will stay with us for two days.) I rushed to Sonechka. They all were very glad too and congratulated me instead of you. They had the opportunity to congratulate at least me, and I, poor thing, had nobody to congratulate. And I wish I could kiss you all over your dear face. [...] I hope that the telegram of Leyonova and Shostakovsky didn't exaggerate things. I'm looking forward to hearing from your own letter how it all went on. I'm very glad that mother came to us. We had fun together. [...] I should kiss you all over and pet your head for your writing so often. I'm so upset that I haven't heard your overture to *The Maid of Pskov*. You should promise to play it next year. But it's such a long time to wait. I can say that we all are behaving ourselves. [...] Now I'll be looking forward to the results of the second concert. I hope it will go smoothly. But even more important is that you come home as soon as possible. Then I could say, "Now my dear is calm." Mother kisses you. Mishka keeps on singing in the mornings and recording notes from time to time. Do you have time for yourself in order to see the sights of Moscow? Are they pestering you too much with work? You should visit the anthropology exhibition that just opened there. They say it's great.

Good-bye. my dear. Don't get a cold in your new coat. Please take care of yourself. I'm embracing you and kissing you heartily.

The composer described the events of the concert in detail in a letter dated 4 April:

My dear,

Yesterday's concert succeeded more than I had expected. When I appeared I was greeted wonderfully. Then "The Hymn" was played three times. The musicians played standing up, and I was facing the audience and wearing gloves. When "The Hymn" was finished I took off the gloves and turned to the orchestra. The overture was played beautifully, smartly, and without incident. (To my mind it is much better in this current orchestration.) After the overture I was called for three or four times. Then Shostakovsky played the concerto of Henselt. He made some mistakes in several passages, as he forgot what should be played further on, but the audience didn't notice it. Somebody from the first row asked me to hand a garland to him and show him a new grand piano to be presented to him. [...] *The Fantasy on Serbian Themes* opened the second act. They played wonderfully well. The audience demanded an encore and I obliged them. (I forgot to tell you that at the beginning of the second act the audience demanded "The Hymn" again,[13] and of course their wish was granted.) [...] When the concert was finished everyone was called to the stage, so I bowed again. The theatre was packed and decorated with special lights. In the intermission I was ordered to visit Kavelin, the general manager of the theatres. He begged me to play "The Hymn" if the audience demanded it, as if I hadn't known this. When the concert was over (it was about midnight) we went to a restaurant called the Hermitage where we celebrated till 4 a.m. Of course Shostakovsky's friends, Blaramberg and Gridnin,[14] were there. We drank a lot of toasts, told jokes and anecdotes about the vagaries of Moscow musical life. All of a sudden Daria got the idea to send a telegram to you. (By the way, she was toasting you at that moment.) [...] I hope the telegram didn't frighten you. My dear, I remembered you often during the concert. You would have been pleased with it. It's a pity Lyadenka, Borodin, and Bach were not here![15] The audience greeted me heartily, much better than in Petersburg, but it seems they don't have musical intellectuals here. [...] Can you read some parts of this letter to Lyadenka and other friends, to mother and our relatives as well? When am I supposed to get a letter from you? My dear and sweet! Kiss the children for me. What about Mishuk? Does he study his music scores? Is Sonya the same little rascal? Has she stopped coughing? Is Andrey still so happy? I think of you very often! I'm enclosing a poster. I'll write to you again tomorrow.

Till tomorrow, my darling. Write to me.

But the letter from Nadezhda arrived already that evening, and so the composer again took pen in hand:

My dear, I just came into my room and found a letter from you. I wanted to deal with my business but even so I couldn't help chattering again with you although I've written to you once today already. I came home yesterday at 4 a.m. after the party and went to bed immediately. I woke up feeling fresh just a little while later, at 7:30, but I realized that I had slept too little and kept on lying in bed until I fell asleep again and got up only at noon. After drinking coffee and writing to you I went to see Shostakovsky. [...] Write to me, my darling, whatever comes into your head. I kiss you, my Nadyushonok. Kiss the children for me.

Before sending this letter on the following day he added: "The weather is a little better today. Maybe I will be lucky and can walk around Moscow a little. This hotel is very nice. I'm living 'in the heavens' in room 106 (it costs a ruble and a half a night!). Everything is perfect. I ate Moscow *kalachi*;[16] our St. Petersburg *kalachi* are not any worse and in fact hardly different at all."

Although Rimsky-Korsakov was very busy, he did find some time to walk around Moscow and to visit the Kremlin. He described this in his next letter:

What beauty! St. Basil's Cathedral, with all its towers, impressed me greatly. I even visited the Cathedral of the Archangel.[17] It turned out I'm pretty good at finding my way around Moscow's confusing streets, and even after walking around a lot I managed to return to my hotel. [...] I think you've just come home from the literary evening and now you are having tea with Lyadinka. They wanted to postpone the concert until Tuesday, but I insisted on holding it on Monday. Otherwise, it would be too long to wait. I'm missing you more and more every minute and I'm dying to see our children. I kiss you, my dear Nadya. I can imagine clearly that they are sleeping now: Mishuk, then Sonka is lying across the bed and Andryushka with his hands crossed. Kiss them for me.

Nadezhda replied:

Lyadinka called on us yesterday. He came about 4 p.m. and stayed for dinner. That night we went to the literary evening together. The evening was a mess, as most charity evenings of such kinds are. They started half an hour late; all the participants were late, and some of them did not show up at all. [...] The program was as follows: singing, reading, etc., in total thirteen performers. [...] From the reading section we listened to: Mordovtsev, who read his new historical novel. It was too long and too boring. He reads horribly. Plescheyev, who recited his poems. There were two old ones and one new. He was very good. Well, I liked the poems at least, but he also reads rather badly, he even gestured a lot. Potyokhin, who read an episode from his novel *A Sick Woman*. It was very good and he reads perfectly, but I did not like the way that he changed voices like an actor while reading and generally conducted himself as if he were an actor on the stage.

And last, Dostoyevsky.[18] I thought I wouldn't have enough patience to wait for his performance as the evening lasted for an unbearably long time. But it was worth the wait! He reads superbly, in a simple but so eloquent manner. Despite the fact that he is very weak and sick and coughed a lot while he was reading, he articulated perfectly, not missing a single word. He read an extract, which is not published yet, from his latest novel, *The Brothers Karamazov*. Judging by that extract, the novel must be very good. At least I liked this extract very much. All the participants were greeted well. But Dostoyevsky was greeted like nobody else! After his reading the room was abuzz with excitement. He was presented with a wreath of laurels, he was called onto the stage repeatedly, and even the men waved kerchiefs and scarves. And can you imagine, our calm Lyadov was one of the most excited? So great was his delight that he got up on his chair, stamped his feet, and applauded till the pain in his hands stopped him; to make a long story short, I had to use all my strength to drag him home. There were some more performers to follow, but it was so late—11:30 p.m.—that I hurried home. Lyadov said that he was not interested in any other participants, and we left for home together. I was very glad that we went back together, as it would be very unpleasant to go by myself. I think that I bored Lyadov while we were riding home.

Good-bye, my dear. Keep on writing as often as possible. I'm kissing you.

Rimsky-Korsakov responded as soon as he received her letter. He informed his wife about his trips to visit Repin in Khamovniki and, at the request of Sophia, to see her friend Anastasia Bestuzheva in Plyuschikha.[19]

Khamovniki and Plyuschikha are rather far, but I went on foot and wandered around Moscow's streets until I became tired. It turned out I remembered the place quite well after my journey to Moscow with Balakirev. So, all these Prechistinkas and Molchanovkas and so on didn't confuse me.[20] Then I went home and read your letter. [...] Could you write me if Sophischa asks about me sometimes?[21] Kiss them all and my mother. My bow to Uncle "Oh!," Sonechka, and Semyon Dmitriyevich. I kiss you my darling, sweet, nice Nadyushka.

Your N. R.-Korsakov, 7 April, morning.

The second concert took place on 8 April and met with much the same success as the first. For the first time the composer was given a wreath. The ribbon on the wreath said, "To the creator of *Sadko, Antar*, and *The Maid of Pskov*."

The Rimsky-Korsakov family spent the summer of 1879 at a country house in Ligovo, not far from St. Petersburg. The composer completed his opera *May Night* there and began working on a composition for symphony orchestra entitled *The Fairy Tale*. It was inspired by the prologue to Alexander Pushkin's epic poem *Ruslan and Lyudmila*.

Semyon Kruglikov

Kruglikov became a close friend of the Rimsky-Korsakovs during this period. They met for the first time when the composer began to work at the Free

Music School, and soon after Kruglikov became a regular visitor at the Rimsky-Korsakov home. He used to live in Moscow, but he had come to St. Petersburg to study at the College of Ways and Means of Communication, at the College of Mines, and at the College of Forestry; concurrently he attended the Free Music School. He sang in the music school chorus and became an employee of the school. His dream was to work in the field of music. He studied music theory on his own and was going to enter the Conservatory, but his parents were firmly against it. They considered music a waste of time and demanded that he come back to Moscow. So in the spring of 1879 he left to see them. He had hoped it would be temporary, but his parents insisted that he remain in Moscow. When it became clear that he would not be coming back, Rimsky-Korsakov wrote to him:

> I'm telling you, on my own behalf as well as on behalf of Nadezhda and the Free Music School, that your absence will be very apparent for all of us. We have become very close recently and met very often. We consider you such a true admirer of good music that indeed it is very sad not to see you for a long time and not to discuss all those issues we are equally interested in. On the behalf of the Free Music School I can say that it's a great loss for us, as we won't be able to find another such active and beneficial employee as you.

Kruglikov was phlegmatic, kind, cheerful, and witty. He was a good story-teller and was capable of telling a joke while keeping a perfectly straight face. He was also a gourmet, and had his own nickname in the Rimsky-Korsakov family. One French newspaper, in an article devoted to Russian music, mentioned him as a music critic but spelled his last name Krougliff, and since that time he had been called Krugliff by the Rimsky-Korsakov family. When he came to visit, the children were very happy and cried out, "Krugliff has come! Krugliff has come!" Once little Sonya said to him, "Krugliff, you're the funniest!" And the little girl's compliment became a family joke. Kruglikov was very friendly with the Rimsky-Korsakov children. He wrote to the composer in one of his letters from Moscow: "My best regards to Nadezhda and my dear friends Misha and Sonya. Kiss Andrey for me as we didn't have time to become friends and he just gave me his hand to shake officially." Andrey was just about twelve months old at that time. Kruglikov assisted Rimsky-Korsakov by copying out his musical scores and kept on doing this for some time, even after moving back to Moscow. The composer stayed in correspondence with Kruglikov for about thirty years thereafter. They wrote approximately six hundred letters in total to each other.

Rimsky-Korsakov took a new student in December 1879: Alexander Glazunov, a fourteen-year-old boy recommended to him by Balakirev. Balakirev gave piano lessons to his mother, Elena Glazunova. Rimsky-Korsakov wrote about him, "He was a nice boy with pretty eyes who played the piano clumsily." In his turn, Glazunov wrote in his memoirs many years later: "You can imagine with what youthful excitement I anticipated my first meeting with Rimsky-Korsakov. I was in awe of his creative work and utterly believed in his artistic authority." Glazunov became a private student of Rimsky-Korsakov and had his lessons at the composer's home.

In 1879 Rimsky-Korsakov's opera *May Night* had been accepted for staging at the Mariinsky Theatre. The opening night was on 9 January 1880. The composer had to make nine curtain calls. Levko's songs about "the head" from the third act were encored. The composer, his wife, his mother, and other relatives had seats in one of the boxes of the first circle. Avdotia, a nanny,[22] accompanied them. After opening night this nanny retold the story of the main character, a *pannochka*,[23] to the children with breathless excitement. Sophia wrote a letter to Nadezhda in which she said, "I'm surprised myself how I managed to give birth [*sic*] to such a husband, and public figure, as Nika." Uncle "Oh!," who had long been a leading admirer of Rimsky-Korsakov's talents, presented him with a golden foot holding a pen on the occasion of the premiere. The composer set it on his desk and used it constantly thereafter for writing his compositions, business papers, and letters. Six-year-old Misha was taken to the theatre for the second performance of *May Night* and was delighted.

5

The Snow Maiden, September 1881– June 1884

I'd been always keen on old Russian customs and heathen pantheism to some extent, but now this flame was growing inside me.
—Rimsky-Korsakov, *My Musical Life* (published 1909)

Hardly had the first performances of *May Night* been given than Rimsky-Korsakov began working on a new opera based on the fairy tale *The Snow Maiden* by Alexander Ostrovsky.[1] He read this tale once again and, in his own words, "it struck me with its wonderful beauty." He wrote in his memoirs:

> I'd been always keen on old Russian customs and heathen pantheism to some extent, but now this flame was growing inside me. At that time it seemed there couldn't be a better plot for me or more poetic characters than the Snow Maiden, Lell the herdsman, and Spring.[2] Nothing could have been better except the Kingdom of the Berendeyans with their tsar.[3] No personality or religion could have been better than the worship of Yarilo the Sun God.[4] [...] At first I had just some unclear ideas, then the mood and colors relative to the scenes appeared in my mind little by little, becoming more and more distinct.

In March 1880 Rimsky-Korsakov had to go to Kronstadt, where he conducted two more concerts of the navy band, but at the end of April he went back to Moscow to conduct a concert at the Bolshoi Theatre. In Moscow he visited Ostrovsky and asked for his permission to use his fairy tale for a libretto. Ostrovsky kindly gave his approval.

While in Moscow he also visited Kruglikov, who wrote to the composer after his departure:

My dear Nikolay,

How dreary Moscow seems to me after your departure! I had nearly got used to this dull Moscow, by the skin of my teeth. But you arrived and I breathed in a different smell, of something different, good, something from the old days. […] Everything here became even more disgusting for me (after you left) than it was before.

In Stelevo

In the spring of 1880 Rimsky-Korsakov decided to rent a summer house much farther from St. Petersburg than was his custom. He chose the village of Stelevo, which was about thirty *versts* from the town of Luga,[5] the latter being about 180 versts from St. Petersburg. Having moved into Stelevo with Nadezhda and his children, he became absolutely absorbed in composing the new opera, for which he had sketched some pieces earlier in St. Petersburg. The composer wrote in his memoirs:

> It was the first time in my life that I had spent a summer in a traditional Russian village. Everything struck me. I admired everything there. I was excited with the beautiful location; the pleasant groves of Zakaznitsa trees and the Podberezyevs- kaya; a huge Volchinets woods;[6] fields of rye, buckwheat, oats, flax, and wheat; many tiny villages scattered around; a small river where we bathed; a large lake called Vrevo nearby; bad roads; emptiness; original Russian names for the villages, like Podberezie, Kopytets, Dremyach, Khvoshnya,[7] etc. There was an excellent orchard that had a lot of apple and cherry trees, currants, wild and garden straw- berries, gooseberries, lilac bushes in bloom, plenty of different wildflowers, and unceasing birdsong—in a word, everything around was in full harmony with my then pantheistic mood and my enthusiasm for the plot of *The Snow Maiden*. I saw a wood goblin or its nest in every thick and crooked branch or stump. I imagined Volchinets as a forbidden forest and the bold Kopytets hillock as a Yarilin hill, a triple echo from which one could hear from our balcony as voices of wood goblins and other creatures.

Rimsky-Korsakov wrote to Kruglikov about their life in Stelevo: "We are living well here. […] We are watching plants grow, eating wild strawberries a lot, and having meals out in the orchard. I can say we are having a pleasant time. And we don't see any familiar faces. We don't have any desire to become acquainted with our neighbors; they all seem to be indifferent landowners." Rimsky-Korsakov retained very pleasant memories about his life in Stelevo. He even composed a humorous poem about the summer he spent there. The composer's wife, on the other hand, gave a much different impression about Stelevo in a letter to her elder sister:

> Yesterday a sudden thunderstorm came with a hurricane and we hid ourselves in our rooms. I sat down very close to the window, washing wild strawberries, as it became dark in the room. Nika and Misha were with me in the same room. Suddenly there was a dazzling flash of lightning, and at the same time we heard a frightening crash. The windows were shaking. So hard was it blowing that I was knocked down, together with a chair that I was sitting on. Nika rushed over to me and helped me to get up. I was so frightened. I thought that the blow I experienced would have awful consequences, and that I would become deaf or something of the kind might happen to me. Fortunately everything is all right. I had a narrow escape. I was just scared and very nervous all evening. But today I'm feeling much better. Everybody in the house became alarmed. All of them rushed out from their rooms. We found out later that evening that our gardener was also thrown out of a window; some children fell off some benches that they were sitting on; a milkmaid who was milking a cow at that moment became crazy for a while; to make a long story short, it was something extremely unusual. We were looking for traces of lightning in our orchard, but we didn't find anything. I assume that the lightning struck the ground somewhere where it's difficult to find its traces. Nika said he saw a bolt of lightning moving in the direction of our windows.

The Snow Maiden was composed very quickly, in just two and a half months. Upon returning to St. Petersburg, the composer worked on the orchestration. The work was completed in the spring of the next year. He played his new opus to his friends at home and also presented it at Balakirev's, who wrote to him after the performance:

> It had a tremendous effect in my apartment. To say nothing of my own pleasure and even delight with most of the piece, [...] it was as if the music cast a spell upon my sister. Even old Maria, as it turned out, was moved to dance. She

confessed that while you were playing your "Shrovetide" she was standing before the icons and praying. She expressed her fear that on the eve of the great holy holiday her legs were rocking and only the strength of her belief prevented her from dancing on her "three" legs.[8]

Rimsky-Korsakov wrote a jocular postscript in his response: "I couldn't even have imagined that I would tempt Maria."

Ostrovsky happened to be in St. Petersburg at the time, and Rimsky-Korsakov played his opera for him as well. When Ostrovsky returned to Moscow, Kruglikov paid him a visit. Afterward he wrote to the composer: "I was with him for half an hour and for all that time he was talking only about Your opera. Here are his exact words: 'The music Korsakov has written for *The Snow Maiden* is fantastic. I couldn't imagine anything more suitable for it. It vividly expresses the poetry of old Russian paganism and completely reveals the nature of the snowy cold at the beginning, and then the irrepressibly passionate heroine of the fairy tale.'" Rimsky-Korsakov said of his work: "On completing *The Snow Maiden* I felt that I had become a mature musician and opera composer, who had become able to stand firmly on his own feet."

The arrival of 1881 brought little joy to Rimsky-Korsakov. First there was frustration at the Free Music School. The composer wrote to Kruglikov:

> I don't know what to do with the Free School. There is no money at all. [...] The chorus is very bad in terms of the quality of the voices. There are many old ladies and just a few good men; the tenors are husky. [...] My fondest wish is to delegate my duties to somebody else. But to whom? [...] I don't have any desire to go on with this school. I'm not a specialist in conducting and I don't consider myself a skilled one. If I stop doing this, I won't be upset.

Illness in the Family

Another round of serious family illnesses occurred next. Rimsky-Korsakov wrote to Kruglikov:

> Everything is very bad at home. Andrusha has been sick for a week already. He has a fever every day. His temperature is between 39.5° [103° F] and 40.5° [104° F]. [...] Nadya is extremely worried and is beginning to be rather gloomy. [...]

Moreover, the other children have suffered from the flu and whooping cough. Very bad! I have just sat down to write to you to distract myself. [...] Lately I haven't been doing anything due to Andrey's sickness.

Despite these obstacles, at the very beginning of January 1881 Rimsky-Korsakov presented *The Snow Maiden* to the opera authorities at the Mariinsky Theatre, who approved it for staging. He completed his new composition for symphony orchestra, *The Fairy Tale,* and conducted it in a concert of the Russian Musical Society. He chose an epigraph from the prologue of *Ruslan and Lyudmila.* Due to this, some of the audience at the concert tried to find images in the music of a chained cat walking round an oak and other episodes from Pushkin's prologue. However, according to the composer, it was his own musical fairy tale, and he chose the epigraph just to show that his composition was a Russian tale of magic.

Death of Musorgsky

By the beginning of February all the children had recovered, but other worries came in their turn. Musorgsky fell ill, and Rimsky-Korsakov took his sickness to heart. Musorgsky was in the hospital for a month. All of his friends visited him, among them the Rimsky-Korsakovs. He died on 16 March 1881. The funeral took place at the Tikhvin cemetery of the Alexander Nevsky Lavra.[9] As Tyumenev reminisced: "The public was expecting speeches, but they had none. [...] Only Nikolay, when he was passing by the crowd, said to Stasov aloud intentionally [...] that he would review and edit everything left by Musorgsky and everything that could be completed would be, and then published."

Musorgsky's death came on the heels of the infamous assassination of Tsar Alexander II by anarchists in the center of St. Petersburg. At the beginning of April Rimsky-Korsakov wrote to Kruglikov: "Some days ago there was the requiem for the deceased tsar at the place of his assassination. A very elegant wreath ordered by subscription was placed there. The requiem was sung rather well by our chorus, whereas I had to stand with a baton and 'conduct' an endless number of pauses. Next Sunday we will play the requiem for Musorgsky." In his memoirs the composer mentioned that the manuscripts Musorgsky left behind were a mess, and without proper additional work their publication would have been useless. Rimsky-Korsakov decided to do everything he could to complete the remaining projects and to present them to the Bessel Publishing House, without compensation of any kind.

In Taitsy

Though everyone liked Stelevo very much, the Rimsky-Korsakov family spent the next summer in Taitsy with Uncle "Oh!," the Akhsharumovs, and the Molases. Taitsy, an estate that belonged to the Department for Independent Principalities of the Ministry of the Court, was located near one of the stations on the Baltiisky railway line.[10] Every summer a large house was placed at Vladimir Purgold's disposal on this estate. Rimsky-Korsakov's holiday was interrupted on 1 June, when he had to leave for Nikolayev again for an inspection of the army and navy bands. Nadezhda traveled with her husband to St. Petersburg, saw him off, and returned to Taitsy the next day.

On his way to Nikolayev Rimsky-Korsakov stayed in Moscow for a day, from where he sent home a brief note:

> Dear Nadya,
>
> I arrived safe and sound. [...] How are you? How was your trip to Taitsy? I'm expecting to receive your letter in Nikolayev. Kiss the children for me. Good-bye, my darling Nadyusha. I kiss you heartily.
>
> Your N. R.-Korsakov.

Then, as soon as he arrived in Nikolayev early in the morning, he sent his first letter:

> My darling Nadyusha,
>
> I've arrived in Nikolayev. I am again accommodated in "the palace." I was constantly surrounded with chatterboxes during my trip. From Moscow till Tula I talked to a fellow named Sobolev, a lawyer. I had to introduce myself and, having learned who I was, he began to talk endlessly about music, my compositions, Tchaikovsky, and so on. He got off at Tula. Then my neighbor was a young but seemingly rather stupid officer. However, he had taken part in the fighting at Shipka and had a wounded leg.[11] He said he was going on business to different places where his dragoon regiment had been located and was collecting materials

in order to write a historical essay about this regiment. He said he was doing it at the wish of the tsarina. After some more or less interesting stories about Shipka he started to chew the fat, which bored me till Znamenka, where he got off at last. At Kursk I got a new neighbor. He was a pleasant and smart local landowner. We started talking about current affairs. There was another officer (some count) who joined in the conversation. He was talking such rotten nonsense, which is common with the top officers, that it was just a disaster. When he managed to mention the rumors concerning Tolstoy's appointment again as the Minister of Education and that he was happy about it, I couldn't bear it any longer and just went out. I spent some time on the platform in order not to listen to him and not to have to confront him. When the landowner got off at Kharkov I tried to make small talk with the officer.[12] He was smoking my cigarettes all the way and even borrowed five kopeks. How glad I was to get rid of him! Because firstly I could have (some) peace and quiet and a nap, and secondly, it became possible to read. [...] By the way, two bandmasters of the First and the Second Naval Depots and a company commander met me at the railway station and took me to "the palace." [...]

Good-bye my darling.

My bow to everyone I know.

Your Nika R.-K.

Inspecting the Navy Bands

That same evening Rimsky-Korsakov began writing another letter:

I'm feeling more lonely and bored than in the morning, when I was writing to you. I've come back recently from the Nebolsins'.[13] At home I had tea, finished reading *A Month in the Country* by Turgenev,[14] and experienced such a surge of loneliness that I felt a desire to write to you about it. [...] Now I have just come back from the First and Second Navy Depots, where I held an oversight review of the instrumentalists. That means I had to greet, thank, praise, and, to make a long story short, act as a Khlestakov with his rank of inspector.[15] It's so stupid. I'm not cut out for this role at all. I can't act with the required solemnity and importance. My service at navy inspections is such a fraud that it is just wretched for me! I'm absolutely useless there. The soldiers or sailors, try as they might, put forth their efforts, but good music doesn't come out. They are just stuck in utter mire and there is no way out. And the local authorities are delighted with their music, praised it as if it were the best in the world because the authorities themselves don't have the least idea what they are talking about. Moreover, they wish and even demand that I, Khlestakov on tour, should also be delighted. And I have to praise. Otherwise, I would cruelly offend the poor instrumentalists, as they really put forth great efforts. It's so stupid, stupid, stupid! I could have scolded them, but for what? It could be useful if I could count on improving them, but that's impossible. So, I should be pleased with them, i.e., praise them. Certainly I'm trying my best to praise them as little as possible, that is, not to speak in an overly emotional voice, not to use superlatives, not to shake hands too firmly so as to convey the need for improvement. But who knows? Maybe they don't feel this at all. Maybe they are just pleased that an inspector came and was satisfied, and then everything was all right. I am between a rock and a hard place. [...]

When will I get a letter from you? It is bound to be here tomorrow! Kiss the children for me. I'm embracing you and kissing your neck so that your ears are trembling, my darling Nadyusha, my sweet, don't be upset. Don't carry Andrey in your arms. Could you write more often?

Meanwhile Borodin was in Magdeburg, Germany, and was also in correspondence with Rimsky-Korsakov's wife. He informed her in his letter that there had been a concert conducted by Arthur Nikisch at which Rimsky-Korsakov's *Antar* had been successfully performed,[16] and about his meeting with Franz Liszt. Nadezhda wrote to her husband and recounted the news from Borodin:

My darling, sweet Nika,

I'm in a much better mood today. I've had a lucky day. I got two letters in the morning: one from you and one from Borodin. And in the evening I got a letter from Stasov with some promised books enclosed. The letter from Borodin is very nice and interesting. Borodin said that he added your name to the list of members of the Allgemeine Deutsche Musikverein [Universal German Musical Association], and then he wrote in a lovely humorous manner how he had answered the question "Who is Nadezhda Purgold?"[17] He told them who I am and they asked him to put my name on the list too. And he did! He wrote "a pianist and composer." It's just a shame! He himself called it "my perfidy." Indeed, it's very insidious of him to do so. [...] I don't know myself why Taitsy seems so unfriendly and alien to me. I feel here as if I were a guest. I don't feel like going out and gathering lilies of the valley. I actually have to force myself to walk at least a little, as it is not recommended for me to be seated all the time. Nevertheless, most of the day I stay in my room sewing or being occupied with the children. […] I wish I could go somewhere! I dislike being here so much. I think of Stelevo every day and of our last wonderful summer. However, the children enjoy staying here. […] In the evenings they all play croquet. Sonya certainly can't play yet, she is too little. So she just watches the others play. Andrey is lovely and amusing as usual. Aunt Sonya showed him a dark closet under the stairs for bad children, and he imagined that a "Baba Yaga" lives there.[18] The nanny told him a fairy tale about Baba Yaga a long time ago, but he still remembers it. He is behaving quite well now and has stopped being capricious. […]

Good-bye, my dear friend. Take care of yourself. Don't eat pork and don't do anything foolish. The children kiss you. I'm embracing you and kissing you heartily.

Rimsky-Korsakov visited the Nebolsins (the acquaintances from his last trip to Nikolayev) regularly upon arriving in Nikolayev. They were nice, hospitable people, though the composer considered them to be too much pleased with themselves. Konstantin Nebolsin was a naval officer of the First Depot of the Black Sea Fleet. He was fond of inventing and manufacturing useful devices for his household. His wife, Maria, was a very emotional woman who tended to get excited over the smallest things. She told Rimsky-Korsakov about everything new that had appeared in Nikolayev during the seven years of his absence with such great delight that the composer couldn't but mock her in his letters to Nadezhda.

"I'm So Bored Without You"

Having sent his letter on 6 June, Rimsky-Korsakov wrote another one the next day:

My dear,
Today I'm writing late at night, so this letter will only be mailed tomorrow; therefore, you'll get it a day after the one I wrote yesterday. A whole week has passed already since I heard from you. […] At this moment a cuckoo has just

cuckooed as if it were laughing: *cuckoo-cuckoo-kakakoo*. I'm sorry for the digression. So, I'm going on. [...] I have returned on foot from each visit to the Nebolsins'. It's very good exercise. Tell Semyon that there is a small wooden box for starlings on a tree in Nebolsin's garden. There are two starlings living in it. I saw them with my own eyes and listened to the male starling singing. The starlings don't fight, as Semyon's birds of the same kind usually do; on the contrary, the female sits on the eggs and the male entertains her. By the way, about birds: there are many of them. There is a nightingale in Spassk [where the Nebolsins lived], and my favorite bird lives next to our "palace." It is singing the same musical figures but makes them even longer and sings higher. Moreover, sometimes it just squeaks some particular notes.[19] You might think I'm happy about being here. Not at all. If I'm lucky enough to go to the Crimea it will be nice. But current red tape just sickens me. If I had something new here, it would be different. And at the moment I have none, and to make things worse I'm all alone here. To brighten up my life and fill in your absence with something, I write letters to you every day. I'll tell you how I spent my day today: I got up at 7 a.m., reviewed and rewrote the third act of *The Snow Maiden*, read Gogol's "The Portrait." I didn't go to the Nebolsins' today, thank God. They are very kind but so boring. As for me, I'd rather stay home alone, and with my *Snow Maiden* it's even better than just being alone. At 2:30 p.m. a bandmaster of the second depot visited me and stayed for two hours. He talked a lot about his life. If he was not lying it's rather curious. But all in all he bored me to death.

Why, my darling, do I still not have a letter from you? Are you all right? If I don't receive a letter from you tomorrow I'll send a telegram, I can't wait any longer. Do the children ask about me? Does Andrey ask for me? Don't you carry him in your arms too much? Have you started piano lessons with Misha? If you were a good girl you would sew little and instead you would play the piano yourself sometimes. You ought to be playful sometimes. I think the proof sheet of *The Snow Maiden* must be ready by now. It would be interesting to get a copy when I come back. By the way, about playing: When I packed my pieces of music to bring them to the summer house, I failed to find the ones for *The Maid of Pskov* and decided I would bring them later. I was stupid enough to forget about it completely. If you happen to have a desire to play it, I'm to be blamed that you won't have them. But you could play Schumann and Chopin, or *Biryulki*.[20] I'll be very glad to listen to your playing them when I come back. You know, I'm here virtually without music. I didn't rent a piano this time. It isn't worth it.

Now, good-bye until my next letter. I hug and kiss you. Kiss Mishka, Sonka, and Andrey for me. My bow to everyone. My dear, Nadyushonok, my sweet Nadyenok, my honey darling.

Your Nika R.-K.

Navy Bands Again

Rimsky-Korsakov did not need to send a telegram, as he had received at last the desired first letter from Nadezhda. He responded:

I've got your letter today.

Now I am going to tell you about my activities. Nebolsin took me for my first visit to the bands. All the musicians were out in the courtyard with new instruments. I bowed to them. They responded, "Long live Your Honor." Then Mrs. Nebolsin appeared with some of the other women. Then officers of different ranks came in for the impromptu concert. The band played some compositions: a march, the *William Tell* overture, the sextet from *Lucia*, a solo for baritone, a solo for cornet, and the *Hungarian Overture*. The master [craftsman] from Odessa, who made all of those new instruments, attended. Nebolsin asked me whether I found the instruments to be good. I only saw that they were glittering and that's it. Well, if they glittered then they must be good. I responded, "They are likely to be good." Everyone asked me in turn, "Do you think that the musicians play well?" "Don't you think they play wonderfully?" Maria Nebolsin asked. I had to respond, "Yes, yes. They are good, very good. They've made progress." Nebolsin gave me some money to cover my expenses in handing out five rubles to each soloist, and I praised them officially. I came into the circle of the musicians and told them, "I haven't seen you for seven years and you've made progress," and gave out the money. Nebolsin granted all the rest of the musicians one ruble each and said in a loud voice, "Thank you, fellows." They answered, "Happy to serve, Your Honor." During their performance Maria Nebolsin sighed repeatedly, "Ah, how wonderful! Don't you think it is lovely?! Ah, ah!"

I had hardly finished with the first band when I was invited to listen to the band of the Second Depot, which had been waiting nearby. Now all of the officers of the First Depot hinted that they would be much worse, they could not be even compared to ours, etc. The women even hurried to leave. The farce started again. The band played satisfactorily. Since it was an entirely brass band it was certainly cruder than the first one. But this band was established only four years ago. Therefore, it had achieved good results. Again, I had to give my thanks. The commander of the Second Depot also wanted to appear generous. He granted money as well. I had to give out another five rubles to each soloist and he gave one ruble to all the rest. In one word, it is a farce, simply a farce. But I tell you again. I was not impressed at all. I thanked them incoherently, and my expression apparently did not show any delight. It puzzled the authorities. They wished secretly that I would have been excited. Moreover, my lack of a dignified appearance flustered them a little.

I visited the bands again today. We played the old compositions and studied new ones. [...] We began to plan the concert program. It is likely that two concerts will be scheduled, for 21 and 22 June. I don't know yet when it's best for me to go to the Crimea. [...] Who knows, maybe I won't go to the Crimea at all. I will tell you for sure in some days as soon as everything has been arranged.

Good-bye, my darling, my honey. Kiss the children for me and don't be sad. And could you write at least a little bit more frequently?

It took some time for letters to reach their recipients, but soon Nadezhda and Nikolay began to receive letters from each other more regularly. Rimsky-Korsakov kept on writing every day.

My dear,

I'm so bored without you and I entertain myself a little by writing to you every day. [...] The musicians were engaged in playing at a funeral today, so I didn't have to work with the bands and have been free the whole day. [...] I stayed home all of the morning, then went shopping, had a swim, had lunch at 2 p.m. [...] In the evening I loafed about the boulevard till 10 p.m. I saw some fireflies. The night was wonderful and starlit. Nebolsin and I are thinking of a proper place for the concerts, but nothing has been decided yet. It might be in Spassk or in the Flag Officers' Court or in the Wild Orchard. In any case it will be outdoors, in the evening, with the streetlamps. There is no suitable house to hold a concert here. The hall for naval officers' meetings is too small; the music would be too loud there. The program also hasn't been agreed. I'm certain only about the *Ruslan*, *Don Juan*, and *Norma* overtures. Are you surprised with the choice of the latter? But the thing is, the bands have used up most of their repertoire, but this overture has never been played. For Nikolayev it doesn't really matter how good or bad it is. There will be very good compositions played as well. For example, besides those that I mentioned: the March of Chernomor, "Slavsya" ["Long Life!"], and "Blagoslovenie Mechei" ["The Blessing of Swords"] from *Les Huguenots*. What have you been doing, my dears? Is Mishuk lovely? What about Sophia? How does Andrey behave at table? I've been thinking of you constantly. I wish I could see you. I hope to get a letter from you tomorrow. I'm writing a short letter today as the ink is too thick and hardly writes. Until my next letter. I kiss you and the children many times. I kiss you and embrace you hard.

The next day he wrote:

My dear,

It's a happy day for me today. I've got your letter dated 5 June. I've read it twice already and I will reread it again later. I'm glad that your bad mood has disappeared due to my letters. [...] I spent the whole morning with the musicians. Tomorrow I'll have to be there in the morning and in the evening. It's boiling hot here, +26° C [79° F] in the shade. I went swimming twice today. I went to a market yesterday and today and bought cherries there. I ate a lot of them. I even washed them before eating. (You should praise me for that.) I'm extremely reasonable. I don't eat pork at all. Only once I ate pork sausage, at the Nebolsins'; but it's not harmful. Instead, every day I eat marrowbone and something from mutton. It's very tasty here. [...] And concerning you and my trip, I still hope for this. [...] Although Taitsy is very boring for you, you'd better sew a little and gather flowers a lot. The children are certain to be happy anywhere they have enough space to play. They will find things to occupy themselves anywhere, either in Taitsy, or Stelevo, or in the Crimea. Kiss them for me. I kiss you, my darling sweet Nadyusha. Thanks for your letter. I'm looking forward to the next one. I hug you.

Your N. R.-Korsakov

P.S. I'm writing and listening to a concert of frogs.

This unusually loud "singing" of frogs was memorable for both of them ever since their first trip to Nikolayev in 1874. Nadezhda wrote to her husband on 11 June 1881:

My dear,

I received your second letter from Nikolayev yesterday. What a nice boy you are that you write so often! I don't know why you didn't get my letters for a long time. I've sent three already. This is the fourth one. And Misha sent a letter to you too. [...] The weather is lovely now. But despite this weather I can't walk here and I don't like being here. Taitsy has the atmosphere of Krasnoe Selo [The Red Village], that is, of soldiers. Companies of officers pass the house every day, and you can even meet soldiers if you go deep into the park. Every day in the morning you can hear gunfire for a while. Moreover, several days in a row a bugler disturbed me by blowing his trumpet day and night. [...] As I always live with dreams I still hope for our trip, if not to the Crimea, then abroad. I have been thinking a lot of such a trip particularly today. [...] I've been practicing scales and the Preludes of Chopin these days. And at last I started Misha with music lessons. But I don't teach him anything else much as I see he is absolutely unable to concentrate and can't understand the simplest things, as if his brains have gone for a rest. But he is studying music with pleasure. [...] Andrey sometimes asks where Papa is. He is nice and sweet as usual. Sonya has become a little more courageous. Now she can go out by herself, but still not very far. In general everything is as usual in Taitsy. Semyon tried to train his dogs to be obedient, as before but in vain. He is usually napping and complaining about his job. Sonechka is kind and careful as usual. Uncle "Oh!" gives his firm opinion about everything in his usual preaching manner. The Molas family, as before, are moving backward and getting further and further away from us. [...]

Good-bye, my darling. Could you write what you think of our possible trip abroad? I'm kissing you heartily. Take care of yourself and come back sooner safe and sound. I'm embracing you and kissing you.

Rimsky-Korsakov felt the falseness of his position, especially when he was treated as an official of the highest rank. He described one such incident in his letter to his wife, Nadezhda:

Yesterday, after the musicians, I again played the role of Khlestakov. Some fellow who apparently is director of the orphanage and old-age home decided to show it to me for who knows what reason. He might have thought that I'm the highest authority. He took me on a tour around this place and showed me the halls and kitchens, basements and toilets, etc. He explained to me how the ventilation system was arranged there and how the foundation was built. He just grabbed me. I was trailing after him and from time to time saying things like, "Hmm, hmm; Ah! Well, I know, and again Hmm, hmm." Instead of having a rest at home during the break between my lessons with the musicians and having lunch at the Nebolsins', I had to walk around that crazy place for two hours. I was bored to death. I will stay at home today in peace and quiet.

Rimsky-Korsakov had been keen on astronomy since his childhood, and while in Nikolayev he observed with great interest a comet that had appeared recently. During his first trip to Nikolayev he also observed a comet with his wife. He continued in the same letter: "Imagine! I can't go to Nikolayev without a comet greeting me! Yesterday and two days before yesterday I admired a small but bright comet located to the right of the Great Bear. I think I will be able to observe it for a few more days. It's so beautiful! However, yesterday it was very cloudy and the clouds obscured the view often. But two days ago it was simply glorious."

Vacation in the Crimea

Unexpectedly, though hardly surprisingly, given the increasingly exasperated tone of her letters, Nadezhda appeared at and attended the concerts of the military and naval bands held there on 19 and 20 June 1881. As soon as the concerts were over, the couple went to the Crimea, where they stayed in the Hotel Russia in Yalta.[21] The manager of the hotel was Sophia Fortunato, Stasov's daughter. Nadezhda wrote to her elder sister:

> It seemed that we lived at home, not at the hotel in Yalta. Our rooms were lovely, and besides we spent much of the time with the family. Sophia invited us to tea almost every day, and there was music at night. Nika played his *The Snow Maiden*, Ms. Blaramberg (our old acquaintance) sang, one young pianist played a lot.[22] We had a wonderful trip up into the mountains. It lasted from nine in the morning until 10 in the evening. We rode in seven carriages; we were thirty-three altogether. First, there was Sophia Vladimirovna's family totaling thirteen members; second, there were a lot of young people; and last, there were composers, artists, performers, actresses, and women writers there. By the way, we became acquainted with Sazonov and his wife, and with a writer and Strepetova as well.[23]

Then they went by carriage through Alushta and Chatyrdag to Simferopol,[24] from there to Sevastopol, and then they came back to Yalta. They left Yalta for a short trip of a few days to go to Constantinople (now Istanbul). Nadezhda wrote to Stasov's daughter Sophia: "Our journey to Constantinople was very fortunate. [...] It's very difficult to describe everything in a letter. I would just say that the Hagia Sophia impressed us greatly."

On their way back they reached Odessa on 19 July. Their ship was delayed due to stormy weather. Nadezhda wrote to her sister about the trip: "Everywhere Nika met his old friends or acquaintances among the sailors. Therefore, we felt especially well on the ships. We paid for economy class but we were always upgraded to luxury cabins due to the kindness of the captains, who treated us as if we were royalty." The Rimsky-Korsakov family arrived back in St. Petersburg on 21 July 1881.

6
Transitions and Travels

At first sight [Rimsky-Korsakov] produces the impression of a very strict man…a dry old stick and hard-hearted. But it's absolutely wrong! He is very kind and, what is even more important, he is something pure.

—Mily Balakirev, quoted by Semyon Kruglikov in his diary

Parting with the Free Music School

Rimsky-Korsakov had become increasingly dissatisfied with his administrative duties. Therefore, in September 1881 he resigned from his position as director of the Free Music School after having held this position for seven years. He wrote to Kruglikov:

> I left the School after having intended to do so during the last three years. And the reason for this is that I simply became fed up with it. Much trouble but with few results. The chorus was supposed to grow and improve and, to the contrary, its momentum is decreasing. Its budget is shrinking, and its audience is shrinking as well. I consider it is improper to appeal to the honorable members for cash as the School itself can't grant them any honor. [...] I'm absolutely incapable of soliciting the rich and influential for the School. In this matter I had to rely solely on Balakirev, who alone supported the School by bringing in new members and advocating for it before the mighty. This led to a situation that I felt I could not bear any longer. I can't stay at the School and work for it with all my zeal as I did before. [...] I think it's more reasonable for this huge talent, Balakirev, who is a thousand times more suitable for this job, to take the post and successfully direct the School openly instead of remaining in the shadows and ruling secretly. [...] So I decided to resign, and I did it unexpectedly for the School. I wanted it to be like this, to cut things off abruptly.

By this time Balakirev had resumed his musical life, and he took over the management of the School. On leaving Rimsky-Korsakov received a parting address from the Free Music School that stated: "We are very obliged to You for all You did for the prosperity of our School. We are parting with You in deep respect for Your activities. We assure You that our School will always remember You as a talented and hardworking leader."

A Third Son, Vladimir

The opening night of *The Snow Maiden* was approaching. It was scheduled to take place on 20 January 1882 at the Mariinsky Theatre. The rehearsals were going well; Rimsky-Korsakov was pleased with the performers and the production. Just before opening night Nadezhda gave birth to a fourth child. The boy was named Vladimir, after Uncle "Oh!" Nadezhda was unable to attending the opening night, and she was on pins and needles. Rimsky-Korsakov reminisced: "I was also upset because of this. I even drank too much wine at dinner. I was gloomy and indifferent to everything around me when I came to the first performance. Most of the time I stayed behind the scenery, just paying visits to the director's room from time to time. I didn't listen to my opera, although I came out for the curtain calls, of which there were many." After the third act the composer was presented with a wreath of laurels whose innermost ring was gilded in silver, a symbol denoting high honor.

Tyumenev reminisced about this premiere: "After each act, when the orchestra finished playing, there were several seconds of complete silence, and then the applause began. The applause, low in the first seconds, grew loud and prolonged." The critics' opinions varied greatly, from awful to perfect. After watching the opera, Borodin expressed his feelings in a letter to Rimsky-Korsakov: "The dearest, kindest, nicest, brightest, gold, silver, etc. On Wednesday, Katya and I saw *The Snow Maiden* and we both derived so much pleasure from it that we are filled with delight up to—(I'm showing you my neck)."

The Rimsky-Korsakov family spent the next summer again in Stelevo. The beginning of summer brought little joy. The composer's wife fell seriously ill with mastitis, but they could not obtain professional medical help in this remote place. Rimsky-Korsakov hoped for the arrival of Dr. Tarnovsky, who was supposed to arrive soon at his summer house nearby. Two more days passed, and at last Dr. Tarnovsky and a nurse arrived. The doctor opened and drained three abscesses. After this Rimsky-Korsakov wrote again to

Sophia, and the tone of his letter was quite different this time: "Dear Sonechka, [...] Nadya has become cheerful and calm. She doesn't have any pain. Tarnovsky forbade her to nurse. But it doesn't matter for Volodya. He drinks cow's milk with pleasure. We all hope that everything will be much better after today. It was just awful before! [...] Nadya charged me with telling you that the children found the first wild strawberry on 2 June, and on 5 June some local girls brought us some of them." Nonetheless, Nadezhda's family still worried about her, and her brother Nikolay and the composer's mother soon arrived at Stelevo. Her brother was an artist, and he made a drawing there of the small one-story wooden house in the green countryside where they lived.

Completing Musorgsky's *Khovanschina*

When the crisis had passed, Rimsky-Korsakov worked on completing the opera *Khovanschina*, left unfinished by Musorgsky, and on editing Musorgsky's romances. He wrote to Kruglikov: "Musorgsky is everywhere. Sometimes I think that my name is not Rimsky-Korsakov but Modest Petrovich, and that it was I who had composed *Khovanschina* and even *Boris Godunov*." Later during the summer of 1882, he was invited to conduct two of the concerts, which were to take place during the All-Russian Industrial and Arts Exhibition in Moscow. Sophia and Nikolay stayed in Stelevo to look after the children, and Rimsky-Korsakov, accompanied by Nadezhda, left for Moscow.

In November 1882 Rimsky-Korsakov left for Moscow on his own. He was invited to conduct a concert that took place in the Nobility's Assembly Rooms.[1] His *Fairy Tale* for symphony orchestra was among the other compositions performed at the concert. Nadezhda could not go with him due to Volodya's sickness. She wrote to her husband:

Darling Nika,

I sent you an unfinished letter yesterday as I didn't have enough time to write the letter. I was busy with the children the whole day. Dr. Potekhin came yesterday. He allowed me to take Misha to "the Quartet Gathering" and we had to go to the barber's and to the glover's in the course of the preparations. Volodya is much better now. He is jumping and squealing, and he looks much better. Potekhin hopes that Volodya might get well without taking medicine this time but I don't think it's likely. [...] Misha listened to the music very carefully and makes clever comments sometimes; for example, he said that the viola sounded like the bassoon. [...] Sonya is behaving badly. She studied enough yesterday, but when Potekhin arrived she turned crazy again. She was punished for this; that is, she was deprived of a piece of cake. She has been capricious today already. I don't know what is going on with her. Yesterday I played "My dear friends, I am sorry about this..." for four hands with Misha. While he was waiting for me, he looked out from the other room and said, "Now it's my turn to play." And he started playing everything exactly as you showed him. So if I criticized him he confronted me, saying, "We always do it like this with father." Won't I get a letter from you today? I'm so worried that you have gone away not being well. The first rehearsal must have been finished already. It's a pity I'm not with you in Moscow. [...]

I'm kissing you and blessing you for a successful concert. Dear, could you write me every day?

Your N. R.-Korsakova.

In the spring of 1882 Rimsky-Korsakov submitted *Khovanschina*, which he had completed and edited, to the Opera Committee for their consideration. Although he was a member of the Committee, he recused himself from the vote, since he considered himself to some extent a coauthor, along with Musorgsky. The result was completely unexpected. The opera was rejected without even being evaluated by an expert panel. Rimsky-Korsakov found this decision outrageous and sent a letter to the Committee:

I am certain that the name of Musorgsky alone has already guaranteed that this posthumous composition is of great interest to any musician devoted to Russian art. Moreover, I very much appreciate the ideas in this composition and I am coming to the conclusion that my view of Russian art and Russian operas differs sharply from the views of most members of the Committee. Therefore, I am obliged to proclaim that under such circumstances I do not find it possible to remain a member of the Committee, and I inform You so that you may consider me as having resigned, effective immediately. I would like to receive the financial compensation that I am to be granted for taking part in the previous seven meetings of the Committee in order to donate it to the fund for raising a burial monument for Musorgsky.

Assistant to Balakirev at the Court Chapel

The beginning of 1883 brought more changes in the life of the composer. Count Sheremetev was appointed director of the Court Chapel, and he offered the post of general manager to Balakirev. Balakirev, in his turn, offered Rimsky-Korsakov the position of his assistant. Rimsky-Korsakov accepted the offer, as it would allow him finally to part from the Naval Office completely. The Minister of Court approved the appointment, but Rimsky-Korsakov officially remained in service at the Naval Office and only resigned completely the following year. With his departure, his position as a band inspector was thought to be superfluous. According to the ruling of the Naval Office, "The army and navy bands along with the school have been established properly and the main goals have been achieved." Rimsky-Korsakov commented on his resignation and its financial effect on him in a letter to M. M. Ippolitov-Ivanov, a conductor in Moscow: "On abandoning my post, Shestakov [chief of the Naval Office] has saved 2,800 rubles for the Office and simultaneously he has saved me the excessive trouble of spending this 2,800 rubles on various trivial luxuries and accordingly left me to live on the salary from the Chapel and the Conservatory. It doesn't matter, I will survive."

Upon starting their jobs in the Chapel, Balakirev and Rimsky-Korsakov faced the problem of the upbringing and education of the minor choristers. Rimsky-Korsakov undertook his new duties enthusiastically and began to draft a charter of the Chapel Musical Society, including rules of behavior and a curriculum of courses for the instrumentalists. The coronation of Alexander III was scheduled for the beginning of May 1883, and the whole Chapel left for Moscow to participate in the ceremony. Rimsky-Korsakov wrote to his wife from Moscow on 8 May:

Dear Nadya,

[...] On arriving at the hotel, I got a room overlooking Tverskaya Street so that I could see Iversky Gate,[2] a part of the Kremlin wall, and even the Church of Our Savior. My room is on the fourth floor. [...] Having changed my clothes I went to the Kremlin to see how the choristers were accommodated. They were provided for rather well. I was informed that a part of the choir had to be at Peter's Palace by 4 p.m. to greet the tsar. After visiting the choristers, I went again to a Moscow tavern to eat some *rasstegai* with Azeyev and Smirnov.[3] [...] I will be able to watch the procession of the tsar entering Iversky Gate very clearly looking out of my windows. I'm expecting to get your letter tomorrow.

I kiss you, my darling, and all our children. Could you write oftener, my dear? Your Nika R.-K.

Not only did Nadezhda, Misha, and Sonya write to their father, but his mother wrote to her son as well, as attested by a letter she sent to him in Moscow:

My dear,

I congratulate you on your name day![4] Many happy wishes! I'm praying to God to take care of you and return you to us safe and sound. I have nothing more to write to you. I embrace you my dearest.

Your Mother [...]

The next day he got a letter from Nadezhda:

My dear Nikusha,

Misha was so obsessed with writing to you that he couldn't cope with himself. He tried as he might, but the letter was a mess. He wrote badly, crossed out a lot of words, misspelled a lot, and became so frustrated that he started crying and didn't want to send his letter. I took this letter from him nearly by force and mailed it to you. I assured him that you would pay much more attention to the content than the appearance of the letter. Sonya is his exact antithesis. She wrote as she could without caring about anything and went on friskily romping. All the children ask about you constantly. Andryushonok is still naughty and witty, and sometimes he runs about so much that he becomes exhausted and looks like a boiled lobster. Yesterday Matilda [the children's governess] was not in and it took quite a lot of time for them to go to bed, and Andryushonok insisted on my undressing him. Misha and Sonya asked him, "Why are you against the nanny undressing you?" And he responded to them, "Because Mama is pretty and much younger than an aged nanny." What a boy he is! Volodya is teething. I think this is why he has been sleeping so badly for the last several days. But during the day he has been very happy and playful. He played a lot in his cradle. [...] What have you been doing there in Moscow, my darling? Have you visited our friends? Please, take care of your stomach. Don't eat ham and don't do anything foolish. [...] I wish I could embrace you and kiss you.... And it's so much time to wait for your coming back. It's a pity! I'm looking forward to getting a long letter from you.

Good-bye, Nikusha. I'm embracing you and kissing you in my dreams, my nice boy.

Your N. R.-Korsakova

P.S. I sent a letter about you to Mother yesterday.

Witnessing the Coronation of Tsar Alexander III, 1883

Rimsky-Korsakov was very glad to receive such detailed information about the children, and he always inquired about everything concerning them, even trivial things. In his turn he sent long letters about his stay in Moscow. His letter in the middle of May 1883 informed his family about the coronation of Alexander III:

Yesterday the whole city was emblazoned with flags and other celebratory decorations. Since early morning there were big crowds everywhere: on Tverskaya Street, round the hotel, and up to Iversky Gate. Balakirev and I, dressed up in uniform coats, had only just managed to reach the Kremlin by 1 p.m., thanks to the manager of our hotel, who helped us; otherwise we would have been late. Then we headed to the Cathedral of the Dormition with the choir at 2 p.m. There were soldiers and civilians all over the place. The seating built for this purpose was also overcrowded. We were allocated some special places for the choirs: Balakirev was on the right, and I was on the left one. The procession started out from Peter's Palace at 2 p.m. and reached the cathedral at 3:30 p.m. When the tsar entered the Cathedral, the choir began singing the hymn *People Glorify* while His Majesty and his wife and children were kissing the icons. So we had to move backward to let them pass. There were not more than thirty inches between me and the icons, and they all passed by at this distance. The choir sang the hymn well. After this, the tsar's family left for other churches, and we hurried to the palace, where they were to finish the procession and where we had to see them off with singing. I saw Sheremetev, Philippov, Kaznakov,[5] and many others in the cathedral. By the time it was finished we were very tired and left for home, where I had dinner with Kruglikov in the hotel. Kruglikov and I visited an art exhibition of Vereschagin's. [...] There was some illumination in the evening but just a little. They promised to make a great deal more on the day of the coronation. Tverskaya was full of crowds from morning until night. [...] Today the choristers have been engaged in the rite of blessing the banners in the Armory Palace,[6] but Balakirev and I didn't go there. If Kruglikov comes we will take a boat trip to the Sparrow Hills along the Moscow River. Today in the morning, I was trying to compose a poem to be sung during the Eucharist. Then I went to visit Taneyev, but he wasn't in. I paid a visit of honor to the Governor-General, as Sheremetev insisted. [...] You shouldn't worry about me. Yesterday was the only dangerous day for the tsar and everyone is sure that during the Coronation nothing bad will happen. I kiss you heartily my dear and all of our children. Indeed, what a boy Andrey is! And poor sweet Mishuk, he wrote a letter and cried! I kiss you again, my sweet darling. Take care.

Rimsky-Korsakov was free the next day, so he, Balakirev, and Kruglikov visited the archpriest Razumovsky.[7] Razumovsky presented them with a copy of his book on church singing to the composer.

Rimsky-Korsakov wrote to his wife, Nadezhda, about his visit to the Trinity–St. Sergius Lavra with Balakirev.[8] When the monks there found out that they were from the Chapel, they took special care of them. They granted them unique access to the compound, including a visit to a library where ancient books were kept, and also took them to their remote, secluded Monastery of Viphania (about three miles from the Lavra).

Rimsky-Korsakov wrote of the coronation:

We had to stand in the Cathedral from 7:45 a.m. to 12:15 p.m. We became rather tired, but everyone sang successfully. I saw almost the whole ceremony quite well except for the scene when His Majesty received the Eucharist at the altar. The tsar's crowns are worth seeing. They are all bejeweled and sparkle wonderfully. But I'd better tell you all in detail when I see you. There was an artist named Kramskoy next to me who was charged with making sketches of the ceremony. He was the only one wearing a tailcoat, all the rest were in uniform coats. [...] In general, the event was beautiful and magnificent. In the evening they lit the celebratory illumination, but since it was rainy and windy it spoiled everything a little. What was really tremendous was the bell tower of Ivan the Great lit up to the Cross with Edison electrical lights: bright and serene light without a blue accent. Many buildings were also illuminated well. But yesterday the weather was better and the illumination was prettier. There were crowds on the streets screaming "Hurrah!" up to 2 a.m. I'm writing briefly today as Balakirev charged me to compose a short hymn devoted to sanctifying the Temple [the Cathedral of Christ the Saviour] and I have to complete it today.

Despite the fact that Rimsky-Korsakov was very busy and was seeing a lot of new things, he missed his wife and children greatly. He wrote to his wife: "It's certainly a pity that I haven't seen you for such a long time, a whole week. I will be very happy to see you on my arrival. I think you've already settled down at the summer house, but in any case you will still be busy with arranging things tomorrow. My dear, be healthy and cheerful. I embrace you firmly and kiss your eyes."

In Taitsy Again

So it was fortunate in this regard that, due to the requirements of his new position, Rimsky-Korsakov couldn't travel far from St. Petersburg. He was required, for instance, to be often in Old Peterhof,[9] as boy choristers were sent there for the summer and their lessons were held there. For this reason, the Rimsky-Korsakov family left the city once again for Taitsy. But this time they did not live with Uncle "Oh!" in his house; they rented their own summer house not far from his. Upon arriving, Sophia wrote to her son: "My dear Nika, I'm in Taitsy now. I like the surroundings very much. Nadya is going to write you in detail about how we have moved in, so I will keep silent. […] I embrace you my dear. God bless you. I ask God to take care of you and return you to us safe and sound. Your mother, Sophia."

Indeed, the move to Taitsy was full of adventures, as described by Nadezhda Rimsky-Korsakov herself:

> I should tell you that I was bothered very much by our relocation. […] I had to think of everything, to buy all things necessary, and to pack things for everyone who was moving as well as to make provisions for those who were staying in the city. Every day I went to bed at 2 a.m. in the morning and got up very early. On the day of our departure I had to wake up at 4:30 a.m. So, I was all in. […] As you know the train stops only for two minutes in Taitsy, so Uncle "Oh!" instructed me to find the manager of the station at Krasnoe Selo, to explain to him that I

had a big family with children, an old lady, and a huge amount of luggage accompanying me, and to ask him to lengthen the time of the stop. I did as he said. […] I found an assistant of the station manager (the manager was away somewhere) and explained everything to him. His response to my plea was laughter, but he calmed me down with the words: "You should not worry. Do you think the train will start moving before all the passengers have got off?" Yet everything happened just as I had feared! And we should be glad that nothing disastrous occurred! Upon arriving at Taitsy, the train was to stop for two minutes but it didn't in fact stop even for one! We were all ready and standing in the doorway with our things; the door was opened quickly and Kolya [Nadezhda's brother] got off and helped Mother, then I got off, then Andrey. And all of a sudden the train started moving. So the conductor had to take Sonya off the train when it was already in motion and then he had to jump into the car himself to hold Misha, who was moving forward. In spite of our desperate cries and requests, the train had gone. Therefore, Misha, the nanny with Volodya, the governess, and two servant girls went on the train farther without any money or tickets, which had been already handed in. Can you imagine how I felt?! I was desperate. Sonya and Andryusha were sobbing violently about Misha and Volodya. I was extremely worried about Misha. I imagined how he, feeling despondent, might throw himself out of the window or something like that. You know that he gets extremely excited very easily and the more so in such a case as this, since the move into a summer house is a great adventure and joy for a child. He anticipated this for such a long time and was so anxious to get to Taitsy, the sooner the better. And he was the very person who failed to get off.

P.S. The servants were brought from Gatchina for free and in second class.[10] I had demanded that they should not make them buy tickets and in any case they had no money.

Nadezhda kept on writing about the children:

We're all very delighted with Volodyasha. Since yesterday he has been walking without help, all by himself: he goes to the sandbox, sits down, picks up some sand, stands up by himself, and comes back. And he has become so naughty that the nanny hardly can cope with him. Uncle "Oh!" and Sonechka arrived yesterday. The children greeted them with flowers; they decorated all the rooms with flowers and even made a flower carpet in the doorway. And we threw bird-cherry flowers and yellow field roses before their carriage when they drove in.

Though Nadezhda disliked Taitsy, it was much better for them to be there than in the city. She wrote in her letter to her husband in Moscow: "Spring is such a wonderful season that even Taitsy seems not so bad. The air here is lovely, especially now, when the larch, fir, and pine trees are in bloom. There is a myriad of birds here. In the evenings nightingales and cuckoos sing. And beside them, there is one little wonderful bird, which is my acquaintance and which sings scales in ups and downs as 'à la Patti.'"[11] Sophia also wrote to her son in Moscow: "It is very nice to live here, only we miss you very much. And there are too many mosquitoes here."

The Cathedral of Christ the Saviour was consecrated on 26 May 1883. During the ceremony a new chorus, *Who Is the King of Glory*, composed by Rimsky-Korsakov for the occasion, was performed. The next morning he had already arrived back in St. Petersburg. Nadezhda met her husband at the railway station and then they went to Taitsy. No sooner had Rimsky-Korsakov left Moscow than Kruglikov wrote to him:

How was Your trip, my dear friend? Have you found all of them to be healthy? [...] Moscow became empty after the time of the coronation. Both the decent Western people and the Eastern men, who are wearing fur hats to stay cool in the summer heat, left Moscow. The city became very quiet. Moscow settled down and according to ancient customs, she eats, drinks, commits disgraceful acts, sleeps, snores; in one word, she holds sacred her fathers' legacy. [...] I bow to everyone in Your family, I shake Nadezhda's hand firmly, embrace the children, and I kiss You. Yours always, Semyon.

The summer of 1883 was very disturbing for Rimsky-Korsakov. He wrote to Kruglikov:

I'm in Taitsy now, but I often remember Moscow and you're first and foremost in those reminiscences. What an awfully nice man you are! I have to go often to Peter and to Peterhof, where the choirboys are living, which spoils my summertime quite a lot. And in the summer house I'm sitting in my room engrossed in drafting a charter, surrounded by Potulov's,[12] Razumovsky's and others' books and different brochures published by the Holy Synod.[13] […] Balakirev is getting tired and exhausted from commuting to Peterhof, and from dealing with various bureaucratic and customary affairs concerning the Chapel. Due to this he has become nervous and his eyes look so mean, he is just impossible to deal with right now.

He sent another letter a little later:

We are living well in Taitsy, but the summer is awful. There are no two similar days in a row: we have either drizzle, or sunshine, or showers. What a summer! Although I am staying in Taitsy, I go twice a week to the Chapel in St. Petersburg and twice a week to the young choristers in Peterhof. It's unpleasant to ride on the train so much: I read and read and read in the carriage, sometimes till I'm stupefied. I am not working on secular music, but I'm dealing very much with sacred music. I have drafted a lot but still do not have anything fully completed. I take my drafts to Balakirev, but he keeps them for weeks without looking through them, and if he reads them he begins making a wry face. […] I feel he thinks, "Oh, no! He can't have Holy Paradise in his compositions, as he himself is no saint…etc." I think I will give up hoping for his blessing and will gather a thick book of my arrangements and publish it myself, and let anybody who wants to sing them. What else should I do if I do not feel like composing secular music right now but instead have become obsessed with sacred music? Should my efforts be in vain? In fact, I have been getting tired of Balakirev recently. He runs the Chapel according to custom, but you can't do anything without his approval, and if you did he would become displeased.

Balakirev on Rimsky-Korsakov

At the same time Balakirev was discussing Rimsky-Korsakov with Kruglikov, and Kruglikov recorded Balakirev's comments in his diary:

If only you knew how Korsakov is loved and respected in the Chapel! And can you imagine that they are afraid of him too? I know it sounds strange to us, but some people are frightened of him, and in fact not only in the Chapel. Glazunov's mother, who took lessons with him for some time, also always assured me seriously that she was scared of him. Indeed at first sight he produces the impression of a very strict man. And he seems to be always ready to assure you that he is a dry old stick and hard-hearted. But it's absolutely wrong! He is very kind and, what is even more important, he is something pure. [...] I will say this: he was better before his marriage. She bound his hands and feet and drew him aside from all of us. Before it used to be like this: When he brought one of his new compositions to me and I gave him some advice, he would follow it in one way or another, and everything turned out well. But after the marriage he listened only to the advice of his Nadya. [...] There are a lot of things both in *May Night* and *The Snow Maiden* that I would cut out with pleasure, for example, many stupid things from the part of Snow Maiden herself.

It seems it was very difficult for Balakirev to give up his role as a mentor, whose students should obey without question. As Borodin said once, "Former nestlings grew into mature birds and flew out of their nests a long time ago." Each of them, Musorgsky, Borodin, and Rimsky-Korsakov, found his own way in music and stopped blindly submitting compositions for their elder friend's opinion. They became independent and distinctive. Balakirev was not right about the role of the composer's wife. Rimsky-Korsakov appreciated her opinion and might even become upset if she did not approve of something in one of his compositions. But he nevertheless always remained of the same opinion and did not normally change anything, and even if he did he would do it only according to his own desires. Any such changes were usually caused by his being a perfectionist. This happened with regard to *The Maid of Pskov*, which he edited several times, although Nadezhda always preferred the first version.

During the summer Nikolay and Nadezhda left for Imatra, in Finland, for a short rest. In the autumn the family moved to another apartment, since the previous one on Furtstatskaya Street had become too small for a family with four children. Being an assistant to the general manager of the Chapel, Rimsky-Korsakov was eligible to have a government apartment on the Chapel premises. Unfortunately, the building was being renovated at that time, so they rented an apartment in a building located on the corner of Vladimirskaya and Kolokolnaya Streets, next to the Our Lady of Vladimir Church's bell tower. The move marked the end of their ten-year period in the apartment on Furstatskaya Street.

As Rimsky-Korsakov wrote to Kruglikov, during September the family was still living in Taitsy, whereas he remained in the city and visited the family only twice a week. He barely had time to see how they were doing and stayed for only a night with them. He informed Kruglikov about his work: "I'm busy with the following: (1) I have moved from the old apartment into a new one by myself; (2) I've gone twice a week to Kronstadt to prepare for an army concert scheduled for 7 October; (3) Most of the rest of my time I've been spending at the Chapel, where classes began on 9 September; and lastly, my lessons at the Conservatory have begun."

Even after the family returned to the city and began settling down in their new place, Rimsky-Korsakov was still occupied completely with his duties. According to him, there were a lot of things that needed changing in the Chapel. The teaching of church singing had been organized by one of the previous Chapel directors, Bortniansky.[14] Illiterate boys, brought to St. Petersburg from different corners of the country, were usually both oppressed and ill-bred. If they lost their voices, their fate was unenviable: they were expelled. Since they were taught to play instruments just a little, and yet they were not used to work, they became bad replacements or just scribes, or servants if they were lucky; most became beggars and drunkards. Rimsky-Korsakov did his best to prevent such things from happening. He was so busy with his service in the Chapel that he did not have time for composition. Stasov wrote to Kruglikov: "Mily and Rimsky-Korsakov do nothing but deal with their damned Chapel." In his turn, Rimsky-Korsakov also wrote to Kruglikov:

> I'm very busy with the Chapel and I'm not composing anything, for I don't have the desire. I think that actually I have put a full stop to composing after *The Snow Maiden*. All those romances, concerts, and sacred music; all that is just a memory of the past. At this very moment my head is completely empty. And even if I start thinking of something musical I get tired immediately. [...] But I like being absorbed in the issues concerning the Chapel, and I'm very glad that everything is going better there.

Discharged from the Naval Office, 1883

Rimsky-Korsakov conducted his last concert as the inspector of army bands in Kronstadt in October 1883. He was officially discharged from the Naval Office on 9 March 1884. At the end of March he gave up his duties not only with the military bands, but with the Musical Society as well. Many of

Rimsky-Korsakov's friends became very concerned that he had stopped composing. Kruglikov wrote to Rimsky-Korsakov: "You should not become dejected. You ought to spur yourself and take up composing something that is worthy of You, like an opera or symphony. I tell you again, it just seems to You that you do not want to compose music." And his next letter sounded the same theme: "With all my heart, I wish You, dear fellow, to spur Yourself and even force Yourself to compose some secular music. I am certain that after the first passages You will begin to take a great interest in this and soon will please us with something huge and very good. Cheer up, don't become lazy. Really and truly, it's too bad and too early for Your age."

But the remonstrations had little effect. On the contrary, his family life took precedence. He even produced several new family performances, a program for one of which survives to this day. It took place in the beginning of January 1884, and two plays were staged: *Two Sashas*, or *The First of April*, and Zombie. The performers were eleven-year-old Misha, eight-year-old Sonya, and six-year-old Andrusha.

Another Daughter, Nadezhda

The Rimsky-Korsakov family had to spend the summer of 1884 in Taitsy again. In June 1884 another child was born. The daughter was named Nadezhda, and so she was later called Nadezhda Junior. Rimsky-Korsakov wrote about this event to Kruglikov in his usual humorous manner: "Number 5, it's quite a lot. There are only three operas." Rimsky-Korsakov again went to Peterhof to teach the choirboys twice a week as he had done the previous summer, giving a course in harmony. He was not satisfied with Tchaikovsky's harmony textbook, so he began writing his own. His textbook was completed by the end of August and published in the autumn of the same year. His creative work as a composer was still in hibernation.

7

Completing the Work of Others, 1884–1889

*Such a great artist [as he] should not forget about himself completely
and be roofing a stranger's house but leaving his own home unprotected.*
—Vladimir Stasov to Nadezhda Rimsky-Korsakov, summer 1887

The dissension between Rimsky-Korsakov and Balakirev continued to get worse. Kruglikov wrote to the composer, commenting on their conflicts:

> Maybe if I had the same close relations and frequent meetings as You do with Balakirev, I would take the view You are beginning to have of him. However, I like Balakirev very much from my own experience dealing with him. He is dear to me and I consider him to be a very fine fellow. However, I have noticed some unattractive and hard traits in his character, his despotic tendencies, which hint at stubbornness, etc.

Rimsky-Korsakov responded: "Oh, Balakirev! The person you have liked so much as a musician, as a superior and even as a man I am getting more and more disappointed with. How I laughed to myself reading your warm words about him. It's very difficult to explain everything in a letter."

Rimsky-Korsakov was extremely busy. He did not have any time either to write letters or to compose music. His teaching load at the Chapel and the Conservatory was about twenty-six hours per week, and in addition he had other administrative duties concerning the Chapel. At the beginning of the next year he wrote to Kruglikov: "I haven't composed any music since early autumn, as I don't have any desire to do so; nothing interesting comes to my mind. I have tried, but the result has turned out to be so disgusting that I've begun to yawn and get tired of it in five minutes." He was very concerned, however, about how slowly Borodin was composing his opera *Prince Igor*. Borodin devoted much time to his principal activity, chemistry, and constantly laid his music aside in its favor. Rimsky-Korsakov used to joke about it: "He's composed *Igor* just a little, and he is sorry just a little." To the question of whether he had arranged one piece of the opera or another for the orchestra, Borodin habitually made a joke: "Yes, I arranged them from the piano onto the table."

Rimsky-Korsakov, meanwhile, was completely absorbed in his work concerning the Chapel. His former student Nikolay Sokolov, a composer and an instructor in the Chapel, reminisced:

> [Rimsky-Korsakov] conducted the student orchestra [...] or trained one of the orchestra's groups, arranged various pieces of music for the student groups, checked how much music notepaper and how much notepaper they had. He was engaged in getting the library in order; he ordered, traced out, handled, distributed, and sent out various musical instruments for repair. He dealt in person with other teachers and students, all of whom he knew as well as he did his own children, and with dealers, etc. He was pulled to the right and to the left, and he was nearly torn into pieces. Sometimes he became so confused with different matters that he had to repeat one and the same phrase in different tunes for some time in order not to forget. [...] Such devotion and the hard work that Rimsky-Korsakov performed were contagious for everyone in the Chapel. His personality and the comfortable atmosphere that he created won everyone's hearts and encouraged them all to work harder. [...] Rimsky-Korsakov judged all work impartially. He did not have any "favorites" or students he "disliked." [...] To get a complete picture of his unique and easygoing way with students, one only needed to observe how he led a company of students of various ages and personalities in his orchestration class.

Rimsky-Korsakov was a man of absolutely even temper. When he rebuked either his students or his children, he never raised his voice and always corrected them patiently. His former student Gnessin remembered the composer telling them during his classes at the Conservatory:[1] "You know how your nanny used to say, 'I will undress you, put you to bed, sing a lullaby to you, but you will fall asleep yourself'? I will do the same: I will explain, describe, give examples, show you everything, but you will compose the music yourselves." Rimsky-Korsakov never used rude words or told obscene jokes, either in letters or in everyday conversation. He could judge people's deeds strictly but would never show his temper or make coarse comments. Rimsky-Korsakov's emotional reserve carried over into friendly relations as well: he did not show his feelings openly. In spite of this, his friends greatly appreciated his friendship. It was Rimsky-Korsakov whom Alexander Glazunov's mother called to be with her son when Alexander experienced difficult times in his life. Rimsky-Korsakov, his teacher, would stay with Glazunov for long hours each time.

The summer of 1885 arrived, and the Rimsky-Korsakov family again went to Taitsy for the summer. Once again the composer was engaged only in the activities of the Chapel and did not compose anything new himself. Instead of music, he composed humorous verses about Taitsy and the different things that happened there during the summer. He made rhymes about Taitsy itself, its perpetually inoperative clock tower, and about the fireworks displays organized by Uncle "Oh!" Although "Oh!" was rather old by this time, he was still very enthusiastic and spent his energies developing various family entertainments, such as performances where the leading parts were taken by his grandnieces and -nephews.

Stasov was indignant about the composer's apparent laziness and wrote to Lyapunov,[2] a fellow composer: "Rimlyanin[3] does not do anything. [...] It's the end of the summer and he doesn't lift a finger. And till now he hasn't been doing anything except making some arrangements for church choirs and for his choristers (The devil take them! They just prevent Rimlyanin and Mily from doing anything decent in music)." Kruglikov was also worried that Rimsky-Korsakov did not compose any new music: "It is inexcusable to bury your talent. You should agree it is too early for you to finish. [...] You should cheer up and take heart."

Experiencing the Caucasus

An important musical event occurred at the beginning of 1886 with the performance of Musorgsky's opera *Khovanschina*, staged according to Rimsky-Korsakov's completed and revised version. The performance was produced by the Muzikal'no-Dramaticheskiy Krujok (Music and Drama Group) of St. Petersburg. They held eight performances that year. The Rimsky-Korsakov family again spent the summer of 1886 in Taitsy, although this time Nikolay and his wife did not stay there most of the time. They left the children with the composer's mother and set off on a journey to the Caucasus, which lasted about two months. They went along the Volga River by boat and visited Nizhny Novgorod, Kazan, Simbirsk, Samara, Saratov, and Tsaritsyn.[4] Then they went further, overland, to Kalach-on-the-Don, Rostov-on-Don, and Zheleznovodsk. From Zheleznovodsk they took side trips to Pyatigorsk and Kislovodsk and hiked into the mountains of Beshtay. They left for Vladikavkaz from Zheleznovodsk, and from there they traveled by road along the Georgian Military Road to Tiflis.[5] Then they went to Borjomi, from there to Batumi, from there to Yalta by boat, and from Yalta started their journey back to St. Petersburg. All this time Sophia kept up a stream of letters informing them about their children. About twelve-month-old Nadya she wrote: "She can eat carved meat all by herself and wild strawberries with a spoon. She has become simply a 'grande demoiselle'!" At the end of July Nikolay and his wife returned to Taitsy. The trip was so impressive that he described their long voyage in a humorous poem; this time his wife also decided to try her pen and created some verses about the trip too.

A Patron: Mitrofan Belyaev

Rimsky-Korsakov got involved in attending the musical Fridays that had been organized by Belyaev beginning with the 1883–1884 season, when the two first became acquainted. Belyaev was born into the well-to-do family of a timber merchant. He was considered an apostate, being absolutely uninterested in the timber trade, and on his leaving the business he received a rather large share of the capital.[6] He had been an aficionado of music since early childhood and could play the viola quite well. Belyaev devoted all his life to the service of his hobby. He was fond of playing in a quartet and held meetings of his friends—quartet players—on Fridays. Belyaev's Fridays were never canceled. If somebody could not come, a substitute would always be found. When Belyaev heard Glazunov's First Symphony, he became so excited that he decided to establish a publishing house in Leipzig, Germany, to publish this symphony and the compositions of other Russian composers. Glazunov composed his First Symphony after just two years of private lessons with Rimsky-Korsakov. The symphony was performed successfully at a concert. Rimsky-Korsakov wrote in his memoirs: "Stasov was excited and showed his delight noisily. The audience was shocked to see, when the composer was called to the stage, that he was wearing a school uniform."

Belyaev's patronage of the arts was not limited to publishing. Soon, following the support of Rimsky-Korsakov, Belyaev also set up and sponsored the Russian Symphony Concerts. He raised funds for poor composers and established an annual prize in honor of Glinka for the best musical composition of the year. Moreover, he paid the money for those prizes anonymously, using Stasov as his intermediary. Stasov was the only one who knew the source of the funds for those prizes. Usually, at the end of the season Belyaev organized a free lottery consisting of the volumes he had published for the regular visitors at his Fridays.

Rimsky-Korsakov wrote about Belyaev in his memoirs: "Belyaev attracted people with [...] his personality and his devotion to art. His money was just a means to achieve his high and unselfish aim, which made him the attractive center of a musical circle." Borodin, Lyadov, Glazunov, and Stasov also began to attend Belyaev's Fridays. Those evenings became more interesting, their repertoire became broader, and new quartets were performed there. For example, the First Quartet of Glazunov was played for the first time at one of the Friday evenings. As time passed, Rimsky-Korsakov turned into the leader of this new musical circle. The customary agenda for one of Belyaev's Fridays consisted of a musical part, which lasted till 1 a.m., followed by a special banquet with champagne. Sometimes they began playing music again after the meal. Belyaev's name day was 23 November, and it was always celebrated with a special banquet. On the occasion of that name day in 1886, four friends, Borodin, Rimsky-Korsakov, Lyadov, and Glazunov, composed and presented a string quartet to Belyaev based on the theme *Be-la-ef* (the notes *do, la,* and *fa*). The quartet was played before the dinner with the participation of Belyaev himself. Borodin wrote to his wife: "We prepared a surprise for Belyaev and we four composed a quartet on the theme Be-la-ef. Korsakov composed the first part, Glazunov—the final part, Lyadov took the scherzo, and I composed a Spanish serenade instead of an Andante. [...] Everything was very lively, original, and extremely witty but very musical at the same time. And the most important thing was that it was composed very charmingly at one stroke."

Belyaev, who did not expect such a wonderful surprise, was very touched. After the dinner they played this Quartet once again. During Christmas that year Rimsky-Korsakov made drafts of his *Fantasy on Russian Themes* for violin and orchestra. He did not compose anything else but instead worked out many arrangements of various compositions for the student orchestra at the Chapel.

Another Loss: Borodin

The beginning of 1887 brought a sorrowful event: on 15 February Borodin died completely unexpectedly. It happened during a merry masquerade held at his apartment in the Medical-Surgery Academy. Rimsky-Korsakov immediately took up working on the completion of Borodin's opera *Prince Igor* for publication, along with his other compositions, which were still awaiting publication. After the funeral Rimsky-Korsakov and Glazunov sorted out all of his remaining manuscripts and divided up the work needed to complete the opera for performance. It was also agreed that Belyaev would publish Borodin's compositions. When the opera *Prince Igor* was published, Belyaev presented Rimsky-Korsakov with a copy of the score inscribed: "To the Highly Respected Rimsky-Korsakov, due to whose talent and love for the deceased and his unselfish hard work, the world can have this opera published. From the publisher." At the same time, Lyudmila Shestakova presented him with a decorative baton with the names of Dargomizhsky, Musorgsky, and Borodin engraved on it as a sign of her immense appreciation for Rimsky-Korsakov's work on completing and editing the compositions of those composers.

March 1887 was a month of celebration for Rimsky-Korsakov. On his birthday, 6 March, there were many guests at Rimsky-Korsakov's home; among them was Pyotr Tchaikovsky, who in fact had become quite a frequent visitor by that time. Later that month there was a celebration of the twenty-fifth anniversary of the Free Music School. A commemorative concert was held, followed by a celebration in honor of Balakirev and Rimsky-Korsakov. The composer was presented with an inkstand in the shape of a bell.

Nikolskoje

That summer the Rimsky-Korsakov family rented a house on the bank of Lake Nelay in Nikolskoje, not far from Luga. The composer had to visit his choristers once a week in Peterhof, and on those occasions he would stay for a night with the Glazunovs, who spent their summers there. Rimsky-Korsakov worked hard on completing *Prince Igor* in Nikolskoje. In an odd coincidence, a total solar eclipse, like that mentioned in the plot of Borodin's opera, occurred that summer. Unfortunately, owing to bad weather the effect was not as great as had been described in the opera. The composer's wife complained in a letter to Stasov: "Nika is busy only with 'Igor.' That is good but annoying at the same time, as he is not composing anything of his own. And it's even more annoying as he is now in favorable living conditions." Stasov responded to her complaints:

> He deserves to be honored and glorified. There are only a few people in the world like him, such a great friend and artist. If it were not for him, two of the greatest Russian compositions, *Khovanschina* and *Igor*, would be waiting in vain for their hour. [...] But: such a great artist as he should not forget about himself completely and be roofing a stranger's house but leaving his own home unprotected.

Confounding his wife, though, that summer Rimsky-Korsakov in fact created a substantial composition for symphony orchestra—the *Capriccio espagnol*.

In the autumn of 1887 the first symphony concert to commemorate Borodin was held. Rimsky-Korsakov conducted the concert, in which only Borodin's compositions were played, among them the overture and the Polovetsky March from *Prince Igor*. These were performed for the first time. Glazunov and Rimsky-Korsakov were presented with wreaths.[7] Ekaterina, Borodin's wife, presented a silver baton to Rimsky-Korsakov. Soon after this concert, Ekaterina Borodin also died.

Capriccio espagnol

In preparation for the next Russian Symphony Concert, the orchestra began to rehearse Rimsky-Korsakov's *Capriccio espagnol*. After the first part, the musicians applauded the composer, and during the rest of the rehearsal they applauded several more times. The composer later reminisced:

> I asked the orchestra for their permission to dedicate this composition to them. Their response was total delight. During the concert itself, this composition was

played with a level of perfection and such enthusiasm that was never again reached in any of the following performances. […] Although the *Capriccio espagnol* was rather long, the composer was repeatedly called to the stage.

Tchaikovsky attended that concert. He presented a wreath to Rimsky-Korsakov, on the sash of which was written: "To the greatest master of orchestration from his sincere admirer." The newspaper *Grajdanin* (*The Citizen*) wrote that "the *Capriccio* eclipsed all of the rest of the compositions in the concert with its shining sound."

A Third Daughter, Masha

The Rimsky-Korsakov family was still growing. In January 1888 another child was born, a daughter named Masha. So it seemed that everything was going well, but the composer was nonetheless in a rather melancholy state. He was not alone in this. Glazunov was also disconsolate, and even he became worried about Rimsky-Korsakov's frame of mind. After he attended a church service in memory of Borodin, which took place on the first anniversary of his death, Glazunov wrote to Kruglikov: "Everything seemed to be depressing; […] somebody was missing. That very missing somebody is Borodin. […] Rimsky-Korsakov is still moping about because of it. (But this is only between us) […] it's just impossible to approach him: if you ask for advice, he answers that he can't help at all. Before, Borodin used to visit him, and after his visits Nikolay would become enlivened, but now nobody can stir him up."

Scheherazade

Nevertheless, in the summer of 1888 Rimsky-Korsakov left for his summer house with the intention to create two new compositions for symphony orchestra. He planned a symphonic suite to be called *Scheherazade* on the themes of some tales from *A Thousand and One Nights* and an overture to be known as the *Russian Easter Festival Overture* on the theme of the traditional Orthodox holiday. He had been thinking about those two compositions since the previous winter, but his work on *Prince Igor* prevented him from composing something of his own. Now, when he was in the summer house in Nezhgovitsy (about eighteen miles from Luga), far from the bustle of city life, he composed his *Scheherazade* in just twenty-four days. This remarkable programmatic composition is distinguished by wonderful scenes of the ocean depicted in music that expresses its various states. Upon completing the piece, the composer wrote to Glazunov:

> My dear friend, don't become angry with me for my decision. I'd like not to show You my composition (it goes without saying that you may include anybody else you like as well), but to make it a surprise. I'd like to arrange so that everybody will hear it for the first time at the rehearsal for Belyaev's concert. [...] So, I have finished the suite but now I'm as poor as Job; my head has become absolutely empty—not a single musical thought is left there.

Despite this assertion of his creative exhaustion, by 20 August Rimsky-Korsakov had also completed the score for his *Russian Easter Festival Overture.* Rimsky-Korsakov described it:

> The Overture combines the memories of ancient prophecy, of biblical stories and a general picture of the Easter church service with its "pagan joy." Does not the dancing and skipping of the biblical King David before the Ark express the mood and feelings of the same sort as idol worshippers' sacrificial dances? Aren't Russian Orthodox bells the same as instrumental church dance music? Don't the trembling beards of priests and church readers wearing white vestments, singing *Beautiful Easter* in the tempo of *allegro vivo*, bring to your mind a picture of pagan times?[8] And all those Easter cakes and *paskhas* and lit candles.[9] ...How far from philosophical and social trends of Christian doctrine all this lies! This legendary and pagan side of the holiday, this transposition from the dark and mysterious eve of Holy Saturday to the somehow unrestrained pagan but still religious joy of the morning of the Holy Resurrection, is what I have tried to illustrate in my Overture. [...] To appreciate my Overture at all, it is necessary for the listener to have attended Holy Matins [*zautrenya*] at least once. Moreover, it should be a matins held in a cathedral, where crowds of people of different social standing gather and where the service is celebrated by several priests. Moreover, it should not be in a small church, but in a cathedral. Nowadays many intelligent listeners lack this knowledge, to say nothing of those who are of other faiths. My impressions are rooted in the days of my early childhood, spent very close to the Tikhvin Monastery.

There was another story, told to Rimsky-Korsakov by Sokolov, which struck him. The composer retold it as follows: "A half-drunk fellow stopped before the bell tower of Our Lady of Vladimir Church while the bells were pealing loudly, and at first he started crossing himself, then he simply stood still, caught up in deep thoughts; and then all of a sudden he started dancing with the sound and rhythm of the bells. Indeed, what a holy joyous scene!" At the end of the year, both compositions, *Scheherazade* and the *Russian Easter Festival Overture*, were performed successfully in concerts.

Unfortunately, Rimsky-Korsakov did not take care of his health very well. Since his early childhood in Tikhvin, the composer had been very healthy. However, after graduating from the Naval Academy he became a chain smoker and was unable get rid of this bad habit for the rest of his life. Sophia Rimsky-Korsakov was glad to be with her beloved son, and she felt well in the country, but it was of course difficult for her to endure the atmosphere of a family with so many children. She wrote to Tikhvin: "There is only one inconvenience for me here—the children's noise. It is especially unbearable for me as I have become used to the company of my old ladies and to silence." She had only two children herself, and they were raised by her one by one, since, when the younger one was born, the elder was already a naval officer and living by himself. Now she was living in St. Petersburg with two old women, Narzissa Bauer (the mother of Maria, widow of her elder son) and Matilda Bauer, a sister of Narzissa.

Yet not everyone was as concerned for Rimsky-Korsakov's health as Sophia. Glazunov, for example, wrote to Kruglikov:

> Regarding the fact that Rimsky-Korsakov has taken a leave from the Chapel for two months, Balakirev is telling everyone […] about his extreme displeasure and complaining that, due to Rimsky-Korsakov, he has to spend the whole summer in Peterhof. What a disgusting thing! How is it he cannot understand that Rimsky-Korsakov needs a rest, and that he has been bending over backward while Balakirev was idling? And why should he gossip about this?

Mlada

On the second anniversary of Borodin's death, all of his friends gathered at the cemetery of the Alexander Nevsky Lavra (monastery), where a memorial monument was to be erected on that day. That evening Stasov, Glazunov, Rimsky-Korsakov, Lyadov, and Belyaev met at Borodin's former apartment, where A. P. Dianin, his former student and successor at the Medical and Chemistry Academy, was then living. His friends wanted to be together, to play some of Borodin's compositions to commemorate him in their own way. Among the uncompleted compositions left by Borodin were some drafts of an opera-ballet to be called *Mlada* (*The Young Girl*). S. A. Gedeonov,[10] who was the director of the Mariinsky Theatre from 1867 to 1875, had ordered this opera-ballet several years earlier. The opera was supposed to be composed cooperatively by four composers, namely Borodin, Musorgsky, Cui, and Rimsky-Korsakov. Each was to compose one part. Then Gedeonov resigned as director, and work on the opera was stopped. The composers had only some preliminary drafts to work with. During the evening's discussion in Borodin's apartment, Lyadov suggested that the plot of the opera itself seemed to be tailor-made for Rimsky-Korsakov and that he should complete it alone. Stasov described this event in his letter to his sister as follows: "Suddenly R.-K.'s cheeks flushed and his eyes beamed when Lyadov suggested that he should compose the opera *Mlada* using the old plot. [...] Rimlyanin crossed the room with his wide steps, came up to me, and said, "That's what Lyadov has suggested!' And I asked, 'And what? What?' 'Yes, I will do it!' he replied." Stasov also commented on this incident in his letter to Glazunov: "I [...] was jolted. Never before have I seen Rimlyanin flushed and his eyes lit up in such a way. [...] You should know how such moments can leave deep impressions in your mind and heart!!!"

Upon coming home that evening Rimsky-Korsakov took a new notebook for his music drafts and made an inscription: "For the opera *Mlada*. N. R.-K. Conceived in the apartment of A. P. Borodin, on the advice of Anatoly." He began working on this new composition with zeal. Stasov assisted in getting an old libretto of *Mlada* and Rimsky-Korsakov conceived the scenes one after another very quickly.

The relations between Rimsky-Korsakov and Balakirev were becoming more and more strained. One unpleasant incident occurred when Balakirev came into the classroom during a lesson Rimsky-Korsakov was teaching on orchestration. Balakirev remarked that the students were not playing suffi- ciently in tune. Rimsky-Korsakov blew up and responded to Balakirev harshly. After the incident, Balakirev wrote to the composer:

Dear Nikolay,

I am very sorry that my remarks, very harmless in their substance as well as in the manner in which I made them, became the cause of such an outburst of indignation on Your part, which You were not shy to express even in the presence of students. […] Is it worth getting into a frenzy just because I expressed my opinion in a very innocent manner about the boys' playing a little more cleanly and in tune? […] I ask You to calm down and not to become upset over nothing.

Rimsky-Korsakov responded:

Dear Mily,

I fully understand that my behavior was rude and indecent. If I had not received Your letter I would certainly have apologized in person. Recently I have become very annoyed. I always express myself either in an absolutely despondent way or, vice versa, through my rough and stupid actions. […] On the other hand, I notice that You are constantly displeased with my activities concerning my classes in orchestration, my work with the students' orchestra and the students' evenings. It seems that on each occasion I receive some kind of reprimand from You. I am doing my best, and in my estimation, I perceive that the work is going well, not poorly. […] If You nonetheless seek to deprive me of my independence, I will lose my zeal and become useless to You.

In the middle of May 1889 the Rimsky-Korsakov family moved into a summer house, again in Nezhgovitsy. But Rimsky-Korsakov had to stay in the city. He wrote to Kruglikov: "You know that I'm going to compose the opera-ballet *Mlada*. I have made numerous preliminary drafts but when I will have time to deal with the opera properly I don't know. I'm about to go to Paris, then I will have to commute to the Chapel in Peterhof, then I'm going to move into a government apartment, and then again I will be 'grinding a street organ.' The devil take it!"

Belyaev decided to organize two Russian Symphony Concerts in Paris during the International Exhibition to be held there in May 1889, and he invited Rimsky-Korsakov to conduct them. Nadezhda was not sure whether or not she would be able to accompany her husband. Upset, he wrote to her: "Dear Nadya, is it true that you've changed your mind and decided not to go to Paris; is it so? I've been thinking the whole day of this and I can't accept it.

I've spoken to Uncle 'Oh!' He said you should go. I'm getting very sad with the thought that you might not go with me." Fortunately, the composer's mother agreed to stay with the children, and Nadezhda managed to accompany her husband. On 30 May they left for Paris. They traveled with Glazunov, the pianist N. S. Lavrov, and Belyaev himself. On 1 June they arrived in Paris. They stayed at the Hôtel l'Albe on the avenue d'Alma.

Paris

Rimsky-Korsakov wrote from Paris to his children in St. Petersburg: "We spent the evening at the hotel as we became rather messy during the trip and had to bathe, and certainly we were rather tired." The next day, from early morning, they walked around exploring Paris and had breakfast in an expensive restaurant. "Then I went on some business with Belyaev. [...] Then we were at the exhibition till 6 p.m., where we admired the Eiffel Tower. [...] In general the whole exhibition, which we visited just briefly, is very attractive and interesting. [...] After dinner, i.e. at night, we were at a *café chantant*, which we didn't like."

The concerts were scheduled for 9 and 16 June 1888, so they had time to explore Paris. The composer's wife wrote to their eldest daughter: "We are leading a healthy life here: we are walking the whole day so that we become so exhausted by the evening that we barely have strength to go to bed." A typical day unfolded in the following manner: they would get up about 8 a.m.; about 10 they would have weak coffee with milk; about 1 p.m. they would take lunch; at 7:30 there would be dinner, with no meal following.[11] Nadezhda continued: "Between meals we are always visiting something or watching something. We have been to the exhibition several times already. We visited the Louvre and saw sculptures and paintings there. We were at a *café chantant*, at the Circus, and we took a trip to the Bois de Boulogne, we were at the races, and generally we just walked around the city, shopped, etc. Besides, father has to pay some visits."

While they were in Paris, Rimsky-Korsakov became acquainted with Léo Delibes, the French composer, as well as some other composers and musicians. At the first rehearsal, when all had gathered, it turned out that there were no music stands, causing them to waste two hours. However, the rehearsal went off successfully. The musicians applauded the two composers after they played

Antar by Rimsky-Korsakov and the symphonic poem *Stenka Razin* by Glazunov. In the evening of the same day, the editor of the newspaper *Paris* gave a dinner in honor of the Russian musicians. Before the concerts of Russian music, there was "a living advertisement"—dozens of boys shouting loudly through the streets, "A hundred musicians under the conductor Rimsky-Korsakov!" The concerts took place in the Palais du Trocadero (which no longer exists). According to Glazunov's memoirs, while they were in Paris, Rimsky-Korsakov was the subject of great ovations. The Russian musicians were constantly invited to various banquets and to attend Paris salons. Glazunov wrote to Kruglikov: "The second concert can be considered a triumph for Russian music, in my opinion. Distinguished musicians in the boxes exchanged glances and smiled with delight listening to our music. [...] Lavrov's playing at the concert conducted by Rimsky-Korsakov was interrupted several times with loud applause."

Nikolay and Nadezhda Rimsky-Korsakov attended the reception, hosted by the minister of art. At the dinner in honor of the Russian musicians hosted by Édouard Colonne,[12] a well-known conductor, they met Jules Massenet, Ambroise Thomas, and Gabriel Fauré. The Rimsky-Korsakovs went to the Paris Opéra, where they saw the opera *The Storm* by Thomas, based on Shakespeare's play *The Tempest*. They also attended Massenet's opera *Esclarmonde* at the Opéra-Comique. In addition they visited the Paris Conservatory and its library. When they visited the exhibition, Rimsky-Korsakov was especially attracted by two things: the sound of a reed instrument played in a group of musicians at a Hungarian café, and the beating of a big drum that was produced by an African in an Algerian café to accompany a female dancer who was performing a dance with a dagger.

Nikolay and Nadezhda were the first of their group to leave Paris, but on the way home they stopped in Switzerland, in Lucerne and Zurich, and in Austria, in Salzburg, where they visited Mozart's house and the salt mines. At the beginning of July 1889 they returned to Nezhgovitsy. Nikolay's mother and the children were already there by then. Stasov wrote to Kruglikov: "Rimlyanin hid in a remote corner, far from Luga in his summer house, and he didn't meet anybody, neither did he pay visits or go out." Indeed, as soon as the composer returned to St. Petersburg, he left for Nezhgovitsy and took up composing *Mlada*. Stasov wrote to him there: "I believe and confess that it will be something very nice, as I saw how it burned inside You then in Borodin's rooms and you were hit by a big wave (The Ninth Wave)."[13]

In the middle of August 1889 Rimsky-Korsakov completed *Mlada*. He wrote to Kruglikov:

> Kindest, nicest, and best Semyon Kruglikov,
>
> [...] I've really completed *Mlada* in the narrow sense, but there is the so-called orchestration left, which nobody except Glazunov considers composing or at least a continuing stage of composing. But truly it is composing. If an artist sketched his picture with a pencil on a canvas in detail, would it mean that the painting had been finished and he should just color as children would do? Very often it happens so that the most important thing is the coloring, the lighting. Moreover, the real expression can be achieved only in colors, to say nothing of the fact that during this work you might alter something and it is itself a rather great job.

That summer, in 1889, the renovation of the Chapel premises was finished, and upon their arrival back in Petersburg the Rimsky-Korsakov family moved into a new government apartment on Bolshaya Konushennaya Street. As the family was by now quite large, the new residence consisted of two apartments joined by an inner stairway. The rooms there were small, so they rearranged them as living rooms; one of them had a grand piano, and they called it the Grand Hall. Ten years earlier Stasov had bet Rimsky-Korsakov that one day the composer would become the director of the Chapel and would live in a government apartment. They had agreed that if Stasov won, then Rimsky-Korsakov would "have to treat Stasov honorably and present him with the first cup of yellow Imperial tea at a price of 12 rubles per pound in front of the public in the main hall of that very apartment." Stasov did not know himself what made him predict this. In any case, Rimsky-Korsakov did become the assistant to the general manager of the Chapel and moved into an apartment belonging to the Chapel, so he offered that very cup of yellow tea to Stasov at his housewarming party.

8
Recognition, 1888–1891

I have done it all: mermaids, wood goblins, Russian pastorals, round dancing, rites, conversions, oriental music, nights, evenings, dawns, birds, stars, clouds, floods, storms, evil witches, pagan gods, ugly monsters, hunting, receptions, dances, priests, idol worshipers [...] and so on and so forth.

—Rimsky-Korsakov to Semyon Kruglikov, 1890

During the first musical soirée in his new apartment, on 30 September 1888, Rimsky-Korsakov played *Mlada* to his friends. Anticipating this event, Stasov wrote to Glazunov: "I've been longing all this time to find out where all of his soul's confusion and talent's anxiety have led. [...] And I've been thinking to myself: 'And what if nothing great comes about despite everything?'" Nonetheless, the music of *Mlada* impressed everyone.

In Moscow

In October the composer left for Moscow to conduct some concerts of the Russian Musical Society. The day after his departure, Nadezhda wrote to her husband:

Dear Nika,

I sat down to write very late, so I'm not sure if this letter can be posted today or tomorrow. The thing is I have received guests today. [...] Uncle "Oh!" brought a wonderful housewarming present: a sweet pie with a silver saltcellar and, in addition, a large nickel samovar with a tray and a slop basin. What a luxury! Uncle "Oh!" liked our apartment very much. [...] The children became outrageously naughty when Uncle "Oh!" came. [...] I woke up several times during the night today and wondered how your trip was going.

Good-bye, my dear. I am kissing you. Take care. Don't catch a cold and watch out not to be overfed with Moscow *rasstegai* and dinners.

One morning before a rehearsal, Tchaikovsky visited Rimsky-Korsakov at the Grand Hotel Moscow, situated not far from the Iversky Gate. They dined together and then went to the rehearsal. Rimsky-Korsakov wrote home: "I had dinner with Tchaikovsky. Eating, eating, drinking, eating, etc."

Although Rimsky-Korsakov and his wife had not parted long before, nonetheless, they worried about each other very much and wrote to each other almost simultaneously. From the composer: "Dear Nadya, I didn't receive any letter from you yesterday, or today either. Why are you not writing regularly?" From Nadezhda: "Darling Nikusha, I haven't received a letter from you today. Why? Are you all right?" In the same letter Nadezhda sent her husband news from home:

> The children are healthy, Thank God. Volodya is behaving very badly today. He was so naughty while I was out that he was even punished, that is, he hasn't received a piece of cake. While I am writing to you Masha is taking a bath, Nadya is knitting next to me, and Volodya is cutting out soldiers from paper. Andrey and Sonya are doing their homework, and Misha just had lunch and went back to school again. They are rehearsing a new play for May's birthday concert.[1] Misha is participating, and he is acting the part of Chichikov in a scene with Plyushkin.[2] Misha is Chichikov! It is funny! I wish I could see that play. See you soon, my dear. I'm kissing you. I hope the concert will be a success.

The Moscow concert in October 1888 received a glowing review: "The first symphony concert at the Nobility Assembly Rooms, conducted by the most talented proponent of the New Russian music, N. A. Rimsky-Korsakov, went off successfully and revealed a great musical event. [...] The *Capriccio espagnol* by Rimsky-Korsakov, his latest achievement in orchestration, was an excellent finish for a perfectly constructed program."

Rimsky-Korsakov's activities as a conductor were keeping him quite busy. A few days after arriving in St. Petersburg, he conducted the first purely Russian symphony concert. Before the end of 1888 he had conducted three more concerts, and he led two more in January and February 1889.

Misha (and later Rimsky-Korsakov's other sons) studied at a well-known private school of the day, established by Karl May. The school was located on Vasilevsky Island in St. Petersburg and was famous for its brilliant curriculum and well-organized teaching procedures. May, the principal, was completely devoted to his school. He set forth certain major principles for the upbringing and education of the students in his school: respect for each student's personality, love for each pupil ("first to love, then to teach"), development of each student's individual abilities, and provision of a democratic atmosphere in the school. Students who were from well-off families and had their own carriages were forbidden to arrive in them at the school doors. They had to park their carriages around the corner before reaching the building, and then walk to school as most students did. Every morning May stood on the stairs and greeted each student with a handshake. However, if a particular student was behaving badly, May did not extend his hand to him, hiding it behind his back; this was considered by the guilty student to be a severe punishment. The school was equipped with excellent laboratories and workshops. The boys were engaged in different group activities and took field trips together, gave performances, and every year celebrated May's birthday with some kind of concert. May eventually gave over his post to Vasily Krakay,[3] a history teacher. Upon leaving his post, May wrote to Krakay: "I can hope and expect that You, Vasily, will maintain the present atmosphere of this school so I can rest in peace and trust You completely with my beloved school." May himself stayed with the gymnasium as a geography teacher until he died in 1895.[4]

A Seventh Child, Vyacheslav

In December 1889 Nadezhda gave a birth to their seventh child, a boy named Vyacheslav (Slavchik for short). The following year was very hard for the family. Various illnesses haunted them. At first two-year-old Masha was ill, then six-year-old Nadya came down with scarlet fever. Rimsky-Korsakov wrote to Kruglikov: "I'm staying at home with my wife and taking care of the child. We have dispersed the other children to relatives. The house is empty. I have given up all of my activities."

Rimsky-Korsakov's relations with Balakirev were getting worse. Balakirev hinted at leaving the Chapel and hoped that Rimsky-Korsakov would take over from him. The composer commented on the matter in a letter to Kruglikov:

"An acquaintance of Belyaev says, 'When I'm promoted to the rank of general, tell me "you're a fool."' And I will ask him to say the same to me if I'm promoted to be in charge of anything. I'm saying this concerning Balakirev."

A Journey to Brussels

In March 1890 Rimsky-Korsakov was provided with some distraction from his St. Petersburg worries by a journey he took to Brussels, where he had been invited to conduct a concert of Russian music. His friends congratulated him on this occasion. Belyaev even organized a farewell party at his house. Stasov could not come but sent a letter, which was read during the special champagne dinner. Stasov asked Belyaev to wish the composer "that in the future, Rimsky-Korsakov will be invited many times to Paris, London, Berlin, Vienna, Madrid, and Rome to glorify Russia and to ram our excellent music into European heads." On 20 March Rimsky-Korsakov left for Brussels. Although the children had mostly recovered from their illnesses, the composer's wife did not go with him due to the needs of the family.

On his arrival in Brussels, the composer wrote to Nadezhda:

My dear,
I arrived in Brussels at 4:17 in the morning. On the order of d'Aust,[5] a commissioner from the hotel met me at the railway station. In the hotel room, I found a letter and a business card from Berendey (!) himself. The last name of the director of the concert turns out to be Beréndès. He informed me that he would pick me up at 8 a.m. to accompany me to the rehearsal. After settling my things, I had a nap, although I had slept well in the train. At 8 a.m., while I was having coffee, Berendey came in and we went out. The rehearsals are being held in a concert hall, not in the theatre where the concert itself will take place. There I was met by d'Aust and Dupon, a former bandmaster of the opera house and the present conductor of the Popular Concerts. Dupon introduced me to the orchestra. [...] After the rehearsal I had breakfast with Dupon, who seems to be an excellent musician. And today I'm going to have dinner with him at the home of one of his friends, a music lover. On the way he showed me around the city a little. The city is very elegant. It is situated in the hills, and with its surroundings it reminds one of Paris. [...] Now I will tell you about my trip. On the way it was very cold (not in the train, but outside). Starting with Berlin, I could see green

grass and trees in bloom. In Berlin I had time to walk along Unter den Linden and to see the aquarium. The city is wonderful, but it seems to be a little dull and barracks-like. There are beautiful houses on the main streets. I was in Cologne at 10 p.m., so I only managed to see the outside of the cathedral. [...] I'm afraid you're still anxious and frightened that the scarlet fever might return. Try to be a good girl. Don't worry and rest well. Could you write to me about yourself and the children as often as possible, every day? No sooner had I written those words than I got a telegram from you: "Tout va bien." What a wonderful thing the telegraph is! Now I know what is going on with you today. [...]

Goodbye, my darling. Kiss all the children for me and sing to Slavchik. I embrace you. Be healthy.

Your N. R.-Korsakov,

23 March, 2:30 p.m.

Rimsky-Korsakov wrote more about his life abroad in his letters:

My dear,

I'm starting with "Ugh—!" which I'm saying in a long way and very affectionately. Yesterday I spent the evening with Dupon at the home of his friend Collard, who is a music fan and a rich merchant. There were also other people there. We sat down at table about 8 and stayed till 11! We were eating, eating, drinking, and drinking endlessly. Ah, how much they eat and drink! Indeed, even more than Russians! They eat small portions but in total so much, the devil take it! After several nutritious dishes, and after the fried potatoes, they served ham. And what ham! Never before have I had more delicious ham! It tastes better than any other kind of ham we tried before, just as Glazunov's herrings taste better than any other herrings.[6] We drank some strange kind of burgundy wine, which must be poured in such a delicate way that it requires a special device, the rotation of which makes the bottle incline very slowly. How stupidly fancy! I had to speak French the whole evening, which I did, mixing phrases with thoughtful "mhhhh"s in order to sometimes show agreement or to pretend that I understood everything to keep the conversation going. It's so stupid! I had even to argue, defending Liszt from their attacks. They don't like him here. They like Beethoven, Berlioz, and Wagner. They paid a lot of compliments to Russian music, which they seemed to know. For example, Collard has all of my compositions.

However, they don't appreciate Glinka. [...] As far as I can see, he is not in favor; it seems more likely to be the opposite. They like Borodin to some extent. They praised me (very) much, but they might just be trying to flatter me. [...] Certainly, they say all of this in a very subtle, kind, and nice manner compared with our way: "he is a scoundrel, villain, fool, etc." But in general they have obscure ideas about Russia, though there were two people there who had lived in Russia for ten years. [...] We stayed at Collard's until 1 a.m. I was exhausted and sleepy, and I have to get up at 7 a.m. to be at the rehearsal on time. Today we played the *Russian Easter Festival Overture* and *Capriccio espagnol*. The first we studied a lot. I've set the world on fire with both of them, and the musicians applauded a lot. [...] On Saturday there is to be a final rehearsal before the public, without any stopping [in the music]. Can you imagine, [it's] especially for Englishmen! That is the custom here. The Englishmen do not go to concerts on Sundays and so for them they arrange paid rehearsals on Saturdays. [...] Tomorrow I suppose I'll be left in peace. I'm very glad about it. I will work on the orchestration of *Mlada*. Or, I suppose, I'll go first to see a local art museum, where there will be only Rubens, Rubens, and more Rubens. Yesterday Dupon and I walked about the city streets for a considerable time. The city is really marvelous. It reminds me of Paris. It is clean, cozy, [and] lovely, with beautiful buildings and shops. The streets are busy; people are wandering [about and] singing. I think it's the happiest and most advanced country in the world.

And the same day:

My dear,

I have written to you today already; nevertheless, I am sitting down writing [to] you again. You can't believe how pleased I am with today! I was alone the whole day. How nice it is! I was alone [but] I was not lonely: I was with you, the children, and my friends. I feel extremely lonely surrounded by all those French and Belgian chatterboxes. I had breakfast alone, then I worked on the orchestration of *Mlada*, then I wrote a letter to you, then I had a nap, then I walked along the streets alone, then I had dinner alone, and now, at some minutes past eight in the evening, I'm staying in my room alone. In one word: it is happiness. Tell our children that they should study French and German hard so that when they are abroad they can speak fluently and easily defend Russia against foreigners who don't have the least understanding of Russia but judge her without discernment, and you have either to keep silent or almost even to agree since you don't know the language. They are very polite, but through this politeness you can feel [they have] some strange desire to pull strings for you, [to do you] a favor and so on. They give you the notion that they are superior to you: you can feel this in everything; they are so arrogant, but for all that, as [with] most arrogant people they are very stupid, as they think that nobody notices this. Certainly, I bored Dupon, and that's clear. It's difficult for me to speak to him, he can't force me to keep on with clever conversation, but his stupidity is in the fact that he doesn't even suspect that he himself bored me much more than I did him. And after all, I know him and understand him, and he doesn't know me and does not understand me. They say that they value Russian music, that Russians have done a lot, but it sounds like it is said with some note of self-defense. They are stupid! They cannot appreciate that Russians have done so much that they have never even dreamed of! If they did understand, they should have admired and venerated and they would value each Russian note as if it were made of gold, [in the same way] that they value Wagner. […] Certainly, it's just my own proud opinion and nothing more than that. But at this moment I feel this so clearly that I couldn't but tell [you] all that. […] Good-bye. I kiss you and the children.

Your N. R.-Korsakov

P.S. The weather is very nice. Everyone is wearing summer coats and so am I.

The next day Rimsky-Korsakov wrote again:

My dear,

I haven't had a letter from you today. And I myself was not going to write to you today, nevertheless I'm writing. In the morning until 10, I was dealing with *Mlada*. Then I went to the art museum. They have mostly Flemish artists and, by the way, my favorite Rubèns (as they pronounced it here). There are a lot of strange paintings that seem to be created by Suzdal icon-daubers of the Flemish school.[7] I found some of them very funny. I'll draw one of them. Here it is. This is the Ascension of Christ. At the bottom, you can see different people looking up, and above them, there are only legs: that is Christ rising up and you can see only the legs at the bottom of the [picture] frame. What a laugh! […] after the museum, I went to see d'Aust. We had lunch together and then rode around the city and through a huge park, the Bois de Cambre. […] D'Aust seems to be very nice. It was my pleasure to visit him. Though he is rich, he lives in a very domestic and simple way. He has two little children, eight and eleven years old. He is a great admirer of music. He knows Russian music well and has almost every Russian composition at home. He must be very keen on music. […] At this very moment there are large posters about the concert with my name on them in the streets.

The composer's wife complained about not receiving letters from her husband for a long time: "I'm longing to find out how your musical affairs are proceeding there. […] All of the children spend the whole day at home now, and therefore there is certainly much noise. They intend to fast and attend divine service during Holy Week." The composer answered: "Could you arrange it so that they will fast on St. Pantaleon's Day?[8] I think the priest will have to pay a visit to us at Easter, so receive him as well as possible." His next letter shared new impressions from abroad:

> The Théâtre de la Monnaie is very good. But they have Parisian customs: when you buy tickets you don't know where you'll be seated, and there is too little space and you have to go out to smoke or drink anything. I will go to see "The Sailor—Wanderer"; it is interesting to wonder what it will be like there. Today at 9 a.m. I went to see Antwerp. It's just an hour's trip and I've just returned from it. It's a nice town, but it's more Flemish than French compared to Brussels. I was at the cathedral. It's a beautiful Gothic church where they have a lot of Rubens. But the most interesting thing to see there is the Plantin Museum. It's an ancient printing house established in the 1500s, which is a museum now. You can see their different samples of publishing from those times, letters, fonts, and other things; they have a lot of etchings of Rubens, copper and wood fretwork and so on. Everything is saved as it was three hundred years ago: rooms, furniture, stoves. […] I'm getting used to Brussels. I came back from Antwerp to Brussels as if it were my home. I have become acquainted with Brussels well enough and can go anywhere alone, as I have a clear picture [of it].

Nadezhda could hardly believe that everyone at home was healthy now and that the children could go for a walk every day. But nobody visited them except Belyaev, as they were afraid of catching infections from visitors. Rimsky-Korsakov's mother was still troubled by a pain in her cheek and did not go out. All this weighed on Nadezhda's mind. Nadezhda was also worried about her husband, the Brussels concert, and about the success of *Capriccio espagnol*. She wrote: "Please God that everything will proceed well and the public will like it." Rimsky-Korsakov wrote that Dupon liked his music and the compositions of Glazunov and Musorgsky, but he liked Cui's and Balakirev's music much less. He added: "It seems that we are getting friendly with the Belgians, and they all repeated that I must come here again next year and that right now it's just a first step. Could you write to Stasov about this? He will be glad. How is his health now? Yesterday I was interviewed by a journalist, today another one will come. I'm glad that I didn't have to go [to them] myself and that they have to come to my place."

The concert took place in the Théâtre de la Monnaie on 1 April 1890. It was a great success. The theatre was so full that some of the audience had to stand. There were musicians from Liège and other cities in Belgium. At first the audience greeted the composer rather indifferently, but later they applauded loudly. He was presented with a wreath as a musical flourish was played. He parted from his Belgian hosts in a friendly manner. On 4 April Rimsky-Korsakov returned home.

An Extremely Dangerous Condition

Upon his return Rimsky-Korsakov was met with another round of family illnesses. Nadezhda was seriously ill with a throat infection, and her husband had to look after her. He wrote to Kruglikov: "Dear Semyon, [...] Nadezhda was in an extremely dangerous condition. There was a day when we were about to make a tracheotomy as there was a danger of asphyxia. She couldn't even drink any water for six days, to say nothing about eating. Now she is better. She can eat and even move round the house. [...] You are so kind! You're one of the few who are interested in Nadezhda's state of health, most just don't care." Some days later, the composer wrote again:

> Your letter, where you expressed your happiness about Nadezhda's recovery, reached me in one of the hardest days. The throat infection recommenced with its previous force: a boil formed in her larynx right next to the glottis. Again, we called in the doctors and surgeons (in case of emergency). In addition, Andrey is sick with scarlet fever and the whole house is in a mess. It has been utterly awful! At this very moment it's more or less tolerable. The boil was treated in time and a possible asphyxia was avoided, and Nadezhda is now on her way to recovery

again. Little Andrey has been diagnosed with scarlet fever of "moderate danger" but he is supposedly recovering "well" (!!). We have to live now being happy about the fact that "under such awful conditions more serious danger did not occur." What a grim fate! As for believers, it's just a mere mockery of Him whom they believe in! Upon receiving this letter, don't become happy for me and my family. I'm very far from the thought that the end of our dark road has already approached. I have given up all of my official business and private work. The house now is simply in the confusion of Babylon.

In fact, Andrey's recovery was progressing, albeit very slowly, and Nadezhda too was getting better little by little, but she was very weak and could not look after Andrey. Rimsky-Korsakov had to carry everything on his broad shoulders. He wrote to Stasov: "Everything is extremely bad at home. You can imagine Nadezhda's mood, [because] due to her own illness [she] can't look after her sick son." The composer turned himself into a nurse. He was not able to concentrate on anything else and could not deal with his musical work or even play: isolating the sick ones meant their "grand" hall was converted into a bedroom, his study into a children's room, and so on. He complained to Kruglikov: "It's awfully bad, everything is just awful. I do not believe that the misfortune, which has been pursuing my family since winter, will ever come to an end. It seems it will be like this forever: illness after illness, if not worse. I sat down to write to you since I don't know what to do with myself or what I can do to slog through this dreadful time."

Rimsky-Korsakov felt bitter about the fact that his friends Glazunov, Lyadov, and Belyaev showed a callous attitude toward him and his wife. They were afraid to visit them to inquire about how the sick family was doing. Balakirev actually and bluntly told the composer that he did not care about his family. Rimsky-Korsakov wrote to Stasov: "I'm sure if I became blind or had to leave them for any reason, half of my musical friends would forget about me as they would about any old person. The devil take them." Stasov responded: "No, dear fellow, You shouldn't speak like this, to think that anybody among those whom You consider Your friends right now would ever be able to forget about You. No, no, no, and a thousand times more no! You have fixed Yourself so firmly in their memory, in their heads and the souls of each of us, that we will never be able to forget about You either together or individually!!!" The composer's wife commented on this later in a letter to Stasov:

Rimsky-Korsakov did not mean that he would be forgotten by his friends as a musician. He meant personal relations, and unfortunately, in our case according to the old saying "A friend in need is a friend in deed" their friendship has failed the test. As concerns my own life and the life of our children, it is absolutely clear that our friends do not care at all. [...] But they should understand that all of our family troubles have influenced Nika and made him extremely upset. So if they truly liked him, they would have come around to find out about his state and encourage him by showing their compassion for his family.

By the beginning of May 1890 Nadezhda had almost recovered; nevertheless, Rimsky-Korsakov wrote to Tyumenev that he did not have any opportunity to take up playing music even in the "healthy part" of the house.

Andrey's health was again getting worse; he had hardly recovered from scarlet fever when he came down with severe diphtheria. Rimsky-Korsakov wrote to Kruglikov seeming at a loss: "Should he come to a bad end? I'm in such a condition that I can't find a place to rest. Why should this awful disaster have occurred?! You can't even imagine how much I love him these days." Kruglikov was extremely sympathetic: "My dearest friend, you should hold yourself well in hand. Don't let despair and depression weigh you down. It is useless: it will not help [and] You could endanger your own health."

"I Can't Compose at All"

At last Andrey's condition began to improve, and the composer wrote to Kruglikov:

> I'd like to tell you that now, when Andrey has got over the crisis, I feel such a huge starvation of my musical heart that I can't even describe it. I'm eager to deal with my class in orchestration, which I had to abandon at the most important moment [the first serious graduate examinations], I'm even glad to give lessons in the boring Conservatory. But the most important thing is my unhappy composition of *Mlada*, the work that was interrupted so many times in the cruelest manner. When I will undertake working on it [again], I don't know myself. The apartment is in a mess, the children are dispersed in different houses. I should gather them and prepare everything to transfer them to a new summer house as soon as possible, while they are more or less well. I could add that there are some

more minor troubles and worries: I have to find a new cook, replace a laundress, etc. All this seems just a trivial matter to an inexperienced Glazunov who is courting Conservatory girls, but you will certainly understand that in family life a laundress may well influence musical art; first you should find her, as you can't live without her, and only then you can compose.

It goes without saying that [one's busy] life limits composing, which is as delicate as a precious flower. But this very thing is why one is living on this earth, or at least one imagines that it is so. Dealing with any trivial matter, of which one constantly has a great deal, I may have to go for example to the Conservatory at a certain hour to conduct a lesson, or to the Chapel and surround myself with its atmosphere, undertake some activities, for which I created the attraction in any case, but I can't compose at all. It's too subtle a thing. [...] If one has some experience one can conduct a concert when the atmosphere at home is unfavorable, as it is some kind of service, merely carrying out one's duties. But composing is a matter that involves the soul; it is much more delicate than any other business such as dealing with [some] scientific or mental activity. Certainly raising children, taking care of their health and the well-being of the family is a thing of greater importance than even mighty musical compositions. Nonetheless, you will understand my heart's starvation; you will think how much my heart hurts because my creative work has been interrupted. [...] In the most dangerous and serious moments of one's life, this feeling remains silent; but when the danger is over and only the consequences and inconveniences of it are left, my soul's sufferings conquer me utterly.

This year has been extremely unlucky for me: I can't avoid dangers, great worries, and scrapes. And all this fell upon me in the midst of *Mlada*, which is likely to be my last composition. [...] I will have nothing to compose after *Mlada*. I have done everything I could within the limits of my talent. Before *Mlada* I had some gaps to fill in, now nothing is left. I have done it all: mermaids, wood goblins, Russian pastorals, round dancing, rites, conversions, oriental music, nights, evenings, dawns, birds, stars, clouds, floods, storms, evil witches, pagan gods, ugly monsters, hunting, receptions, dances, priests, idol worshipers, tracing the musical development of Russian and various Slavic elements, and so on and so forth. By completing *Mlada* I have filled in all the gaps. I have nothing to compose anymore. It's not worth repeating the old or washing it away. I'd better do like Rossini and simply stop. I don't want to be like old voiceless singers who keep on singing after [their] twenty-fifth, thirty-fifth or forty-fifth anniversaries. [...]

I love *Mlada* for its being the last, for that possibility to say everything that I haven't said before in music. And circumstances disturbed and hindered me from doing so, and therefore, it's especially painful.

Kruglikov argued:

Oh no, my dear [friend]. That example with Rossini should be sent to hell. First of all, why should he be a model for Korsakov? Who is that Rossini? A dissipated Italian who ordered dried mushrooms from Russia [in order] to cook some extravagant sauce in Paris? And secondly, the author can't judge his own compositions. He can't give up composing unless he becomes deaf, paralyzed, and incapable of giving birth to any tiny musical thought, which can be worthless in his opinion, but which in fact, might be even of more importance than [those] previous ones.

The composer's mother was beginning to show her age. On Rimsky-Korsakov's birthday Sophia wrote in a weak hand: "My dear Nika, today is your birthday, but you will get this note only tomorrow. You know that today my memory is very poor. Usually those who congratulate a birthday person give him presents, but I am expecting my son to present me something, what exactly I will tell you when I see you. The thing is very amusing. God Bless You. Your Mama, S. R.-K., 6 March." In the beginning of April 1890 she shared a thought with her Tikhvin friends: "I'm thinking of spending the summer with my son in the Luga region, at the same place where we were last year. [...] He, my darling, is very rich in children. He has seven now. The youngest is three months old. [...] All of his children differ greatly, but it seems none of them has shown the same passion or talent for music that their father has. However, they all have a very good ear. [...] Thank God, he has a government apartment; it's a great assistance to him." She was getting weaker by the day, but the composer still took her to his summer house in Nezhgovitsy with Nadezhda and all of the children.

Death of His Mother, Sophia

As usual, owing to the examinations at the Conservatory, Rimsky-Korsakov had to return to St. Petersburg. He moved to Nezhgovitsy only at the beginning of June. Here at last he undertook further work on *Mlada*. But in the middle of August Sophia felt so ill that Rimsky-Korsakov brought her back to St.

Petersburg to be closer to her doctors. Just then Balakirev decided to go to Yaroslavl for a rest and delegated all of his duties to the composer. Glinka's sister, Lyudmila Shestakova, and some others tried to persuade Balakirev not to leave at that time, since Rimsky-Korsakov was facing considerable personal difficulties: his family was in Nezhgovitsy, his mother was languishing in St. Petersburg, and the Chapel was still in Peterhof. Stasov described Balakirev's response in a letter to Stasov's brother: "It's not my concern! His mother is nearly ninety years old now; he should have been ready for her passing away a long time ago." Stasov commented on this further: "Everywhere he shows just unbelievable and uncaring cruelty. And all the while he is proclaiming Christianity, eating communion bread, reciting prayers and lighting candles before the icons." What is more, this was not the full extent of Balakirev's hypocrisy, as Rimsky-Korsakov revealed in a letter to his wife in Nezhgovitsy:

My dear Nadya,

I am sitting in Peterhof as if I were in prison. However, today I visited Belyaev, and tomorrow I am going to the Conservatory in St. Petersburg. As I said, I am living as if I were in prison because our English Palace and my room is certainly a prison.[9] I have nothing to do, so I am staying in my room almost the whole day polishing and revising the fourth act of *Mlada*. I do not feel like going out at all. The park is just annoying for me. I have nobody to speak to. Balakirev is still here, although he handed over the administration of the Chapel to me; he comes twice a day to the office and writes some letters. On my arrival in St. Petersburg [Friday, 24 August] I visited Mother; she felt a little better. Tomorrow I am going to [see] her again. [...] The Chapel is returning to St. Petersburg on 4 September, as arranged before. [...] Balakirev certainly might have asked me to be here five days later. I wish he would go away as soon as possible. [...]

P.S. Having written this letter I went to bed, but I was woken up by a telegram [...] that Mother is very bad, and they have asked me to come over. I got on the train at 12:45 a.m. and was with her by 3 p.m. I found her extremely weak. I slept on the sofa in her room. She moaned all night. She is so weak that I could not make out what she was saying. By morning she was a little better. At 9 a.m. the priest came and gave her the Eucharist. The doctor is expected at 2 p.m. I think she is enduring her last days. At night she asked about you and the children. Today, if nothing happens, I will stay in Peterhof for the night.

Your N. R.-K. Monday, 10 in the morning.

Nadezhda wrote from Nezhgovitsy: "I'm so sorry that I don't know anything about you: whether you've settled down comfortably, whether you have everything you need like a pillow, a blanket, bedding, etc., as you haven't taken anything with you. This Palace might be damp and cold and you might catch a cold there. P.S. I've just got your letter. It's terrible that Mother is so ill."

Sophia could not speak at all on her last day. She died on 30 August at the age of eighty-eight. The next day, the composer's wife, together with Misha, their eldest son, and eight-month-old Slavchik, whom she could not leave in the summer house, arrived in St. Petersburg. The composer's mother was buried in the Smolensky cemetery, next to the tomb of her elder son. Many years later Misha recalled that he saw tears in his father's eyes when the remains were placed in the tomb. Sophia left a will entitled "Posthumous Wishes, written in the year 1887 on 9 January." She was eighty-five years old then and wrote her will with fairly firm, neat handwriting:

> I ask my son Rimsky-Korsakov to fulfill the following:
>
> I wish my tomb not to have a monument, but only a simple cover like the tomb of Andrey Petrovich. [...][10]
>
> The icon of the Tikhvin Holy Mother, which is smaller, must be given to my son, Nikolay. His grandmother blessed his father with this icon at the time of our marriage. The bronze crucifix that used to hang above Andrey Petrovich's bed and was on his chest when he passed away (he used to take it with him everywhere he went), and that after his passing was always near my bed, I also leave it for you, Nika. I'm also leaving my favorite bronze clock to my Nika, so he can remember me fondly. I ask you to save it and set it on your desk. [...] The watch I'm wearing I am giving to Misha when he turns eighteen years old. The dressing case, golden brooch, and purse decorated with beads of birds are for Sonya. The silver holder for fifteen-kopek and ten-kopek coins is for Andrusha. The silver knife with the letter S and the dessert spoon are for Volodya. The silver and gilded milk jug, the silver ring for napkins, the silver purse with five-kopek coins, and the little teaspoon are for Nadya Junior.

Thus Sophia bequeathed her modest belongings.

At the end of September Rimsky-Korsakov played *Mlada* to his friends at his home. Over the next three weeks he attended rehearsals of Borodin's opera *Prince Igor*, which he and Glazunov had completed and which was to be staged at the Mariinsky Theatre. The opening night was 23 October 1890. Rimsky-Korsakov took several curtain calls during the first and the second performances. M. Ivanov wrote a review in the newspaper *Novoe vremya* (*The New Times*): "Russian art owes much to Rimsky-Korsakov, who, by the way, has organized and completed a third opera on behalf of the deceased composers: the first two were *The Stone Guest* and *Khovanschina*. This is a rare example of that very selflessness, which along with the feeling of respect for a certain idea, could be best of all characterized with the conception of the German word *Pietät*."[11]

Losing a Son

Unfortunately, it was not yet the end of an incredibly unlucky year for the Rimsky-Korsakov family. Doctors diagnosed three-year-old Masha with pulmonary tuberculosis, which they had at first confused with pleurisy. In the beginning of December their youngest son, Slavchik, who was only about a year old, died from a brain disease. As usual, Kruglikov was there to express his condolences: "My dear friend, kind, dearest Nikolay! I've just got a letter from Stasov, who informed me of the sorrowful events that occurred in Your family. There are such moments in one's life when one does not want to hear any words even from a sincerely loving and truly faithful friend. I understand this and so I keep silence. Let me just embrace You heartily and shake Your hand with compassion. My heartfelt wishes to Your family."

A Twenty-fifth Anniversary

Preparations had been under way since September to celebrate Rimsky-Korsakov's twenty-fifth anniversary as a composer. The actual date was 19 December 1890, since on that day in 1865 his First Symphony was performed for the first time; however, the official banquet in honor of the composer was scheduled for 22 December. Many musical institutions expressed their desire to participate in the celebration. One can imagine in what kind of mood Rimsky-Korsakov and Nadezhda were in when they had to receive the congratulations and participate in the anniversary activities. On the advice of Stasov, Shapiro (a famous St. Petersburg photographer) displayed a large portrait of Rimsky-Korsakov in laurels in the window of his photo studio on Nevsky Prospect.[12]

Stasov. This address was given the name "The Golden Leaf." Count Sheremetev, the director of the Chapel, congratulated Rimsky-Korsakov on its behalf.

His Conservatory colleagues also presented Rimsky-Korsakov with a gold pocket watch with an inscription. The students of the Conservatory presented a large photo album in a plush cover decorated with silver and enamel and with a picture of a gonfalon and the musical phrase "The strings are sounding the glory" (from *The Snow Maiden*).[13] The album had photos of his students. And in response to a petition by Balakirev to the Ministry of the Court (via the assistance of Count Sheremetev), Rimsky-Korsakov was granted a special pension in the amount of 1,500 rubles per year "as a reward for his twenty-five years of useful service to music." The Naval Office did not congratulate the composer. After the concert there was a special dinner in his honor. The menu contained a large selection of fancy hors d'oeuvres, bouillon, pies, fish, cutlets, ice cream, and coffee. The menu card was decorated with musical notes and the dates 1865–1890 and crowned with the figure "XXV." The dinner took place in the Kontana restaurant.

Balakirev: Quarrel and Estrangement

In response to this celebration, the Rimsky-Korsakov family gave a special dinner at their home for a small group of close friends on 6 January 1891. On the eve of that day, Rimsky-Korsakov visited Balakirev to invite him to the dinner. Balakirev refused, saying, "No, I will not come to you." This sharp denial was caused by a trivial event that had happened some days before. The composer had sent the following letter to Balakirev:

Dear Mily,

In accordance with your wish, I asked Belyaev about the terms for publishing Lyapunov's Symphony. I wanted to tell you this in person, but you asked that I do it in writing. I asked you not to become angry with me if I did not do this in person. [...] The direct way to Belyaev is open to everyone. My informing you about the terms only in writing will make me a possible intermediary in something that is certainly not my business and that I do not wish to be involved in. By declining to give you the terms of the agreement between Belyaev and Lyapunov in writing, I asked you to let me excuse myself from telling them to you in person as well.

This letter outraged Balakirev. He responded:

Nikolay,

Your unexpected visit to me yesterday and even less expected invitation for dinner, after I had received that outrageous letter from You, made me so excited that in that condition I could have given away too much and missed the essence of our conversation. Therefore, to settle our relations I find it necessary to inform you of the following: The resumption of our personal relations is impossible not only for me but also for You. Since You gave me clear notice that You think of me as being capable of playing tricks on You and that in dealing with me You should keep Your ears pricked up, would it not present a lie on Your part not only to offer an invitation for dinner but even simply for You to be my acquaintance? But there is a walk of life where we should not be parted. That is the Chapel. I am certain that I will be capable of appreciating the benefits received from the service of my subordinates irrespective of my own personal relations with them. So, for the sake of those benefits that are received from our official alliance for our dear children entrusted to our care, that alliance should not be broken. Friendship is friendship, but duties remain duties!

And for the sake of those interests, I think that nobody in the Chapel should find out about our clash.

M. Balakirev.

Rimsky-Korsakov responded:

Mily,

Upon my leaving you on Saturday and looking back on our past relations, I came to the conclusion that our exceptionally official relations were established a long time ago and they had been established gradually. Our conversation about the topic of my letter simply confirmed these relations. Nevertheless, it does not prevent us from undertaking our official business in concord and even in a friendly manner. Hence, now nothing should have to be changed. Certainly, nobody should know that we have broken off our personal relations. Let it be like this.

N. R.-Korsakov.

After this exchange the greeting "dear" in their letters was replaced by "To the General Manager of the Court Chapel, Sir Balakirev" and "To the Assistant of the General Manager of the Court Chapel," respectively. It took a long time for them to use friendly greetings again in their letters. Despite this personal quarrel, Balakirev was delighted with Rimsky-Korsakov's *Mlada*. The opera-ballet was published at the beginning of the next year, and when P. Olenin, an opera singer, visited Balakirev, he saw the score of *Mlada* on the reading stand of the piano. Balakirev played the Prelude to him. Olenin reminisced: "He was excited. He exclaimed, 'It's a work of genius!' Then he played the dances of Cleopatra and gave the same exclamations and expressions of delight." The breaking off of relations with Balakirev coincided with a period of difficult family troubles for the composer and added much more unhappiness to Rimsky-Korsakov's emotional life at that time.

9

"I Fell Out of Love with Music," 1891–1892

I'm looking at the future of Russian music in general and the young Russian School in particular with great doubtfulness and distrust [...] I'm certain that it is already showing its age or at least it will grow old rather soon.

—Rimsky-Korsakov to Semyon Kruglikov, 1892

In February 1891 the third act of *Mlada* was performed successfully in concert. After the concert the board of the Imperial Theatres decided to stage it at the Mariinsky Theatre. But this did not bring Rimsky-Korsakov much joy. The composer was in low spirits because of several recent sorrowful events: the sickness and losses in his family and the clash with Balakirev. Owing to the illness of their youngest daughter, Masha, the family decided to spend the summer in Switzerland. Having received a leave from the Chapel for two months, Rimsky-Korsakov and his wife and children left for Lucerne. They stayed at the Hotel Zonnenberg, forty-five minutes' walk from Lucerne. The hotel was located at an altitude of 800 meters (2,625 feet) above sea level. It had a beautiful view of Lake Lucerne and other lakes in the valley, as well as the snow-capped peaks of the Alps. Then the Rimsky-Korsakov family went to Engelberg, in the central part of the country. But the weather there was so bad that they moved to the Italian part of Switzerland, next to Lake Lugano.

During his stay in Switzerland, Rimsky-Korsakov did not compose anything new. He just completed the orchestration of several of his romances and began to work on a third version of *The Maid of Pskov*, since he did not like either the first or the second version. At the beginning of August Rimsky-Korsakov returned to St. Petersburg, leaving his family at the Zonnenberg. On his way home, he wrote to his wife: "Dear Mama,[1] I'm writing to you at the railway station in Frankfurt. I have two spare hours and I got the desire to kiss you all by this letter." He sent another greeting card on his way home: "Dear Mama, I'm in Berlin and extremely bored. I arrived at 5:30 and I am leaving at 11. I have nothing to do at all. I walked along Unter den Linden, tried to go to the Tiergarten, but I don't like anything. Today is Sunday. All the shops are closed; I can't even buy an umbrella. There are crowds on the streets as in St. Petersburg on the Nevsky Prospect. I had to walk slowly."

Nadezhda wrote back that they were settling down well at the Zonnenberg:

> It's good that we are here again, there is only one thing…it's so sad to be without you. We are enjoying wonderful views here and you, poor boy, are still traveling and traveling, becoming tired, exhausted and all alone. I climbed a mountain a little today to look at Mount Pilatus and suddenly I felt as dull as ditchwater and I even cried a little. I'm looking forward to your letter. [...] Good-bye. I'm kissing you heartily, my darling. Take care of yourself and pay more attention to yourself. Could you write as often as possible?

Rimsky-Korsakov was in a terrible mood. By the end of his journey the weather was very poor, and it was raining hard. Upon his arrival in St. Petersburg he wrote:

> My darling Nadya,
>   [...] On reaching the border, I felt the usual disappointment: everything is plain, poor, and gray. [...] I found Petersburg also much too official and unattractive (the same as Berlin, by the way). I can't but think of mountains and hills, vivid surroundings and villages, beautiful water and clear blue sky. [...] I imagine Volodya and Andrey skipping to the lake and you and Nadya roaming in the woods. [...] Sweet Volodyaka burst into tears when I was leaving! I hug you and kiss you.
>   Your N.
>   P.S. Misha, take care of mother!

By that time, Misha had finished high school with a silver medal and had become a student at the Department of Physics and Mathematics at St. Petersburg University. As soon as the composer received his wife's letter from the Zonnenberg he answered her: "Now I can follow your life in my thoughts.

I imagine the children playing with Lily; you walking in the woods and on the slope of the hill with Nadya; you admiring the view and watching the trains appearing at Lac Rouge; the bells of Krisne and Lucerne; at last you all sitting together at table. If you lived in another place everything would be unclear for me, hazy, and because of this I would be worried."

Nadezhda was worried about her husband's mood and about his lack of desire to compose. She tried to encourage him:

> My darling Nika,
>
> I'm so glad that you arrived in Berlin safe and sound. Now I'm looking forward impatiently to receiving your letter from St. Petersburg. It's much better to know that you're at home, though it's a pity you're so far away. You must certainly feel the same, but I calm down with the thought that maybe being alone and free you will compose something new and nice and will restore what you tore up, to my great grief, in Frankfurt. I'm growing especially sad when I go for a walk due to the fact that you're not here.

Soon Nikolay sent another letter: "Balakirev is on vacation starting today but actually he is going to leave only in two days. [...] I'm as meek as a lamb with him, fulfilling your wish. But it seems I have never had a greater desire to leave the Chapel than now. Should I be servile to an insane person and play with toys instead of carrying out business? We'll talk about this when we meet. I kiss the children. I hug you, my darling."

Rimsky-Korsakov was living in Peterhof, but he traveled to St. Petersburg and visited the Smolensk cemetery. He informed his wife: "The tombstone is ready. I ordered them to edge the tombstone with turf and plant some flowers, so by 30 August Grandma's tomb will be ready." In accordance with his mother's wishes, the tombstone was very plain, made of marble with an engraving.[2] The first anniversary of Sophia's death was approaching. On that day Rimsky-Korsakov arranged a church service to sanctify the new tombstone to be placed on the tomb.

The composer continued in the same letter that Balakirev was still in Peterhof, that he had not left yet, although he was already officially on leave, and that Balakirev still visited the Chapel occasionally "and certainly received reports from his spies. I won't tell him anything, as he could always answer that he is on vacation since 9 August, as he told me already. But I'll try to set

Lyudmila Shestakova upon him, who will write to him something like: 'Mily, I love you, but you've pulled a swinish trick.' Or something like that."

His next letter was about his visit to Glazunov at his summer house in Ozerki, where they walked in the Shuvalov Park and passed the church where the Rimsky-Korsakovs were married, and rode on a steamboat on the lake.

> I have a lot of good memories, but nature is still gray, the water is gray, even the grass is gray, the trees are somewhat short and thin, the foliage is scanty. Peterhof is the dullest of places: the "barn" of an English Palace, the choristers and my barn of a room. The only thing that entertains me is my occasional trips to St. Petersburg. And today I'm going there. I'll visit the theatre and find out about *Mlada*. [...] I haven't yet undertaken anything, even *The Maid of Pskov*. [...] The music that I happened to hear didn't impress me at all. Glazunov asked me to correct the proofs of his *Oriental Rhapsody* and I'm doing this with great laziness. I don't like this composition. I began reading *Anna Karenina* (!) [...] By receiving your letters every day and with my awareness of the conditions at the Zonnenberg I feel somehow that you're all right. It's vexing that if it were not for that strange growth of Balakirev's bossy arrogance, I might have been with you till today. You ask about my cough, it's in absolutely good order, i.e., it's as usual, neither more nor less. [...] I'm always anticipating 10 a.m. anxiously, as that's when they bring the mail.

Approaching Crises

Nadezhda was worried about the problems at the Chapel caused by her husband's clash with Balakirev. She wrote that she would be very glad if her husband left the Chapel: "How you would enjoy today if you were here! The weather is marvelous: hot, clear blue sky, all the snowy peaks are unimpeachably pure and exceptionally pretty, as they have even more snow after the last snowfall. At sunset everything was bright pink. [...] Why did this repulsive B. steal so many days from you? We could have been together the whole week! [...] Good-bye my dear, I'm so glad that you write to me every day." Indeed, Rimsky-Korsakov began each day writing to his wife, and then he attended to the Chapel affairs and worked on the schedule of classes for the coming term. He gave up composing music completely. He did not touch the piano or even edit *The Maid of Pskov*. He wrote:

When I was abroad, I thought that I missed music. And now it's turned out that I don't need it at all. I don't know why it's happened. There is a railway timetable for St. Gotthard with pictures of Monte Generoso, which you know well, on my desk. I like to look through it very much. It reminds me of all of you, and of our life abroad and all those wonderful places we've visited. I must have become so lazy, I don't do anything. Well, I'm reading *Anna Karenina*, but it doesn't count. [...] Kiss Andrey for his being affectionate, Volodya for his being a nice boy, Nadya for her remembering me, and Masha for her being a sweet girl. [...]

P.S. Misha, take care of mother. Tell Andrey and Volodya to behave themselves on the way back home.

Nadezhda responded: "It's very bad that you don't undertake writing any music and do not walk. I don't believe that you have suddenly become lazy. I think you're just not in a good mood; but you should try to adjust yourself." Shestakova wrote to Rimsky-Korsakov that Balakirev had visited her and she told him, "Haven't you left? If not, then why did you separate Korsakov from his family? Only God knows why!"

Rimsky-Korsakov had still lost his enthusiasm for music. He attended the rehearsals of the choral parts for *Mlada* at the Mariinsky Theatre and shared his opinion with his wife:

It's so strange! I listened to the choruses of *Mlada*. They sang well and the choruses sound good, but I remained absolutely indifferent to my own composition. I disliked it! All in all, I notice a great change in myself after my trip abroad. I had a rest and I fell out of love with music, and everything I hear now I don't like. I listened to *The Kremlin* [by Glazunov] played for four hands—it's boring. I proofread the *Oriental Rhapsody* of Glazunov—it is petty and worthless. The romances and a quartet of Sokolov are cold and lifeless. To make a long story short, beautiful harmony, complications, melodic phrases do not touch me. Everything seems cold and lifeless to me. *Mlada* is as cold as ice. But a quartet or a symphony of Beethoven is quite the opposite! The techniques and development here are structural, and there is life and soul running throughout the whole composition. I can say the same about Chopin and Glinka and (just imagine!) about the Italians with their sextet from *Lucia* and their quartet from *Rigoletto* and all their tunes. Indeed, there is life there! "La donna è mobile"—this is music, but Glazunov's [music] is only technique and has a conventional beauty that conforms to current fashion and tastes. I think that part of the Russian School is not music itself but consists only of cold and clever inventions.

Beethoven, Glinka, Chopin, the Italians, and certainly many works of other composers such as Schumann and Haydn (you can understand me) are not tobacco; you can't grow out of them. But the Russian School, with minor exceptions, is just like the tobacco habit. I probably should not compose having thoughts like this; on the other hand, if my thoughts are correct then I'd better give up. Certainly, you never should interfere with events; everything will be cleared up by itself. But I think at this very moment a considerable amount of truth comes out of my mouth. My heart, don't have any regret about my tearing up the notebook in a fit of stupid anger and that I can't remember its contents now. Really, everything that was written down there is not worth a pin, as they were samples of undesirable invention.

The same evening Rimsky-Korsakov continued:

I was the whole day in the "lovely" English Palace and early in the evening went to St. Petersburg to spend a night in better surroundings and to eat tastier food since the meals of our choristers might otherwise become boring. When I wrote to you about my thoughts concerning music in the morning, I didn't mention Liszt or Wagner. I haven't heard the compositions of the former lately, so I can't predict exactly what impression they will make on me. I think that his *Danse macabre* will keep its full strength, but about many of his compositions I would feel cold breath, I'm sure. Of Wagner I heard part of the songs of the Rhine Maidens from *Götterdämmerung*, which Glazunov played. It's lovely. I think that the forging of the sword and many other compositions, such as the Allegro from the overture to *Tannhäuser*, would impress me in any case, but they are just small parts of the music that burn brightly; all the rest would seem brainy, speculative, and cold. However, I should test it.

I'm afraid that during my time abroad I did not take enough of a rest from music, I did not grow out of it enough. If I had not heard [music] for even a longer time, I might have developed a much more refined taste, or, it's better to say, a more refined perception; that kind of perception which is able to distinguish God's divine spark from a simple oxygen compound.[3] They say putrefaction and oxidation are also burning. But there is a difference. I remember that until today I liked all the compositions of Glazunov. I could find shortcomings in them—prolixity, exaggerations—but I couldn't understand how others were not able to like many of his compositions. And that happened because others' sharp perception of God's divine spark had not been deadened, and mine didn't exist at all. God's divine spark can exist even in an operatic melody. Strauss has it to the highest degree. Taste and the spirit of the time, fashion and a relatively noble style are quite different terms. However, we often confuse the ability to satisfy these terms with God's spark. Look what came out of me! You might even become annoyed with me. I have been talking to you about this issue, but it's impossible to say everything in a letter.

My darling, my heart, Nadyushonok, mother, Mama, good-bye. I kiss you on the eyes.

Rimsky-Korsakov was expecting the arrival of his family and was happy to be seeing them soon. As usual he worried about their journey back to St. Petersburg. In his last letter to them, which he had already sent to Berlin, where the family had to change trains, he wrote:

You're leaving today and I became frightened for you. Certainly I don't think that something bad might happen to you, but I imagine: you don't take care of everything; you don't sleep the whole way; it might become cold; conductors might be rude; and then Russian customs; currency exchange—all this will make you anxious. Poor you! Poor Mama! Russian rail carriages are large, and they might put strangers there who would demand that the windows be opened when it's impossible, and so on and so forth. Be healthy, my dear. You should notify me at what hour you're arriving at St. Petersburg.

The composer received another blow from Balakirev. Balakirev cut his salary in half because Rimsky-Korsakov had moved into a government apartment. The composer discussed the issues that occupied him in a letter to Kruglikov:

My relations with M. A. [Balakirev] are the same, hostile in essence, but seemingly decent though not always. During the summer I had a complete rest and did not compose anything and became rather cold to Russian music (but certainly not to everything). I'm interested in *Mlada* just a little, more as if it is my duty. Do you know what Russian music does not possess?—Soul. And Beethoven has a great soul. Beethoven is the greatest and the most wonderful composer. You think,

"Here is a wonder indeed!" Yes, it's a wonder. Whenever I'm listening to the Eighth Symphony in the orchestration class, for the thousandth time in my life, or I'm playing some pieces of the first sonatas for my students to draw their attention to the form, I feel I'm being filled with this wonderful music. What a flame, a life, and a soul! Glinka is also wonderful, and Chopin as well. Do not think that I just reject all the rest bluntly; nothing of the kind. But the younger generation of musicians, indeed, has little value.

The composer began working again on the second revision of *The Maid of Pskov*, but he still did not compose anything new. Simultaneously he undertook the editing of Musorgsky's opera *Boris Godunov* with the hope it would be approved for performance in the Mariinsky Theatre. The opening night of *Mlada* was rescheduled for the 1892–1893 season at the Mariinsky Theatre.

Since the autumn of 1891 Yastrebtsev had become a frequent guest at Rimsky-Korsakov's house. He described his first visit as follows: "13 October 1891. At last the day I was longing for has come. Certainly I was so anxious that I could not sleep all night. At last, the thing for which I have been striving for several years in vain is to occur. It was just some minutes past 10 in the morning when I rang the bell of apartment 66 [the apartment of Rimsky-Korsakov]. I won't describe that state of bliss I experienced on that notable morning; I just will say that never had I been happier in all my life. All my cherished wishes had been granted." During the visit Yastrebtsev did not discuss everything he would have liked to know about Rimsky-Korsakov's opinions—but almost everything. He wrote: "It was time to go, but I was sitting and sitting. I felt awfully good. I can't believe it. Sometimes common mortals are granted such utterly happy moments! At 11:45 I forced myself to get up and said good-bye. Rimsky-Korsakov saw me out, helped me with my clothes, and said, 'You are welcome. If you should have the desire to discuss something you can visit me informally any time. I will be glad to see you and talk to you.'"

In the spring of 1892 Rimsky-Korsakov wrote to Kruglikov that he had finished reediting *The Maid of Pskov* and had been dealing with the editing of *Boris Godunov*, *The Stone Guest*, and *Sadko*:

You see that I've done a lot of new (!!!!!) things and will do more. Hence, I'm teaching, studying myself, giving instructions, and being instructed myself; I'm getting angry at many things but I'm taking an objective view of many others. I'm developing and nursing a feeling of utter disgust for Balakirev (with much success). I'm looking at the future of Russian music in general and the young Russian School in particular with great doubtfulness and distrust, or, even better, I'm certain that it is already showing its age or at least it will grow old rather soon.

The Rimsky-Korsakov family spent the summer of 1892 again in Nezh-govitsy. The composer was still not in a creative state of mind and did not compose anything. According to the words of Nikolay Sokolov, "There was some notable change in him. [...] N. A. has been gradually losing interest in everything. He became bored and languid. One could notice the notes of unusual exhaustion in his voice when he spoke either officially or in private conversation. [...] Soon he began complaining about [...] being incapable of composing any longer."

Rimsky-Korsakov turned to the issues of aesthetics and philosophy. He meant to write about aesthetics in music. Since he considered himself insufficiently knowledgeable on this topic, he became engrossed in studying the works of Hanslick, Lewes, and others.[4] He wrote several articles about music, musical education, and musical creative work. He found Sokolov to be an attentive listener and a good conversationalist with whom he could discuss the issues that interested him. Sokolov reminisced later: "First our topics were limited to art. [...] We exploited our imaginations to the fullest extent, trying to solve aesthetic mysteries. But we did not even notice how we became involved in other issues in other fields. [...] With the courage of dilettantes we came into a vicious circle dealing with taste and reasonableness, license and concealment, [...] aimless existence and perfectionism, holiness and divinity." All of these complicated issues intrigued the composer. Sokolov asked himself whether this continuous, restless, and infinitely persistent work of the composer and his slaving for others was an instinctive attempt to flee, to hide from the "damnable questions of life."

Illness

At the end of August 1892 Rimsky-Korsakov's intense work caused him to experience some disturbing symptoms: the composer felt some strange surges in his head; his thoughts became confused; he lost his appetite; if he stayed alone he became occupied with unpleasant obsessions; he became interested in religion; and he thought of making peace with Balakirev. The composer recalled later: "One bright morning I felt extremely exhausted followed by some surge in my head and utter confusion in my thoughts. It made me very frightened." Nadezhda pushed him to cut off all his philosophical studies. It helped. According to Rimsky-Korsakov, he returned to St. Petersburg "sane." Despite the doctor's advice not to undertake any more studies, the composer resumed his philosophical studies and zealously read the works of Hennequin, Spinoza, and Spencer.[5] He again became obsessed with the idea of writing his own book.

At last, on 20 October 1892, the first performance of *Mlada* took place at the Mariinsky Theatre. The house was packed, and the opera was a great success. According to Yastrebtsev, Rimsky-Korsakov received fifteen curtain calls and five wreaths: the largest one was from his friends, and then there was one from Shestakova with a sash that she had woven herself, one from the Muscovites, including Kruglikov, and two more from some young composers, including Yastrebtsev. After the performance Rimsky-Korsakov's closest friends gathered at his apartment. The following day the artists of the Mariinsky Theatre gave a dinner in his honor at a restaurant called the Bear. There were many toasts; the most surprising one was given by Pogozhev, the manager of the board of theatres, who called the opera-ballet *Mlada* an "archaeological" one. The score of this opera is extremely complicated, and, as the *New Times* noted, the composer should consider himself really fortunate since no other theatre could have performed *Mlada* as well as the Mariinsky. In spite of its success, however, the opera met strong opposition in the press and from season ticket holders, who mostly belonged to the elite and did not like *Mlada*. One woman subscriber asked Tchaikovsky his opinion about *Mlada*; he answered: "Certainly, as the general audience is foolish and undeveloped in terms of art, they do not like this composition. Meanwhile, for us musicians, there is much to listen to and to learn from [*Mlada*]."

Rimsky-Korsakov's health and emotional attitude had not improved. He became extremely exhausted and absentminded. Once while speaking to Yastrebtsev he couldn't remember the title of his own opera *The Snow Maiden*. Another time he asked Yastrebtsev why he had not come to see him in his room after the concert, when indeed Yastrebtsev had visited him and spoken to him. As the physician Alfons Erlicki said at the time,[6] Rimsky-Korsakov's whole body had become seriously imbalanced and his multiple sclerosis was progressing, which caused his depression and led him to believe that he was incapable of composing. Soon after the new year the composer wrote to Kruglikov:

I can tell you that these days I'm busy curing myself, under the doctors' guidance certainly. The treatment is to be long: I should take iodine, move about as much as possible, and the most important thing is not to do anything. As long as the odd surges in my head still occur I have to be continually examined by doctors. They have diagnosed overexertion and prescribed the treatment I mentioned above. I have to continue with this treatment until the summer; in the summer they are going to examine me again and prescribe another treatment for the summer; then in the autumn they are going to examine me again and then ????
If you ask me what I've been doing, I [will] answer I'm walking out in the frosty weather for hours; in any case the air is very bracing for me. I wonder if it is doing me any good.

The sicknesses of his family members also continued to discourage him from composing. Andrey was ill again, Masha was not getting any better, and his wife had an earache.

At the end of January 1893 the Bolshoi Theatre in Moscow was preparing for the opening night of *The Snow Maiden*. Rimsky-Korsakov left for Moscow several days before opening night. He went straight from the railway station to the rehearsal at the Bolshoi Theatre. There he was introduced to the artists, and the orchestra played a flourish. He was very satisfied with the artists and the orchestra and he shared his impressions with Nadezhda in a letter:

The Snow Maiden as an opera made a very good impression on me. I can say that those who don't like *The Snow Maiden* do not understand my compositions at all nor me. I will tell you (in confidence) my purely biased opinion: *The Snow Maiden* is the best opera after Glinka's and not only among Russian ones but in the world. Everything in it is good; it is theatrical, musical, and balanced. Don't consider this as conceited. However, those who like it and praise it, and find it nice, fresh, etc., do not appreciate it enough or value it enough, since they do not comprehend to what degree it is expressive, picturesque, sincere, and beautiful; and at the same time it is successfully constructed and harmonic in every way. In addition, it is huge. It does not possess anything pretentious, showy, exaggerated, or overemphasized. I do not know how it happened that, its author having relatively little talent and artistic temperament, managed to compose the opera to be as it is, but it's true. If you don't agree with my opinion of *The Snow Maiden*, well, maybe you will one day. This luck with *The Snow Maiden* I can explain only by the fact that its plot was exceptionally well matched to my sensibilities and that I undertook composing it when I had become fully developed. I couldn't compose anything like it again. *Mlada* is already on the decline, in spite of its great brightness: it gives off light but not heat, with the exception of some pieces. [...] I remembered you often during the rehearsal. It's such a pity you're not here.

Rimsky-Korsakov had a very busy schedule. He wrote to his wife:

Today I'm going to listen to the children's orchestra of Erarsky at noon, then at 2:30 p.m. I'm attending a concert of the Russian Musical Society (Safonov has invited me to his box);[7] in the evening I'm listening to *May Night* (they decided to perform it for me), and after the opera I'm having dinner at the Hermitage [restaurant], which is organized by Mamontov and his former singers who performed *The Snow Maiden*. Tomorrow I'm having dinner at Safonov's; in the evening I'm likely to be at the theatre with Pryanishnikov. On Wednesday [the morning after opening night] the artists of the Bolshoi Theatre have invited me for breakfast. I'm going to catch the 4 p.m. train and arrive in Piter at 9:10 a.m. Don't forget to prepare my court dress coat, a rapier, and a waistcoat. I'll have to rush to the Sheremetev Palace as soon as I get home and change my clothes. It's a disaster!

But all of a sudden Nadezhda arrived unexpectedly in Moscow and attended not only the opening night of *The Snow Maiden* but the following breakfast in honor of her husband as well. On 29 January the sixth performance of *Mlada* took place at the Mariinsky Theatre. Although the ordinary public liked it, it was the last performance of the opera. Gennady Petrovich Kondratyev,[8] the general director of the Mariinsky Theatre, wrote in his diary that the opinion of the tsar's court was against *Mlada*: "It's just sheer happiness that this opera has ended! These words described the impression received about the opera." *Mlada* did not please the tsar's court.

Rimsky-Korsakov shared his thoughts with his close friend Kruglikov in a letter dated 1 February 1892:

> Dear Semyon,
>
> I'm sure my letter will surprise you. I ask you to keep the information to yourself for some time. The thing is: (1) I've been thinking for a long time of abandoning my service at the Chapel. On 2 February 1892 I will have served at the Ministry of Court for ten years and will receive the right to resign with a considerable pension. At the same time I feel a growing moral necessity to leave the Chapel, where I'm not able to do anything else useful, having done everything I could already. At this moment I feel only the impulse to resign. (2) The business at the St. Petersburg Conservatory is moving toward disaster: you can't even imagine what kind of slumber, laziness, and hopelessness rule there. (3) The group of St. Petersburg musicians (the former Mighty Handful) is entering a new stage that seems to be alien to me.[9] (4) All in all I am feeling the need for some kind of renewal, in other air, and less dark and cloudy winter days. I think I will become cheerful in other surroundings; maybe I would begin to compose again, and so on. You know that I love Moscow, not only because of its meat and fish pies but also for its somewhat more youthful and energetic life.
>
> You Muscovites think the opposite; however, we St. Peterburgians can see it more clearly, as we know very well our tired and listless St. Petersburg. It's not just my own opinion. Moscow produces the same impression on others as well, for example Repin. I wish I could leave the Chapel, move to Moscow (take an apartment in one of the side streets), and become a professor of the Moscow Conservatory, for which I think I'd probably be a good match. [...] Don't you find all this strange? I wish to become a Muscovite at the end of my term, I wish and that's it! The same is true of my wife. We long for something new. The old is unbearable.

The composer began negotiations with Balakirev about his resignation. Balakirev promised to do his best but asked him not to submit the application till autumn. At the same time Rimsky-Korsakov's mood seemed to be improving. He wrote to Kruglikov again:

> My dear Semyon,
>
> [...] We are not going to move to Moscow. But why not dream of it for two or three days? And now it's time to deal with reality. And this reality is that—try

as I might to part from the Chapel, I still can't abandon it. I'd better stop being a milksop, unwell, annoyed with Balakirev, and start working. That's it. It's very easy to do something stupid and impulsive, but then it would be impossible to correct it. Indeed, the grass is always greener on the other side. But it's still true that St. Petersburg is good for nothing. However, you can do business here, and it depends only upon yourself. In one word, it just [depends on your] morals, and [if you have] any morals [they] are in any case good for something.

Rimsky-Korsakov kept on working in the field of the aesthetics of music, and he was writing his memoirs as well. At the end of February 1892 a musical evening was held at Rimsky-Korsakov's house, and many people gathered there. Some pieces from *Mlada* were performed. Alexandra Molas sang several romances. The composer received several guests on his birthday: Belyaev, Lyadov, Sokolov, Glazunov, and an unexpected one, Antokolsky, a sculptor. They finished only at about 3 in the morning. At the end of March the composer's wife left with her youngest daughters for Yalta to spend the summer there. She took with her Olga Mragushina to help her with the children. Olga had been living with the Rimsky-Korsakov family for several years as a tailor and housekeeper. This journey was thought to be essential for Masha's health. The next day after their departure Rimsky-Korsakov wrote to his wife:

My darling Nadyusha,

No sooner had you gone than we became very sad. We spent the whole evening yesterday in a strange mood. We colored eggs and then had tea with snacks at 8 p.m. The children went to bed early. Everything seems to be as usual except for that unusual emptiness and silence that has come upon the whole house. Masha is not misbehaving, Nadya is absent, but the heart of the house is gone, i.e., you are not here. I was thinking about you the whole evening: how you were traveling, what stations you were passing through. I imagined how anxious you would be, how you must be frightened for Masha and constantly busy with something. She might have a fever; she might be sad that her doll was left at home. The first is unfortunate yet is normal, and the second would soon be over, much ado about nothing; you are torturing yourself because of that. At night you must be too worried to sleep, so you are just dozing off from time to time, and nothing can help you. Today we got up early. The Easter cakes turned out to be delicious, and the eggs are pretty.

Nadezhda sent greeting cards home on her journey, whereas her husband kept on writing letters every day to her in Yalta. "When in the summer I return to an empty house I do not feel such a kind of emptiness as I feel now. In the summer the apartment just seems to be a barn, empty premises and nothing more. But now it is not a barn, but our home, and the family is here, and so the lack of your presence is seen so strongly and unpleasantly."

Visit to the Studio of Ilya Repin

In those days Rimsky-Korsakov regularly had to visit Repin's art studio, which was located not far from St. Petersburg's Kalinkin Bridge. Repin was working on a portrait of Rimsky-Korsakov ordered by Belyaev. The artist managed to depict Rimsky-Korsakov's appearance as he looked in that difficult period of his life, in a state of exhaustion and depression. Later, after Belyaev died, the portrait became part of the collection of the Russian Museum in St. Petersburg.

To play in a trio with his younger sons was a kind of relaxation for the composer. Volodya took violin lessons, and Andrey took violoncello lessons. But even playing in the trio did not prevent Rimsky-Korsakov from thinking constantly about his wife, about her difficult trip, her worries about Masha, and her being emotionally worn out. Nadezhda, the girls, and Olga took the train to Sevastopol, then traveled by ship to Yalta, where they settled down in the premises of Dr. Veber's boardinghouse. Their cottage was not far from the main building, which was completely occupied by sick people. Nadezhda wrote home to her husband in St. Petersburg:

> Our little cottage has four rooms and four balconies. It's surrounded by trees, but they are still completely bare. The rooms are small but cozy. The furnishing is very simple. It reminds me of the typical furniture of summer houses: the wardrobes are old, the lockers have no keys, the curtains can't be lifted after they have been drawn as the cords are too short, etc. There is a water closet here now as well as bells to call for service. It's good that we are all living separately and attend the common dining table only for lunch and dinner, and in the mornings and evenings they bring a samovar to the house for us, so we have tea and coffee at home. They have been bringing all of the meals to our house for Masha.

Moreover, Nadezhda got a terrible cold, which made Rimsky-Korsakov extremely worried, and he wrote:

> I've decided that I will send you a telegram from time to time (for example, once a week) with a prepaid response. When we are living in St. Petersburg we buy some fancy sweets sometimes or allow ourselves some extra entertainments, and in this case, when we are apart, recent news is a necessity. If I don't ask about Nadya, it's just because she is assumed to be healthy. Masha is our poor sick girl and you are a mother-martyr. [...] I embrace you, my dear. The most important thing is you should be calm and healthy.

Nadezhda could not attend the common dining table for some time, and they had all their meals in their cottage. She was very glad about this situation, as the people who sat at the common dining table were not the best company. As she wrote to her husband: "There are only sick people around. One is absolutely voiceless, he can only whisper. The other is coughing awfully and spitting. All the women are thin and pale. However, the hostess is nice, lovely and easygoing."

On the other hand, the family members in St. Petersburg were occupied with different activities. Misha was taking examinations for his second year of study at the university, and Sonya was cramming in preparation for her final examinations at the private school of Stoyunina.[10]

Rimsky-Korsakov sent some news about himself in a letter to his wife:

> I've been writing a little about aesthetics during this week. But I've decided to give it up as I'm at my wits' end and I don't have any strength to cope with it and meanwhile I'm feeling tired. I have wound up all my writings and put them aside. I talked a lot with Repin about it. He advised me to write separate notes and write down my thoughts without any system, something like a diary. It really might be easier and better if I do it at odd moments. And in the manner I've conceived to do it, it's just impossible and it's harmful for my head. In any case I've decided to postpone this writing for a while and to undertake something interesting to distract my attention, namely working on *Boris*. It will force me to forget about my interest in philosophy and my search for the beginning of all the beginnings. I've been taking iodine since yesterday and I will be taking it until I leave for Yalta. Sigh. I hope to get your letter as soon as possible.

Nikolay Andreyevich Rimsky-Korsakov, 1900.

Mitrofan Petrovich Belyaev, a music publisher and leader of a musical circle that included Rimsky-Korsakov, 19 December 1887.

Lyudmila Ivanovna Shestakova, Mikhail Glinka's sister, who met Rimsky-Korsakov at Vladimir Stasov's birthday party in January 1866.

The program of the concert dedicated to the twenty-fifth anniversary of Nikolay Rimsky-Korsakov's musical activity, 22 December 1890.

The menu of the 22 December 1890 dinner celebrating Rimsky-Korsakov's twenty-fifth anniversary as a composer.

В честь

Н. А. Римскаго-Корсакова.

SOUPER

du 22 Décembre.

Hors-d'oeuvre riches.
Consommé Borschok.
Diables et Rissolles.
Turbot de la Manche, sauce crevettes.
Cotelettes maréchal aux truffes.
Glace Caroline.
Café.

Top: The composer's study in the last apartment in St. Petersburg used by the family after the summer of 1893.

Right: Vladimir Ivanovich Belsky, who began writing librettos for the composer after 1895.

Top: The main house at the country estate at Smerdovitsy, where the Rimsky-Korsakovs spent the summer of 1896.

Right: Nadezhda Ivanovna Zabela, Princess Volkhova in Rimsky-Korsakov's opera *Sadko*, in 1898.

Left: Drawing of Nadezhda Nikolayevna Rimskaya-Korsakova by Elisabeth Boehm, 1898.

Bottom: The Rimsky-Korsakov children in 1900. Left to right: Andrey, Vladimir, Nadezhda, Sophia, and Mikhail.

Soirée of the art and music critic Vladimir Stasov, 1902. Rimsky-Korsakov and Glazunov are standing at the back, far left; Fyodor Chaliapin is singing behind the pianist; César Cui, in uniform, is leaning against the piano at the center; and Stasov is sitting in peasant costume.

The main house in the country estate at Krapachukha.

The Rimsky-Korsakov family—two parents and five children—at Krapachukha, 1903.

Nikolay Rimsky-Korsakov in
the park at Krapachukha, 1903.

A Cold and Windy Spring in Yalta, 1892

The spring of that year was unusual for the Crimea: cold and windy. Masha was to be kept indoors. Nadezhda wrote on 5 April 1892:

> Thank God, at last today is sunny and +10° [50° F], although the wind is still strong and cold. I allowed Masha to spend some time on one of the balconies that is covered with canvas and so is more protected from the wind than the others. She had a 38.2° [100.8° F] temperature yesterday. [...] I set her down onto a chair, put a warm blanket over her legs and we stayed there for a half an hour. [...] Now I'll tell you how we've settled into our house and how we are spending our time here. I sleep in one and the same small but cozy room with Masha, Nadya sleeps in the next room, which is nearly the same as ours. We keep our doors open at night so that we can see each other lying in bed. The next room is a kind of living room, and then across a little corridor there is Olga's room. It is narrow and small but it has everything she needs. In the morning about 9 they bring a samovar and coffee for us and milk for the children. They drink it as they are served and I come at 9:15 to have some myself; and then I'm occupied with Masha. After noon we are served lunch in our rooms, and at 6—dinner. After lunch I write letters to you and usually it takes me a lot of time, as Masha disturbs me every minute. [...] Every day Mrs. Verber [the doctor's wife] visits us, sometimes even twice a day. I'm very grateful to her for her attention to us and her kindness. After 8 we are served tea. Masha has her milk earlier, at 8 p.m., and goes to bed, and then Nadya goes to bed at 9. I read in the evenings, but I fall asleep here much earlier than in St. Petersburg. I'm feeling so well now that I have already forgotten about my being sick. [...] For God's sake, don't worry and don't study too much, otherwise I'll be constantly worrying about you. I'm so glad that I receive letters from you every day.

Nadezhda, who looked so slim and fragile, in fact seems to have had a very strong constitution and faced everything with fortitude. Even so, while she tried to be cheerful, she needed her husband badly: "Oh Lord, I wish you could come sooner!"

Nadezhda often related humorous episodes in her letters to her husband:

> The doctor asked for some paper to write out a prescription. (He is keen to prescribe as many absolutely unnecessary medications as possible, and he made a

huge list of them.) I was lying in bed. Everyone was searching for some paper. The room was in a mess. They couldn't find anything suitable. At last they gave him a piece of paper. He wrote on the whole page, turned over the paper to write more, and found there was a goose drawn there. Masha and I had drawn it the day before. Laughter and again searching for paper. [...] The weather turned absolutely crazy. Yesterday there was a storm. I woke up today at 8 a.m., the sun was shining, I lifted the curtains and—everything was covered with snow! The temperature is just +2° [36° F], and in our rooms as low as +10° [50° F]. [...] Good-bye my darling, my sweet, I'm kissing you thousands of times.

The house they were residing in was in fact not suitable for such cold weather. The walls were thin, and the four balconies let in drafts. Despite the fact that they heated the house well, it became very cold by the morning.

Nadezhda regretted not seeing the portrait of Rimsky-Korsakov that Repin was working on. She asked her husband whether he was pleased with it and what his opinion of Repin himself was. She was very worried about his health and wondered how he was feeling. The composer responded:

I haven't been thinking about philosophy or aesthetics much this week. I have orchestrated the girls' chorus sung in Marina's dressing room [the character from the opera *Boris Godunov*]. It was not difficult, but it helped to keep me away from my philosophical thoughts. My head is still not always clear. I can't decide what causes my feelings of being unwell: tiredness, stomach problems, lateness going to bed, or annoyance. In any case there is nothing really bad, and it even seems to happen less often now than before. I think that when I come to you in the Crimea I will recover. We should only walk more there.

Rimsky-Korsakov was very busy in St. Petersburg:

Beginning today I'm dealing only with examinations for the next two weeks: from 9 a.m. to 1 p.m., then from 2 till 5 or 6 p.m., I have to go to the Conservatory to give lessons that I missed giving in the morning. In a word, I have free time only from evening tea till the time I go to bed. You shouldn't worry about me, though it won't hurt me since those activities make one tired only from their being boring and monotonous, but they are not tiresome for my head. [...] Don't think that my worries about you made my situation worse. It's not like that.

On 13 April he wrote again:

> The past two days, although I was very busy, I've been feeling well and I don't
> have any of the same occurrences in my head. I think that teaching is useful for
> me, or it's my usual state, to which my head and my body have become adjusted
> for a long time. It seems that I must not be cut out for all those books on
> philosophy and aesthetics. What have I done this year? I just spoke and spoke,
> talked and talked. I'm an old chatterbox, and that's it. If you try to read my
> notes, you will see they are the notes of a mad Poprischin.[11] In order to do
> research in this field you should start it when you're young or have had a good
> background. And in the manner that I did it, it's not worth the effort. I become
> tired after examinations, but this weariness is of a healthy kind and I even have a
> desire to undertake some music, despite the fact that all day I've listened to wrong
> notes on the violin. Volodya is taking his examination in a day (on Thursday)
> and our merry boy is anticipating it with pleasure. Sweet Volodya!

Volodya's examination was to be on playing the violin. His teacher was Vasily
Zolotarev, a graduate of the Chapel.

About Repin, Rimsky-Korsakov wrote: "He is very nice and intelligent.
I've discussed art with him very much, and his views are not odd or awkward
like Stasov's. My portrait is unlikely to be completed before summer. The
portrait is very true to life. He is putting the final touches on the face now
and the canvas is covered completely."

Meanwhile, his wife was witnessing her daughter suffer with her illness:
"My dear Nika, I don't even know what to write to you. Everything is the
same, the same boredom and misery. Masha is not getting even a little better—
the opposite: in my opinion, she is getting worse. [...] She is coughing much
more now, and her breathing is becoming more labored. [...] She is usually
merry and cheerful before dinner, but that is a poor consolation."

The weather in the Crimea was still awful. Nadezhda began to wonder
whether it had been a good idea to take a sick child so far away from home if
it resulted in exposing her to such unpleasant weather. Would it have been
better to stay in St. Petersburg? She wrote: "The most unfortunate and unhappy
idea was to come to this damned Yalta, where the climate has turned out to be
so bad. I do not know when it will be possible to escape from here. I wish we
could go to Italy." The doctors tried to calm her down, saying that it would

take time for any improvements and that they had to be patient. But Nadezhda was desperate and could not think of anything but Masha's condition. Nikolay wrote to his wife:

> My dear Nadya,
>
> Your letter made me very sad. If the reason for your being depressed was just your missing the children and me, we could cope with this, as I feel the same. But it is aggravated by poor Masha's condition. It is a waste of time staying so far from home, and the inconveniences of that life, which is not improving her health at all. […] It is very good of you to speak frankly about your thoughts and your mood. You should not pretend to be joyful when you are far from being so. […] You seemed as if you did not wish to go there, as if you did not trust the doctors' advice, and it seems you were right. You're always right in such cases, being guided by some unerring sixth sense.

Nadezhda reminisced to her husband that they had been in Yalta before, under other, more fortunate circumstances: "Do you remember how happy we were here the last time? But I am sure when you come to us it will be better here again. I received your letter in which you called yourself an old chatterbox. It is not true, and don't you dare to talk like this. I am kissing you right on your lips. Kiss the children for me." He responded: "My heart! It is awful that you are there all alone. Certainly, you will be in a bad mood if Masha feels so bad. I am dying to flee to you for a while, but it seems impossible. My heart, don't become desperate, maybe everything will be all right."

Repin suggested that Rimsky-Korsakov's children come and see the portrait. Sometime later they visited Repin, and they liked the portrait very much. In 1895 this portrait was exhibited at the Peredvizhnaya (Mobile) Exhibition. Volodya and Andrey passed their examinations well, in violin and violoncello, respectively. The composer made an arrangement of the song *A Birch Was Standing in the Field* for them with different variations, as he had heard them try to play it by ear. He wrote to Yalta: "Don't think it's a real composition. It's just a thing to amuse and entertain them."

Rimsky-Korsakov's wife still could not send any good news. Masha was getting worse. Nikolay tried to do his best to support her: "My darling Nadya, I received your sad letter today. […] Indeed, I cannot but become upset due to the sad news. Masha's situation is very bad, and there are still no benefits from your staying there. How awful it must be for you to comprehend everything and endure everything being so far away!"

Rimsky-Korsakov was longing to join his wife, but his work at the Conservatory did not yet allow him to leave St. Petersburg. He was still debating with himself whether to leave the Chapel or stay. He thought he might teach a class in orchestration starting in the autumn. When Balakirev learned his intention he sent a letter to Rimsky-Korsakov in which he asked him not to do this, under the pretense that the composer's health was poor, his nerves were strained, and those classes would only be harmful for him considering his propensity to become extremely irritable. Rimsky-Korsakov understood that Balakirev was hinting at his desire to part from him. Nadezhda agreed with her husband: "I also interpreted Balakirev's thoughts about your health in this way. This is a kind of way to get rid of you. I think you have to resign."

The Loss of a Daughter

As time passed, Nadezhda's mood changed, along with Masha's condition. Even the slightest reduction in the fever, which was constantly higher than 38° C (101° F) and sometimes ran as high as 39° C (103° F), was the cause for some hope; but every time that hope was illusory. The thought of her husband arriving soon encouraged her. She was anxiously counting the days before their meeting. She urged her husband to join them, the sooner the better: "Everything is the same, the same bad situation. Masha is not getting better. The weather is cold. Masha did not go out today. Her fever is 38.6° C [101° F]. Come sooner. It's getting unbearable for me to stay here alone." And the next letter:

> My dear Nika,
>
> I can't stand being here anymore. Yesterday I didn't write everything on purpose; but today I can't but write you everything as it's too unbearable for me. I cannot keep it to myself any longer. From the doctors' opinions, I understood that Masha is not going to recover, and I am afraid that here, in this damned Yalta, she has become infected by consumption. [...] The infection has already moved from her lungs to her intestines; that means she cannot be cured. So why should we stay here? It is always better to die at home than in a strange, faraway land. We'd better get away from here before we are all infected with consumption. [...] It

was unforgivable stupidity for me to agree to bring a sick child here, so far away from home. It has turned out that we brought her here to perish. I am writing all this to you as I am feeling so awful, more terrible than I have ever felt before. Please, forgive me if I'm writing nonsense to you.

Masha's doctor, a Dr. Verber, spoke to Nadezhda, trying to console her, and persuaded her not to give up hope. But the picture was clear to her now. She wrote to St. Petersburg: "Now I'm inseparable from her. I do not leave her side for a second. I feel so sorry looking at this poor sweet girl. And she is so diligent: she is constantly busy with something, now she is sewing a dress for her doll. We call her Nadya's governess, as she is constantly making remarks to her at table and they are always reasonable. She herself behaves perfectly at lunch and dinner. She is such a kind, beautiful girl."

Meanwhile, the children who were home in St. Petersburg were still occupied with their examinations. Rimsky-Korsakov wrote to his wife:

> Yesterday Sonya passed her last examination successfully, with a C in Russian. She is pleased, and I am very happy for her. I decided to congratulate her on this occasion and presented her with *Les Huguenots*, which she had been dreaming of. [She had begun studying singing some time earlier.] Andrey passed a written test in Russian yesterday. We do not know the result yet, but it seems that everything will be all right. Today he is taking an examination in the Russian and Slavic languages (an awful exam). It is a pity to leave the children, but I am dying to see you. Good-bye, my darling. I hug you.

This letter, dated 11 May, was the last before his departure for Yalta. He arrived in Yalta on 16 May 1892. His leave, which officially lasted for two months, was prolonged for another month until 20 August owing to his own poor health. Masha's condition had not improved by the time he arrived, and the parents were unable to decide whether they should attempt to return to St. Petersburg. The composer wrote to his eldest son:

> To insist on returning to St. Petersburg right now means depriving Mama of the last hope. On the other hand, if there is no hope, in any case we ought to do our best to lengthen the life and postpone the end. [...] Certainly Masha is the center of our world now, and the main figure is Mama, so I will only assist in whatever

mother is going to undertake. And she will act as she feels is best at that moment when she will have to make a decision.[…] I cannot do anything these days. I wander about the room or sit down and smoke like a chimney. I undertake this or that and give it up as being unnecessary.

The day when Rimsky-Korsakov was required to depart for St. Petersburg was approaching. Misha and Sonya came to Yalta to replace him. On 20 August the composer left for St. Petersburg, but en route, in the northern Ukrainian city of Kharkov, he received a telegram that Masha had died. He went back to Yalta and sent a telegram to the Chapel that his leave would have to be prolonged. Having buried Masha in Yalta, the family returned to St. Petersburg and then to Taitsy to spend the rest of the summer there.

On 6 September Yastrebtsev wrote: "On my way to the bank, I saw Rimsky-Korsakov in the distance, going to the Conservatory. He looked very worried, his eyes were looking off somewhere into the distance, seeming to see nothing. My first impression was that he's lost some weight."

Parting from the Chapel

Rimsky-Korsakov's intention to separate himself from the Chapel remained, and he began looking for new accommodations. In mid-September he submitted an official memorandum to Balakirev: "At present I am living in a government apartment.[…] My family—my wife and my children, as well as I myself—have been repeatedly sick, and two of my children have passed away. There is a cold corridor in the apartment that is the source of all the illnesses. Moreover, almost all of the stoves produce smoke indoors.[…] Therefore, I plead for permission to leave this apartment and move to a private one." His service in the "devout but bigoted Chapel," as the composer called it, was getting more and more unpleasant. Rimsky-Korsakov considered it to be harmful to his health due to constant irritation. He wrote to Kruglikov sometime later:

> Since last year I've been suffering from overexertion, which is related to my arterio-sclerosis, from which I have started to suffer too early for my age.[…] Everything about the Chapel is disgusting for me, that is, all its rules and regulations. My relations with Balakirev are more than just cool. I can tell you that nothing

extraordinary has happened recently. However, my disgust with everything that occurs there is gaining momentum. Generally, I have nothing to do there; I'm ill-suited for the position.

Once the decision to depart from the Chapel had been made, Rimsky-Korsakov had to go through all the official formalities. He informed Kruglikov about his resignation:

> They are gossiping about my leaving the Chapel. They blame Balakirev, suppose that there has been a quarrel, etc. The formal reasons I'm doing this are as follows: I do not feel well and I'm exhausted. I have thirty-three years of governmental service and am leaving because of sickness. This gives me a considerable pension plus the additional bonus granted to me by His Majesty on my twenty-five years of beneficial service to Russian music. I will free myself from service in order to have time to spare for composing without being overexerted. Don't you think these reasons are well grounded?

Stasov in his turn wrote to Kruglikov:

> R.-Korsakov has parted from the Chapel! I think it's just awful! That is what poor Rimsky-Korsakov was forced to do by the behavior of this canting hypocrite and false Christian Balakirev. He has been torturing and haunting him for several years in a row. […] And all of it just because he has lost his previous prestige and power over the new Russian music school. […] By the way, I should mention that R.-Korsakov is just worn out and exhausted. He has become drawn into some kind of mysticism during the last year! He urgently needs to get back to his old self.

10
Return to Musical Life

If only you composed again! Now I am sure that for me there is no ideal real music but yours. It would be very sad if you had just six operas.

—Vladimir Belsky to Rimsky-Korsakov, 1896

In the late summer of 1893 the Rimsky-Korsakov family rented a new apartment in a building on Zagorodny Prospect, with its premises located in an inner courtyard so that noise from the street did not bother them. Rimsky-Korsakov was the first to move in on 19 September. The family was still in Taitsy and was reunited in the new apartment on 30 September. The sunny, spacious rooms, the quiet surroundings, and the trees visible from the windows, together with the end of his Chapel responsibilities, helped the composer to regain his needed peace of mind and to revive his aspirations, According to Sokolov's memoirs, "Rimsky-Korsakov again was cheerful and in good spirits, laughing and telling jokes carelessly. He repeated the old saying 'a trumpeter should trumpet, a fiddler should fiddle,'[…] which implied that 'a composer should compose.'"

The largest room in the apartment served as a living room; the next one was converted into a dining room. They put a grand piano in the living room, hung portraits of Russian and foreign composers on the walls, and arranged the furniture comfortably. The dining room was decorated with family portraits, including those of Nikolay's and Nadezhda's ancestors. The study of the head of the family was arranged in a room having a common wall with the corridor. There was a desk at which he composed. (He never composed at the piano; he used it only for playing his compositions.) There was a desk for the composer's wife where she made arrangements of his operas for voices and piano and assisted her husband with the correction of his proofs. The composer's desk accommodated many items: the old travel clock he had inherited from his mother; the inkpot with a gilded plate presented by Uncle "Oh!"; photographs of his wife and children; a small ornamental box brought by his brother, Voin, from the Far East; a blotting pad presented by Shestakova; piles of books; a lamp with a special cap to protect his eyes from the glare; and a bulky ashtray shaped like a dragon.

The day after they moved into the new apartment, the Rimsky-Korsakov family received their first guests: Yastrebtsev and Nikolay Shtrup. The latter was a student of the faculty of mathematics at St. Petersburg University. He had been fond of Russian music since his early years. He was a stepson of V. I. Lomansky, an academician, and he organized meetings of a student musical circle in his stepfather's house. Rimsky-Korsakov's compositions occupied first place in that circle. Yastrebtsev joined Shtrup's circle when he was a student at the Technical College. For his part, Shtrup was a private teacher of Rimsky-Korsakov's children Andrey and Volodya, and therefore visited his family quite often.

A Busy Musical Life

Rimsky-Korsakov's musical life soon became very active. He started to conduct Russian Symphony Concerts again. This was prompted partly by a tragic event. In November 1893 Tchaikovsky died in St. Petersburg. It happened soon after his Sixth Symphony was performed for the first time. Under such circumstances, Rimsky-Korsakov considered himself morally obliged to play the music of the deceased composer in his honor. The new season of Russian Symphony Concerts opened with a concert consisting exclusively of Tchaikovsky's compositions and conducted by Rimsky-Korsakov.

Rimsky-Korsakov had submitted a letter of resignation [from the Chapel —*Eds.*] on 3 November 1893, but he was not released from his duties until 19 January 1894. Two days later the official farewell meeting was held. His colleagues greeted him with a loaf and salt in a silver saltcellar on which were engraved the dates of his service in the Chapel.[1] Balakirev sent a letter of thanks. However, he did not come to say good-bye to the person who once was his beloved student and friend. Here is the text of his letter:

Highly Respected Nikolay,

I am very sorry that my being unwell does not allow me to attend the farewell party organized by the Chapel in Your honor. Owing to this, I am addressing You in writing to express my sincere gratitude for Your ten years of hard work on the inspection of the music classes in the Chapel. If the deceased Lvov began them, then You are the second founder, since the music classes we founded in the Chapel a decade ago did not meet the requirements of the time in any way; therefore, there was an urgent demand to set them right.

You carried out the task You had been entrusted with brilliantly. Now, due to Your industrious service, the Chapel has perfectly organized music classes with a curriculum equal to Conservatory courses. Your name will remain forever in the history of the Chapel and will occupy one of the most honorable places there.

The next day Rimsky-Korsakov visited Balakirev. According to the words of Nadezhda, which were recorded by Yastrebtsev, "Balakirev was happy to see Rimsky-Korsakov and they even kissed each other. Suddenly Mily's behavior changed beyond all recognition. He even offered him tea." Yastrebtsev asked himself: "Is it possible that they will become friends again?"

On 21 January 1894 Rimsky-Korsakov, being disappointed in his results so far, burned all of his papers concerning aesthetics.[2] At the end of January Rimsky-Korsakov left for Odessa, accompanied by his wife, where he was to conduct symphony concerts. Upon his arrival there was a concert in his honor in the building of the Stock Exchange, organized by music students of the Odessa branch of the Russian Musical Society. After the concert he and Nadezhda were invited for a special dinner. Nadezhda described it in her letter to her eldest daughter: "There were many toasts very flattering to Father and even some in my honor. One gentleman spoke for a quarter of an hour and described in his toast all of Father's musical life. All this is good, but I was very bored. The society was absolutely unknown and might be insincere, and I don't like such special dinners in general."

The concert took place on 12 February 1894. Nadezhda wrote that they "were invited to a ceremonial dinner but luckily managed to decline the invitation." At that time the mayor of Odessa was Pavel Zeleny. He was a former naval officer and the captain of the clipper *Almaz*, on which Rimsky-Korsakov sailed after graduating from the Naval Academy. Neither the officers nor the cadets had liked him, to say nothing of the sailors. He was rude and mistrustful. He did not flog them but had them beaten with fists and otherwise abused. Rimsky-Korsakov reminisced: "I wouldn't have been glad to see him; fortunately for me, he was away on business." The ceremonial dinner, which the Rimsky-Korsakov couple escaped, was given by Zeleny's wife.

Nadezhda continued in her letter: "I'm very worried about today's concert. They had fewer rehearsals than before the first one. [...] However, Father is exceptionally patient and calm. Thank God he has such a moderate temper."

The trip to Odessa refreshed Nikolay. By 6 March, his birthday, he was in good spirits. The first music meeting was held that day in their apartment. Twenty-five people attended, including Lyudmila Shestakova, who was quite old by that time but looked young for her age.

Christmas Eve

A month later there was a performance of *May Night* in the Molas household. This opera had finished its run on the stage of the Mariinsky Theatre much earlier. During the performance, Rimsky-Korsakov was struck by the idea of composing a new opera on the plot of another Gogol tale—*Christmas Eve*. He undertook the writing of the libretto by himself. Soon he had the first draft of parts of the new opera. He kept his work secret for some time, but eventually the desire to share it with one of his friends defeated him. In the beginning of May, Yastrebtsev, Shtrup, and P. A. Trofimov, a music critic, paid a visit to the composer. Without revealing the secret, Rimsky-Korsakov played the prologue he had composed to the new opera on the piano and asked them to think what it might have been. As Yastrebtsev recorded: "We all decided that the music depicted a clear, cold, starlit night and serene silence."

After this Rimsky-Korsakov revealed the secret, but he did not want to make it public. He responded to a letter from Kruglikov:

> Dear Semyon, I'm so sorry! But when I'm beginning to compose a new opera I grow rude, ungrateful, capable of a small or moderate amount of swinishness, and so on. And I'm occupied with a new opera. But I won't tell you the title as I am not telling it to anyone and I ask you to keep this knowledge secret. And for this reason, that is, being infected with some swinish behavior, I did not respond to you. And even now it's not really a response; just a hello and I shake your hand in my thoughts. I wish you and your family all the best.

A Summer in Vetchasha

As was his custom, Rimsky-Korsakov composed mainly during summers. That year the Rimsky-Korsakov family for the first time spent the summer in Vetchasha on the estate of S. M. Ogareva. This estate was located in one of the most picturesque areas of the Luga region. A long time before, Vetchasha had been an estate of the Tatishchev family.[3] The estate was purchased later by Fyodor Ogarev, a colonel and a remote relative of the poet N. P. Ogarev. It was bought in the name of his wife, Sophia. The vast park of Vetchasha consisted of a low ridge along the bank of Lake Pesno, which had a great number of very old trees. The shady alleys, sunny meadows, and fruit orchard were very attractive. Bushes of white, pink, and crimson roses flourished there. The main house, which Ogareva let to Rimsky-Korsakov, stood high above all the others, as it was at the top of a hill. The manager of the estate was Martyn Strauss, a perfect estate manager. Sophia lived in Vetchasha with her son Mikhail and daughter Maria. Her other daughter, Anna, was by now married and lived in Pskov, but she too came there for the summer. Sophia was old and so nearsighted that she was unable to recognize a person at a distance of more than two or three steps and even to distinguish a man from a horse. Mikhail, the son of the property owner, seemed to be mentally unfit. They said that he had lost his mind due to an unhappy love affair when he was young. Although he was very meek and peaceful, he had a reputation as a skirt chaser. To nineteen-year-old Sonya he used to say, "If I were the sun I would incinerate you."

Rimsky-Korsakov reminisced about Ogarev's estate:

> Vetchasha is a lovely place: the wonderful large Lake Pesno and the huge old orchard with century-old lindens, elms, etc. The house was sturdy and built awkwardly, but spacious and comfortable. [...] The swimming there was wonderful. At night the waters of the lake clearly reflected the moon and stars. There were many birds. I was the one who found the estate, and I liked it at first sight. There were two villages nearby: Zapesenie and Polesno. There was also another estate, Loubensk, which belonged to Mrs. Bukharova. The forest was a little far away but beautiful.

It was raining hard on the day of their departure. The composer's wife, Nadezhda, and the children had to ride about twelve miles in carriages in heavy rain from the Plussa station on the Warsaw railways, so her first impression of Vetchasha wasn't good. She even hesitated whether they should go any further or return straight away. Andrey joked that they might have returned to St. Petersburg on the same train. Rimsky-Korsakov wrote to them: "We are all right here. I feel good but I'm missing you. The weather is outrageous!

What terrible luck! I'm waiting for Misha's arrival impatiently to listen to his story about your journey. I can imagine how sad you are. I kiss everyone."

The next letter said: "My dear Nadya, Misha arrived and told me how you all got wet. It's awful. But I suppose everything was all right in the end."

Soon after his return, Mikhail went to Solovki to work at the local biological laboratory for the whole summer. Rimsky-Korsakov stayed in St. Petersburg, as he had to give examinations in the Conservatory. Nadezhda wrote to her husband from Vetchasha:

My dear Nika,

We have settled in well here. The summer house is very comfortable and spacious. The landlords are surprisingly attentive and courteous. If I just hint at some kind of request they fulfill it immediately. It's a pity that the weather was awful. [...] The orchard is beautiful. There are many wonderful old lindens there. They have put some gym devices in the yard and all the children hang on them almost all day long, including Sonya. Today a queer thing happened. Yesterday Sonya sang and I played "Cherevichki" ["Shoes"] and everything was OK. Today in the morning Sonya sat down at the piano and started singing and beating the keys—no sound at all. Sheer sorcery! That is, all the notes sound as if ten left pedals are being pressed. [...] We don't know how to fix it and are very upset that we're left without a piano. Mulbakch might have sent us a spoiled one.

However, Mulbakch was not to blame. The Rimsky-Korsakov family rented a piano for the summer from him every year. This piano had a moderator, and Nadezhda did not know how to use the device. The next letter continued the story:

Andrey restored the piano by accident. He happened to move a screw near the keys and everything was made to work by some magic. We were absolutely happy about that. To be without a piano in this awful weather would just be a disaster. The children make me play their favorite operas: *Igor*, *Mlada*, etc. Today I took out some sonatas of Beethoven and played them several times with great pleasure. But our children don't like this kind of music very much. For me these sonatas are very dear, not only because of their beautiful music but also because they remind me of my childhood. They carry me away to that happy time.

When Rimsky-Korsakov came to Vetchasha, he devoted almost all of his time to the composition of *Christmas Eve*. He also spent some time walking and swimming. Yastrebtsev, who visited him there, made the following note: "Today our company, including Rimsky-Korsakov himself, climbed trees and played games after evening tea.[…] In the morning, about 7:45 a.m., Rimsky-Korsakov was already swimming."

The Legend of Sadko

In the spring Rimsky-Korsakov received a letter from Nikolay Findeisen, a historian of Russian music and the publisher of the *Russkaya muzikalnaya gazeta* (*Russian Musical Gazette*), in which he suggested that Rimsky-Korsakov should think of composing an opera on the legend of Sadko, which Rimsky-Korsakov had used a long time ago for the composition of his symphonic poem for orchestra (1867). Findeisen believed the story was perfect for an opera. The draft plan for a possible opera was enclosed in the letter. Rimsky-Korsakov liked the idea and he was inclined to challenge himself with composing it. He said later that he was occupied with composing his opera *Christmas Eve* in Vetchasha but that some thoughts concerning *Sadko* also occurred to him there. "I remember that the place where ideas about *Sadko* usually struck me was a long wooden path from the shore to the bathing house by the lake. The path went through the reeds. There were huge bent willows on one side and a beautiful view of Lake Pesno on the other side. The scenery encouraged me to dream of *Sadko*."

When Stasov found out about that, he wrote to Rimsky-Korsakov in excitement: "Dear, dear, dear, and ten thousand more times dear Nikolay! That's it! Are you composing two operas at the same time? Well, I'm applauding and happy for You. All decent people would be. Look at […] Beethoven: this man wrote his Fifth and Sixth Symphonies simultaneously. My excitement rises to triple fortissimo.[…] And I'm sure it will be Your super fundamental work, Your Ninth Symphony."

Rimsky-Korsakov responded: "I'm not composing two operas, only one— *Christmas Eve*. And I will compose *Sadko*.[…] You missed the fact that I've already composed my Ninth Symphony—it's my opera *The Snow Maiden*."

By the time he returned to St. Petersburg, the preliminary draft version of *Christmas Eve* had been almost completed. Rimsky-Korsakov reported to

Kruglikov: "I have spent the whole summer in the remotest place. And as you will see, I've worked out quite a lot. I wrote to you before that I was undertaking the composition of a new opera. The idea came to my mind on 10 April, and on 16 August the opera in four acts, nine scenes was completed (certainly only in draft). My opera is based on that very tale of Gogol's, *Christmas Eve*."

Nikolay's revived activity as a composer was a great source of joy for many people. Shestakova even held a special dinner to celebrate the completion of the new opera *Christmas Eve*. Rimsky-Korsakov presented his new opera at the end of November at his own house. Glazunov, Stasov, Lyadov, Belyaev, Yastrebtsev, Shtrup, the Molas family, and some other people were there. Yastrebtsev noted: "The music started about 9 and finished at 1 at night. There was only one long interval between the third and the fourth acts. It lasted more than an hour, and we had tea during it."

Glazunov remained indifferent to the opera. In his opinion, it was unsuccessful. Stasov was dissatisfied as well.

In November 1894 Anton Rubinstein died. His remains were placed in the Trinity Church, and a twenty-four-hour honor guard was organized. At night on 16 November Lyadov and Rimsky-Korsakov stood guard of honor over Rubinstein from 2 a.m. to 3 a.m. The first Russian Symphony Concert of the season was held to commemorate this outstanding musician. Rimsky-Korsakov conducted the concert.

The end of 1894 was marked by the performance of the complete opera *The Snow Maiden* in Rimsky-Korsakov's apartment. Several performers from the Mariinsky Theatre and a chorus made up of eight singers participated in the performance. E. K. Mravina, a famous soloist of the theatre, sang the part of Snow Maiden, and a famous string player, A. V. Verzhbilovich, performed the violoncello solo in Berendey's cavatina. There were about eighty guests at the party, and the hosts presented flowers to each actor before the performance. The guests were served tea, sweets, and fruits in the intervals. Shestakova provided a great deal of assistance in arranging the party. The guests left late at night.

Now Rimsky-Korsakov was concerned to see that his new opera was performed on the stage. He decided to offer it to the Mariinsky Theatre. It was accepted, but there were some difficulties with censorship. The main problem was that Empress Catherine the Great was among the set of characters in Gogol's novel, but it was forbidden for members of the Romanoff imperial family to be shown on the stage. Rimsky-Korsakov understood that there would be some problems: in his libretto he had omitted the empress's name, and instead of St. Petersburg, he called the city "The Capital." Despite all his precautions, the censor claimed that everyone knew this novel of Gogol and that the empress was obviously Catherine II.

In mid-December Rimsky-Korsakov was at a reception held by Prince Vorontsov, minister of the Imperial Court. He informed Rimsky-Korsakov that Balakirev was going to resign and offered Rimsky-Korsakov the post of general manager of the Chapel. However, Rimsky-Korsakov declined the offer and wrote to Kruglikov: "I just want to be free to compose." He also informed Balakirev about his refusal: "I'm telling You this as I think You will be interested in this information."

During the reception, the prince was in high spirits. Rimsky-Korsakov decided to take a chance and asked him to solicit the tsar's permission for the opera *Christmas Eve* to be staged at the Mariinsky Theatre. The prince promised to assist, and he did indeed keep his word. On New Year's Eve a carrier delivered an official letter: "On the report submitted by you to the Minister of the Imperial Court and on His petition, His Majesty grants the petition. Your opera *Christmas Eve* has obtained permission to be staged at the Imperial Theatre without any changes to the libretto. 31 December 1894."

Rimsky-Korsakov was delighted. That day he made an inscription on a cover page of a new notebook: "*Sadko*. Epic Opera in five acts. 31 December 1894. 1 January 1895. Draft." The composition of the opera proceeded rather quickly. Yastrebtsev wrote on 24 April: "I found Rimsky-Korsakov in high spirits. His opera is growing." Unfortunately, ten days later Rimsky-Korsakov complained to Yastrebtsev about his multiple sclerosis, which he had diagnosed himself, and about an abnormal heartbeat.

That year the family moved to a summer house earlier in the season. On 12 May 1895 Nadezhda together with Andrey and Nadya left for Vetchasha. Rimsky-Korsakov himself arranged for the household utility items to be sent to the summer house by going to the railway station. The next day his wife wrote to him: "My dear, you might be worrying about us. You should not. We have arrived safe and even without rain. Indeed, the clouds moving above were heavy, but they just frightened us. We did not even hear any thunder, and it just drizzled a little. The road is dry and, because of this, very hard. Certainly it is not very pleasant, but it is much better than we had to experience last autumn. We didn't have any difficulty in finding horses."

Nadezhda and Andrey rode in one carriage and the servants in the other. Nadezhda wrote:

> The driver of the second carriage was drunk, and he went to drink more in Kotorsk, where they were supposed to have a short stop; so they arrived much later than us. […] The weather today is as it was yesterday: heat, clouds all around, but no rain. The air is wonderful. Nature is in full glory. The bird-cherry trees are fading, but the lilac is in full bloom, and the cherry trees look as if they were covered with snow, they have so many flowers on them. The apple and pear trees are simply blossoming. Andrey found some lilies of the valley in the garden. […] Now it is the most beautiful time: there are plenty of birds in the garden, and the young green foliage gives a balmy air. And you must be languishing in nasty Petersburg. It is a pity and sad that we are not altogether. Big kisses and all the best. Take care of Volodya.
>
>   Your N.

Volodya had been staying in the city with Rimsky-Korsakov since he took his examinations at the gymnasium. At the end of May they also left for Vetchasha. Rimsky-Korsakov brought many new musical materials with him for his use in the composition of *Sadko*. In addition, they invited a private tutor for the boys' education there. The tutor's name was Henrich Kal, a student of Tartu University in Estonia. He turned out to be a passionate chess player and became Andrey's customary chess partner. Later Andrey even played blind-folded with several players simultaneously after this intensive practice with Henrich. Sonya, Andrey, and Volodya liked riding horses; Zybka was their favorite, the fastest of all the horses in the Strauss stables. Misha graduated from St. Petersburg University that spring.

By the middle of August Rimsky-Korsakov had almost completed *Sadko*. He played several pieces from the opera to Vladimir Belsky, with whom he had become acquainted in the winter in St. Petersburg. Belsky was a well-educated and highly intelligent person, an expert in Old Russian literature and an admirer of Nikolay's music. He was fond of Russian and Arabian fairy tales, legends, and epic poems, and of the works of Pushkin, Lermontov, and Zhukovsky.[4] When Belsky was just eight years old he tried to compose poems, and he started a family literary magazine, *My Leisure*. He began studying at the St. Petersburg classical gymnasium at the age of eleven. By nineteen he was well-read in literature. He graduated from the law school of the St. Petersburg University, then studied mathematics and foreign languages at the same university. By the end of his term he could speak fourteen languages. Maria Chertova, his godmother and a brilliant pianist, gave him music lessons and imparted to him extensive knowledge about Western and Russian composers. When he was a student, he saw performances of *May Night* and *The Snow Maiden* at the Mariinsky Theatre, which impressed him greatly. Vladimir Belsky and his brother Rafail became regular attendees of the musical soirées held by the Rimsky-Korsakovs. Belsky became very excited about the music of *Sadko*. Rimsky-Korsakov discussed the plot of the opera with him, and they were struck by a new idea: to add a new character to the libretto—Loubava, the wife of Sadko. Rimsky-Korsakov asked Belsky to assist him in adding this new part in the libretto. It was the beginning of their collaboration, after which Belsky became the librettist for Rimsky-Korsakov's operas.

Upon returning to St. Petersburg, Rimsky-Korsakov became utterly immersed in the life of the city, but he kept on working on *Sadko*. He wrote to Kruglikov: "You are amused that I'm composing operas as if I were frying pancakes. […] I feel as though I am a lazy student who is cramming before his exam. It is completely possible to pass that exam perfectly when you exceed the age of fifty. I did little, I idled much, I wasted too much time; now I should think of my soul; that means composing what I can and what I'm good at as much as possible. So, I'm composing."

The director of the Imperial Theatres was very pleased that imperial permission had been granted, and he wanted to stage an elaborate performance of *Christmas Eve* in hopes that the court would like it. Despite Rimsky-Korsakov's protests, he ordered the tsarina to be dressed exactly like Catherine II, and the scenery to represent the capital itself, including the Peter and Paul Fortress with its cathedral.

The first dress rehearsal took place on 20 November 1895. The princes Vladimir Alexandrovich and Mikhail Nikolayevich attended the rehearsal. They were outraged that Catherine the Great appeared on the stage and that the Peter and Paul Cathedral, where their ancestors were buried, formed part of the stage scenery. Vladimir said to the actress who played the part of Catherine the Great, "I see that you are my grandmother now." They demanded that the opening night be canceled. However, the first performance was planned to be a benefit performance devoted to O. O. Palechek, an expert of the stage. To save the performance Vsevolozhsky offered to replace the part of the tsarina with that of a prince (!). Rimsky-Korsakov had to agree, although he did not like the idea. He said to Yastrebtsev, "Indeed, they'd better ban all of Gogol's works along with my opera. Then at least I will not be tempted to compose based on his tales." The Rimsky-Korsakov children attended the opening night, whereas the composer and his wife went on a trip to the Islands (a district of St. Petersburg). They found out about the opera's success from their children. Yastrebtsev visited them after the performance and brought them the laurels given by admirers. Most of the reviews were unfavorable. N. F. Soloviev, a critic, considered the opera blasphemous: stars were dancing on Holy Night, the comet was shown as a beautiful woman, and the church reader, who was singing sacred music, was flirting with Solokha. The opera was performed only a few times. It would not be staged again during the composer's lifetime.

Smerdovitsy, Summer 1896

The year 1896 brought another sad event: Uncle "Oh!" died. During the summer of 1896 the Rimsky-Korsakov family had to lease a house in Smerdovitsy, the estate of Baron Tisengausen, since the Ogarevs did not let their house that year. Rimsky-Korsakov wrote:

> In Smerdovitsy the main house was rather, I can say even too, spacious for my family. There was a beautiful park next to the house. The other surroundings were not at all interesting. The wood was sparse, plain and full of tussocks, and it had many stumps. The lake was small, and the water in it was very cold, which prevented us from swimming much. There was a railway line about eighteen hundred feet away from the house and we could hear the sound of trains.

The past winter, with all its worries and hard work, had exhausted Rimsky-Korsakov, and the trouble he had had with the staging of *Christmas Eve* discouraged him from working on *Sadko*. Fortunately, upon moving to Smerdovitsy he was in high spirits and began working on *Sadko* again. Moreover, he was also busy making a new orchestration of *Boris Godunov*. The summer did not leave the family in peace. Nadezhda wrote to Stasov: "Hardly had we settled down when Volodya became sick with the measles. In two weeks Nadya also became sick with it. So I spent time looking after the sick and worrying about them.[…] Moreover, we like the surroundings and the house itself only a little."

Stasov responded: "You seem to experience trouble with your summer house. And I am, on the contrary, very pleased with my stay here.[…] Pargolovo is my favorite place. I have been coming here for fifty years already.[…] Yes, I'm like that bulldog who keeps a thing between its teeth firmly if it grabs it once. Think, for example, about yourself and Nikolay. You are something like Pargolovo for me. And I'm sending my love and friendship to you, my dear Pargolovo."

To make things worse, the landlord of their apartment in the city, where the Rimsky-Korsakov family lived, decided to remodel the house, and Rimsky-Korsakov had to go to St. Petersburg several times to look for a new place to live. Fortunately, circumstances changed, and the family was able to stay in their home. Despite all of the obstacles, Rimsky-Korsakov completed his sixth opera. Belsky was in Vienna at the time and sent a letter to Nikolay: "The dearest, invaluable Nikolay! […] Oh, dear! How impatient I am to hear some news from you concerning your next opera. I'm even itching to find out what plot you would like to use....If only you composed again! Now I am sure that for me there is no ideal real music but yours. It would be very sad if you had just six operas."

Boris Godunov

In January 1896 Rimsky-Korsakov offered Vsevolozhsky, the director of the Imperial Theatres, the opportunity to stage *Boris Godunov*, which he had nearly finished revising, at the Mariinsky Theatre. Vsevolozhsky did not dare to give a response immediately and said that he would need to obtain the highest permission for this. Thus, he promised to discuss it with the tsar as soon as he had occasion. Sometime earlier Tsar Alexander III had deleted from the repertoire of the Mariinsky Theatre an opera that Musorgsky had submitted. According to Vsevolozhsky, this time Tsar Nikolay II frowned and said: "Oh, no. We do not need this opera yet. It is all just the music of Balakirev's school."

It looked as though *Boris Godunov* could not expect to find its way to the Imperial Theatres anytime soon, so Rimsky-Korsakov decided to raise funds for its production with the assistance of the St. Petersburg Society of Musical Gatherings. Not long before the society had staged *The Maid of Pskov* quite successfully. Yastrebtsev recorded the words of the composer: "While I'm collecting money I will orchestrate this opera to spite everyone. And I will do it especially well. It will be my revenge." He worked quickly. On average he produced twenty-three pages of orchestration per day. When Musorgsky composed his *Boris Godunov*, he and Rimsky-Korsakov were especially close and even shared the same apartment. Musorgsky was composing his opera virtually before Rimsky-Korsakov's eyes. His memories from that time helped Rimsky-Korsakov to relive the artistic atmosphere during this period of Musorgsky's creative work and to recreate the main features of his music.

Only six days after the private subscription was opened, Rimsky-Korsakov had already received 1,500 rubles in subscriptions. Pretty soon the sum totaled 2,600 rubles, including the amounts given by Belyaev (500 rubles), Counts Alexander and Sergey Sheremetev (900), Glazunov and his mother (300), and Shestakova and Yastrebtsev (100 rubles). Moreover, Yastrebtsev's mother claimed that if there was a deficit, she would cover it at her own expense. Rimsky-Korsakov refused to take money from Stasov, who offered 100 rubles. The thing was that many musicians thought that Musorgsky's opera should be left in the author's original version, and Stasov was one of them. He was annoyed that Rimsky-Korsakov had edited *Boris Godunov*. In the summer Rimsky-Korsakov wrote to Yastrebtsev that Stasov had ranted and raved after seeing that he had changed the recitatives. Stasov screamed that Rimsky-Korsakov did not have the least idea about them, and that only Musorgsky and Dargomizhsky had mastered them. When Glazunov said that Rimsky-Korsakov was certain to know something about the music, Stasov yelled, "To hell with the music! How do you like it?" Later it was found that the sum of the private subscriptions of 3,000 rubles was exceeded by the sum of 6,000 rubles received from the ticket sales.

Rimsky-Korsakov began to rehearse the opera with the performers and the orchestra. All of the soloists, who were performers in the Imperial Theatres, sang for free. They were not supposed to participate in private performances, and they had to ask special permission from the board of the Imperial Theatres. Vsevolozhsky wrote in his memorandum to the office of His Majesty: "Due to the fact that the performers are not pursuing any monetary rewards in this case, but only the enthusiasm of the group, I do not see any reason to deny the request. [...] Moreover, I hope that the audience will realize, at last, that the new Musical Society is going in the wrong direction."

Count Sergey Sheremetev donated the scenery. Prince Sergey Volkonsky provided the performers with new costumes. Palechek was in charge of the production. The Russian Musical Society allowed the use of the Grand Hall in a new building of the Conservatory for a moderate fee. The St. Petersburg Conservatory used to be on Theatre Street and now was expected to move into a new building.[5] After the first dress rehearsal, at which many musicians and people connected with the world of music were present, Stasov changed his opinion completely. Yastrebtsev wrote: "Stasov seems to be absolutely captivated. When he met Rimsky-Korsakov he kissed the latter for *Boris*."

Now Stasov started telling everyone that Rimsky-Korsakov had indeed performed a great service in honor of Musorgsky, a heroic deed. "How amazing it is!" he said to Yastrebtsev after the rehearsal. According to Glazunov, it was one of the bravest things Rimsky-Korsakov had ever done. Knowing the whole opera by memory, he set himself the goal of achieving in the music the power that he had heard so many times when the composer played it on the piano to such perfection. As Glazunov described it, the composer, a musical magician and wizard, had carried out this task using all his talent and skill and completely as a volunteer.

Opening night was on 28 November 1896, two weeks after the new building of the Conservatory was opened. Rimsky-Korsakov conducted. The part of Boris Godunov was sung by Mikhail Lunacharsky, the part of Varlaam by F. I. Stravinsky. The opera was staged perfectly. The costumes were beautiful, and even the fountain on the stage was real. It was a tremendous success. A group of young people presented a silver baton to Rimsky-Korsakov with the inscription: "28.XI.1896. The work bequeathed by God has been completed." A problem occurred in the orchestra that Rimsky-Korsakov solved in an unusual way. During the first performance a musician playing the tam-tam missed the beat occasionally, but during the next performance this was corrected. In the second performance Rimsky-Korsakov played the tam-tam himself in the orchestra, and M. A. Goldenblum conducted in the place of the composer. There were four performances altogether. In one of them, Rimsky-Korsakov's twenty-year-old daughter Sophia sang the part of a nurse. M. D. Kamenskaya, a famous actress at the Mariinsky Theatre, attended one of the performances. When Rimsky-Korsakov mentioned that the Mariinsky could have staged *Boris Godunov*, she responded, "Today I was telling our fools off the whole day for this." The most special performance was the last one: all the participants were praised and given baskets of flowers and wreaths. Rimsky-Korsakov's wreath was presented by Stasov, Lyadov, Glazunov, Yastrebtsev and his mother, and Belsky. On the sash was written: "To the outstanding interpreter and friend of Musorgsky, Rimsky-Korsakov, on 4 December 1896 from the admirers of Musorgsky and Rimsky-Korsakov."

Yastrebtsev recorded the event as follows: "While the wreath was being handed to Rimsky-Korsakov, the orchestra was playing a flourish, and the soloists along with the chorus who had come before the curtains earlier, were greeting him with applause and 'bravo's!"

This production of *Boris Godunov* gave new life to Musorgsky's opera, which now began its triumphal march all over the world. At first it was staged in the Moscow Private Opera of S. I. Mamontov with Fyodor Chaliapin singing the part of Boris Godunov. Then it was performed in the Mariinsky Theatre. It was also staged in Paris and London with the assistance of Diaghilev. Later productions were mounted in other European countries and in the United States.

The autumn of 1896 marked the twenty-fifth year since Rimsky-Korsakov had started working as a professor at the Conservatory. Rimsky-Korsakov received several congratulations. He was named an honorary member of the Russian Musical Society, which supervised the St. Petersburg Conservatory. In his turn, Rimsky-Korsakov expressed his gratitude and said that, although he was not enrolled in the Conservatory, he considered himself to be an extra student. In a letter to Modest Tchaikovsky, the brother of Pyotr Tchaikovsky, Rimsky-Korsakov commented on his work in the Conservatory: "Frankly speaking, I myself do not think I have performed outstanding services. I like music and I have some ability for it, therefore my service to music is something natural and ordinary. Anybody would do the same if he were me."

Despite all the troubles experienced with the staging of *Christmas Eve*, Rimsky-Korsakov decided to offer his newly completed opera *Sadko* to the board of directors of the Imperial Theatres. However, Vsevolozhsky, who remembered the incident with *Christmas Eve*, claimed again that he was unable to include it in the theatre's repertoire without the tsar's approval and that the production of this opera would require huge expenditures. Rimsky-Korsakov perceived these words as a polite refusal. Nonetheless, Vsevolozhsky reported to Nikolay II on Rimsky-Korsakov's new opera. The tsar asked what kind of music it represented, and Vsevolozhsky answered that it reminded him somewhat of *Mlada* and

Christmas Eve. Nikolay II said, "In this case we do not need this opera. Let the board of directors find something merrier than this one." Rimsky-Korsakov told Yastrebtsev about the refusal to stage *Sadko* in the Imperial Theatre and added, "The most curious thing about the whole story is that today Kondratyev, the director, greeted me without pressing my hand to his chest and did not ask me about my wife." Vsevolozhsky did not find anything better to say to Nikolay than, "Do you know what is good about all this? We managed to escape a lot of troubles connected with staging this opera." S. K. Bulich,[6] a music historian and professor at St. Petersburg University, said, "Well, it means we still have new really talented compositions if they refuse to stage them." Having learned about the misfortune with *Sadko*, Belsky wrote to the composer:

> I dare to calm myself with the thought that try as they might, dark forces can only slow down the wheel of history for some time but they are not able to stop it completely. I believe, sooner or later, your opera *Sadko* will be staged, appreciated and recognized as a classical one. [...] The tsar, Vsevolozhsky, and season ticket holders are displeased with Your music, but I dare to say that their opinion will not be final.

From then on Rimsky-Korsakov decided not to bother offering the board of directors of the Imperial Theatres any of his new operas. In the middle of February 1897 a concert devoted to the tenth anniversary of Borodin's death took place in the Hall of the Assembly of the Nobility. On the advice of Stasov, a large portrait of Borodin painted by Repin was placed on the stage. Rimsky-Korsakov and Felix Blumenfeld conducted the orchestra. On 4 March a reporter of the Moscow newspaper *Novosti dnya* (*Today's News*) informed the readers that the famous composer N. A. Rimsky-Korsakov was very ill. Kruglikov was worried and sent a telegram to Rimsky-Korsakov inquiring about his health. Rimsky-Korsakov answered also by telegram: "Thank you. I'm absolutely healthy and haven't been sick. All lies. Rimsky-Korsakov."

At the end of April 1897 Rimsky-Korsakov and Sonya went to the estate of N. I. Glinka-Mavrin. It was located at a place called Golubkovo on the banks of Lake Cheremenetskoe, about twenty-one miles from Luga. The Rimsky-Korsakov family liked the Luga district very much. Unfortunately, the Ogarevs, their old acquaintances, did not let their country house again that year. Rimsky-Korsakov and Sonya liked the old overgrown orchard and the huge lake there. However, the house he decided to lease instead was in a bad state of repair and required some renovation as well as furnishing. Glinka-Mavrin, the landlord, promised to do his best to make the house ready by 20 May. He managed to persuade Rimsky-Korsakov to pay two hundred rubles in advance (two-thirds of the rent). Nonetheless, in the end the Rimsky-Korsakov family did not spend the summer there. Although Rimsky-Korsakov had paid in advance, when they arrived in Golubkovo it turned out that Glinka-Mavrin had not kept his word. The house was locked, and the landlord had disappeared. They were lucky to find the keys of the house, but the house itself was absolutely unready: there was no furniture whatsoever, and everything was in complete disorder. After spending an uncomfortable night in the empty house, in the morning they left for Luga. They were advised to rent a house in Smychkovo, an estate of Khotinsky, a local landowner. The house turned out to be suitable and just about five miles from Luga. There was a river nearby and an orchard. It was not bad, but it was not as pleasant as living in Golubkovo. They settled down there by that evening. Some days later their son Mikhail left for the Kherson region in the Crimea to take part in some research to be carried out by the entomological committee of the Land Department. Upon overcoming these unexpected difficulties and settling down his family, Rimsky-Korsakov returned to St. Petersburg to conduct examinations at the Conservatory. He wrote to his wife: "My dear Nadyusha, it turned out that Andrey and the nurse had known already about our departure from Golubkovo. […] I've sent a refusal letter to Glinka-Mavrin, but he has not yet come to the city. I hope I never see him again. To hell with him!"

Andrey stayed in the city, since he was to take his final examinations in the gymnasium. Ill luck followed the family: Andrey developed a serious case of pleurisy. Rimsky-Korsakov nursed his son through his illness. He wrote to Nadezhda:

My dear Mama,
    […] I was very worried whether they would accept his average grade for the year. […] I visited Krakay. He said that it might be done. […] I am taking care of this, so do not worry about his examinations and grades. Also do not become too anxious about his sickness. […] I am sleeping in the same room with him. During the day he is moved around the house to keep the air fresh: in the morning he is in the dining room on the sofa, then back in his room, then again

on the sofa. We change compresses every four hours. Be assured that we have taken all of the necessary precautions. I have only a few lessons at this time, so I can come home at the time necessary to change the compress. […] My dear, do not be too worried, […] do not become fearful. Andrey begs you about this. The same from me.

When the examinations at the Conservatory came to an end and Rimsky-Korsakov was able to move into the summer house; Nadezhda returned to St. Petersburg and stayed with Andrey. Although Andrey was seriously ill and did not take two of his examinations, he left the gymnasium with a silver medal.

Savva Mamontov

In the summer Rimsky-Korsakov turned over *Sadko* for its production to Mamontov, the creator of a private opera group in Moscow. This opera group gave its performances in the theatre of Solodovnikov.[7] They had already performed *The Maid of Pskov* and *The Snow Maiden*. Mamontov was a son of a pioneer of railway construction in Russia who took over the business after his father and made a fortune. He invested heavily in railway development, which was one of the most profitable industries in Russia at that time. Mamontov was a great admirer of art as well. He was quite gifted and was good at sculpture; he had also taken singing lessons in Italy. He was fond of the theatre, and he created plays himself that he produced with the help of amateur performers at his home. Mamontov took part in these performances himself, sometimes as an actor, sometimes as a director, and sometimes even as a make-up assistant. The performances took place in his Moscow house as well as at his estate in Abramtsevo, which he purchased in 1870. Many famous Russian artists lived and created their works on this estate: I. Repin, V. Vasnetsov, M. Vrubel, V. Serov, I. Levitan, M. Nesterov, K. Korovin, and V. Polenov, to name just a few.[8] They all took an active part in the performances as artists and performers. The opera *Faust*, its third act to be precise, was the first opera staged by Mamontov in Abramtsevo in 1882.[9] Mamontov himself sang the part of Mephistopheles. In 1885, on the advice of his friends, who witnessed his enthusiasm and successful productions, Mamontov opened a new opera theatre in Moscow. Kruglikov was the mediator between Mamontov and Rimsky-Korsakov in the matter of the production of *Sadko*. In June 1897 Kruglikov wrote to Rimsky-Korsakov:

You know that Mamontov, in Moscow, is a great admirer of Your *Snow Maiden* and *The Maid of Pskov*. He is a man of high taste in art and is surrounded with artists such as Repin, Vasnetsov, Polenov, and others. [...] Mamontov admires You very much, and Borodin and Musorgsky, as well [...] he is dreaming of staging Your new opera. It would be wise of You to trust Mamontov and his new opera theatre. [...] Why don't You try producing Your *Sadko* there?

Rimsky-Korsakov responded:

As for Mamontov, I know him in person and respect him. If he finds it possible to produce *Sadko* and by this to outclass somebody who deserves it, I'll be very glad. It's desirable that they should have a complete orchestra and the necessary number of orchestra rehearsals as well and spend time studying the opera itself. And you could influence him in this matter. He spends money with great generosity on costumes and scenery, but music should be the priority in any opera. Compared with the expenses for costumes and scenery, the sums for some additional instruments and two or three additional rehearsals are minor. The first thing in opera is not the visual spectacle, but the music.

Another letter from Kruglikov came back with Mamontov's words to Rimsky-Korsakov: "Tell Rimsky-Korsakov that I am his true admirer, and if we have enough resources to produce *Sadko*, I assure him that I will make every effort to make both the musical and the visual aspects equally perfect and worthy of the opera and its author." Therefore, the production of *Sadko* became a reality, though not on the imperial stage.

11

From *Mozart and Salieri* to *Tsar Saltan*, 1897–1899

This scene with the aria and the Nymph I wish to listen to only with your voice.

—Rimsky-Korsakov to soprano Nadezhda Zabela-Vrubel, 1898

The Rimsky-Korsakovs celebrated their twenty-fifth wedding anniversary on 30 June 1897 in Smychkovo. They had only a few guests: the Akhsharumovs and Yastrebtsev; the latter came unexpectedly. Yastrebtsev recorded the events:

> We were invited for lunch about 2 p.m., after which we had hot chocolate. Then we went for a walk; at first we roamed along the picturesque banks of the river Luga; then we climbed a high hill with a burnt pine, from where a beautiful view of nearby fields, meadows, and a mill opened up. […] Since the weather was beautiful, they laid a table in the orchard. The special dinner, with ice cream, snacks, and champagne, lasted from 6 to 8:30 in the evening and was lovely and merry. After dinner we went to the hall, where Rimsky-Korsakov played all of his "June" romances and duets upon our request. […] About midnight we went to our bedrooms.

Mozart and Salieri

The composer played seventeen romances, among them a new one, *Nenastny den potukh* (*The Rainy Day Has Faded*), based on the words of Pushkin. Rimsky-Korsakov had completed this romance just the day before, and he dedicated it to his wife. He produced a considerable number of compositions during the summer in Smychkovo, including a large number of romances one after another based on the poems of Tolstoy, Pushkin, and Maikov.[1] In addition, that summer he composed the opera *Mozart and Salieri*. In this opera he succeeded in preserving the full original text of Pushkin's tragedy. He also composed the cantata *The Maid of Svityaz*; two duets, *Pan* and the *Song of Songs*; the vocal trio *Dragonflies*; a string quartet; and a trio for violin, violoncello, and piano. This trio was not completely finished because he decided that he was not very good at writing chamber music, and thus it should not be published.[2]

Upon his return to the city, the composer played his *Mozart and Salieri* to a small group of friends at his home. Later that year, in December 1897, the Rimsky-Korsakov family held a musical evening at which they received fifty guests. Many romances were played, and the new opera *Mozart and Salieri* was also performed. The opera had a great success, and after tea it was put on again. Having learned about this new opera, Belsky wrote to Rimsky-Korsakov from Munich: "The news excited me so that I felt as if I had been captured and carried by a huge beautiful wave. […] Your *Mozart* must be the result of the harmonic mixture of your striving for both powerful realism and expressiveness, and, on the other hand, for your radiant Goddess of Beauty, who emerges from the foam of the sea."

At the very end of December Mamontov's Opera held the first performance of *Sadko* in Moscow. Rimsky-Korsakov did not attend the premiere. But on 29 December 1897 the composer and his wife left for Moscow and attended the third and the fourth performances of the opera. A correspondent of the newspaper *Today's News* wrote: "The third performance of *Sadko* was accompanied by a number of great ovations in honor of its author, who came specially for this performance from Petersburg. After the third act, N. A. Rimsky-Korsakov appeared on the stage during each intermission to storms of enthusiastic applause and greetings."

He was presented with five wreaths, including a silver one from Mamontov. The part of the Marine Princess Volkhova was sung by Nadezhda Zabela.[3] Rimsky-Korsakov was impressed by her fascinating voice and perfect acting. Zabela wrote later in her memoirs: "After the second act I was introduced to Rimsky-Korsakov and received his approval." Her husband, Mikhail Vrubel, worked for Mamontov, and it was he who designed the scenery and costumes for *Sadko*.

Count Lev Tolstoy

While they were staying in Moscow, the Rimsky-Korsakovs became acquainted with Count Lev Tolstoy. Nadezhda was especially fond of Tolstoy's novels. Stasov, who also was with them in Moscow, first introduced them to Sophia, Tolstoy's wife; then they all visited the great writer himself and his family in Khamovniki. Upon arriving in St. Petersburg, Rimsky-Korsakov told Yastrebtsev about this visit, and the latter recorded it:

> When we came into Tolstoy's house, we saw the author of *War and Peace* and *Anna Karenina* wearing his work clothes in his usual manner, above his nightshirt. His hands were very clean, and he had a strong but pleasant fragrance from his soap.[…]During our discussion Lev Nikolayevich became excited: he often grabbed my hands and interrupted me several times.[…]Before tea we had a conventional discussion; but after tea, when Nadezhda and I were going to leave, Lev Nikolayevich forced us to stay. He said that he would like to talk about some issues with me in person. So we stayed. At that point we began exploring the aims of art. We touched upon the problem of beauty, which, according to the words of Tolstoy, was "a rotten stinking ulcer on the body of art." Then Tolstoy said that he couldn't stand Beethoven for his passion and that he was sorry about the fact that he couldn't stop listening to Chopin's music. This very fact made Tolstoy especially sad. Rimsky-Korsakov argued that he, in his turn, was absolutely happy about the fact that he himself worshipped both Chopin and Beethoven, and he didn't regret this at all. Count Tolstoy went on, "First of all, any work of art must be simple and clear in order to be understood easily either by a 'lord' or a 'driver.'" […] Rimsky-Korsakov contradicted him and said that, if even Lev Nikolayevich himself admitted that all art ennobled and improved a person's nature, then he should admit that one couldn't be improved in a downward direction. His novels *Childhood and Youth*, *War and Peace*, and *Anna Karenina* were genuine creations of art, but they were far from simple, and they were full of beauty. Lev Nikolayevich didn't even listen to Rimsky-Korsakov's words, he interrupted him and said that he despised himself greatly for those particular novels and that he considered them worthless. The Rimsky-Korsakovs left Tolstoy at 12:30 at night. Lev Nikolayevich saw them out. When Nadezhda apologized for any inconvenience they might have caused, the great writer responded, "That's all right. Today it was my pleasure to face the darkness in person." Upon

hearing this odd phrase, Stasov became so frightened that he put on Nikolay's fur coat instead of his own and rushed away.

When Rimsky-Korsakov told this story to Yastrebtsev, he mentioned with irony that he would like to engrave those peculiar words of Tolstoy on a gilded board and put it on his desk for further edification. He also said that he would never read Tolstoy's book about art. In his turn, on the day after the visit, Tolstoy wrote in his diary: "Yesterday. Stasov and Rimsky-Korsakov. Coffee; stupid talk about art." It was the first and only meeting of these two great artists.

In February 1898 Mamontov came to St. Petersburg with his opera group. The repertoire of the tour included *The Maid of Pskov, May Night, The Snow Maiden*, and *Sadko*. The latter, just prepared, was to open the tour. The performances took place in the Great Hall of the St. Petersburg Conservatory. Mamontov asked Rimsky-Korsakov to conduct *Sadko*. As soon as the group arrived, Rimsky-Korsakov conducted the rehearsals with the orchestra and the soloists. The first performance of *Sadko* was held on 22 February. Yastrebtsev wrote:

> The theatre was overcrowded. […] The encores were endless. Rimsky-Korsakov was presented with a wreath. When the opera was over, a group of students led by Kholodny, a pianist, came to Nikolay's room to thank him for the great pleasure they had received from his new opera. Rimsky-Korsakov was happy. He shook the hand of each guest and said, laughing, "I am so delighted to please you with my *Sadko*. […] Indeed, Zabela acts the part of Volkhova perfectly. She is just an ideal match for this part. Besides, her singing is full of nobility and poetry. By the way, I am not the only one who has gone crazy over the Marine Princess. Honor and glory to her!

The next day *The Maid of Pskov* was performed, with Chaliapin singing the part of Ivan the Terrible. The opera was a great success, owing in large part to Chaliapin's singing. The day after *May Night* was performed. After the performance Rimsky-Korsakov was presented with two wreaths: one from the performers of the Private Opera company, the other one anonymously with these words on the sash: "To the creator of the fascinating Russian chords."

The Private Opera company performed *The Snow Maiden* as well. Rimsky-Korsakov wished Zabela to sing the part of the Snow Maiden, but Mamontov appointed Paskhalova for this part instead. Rimsky-Korsakov was very annoyed with the director's decision. In addition, he was getting really exhausted by everything. An unpleasant event that happened during the rehearsal aggravated his condition. Yastrebstev described the event:

> During the rehearsal, when they repeated the chorus of the Berendeyans, Rimsky-Korsakov decided to hum the tune in order to show the chorus where they were to start. At that very moment one of the choristers mimicked him in a squeaky voice. Rimsky-Korsakov became outraged. He screamed at the chorus, "It's not my fault that I don't have a good voice. I am not to be blamed. But don't you think that I might have something else, which none of you possess." He was extremely agitated. Rimsky-Korsakov beat on the music stand with the baton so hard that the he nearly broke it in two. When the chorus finished singing the required part from the beginning to the end, Rimsky-Korsakov stood up and said, "Till tomorrow with Esposito!"

Eugene Esposito was the conductor of Mamontov's Private Opera, though Rimsky-Korsakov conducted *The Snow Maiden* in public. Yastrebtsev wrote: "When he entered the place for the orchestra, they played three flourishes. In general, greetings of excitement occurred at the beginning of each act. Rimsky-Korsakov received laurels presented by children before the last act. The inscriptions read: 'Listening to and melting.' These words are from the part of the Snow Maiden."

The Maid of Pskov, staged in March 1898, was the last performance given by the Mamontov group. The performers and the composer as well were called to the stage many times. Rimsky-Korsakov was presented with a beautiful, delicate silver basket with roses and white lilacs. On the bottom of the basket was inscribed: "To Rimsky-Korsakov from his sincere admirers." The admirers remained anonymous. Three days later the Rimsky-Korsakov family held a musical evening. There were about thirty guests, including Glazunov; Lyadov; Stasov; Zabela and her husband, Vrubel; Chaliapin; Belsky and his wife, Agrippina; Yastrabtsev and his mother; and some others. Much music was performed. The guests enjoyed listening to the singing of Zabela and Chaliapin. Rimsky-Korsakov felt he had to tell Mamontov about some shortcomings in the performance of *The Snow Maiden*. He wrote to Kruglikov:

I had a heart-to-heart talk with S. I. [Mamontov]. I told him that I considered music to be the priority in any opera, but for him music was not so important. Therefore, it made me a little indifferent about his affairs. We parted good friends, but I had nothing to do in his opera. […] As usual it turned out that I had made some stupid mistakes, since I was talking from my heart, but I met with the ambitions of a petty tyrant. I have noticed that there is much hypocrisy in the Moscow Private Opera. […] Zabela, who is the best soprano, and who is certainly admired by the Petersburg audience, is not in favor. And the fact that they do not pay attention to the composer's opinions is even worse.

Kruglikov understood that the composer was striving to get the best performance of his music; but at the same time he thought that Rimsky-Korsakov had become too upset and had made a mistake. Kruglikov tried to convince Rimsky-Korsakov that he was wrong:

You know that You are not in favor with the Imperial Theatre board. So You cannot allow yourself to ignore Mamontov, who adores Your music and Your personality. And before the problem with Zabela occurred, the way he had treated You did not annoy You. […] You used to show Your good attitude to the Mamontov Opera as well as to Mamontov himself, and You favored him. You even called him Savva the Best. All in all, you should understand there are no perfect people in the world, and their personal deeds are not perfect either. What should You do? […] You could easily forgive Mamontov's mistake that upset you so much, since he has produced four of Your operas during one and the same season. He has done so much for You. And I could say even more than You did for him. […] I wish sincerely, from the bottom of my heart, that You would make peace with him and everything would be as it used to be. Otherwise I am afraid I might think of You as a less fair person than I used to. And what is even more important, Mamontov can feel Your new attitude to him and [he] might become cold to You and to Your music. Please, don't make me suffer. I really like You very much.

Rimsky-Korsakov responded two weeks later:

Dear Semyon,

    I think you may be surprised that you haven't received my answer to your sincere and friendly letter till now. It's just because I am composing at the moment. You know, when I'm composing, I become insane and don't pay attention to anything, and so, sometimes, I behave awfully. [...] Just forgive me, my dear friend. My attitude toward Savva is absolutely clear to me now. We are not enemies, but we are not close friends. Everything now is as it was before his staging of *Sadko*, and it was supposed to be like this. Previously, I intended to become his adviser, but it turned out to be very uncomfortable for me. We are two different people. He is concerned about visual impressions, and for me music is the priority. We have nothing to be at war about, and I didn't offend him in any case. I am grateful that he has produced my operas; on the other hand, he, in his turn, must be thankful to me that those operas do exist. The public came to listen to the operas, especially *Sadko*. [...] His expenses for production were minor, and from the point of view of the music, their performances left much to be desired. [...] Due to this, I don't consider that I owe anything to Savva. It is just quid pro quo. Besides, I trusted him with good operas, and he presented me with poor performances of them when, by the way, he could have repaid me with the same. I think he will go on producing my operas if I create any new ones. [...] In any case, we haven't quarreled, and you are worried about nothing. I can't understand what you are trying to convince me of. [...] Please don't be angry with me for my long silence. With love, N.

Indeed, when Rimsky-Korsakov composed, he became, maybe not insane, as he wrote to Kruglikov, but rather absent-minded. Sometime later Rimsky-Korsakov sent another letter to Kruglikov and received in response: "It's a miracle that I have got Your letter. The postman had to search for me at the following address: Moscow, Tver Boulevard, the house of Romanov, to Semyon. You are lucky that there is only one Semyon in the house of Romanov, and although he is very proud of Your desire to promote him to become Your relative, he is still called Semyon Kruglikov, who is embracing You and wishing You all the best."

The Tsar's Bride

During the first few months of 1898, Rimsky-Korsakov began composing another opera based on the plot of L. Mey's drama *The Tsar's Bride*. After considering the structure of the opera, he asked Ilia Tyumenev to write the libretto. As usual when Rimsky-Korsakov was in the city, he did not have much time to work on the opera.

A Portrait by Vasiliy Serov

On his birthday, 6 March, Rimsky-Korsakov was visited by Glazunov, Yastrevtsev, and Stasov at noon, and in the evening he attended a performance of *The Maid of Pskov*. That same day the artist Serov began to paint a portrait of Rimsky-Korsakov. The portrait was commissioned by P. M. Tretyakov. Serov made the first sketch with charcoal. He worked at Rimsky-Korsakov's apartment, which distracted the composer from working on his new opera. Rimsky-Korsakov wrote to Kruglikov: "I go to the theatre twice a day. From early morning till noon I pose for Serov. It disturbs me a lot because I can't do my work. Therefore, my composition is at a complete stop. P.S. Three days ago I turned fifty-four years old. It's a pity I wasn't sixteen!"

Serov had been working on the portrait for two months. Rimsky-Korsakov forgot that he could not change his appearance because of this, and he had his hair cut short, as he was accustomed to do in the spring. Serov was shocked when he saw Nikolay's new look. Nonetheless, the portrait turned out to be very true to life. The composer is depicted sitting at the table, as he used to do. Rimsky-Korsakov's children said that this portrait was more realistic than any of his photographs were. His photographs always made him look too strict, and he actually never was. There must have been good reasons why one of his nicknames in his youth was Sincerity.

Rimsky-Korsakov's personal charm was inseparable from his huge prestige as a well-known composer. His eldest daughter reminisced later that from time to time Rimsky-Korsakov received letters from complete strangers who sent librettos to him in the hope that he would compose his operas using them. Usually those librettos were very weak, sometimes even odd and funny. For example, once Rimsky-Korsakov received a libretto composed in verse and titled *The Lady-Warrior*. It had the following text: "Mama is calling for help with stuffing pies; Papa judges everyone on their feet, he likes marching." The cover letter read: "My name is not famous yet. I have composed a play in a minor key. Could you be so kind as to publish it under your name? We can share the profit."

The female Conservatory students were very afraid of Rimsky-Korsakov, especially during the tests, if they did not know music theory and harmony well enough. However, Rimsky-Korsakov had pity on them during examinations. He used to say to his relatives at home:

I don't want to fail a girl. I usually ask something very easy, well-known; for example, the last time I asked a girl student:

"Are there many violins in the orchestra?"

"One."

I asked again:

"Do you think only one?"

I asked, "How many cymbals"?—

"Very many."

The response: "Maybe two."

I gave her a pass. I felt too sorry for her to fail her.

Sometimes a distant relative, a strange old woman named Varvara, who lived in a poorhouse, visited the Rimsky-Korsakov family. She usually came with a big bag for collecting various cookies and sweets that her numerous relatives offered to her. Rimsky-Korsakov never forgot to make sure Varvara had got something tasty. Sometimes she sent utterly odd letters to him, for example: "To the great hall of the Conservatory. To Rimsky-Korsakov. I am starving. I can't eat anything. My stomach has become very thin. Could you send me, please, hazel hens and pies?" In such cases a special packet was sent to her.

The summer season was approaching, and the Rimsky-Korsakov family rented a summer house in Vetchasha. Upon arriving, Nadezhda sent a letter to her husband:

Dear Nika,

It's so pleasant here in Vetchasha. I am so sorry that you three have to stay in that stuffy, dusty, and ugly Petersburg. [...] We found the house clean, and absolutely meticulous. Everything here is as it used to be: even all the nails I put in are in their places. As soon as we arrived we went to the orchard. The apple trees are just superb: they look as if they are covered with snow—there are so many flowers. [...] We were just happy to see the lake again. In general, I feel very content, as if I have returned home. [...] While I was writing to you, mosquitoes have bitten me. There are so many of them this year. There are also millions of frogs. They give us concerts during the days and nights. It reminds me of Nikolayev.

Nikolay, Andrey, and Volodya had to stay in St. Petersburg because their sons were taking examinations, Andrey at the university and Volodya at the gymnasium. Rimsky-Korsakov was giving examinations at the Conservatory. Having passed the examinations, Volodya left for Vetchasha, whereas Andrey was going to visit Latovka, where Mikhail was on business. Michael wrote to his parents: "I am keeping on with my business. The spring was very late this year; therefore the insects appeared much later than usual. Now I am not sure how long I will have to stay here before I finish my research. I hope Andrey will come to see me after passing his examinations. We are expecting him. I think that he will have an interesting and lovely time here and, besides, it would be very useful for him to stay in the south for some time."

Return to Vetchasha

Rimsky-Korsakov arrived at Vetchasha on 1 June. There he became completely occupied with composing *The Tsar's Bride*. He kept the composition of his new opera a secret for some time, but everyone felt that he had been working on something new. Stasov thought it did not matter what opera Rimsky-Korsakov had been composing; the fact itself was of great importance. He wrote to his brother: "Great! He is working again!"

In his turn Yastrebstev wrote: "I don't know what opera Rimsky-Korsakov is composing right now. I have some grounds for believing that it is Mey's *The Tsar's Bride*." Kruglikov also became intrigued. He asked about this new opera on which Rimsky-Korsakov was working in secret, and the composer responded: "You have asked what the title is of my new opera. My dear friend, I am so sorry! I can't tell you. I can just say that I have completed drafts of three acts and now I am working on the fourth. The first act I have finished and even orchestrated already."

Nadezhda decided to go to Yalta to visit the tomb of her daughter. It had been five years since Masha died. At the beginning of July 1898 Nadezhda left for St. Petersburg. When the children went for a walk, Rimsky-Korsakov stayed home all by himself and sat down to write a letter: "My dear Nadya, [...] I have been left alone and the emptiness is boring me to death. I wrote to you, idled in the orchard, and then wrote to you again, then again idled in the orchard and so on. When they came back home, it became much more pleasant."

Nadezhda went to Sevastopol by train. Before her departure she sent a letter to her husband:

I came home at 1:30 p.m. yesterday. The janitor rang the bell but no one answered. He assured me that Katerina, a servant, hadn't left the house. How strange! We rang and rang without any result. The servant started searching for her, and I was guarding my belongings. About twenty minutes passed. […] Katerina didn't open the door. Then I left all the things with the servant and went to the Belsky household. But no one opened the door there either. I left a note for them and returned home. At last I managed to get inside. It turned out that Katerina was roasting coffee beans in Luchinsky's apartment [their apartment was on the floor above]. You see I wasted a lot of time, but eventually I was lucky to get everything done that I had intended. […] Double the usual kisses for you! Kiss Sonya, Volodya, and Nadya for me. I am leaving soon. Goodbye, my dear.

Nadezhda did manage to visit Belsky, however, before her departure. She wrote to her husband that Belsky tried to find out what opera her husband was composing, but she did not reveal the secret and just said that there were three completed acts. Rimsky-Korsakov responded to her letter: "Dear Nadya, although I sent you two letters yesterday, I've decided to write a new one after reading yours written in pencil. I have a great desire to tell you some words. My poor thing! How unlucky you were in Petersburg. I'm so sorry for you! I imagine how you felt sitting on the stairs for such a long time. […] You've left and the house seems empty. The children went to the wood to gather wild strawberries. If you were here you would go with them. Nonetheless, I feel especially lonely today."

The composer's wife sent him several letters while she was on her way to Kharkov:

The train is heading for Kharkov. […] The environs are becoming more beautiful. There are huge hills, peasants are mowing and making sheaves of wheat. Now I can see windmills and purely white houses, which I like very much. There are chalk hills and fields of sunflowers. They are in bloom now and they look so beautiful at a distance. I am reading Drepper's work about Greek philosophers and a story of Zuderman, a German writer, and I am writing to you constantly, maybe too often; but I am traveling all alone and I don't speak to anyone except the conductors. There are only two or three gentlemen in the railway carriage and no ladies at all. Don't think I'm complaining. I like traveling a lot.

What about Nadya and Volodya? Do they speak French and German? Remind them that they should speak as much as possible. How is Sonya keeping the house?

Upon receiving this letter, Rimsky-Korsakov responded:

My dear Nadyusha!

All four of us went to the wood and lay there reading. I read *A Nest of Gentlefolk* and then had a nap. Sonya is looking after me as if I were a child. She is constantly next to me. I feel a little tired from composing and I'm not doing anything these days. [...] Now it's 11 p.m. I'm writing this letter on the balcony. Sonya is also here writing a note to you. Nadya is playing and also putting down some words for you. I often remind the children to speak French and German. [...] I'm looking forward to getting your letter from Sevastopol. [...] I'm embracing you so hard that you even ask me to release you a little.

Andrey joined his mother on the way to Yalta in order to keep her company. They spent two days in Sevastopol and liked the city very much. Nadezhda shared her impressions with her husband:

The city has improved very much since we stayed there the last time. I can barely recognize it. There are a lot of pretty houses now; the streets are lined with white acacias, and there is a boulevard with a public garden there. [...] But the most charming thing there is boating. We haven't taken a carriage yet and we travel everywhere by water under sail. Andrey is doing this for the first time in his life, and he is very excited. We took a wonderful trip to Inkreman. The wind was strong enough. and our boat even took a list. I was frightened a little but then I got used to it. The next day we went to Kherson. And again the wind was strong; but the sea was so beautiful and sparkling. The waters were so rough that I felt a little dizzy. However, soon I got used to it and everything went all right. We sailed both ways. Yesterday when it became dark we sailed by boat to the southern harbor. The sea was calm, and I allowed Andrey to row. We hoped to see the water shining. Unfortunately, it wasn't glowing this time; maybe the moon just produced a little light near the oars. [...] Goodbye, my dear. I kiss you all heartily. Can you write to me about your opera?

At last Nadezhda and Andrey arrived at Yalta. She wrote from there:

My dear Nika,

Yalta made me depressed as I had expected. How relaxed and merry I felt in Sevastopol: I feel so hurt here. I'm tortured with painful memories.[...] Today Andrey and I visited Masha's grave.[...] The cypresses and other trees have grown so high at the nearby graves that they cover the view to the sea from Masha's. But if you move some steps further on the path, the view to the sea is wonderful. The sea is raging today. The wind was very strong. The water started covering the embankment; fortunately, the wind weakened by evening. However, the breakers are still very loud. I can hear the roar of the surf and the awful noise, which makes my heart sick. Moreover, Yalta is associated not only with awfully difficult memories. I consider it to be a breeding ground for disease, although the location of the city is very healthful. I look at each room in the hotel suspiciously and think about the previous residents. I'm not worried about myself, I don't care about myself, but it might be dangerous for Andrey. I'd like to leave the city as soon as possible. Andrey, on the contrary, wishes to see as much as possible.[...] I sleep very badly here. My heart is crying, and I feel so sad. I wish I could be in Vetchasha immediately. I kiss Nadya, Volodya, Sonya and you.[...]

P.S. The disgusting Black Sea is still raging, roaring and furious. This constant noise of the surf is annoying me. Our hotel is on the seacoast and our balcony faces the sea.

Rimsky-Korsakov decided to congratulate Belsky on his name day and invited him to visit Vetchasha. Rimsky-Korsakov composed his congratulations in verse. Belsky arrived in Vetchasha soon after, and Rimsky-Korsakov wrote about his news to Nadezhda:

My dear Nadya,

[...] Yesterday Vladimir arrived and stayed with us. I played for him and sang the opera: all three acts and a piece of the fourth one, which you haven't heard. Sonya assisted me. He liked everything in general.[...] I am very glad about his visiting us. It's not only my pleasure to see him but it also forces me to rest from my opera. And it's very useful just to play the pieces I have composed again and again. It's a pity you are not coming home with Andrey yet, but in any case, your return is approaching and we'll be together quite soon.

Nadezhda and Andrey visited Alupka, and she described their trip in her next letter to Vetchasha:

> The village of Alupka has grown a lot since we were there. There are many summer houses, a large hotel, two restaurants and plenty of small shops. There are a lot of residents, but I wouldn't wish to live there. The air is awful here. The place itself is dusty, stuffy, and overcrowded. The narrow Tatar streets with their dirty *saklyas* are very unpleasant. [...]⁴ We went there along the lower road via Livadia, Oreand, and Miskhor and returned along the upper road in the moonlight. The night was cloudless. In Oreand we made a stop at the Cross Mountain and climbed it. If you remember, it's not easy to climb up to the top, as they are huge stones piled up there. It was especially frightening to climb the mountain in the moonlight. [...] But it was worth doing. The view was unforgettable. The moon was so bright that we were able to see everything in detail. After enjoying the view we went down and rode home.

Their trip came to an end. They went to Alushta by ship; from there they rode in a horse-drawn carriage to Simferopol, then by train to Sevastopol, then again by ship to Odessa, and at last from Odessa to St. Petersburg. At the very end of July the family gathered in Vetchasha. Rimsky-Korsakov wrote in his memoirs: "The summer of 1898 passed very quickly in lovely Vetchasha. The composition of *The Tsar's Bride* proceeded smoothly and easily. The whole opera was completed during the summer."

Rimsky-Korsakov was in high spirits and so absorbed in his music that he even wrote his letters in the form of musical recitatives. He composed one such letter to Andrey asking him to bring some things from St. Petersburg and sent another musical letter to Belsky inviting him to visit Vetchasha. The time passed, and the title of the opera was not kept secret anymore. Kruglikov came to Vetchasha in August, and Rimsky-Korsakov played *The Tsar's Bride* for him. Vladimir, Rimsky-Korsakov's youngest son, remembered the event later:

> You can't even imagine how Semyon listened to the opera, which Rimsky-Korsakov played to him. With what attention, interest, and veneration! When

Semyon wasn't discussing music or the future production of the new opera by Mamontov, he walked with us in the park, picked Indian cress, and ate the flowers, trying to persuade us that they were very tasty. He also gathered currants and gooseberries with us and ate them. Upon returning home Semyon used to sit down on the sofa trying to convince us that he had been fed with the berries as a baby would be fed with mother's milk and now he could only kick his feet as a baby would do. And to prove this he gestured like a baby. This time he arrived in Vetchasha by night train. He decided not to disturb the family at night, and so he spent some hours at the railway station of Plussa, which he called a "hotel." When we all started showing our sympathy about his waiting till morning in a simple village inn, he tried to persuade us, laughing, that he felt very good there, as he went straight to a "clean half," drank some tea, and had some snacks from the "price list." He told the story merrily and heartily but he managed to make it absolutely clear that the cleanliness was of the kind described by Goncharov:[5] "It was very clean there, although full of cockroaches and fleas."

Rimsky-Korsakov had been fond of astronomy since early childhood. While Kruglikov was in Vetchasha, Rimsky-Korsakov taught him how to find different constellations in the sky. Kruglikov left the estate during some bad weather. Since he was supposed to ride on a simple two-wheeled cart, called a *karafashka*, he was offered a raincoat, which Kruglikov named immediately an *inpromocable*, that is, a "waterproof for departing persons."

Having found out about Rimsky-Korsakov's new opera, Mamontov asked Kruglikov for assistance in pleading with Rimsky-Korsakov for permission to stage this opera in his Private Opera. Mamontov wanted him to ask Rimsky-Korsakov to allow the Private Opera to be the first to stage it and not to give it to the Imperial Theatres. Kruglikov's request to Rimsky-Korsakov: "If our dear and honorable Rimsky-Korsakov has nothing against our production, we would be honored to be the first to perform his new opera with all our efforts. Could you write to him that we would do our best, choose all our best voices, and give all of our love to *The Tsar's Bride* of Rimsky-Korsakov?"

At the end of his letter Kruglikov added: "Thank you very much for your heartwarming welcome. I felt very well at your house, and now I can find the constellations of Arcturus, Capella, and Vega. But I can't remember the name of the constellation that looks like a downward 'y.'" Rimsky-Korsakov responded:

"Dear Semyon, if you are pleased with your stay with us, then we are just as excited about your stay. As for me, you know that I like you very much because you are nice, kind, and have a good musical ear, and we have been friends for such a long time." In the same letter Rimsky-Korsakov reminded Kruglikov that the name of the constellation was Cassiopeia.

Nadezhda Zabela visited Tatyana Lyubotovich, a singer at Mamontov's Private Opera. She went there with Savva. Chaliapin sang the whole of Rimsky-Korsakov's *Mozart and Salieri* all alone. Sergey Rachmaninov accompanied him. Zabela wrote to Nikolay Rimsky-Korsakov:

> Rarely have I taken such delight before! The music in this opera is so fine, so touching, and at the same time it is so intelligent, if I can describe music in such terms. My husband also enjoyed it very much. He designed the costumes for the opera immediately and during the dinner we had a toast to the future success of *Mozart and Salieri*. I don't doubt its success at all. […] I am sorry since I think I haven't managed to show you all my excitement about *Mozart and Salieri*. Well, indeed, it created a very good feeling inside me.

At the beginning of September the Rimsky-Korsakov family returned to St. Petersburg. They suffered another sad event that autumn: Avdotya, their favorite nanny, died.

As usual, upon the completion of his new opera, Rimsky-Korsakov felt tired. With regard to the question of the production of his new opera with the help of Mamontov, Rimsky-Korsakov informed Kruglikov: "I would turn down their offer directly in case the board of the Imperial Theatres express their intention to stage the opera. The opening night of this opera must take place in Moscow and be directed by S. I. [Mamontov]."

Sometime earlier Mamontov had asked Rimsky-Korsakov to change the ballet music in one part of *Sadko* to choral music, for he found it difficult to stage dances. In his turn Rimsky-Korsakov refused to change anything in *Sadko*: "It's completed and that's it. The old saying tells us: Take us as you find us. I am too tired to think of *Sadko*. I feel too exhausted to think of *The Tsar's Bride*, though I am keeping on working on polishing it and on its orchestration. I will finish the second act soon. I am still not satisfied with a lot of trivial things in my opera, just owing to the fact that in any case I am not excited about myself in general. I wish I were ten years younger."

These words worried Kruglikov, and he wrote to the composer:

I do not like the mood of both your letters from the city.[...]I have noticed something wrong. They differ greatly from your letters from Vetchasha, as they do not have the same attitude. In your letters I could feel some fatigue, again some distrust in yourself and your abilities. You shouldn't feel like this. Instead of complaining about ink, notepaper, and a pen, just take them as often as possible. You should become as enlivened as you were before, and you should avoid dark thoughts and apathetic tunes. I especially beg you not to be weighed down with the latter. You should give us, those who love and appreciate you and your creative work, an opportunity to admire your desire to compose using new plots as long as possible.

In October 1898 Rimsky-Korsakov spent five days in Moscow, where he conducted the orchestra of the Russian Symphony Concerts. Mamontov invited him to his home, and for Rimsky-Korsakov's sake he organized a performance of *Mozart and Salieri* and *Vera Scheloga* at his place. Chaliapin sang the part of Salieri, Zabela the part of Vera. Rachmaninov accompanied him on the piano. Upon arriving home, Rimsky-Korsakov sent a letter of thanks to Mamontov: "You've managed to spoil me.[...]I appreciated the interest in my compositions and the cordiality much more than the ovations and wreaths."

Rimsky-Korsakov confessed in his letter to Kruglikov: "I've come to think that I'm rather vain. I like being praised and praised sincerely when my compositions are being played. I left them in a mood that seems to encourage me to compose new operas. But it's not true. I should take a rest for a long time or give up composing, since I'm tired and very tired. My vain thoughts and ideas are encouraging me just in an artificial way, and they encourage me for only a little while."

After his visit to Moscow, Rimsky-Korsakov sent a manuscript of Marpha's aria from the second act of *The Tsar's Bride* to Zabela. He wrote:

I'm impatiently looking forward to hearing your opinion about the aria. At first I was brave enough to think I'm composing to suit your voice and that the aria and the part of Marpha were written only for you. And now, I'm afraid I was wrong and that I won't please you. And you wish me to be in an "F major" mood. I can tell you that even "E-flat major" is not bad for me and enough for me at my age. And "F major" is not proper for my age. "F major" is the music of youth and spring, but not that early spring with delicate ice and tiny puddles. It's the time when lilacs are in full bloom and all the fields are covered with flowers. It's the key of daybreak, but again not of that certain time when the light is just born, but when the east is completely purple and golden. Was I good enough in showing my decadent tendencies, "F major" and my pictorial preferences?

Then he sent Marpha's aria to Zabela as well as a new romance, *The Nymph*, which he dedicated to her. He mentioned in his letter: "This scene with the aria and Nymph I wish to listen to only with your voice."

On 24 November 1898 Rimsky-Korsakov completed the orchestration of *The Tsar's Bride*. He wrote to Zabela again: "I'm not feeling tired yet, though I understand that it's just a matter of time. A little later I will feel exhausted and I'll become limp and then I'm likely to pull myself up. Composers are like confirmed drunkards; that is, if they gave up composing they would be healthy, but they cannot and they just dream of not aging. How I'm afraid of becoming old!"

The opening night of *Mozart and Salieri* took place on 25 November 1898 at Mamontov's Theatre. Rimsky-Korsakov did not attend it. The opinions about the opera varied greatly. S. I. Taneyev, a composer, wrote in his diary: "I don't like the opera even a little.[…]The music is lifeless and doesn't impress one at all. It's just a colorless thing. And that after *Sadko!*"

Nadezhda Zabela shared an absolutely contrary opinion: "The impression of *Mozart and Salieri* was […] the following: The audience in the boxes and general viewers were at a loss. They didn't know if they should become excited or not. On the contrary, the stalls applauded much. I heard a lot of good and even delighted opinions about the opera." The newspaper reviews were mainly flattering, but mostly they praised Chaliapin, who sang the part of Salieri. Chaliapin sent a telegram to Stasov: "Yesterday, for the first time, I sang a wonderful composition by Pushkin and Rimsky-Korsakov." *Mozart and Salieri* was a great success. I am very happy."

Kruglikov was excited with the opera:

Your opera, if one listens to it very attentively, is just tremendous. (It's just impossible to listen to it inattentively; nobody even coughed in the audience.) I don't remember that anything has touched me and impressed me more than your *Mozart*. Tears appeared in my eyes, and I had a kind of spasm in my throat. This is a huge composition. Certainly, its intimacy and its omission of common effects are not for the general opera public, [...] but in any case, it's a huge composition, which you should be proud of. The man who managed to compose it hasn't exhausted his talent. On the contrary, his talent is in full bloom, so you shouldn't be down in the mouth.

Mikhail Vrubel was also captivated by *Mozart and Salieri*. To show his admiration for Rimsky-Korsakov's talent, he presented him with the three drawings, in particular the illustrations to the Pushkin tragedy that he had drawn in 1884. These wonderful drawings were hung later on a wall in Rimsky-Korsakov's living room.

The Mariinsky Theatre decided to produce *The Snow Maiden* again. The first performance took place on 15 December 1898. Rimsky-Korsakov considered the production much too elaborate. He attended the first performance, and according to Yastrebtsev's notes the composer was called to the stage twenty-one times. Rimsky-Korsakov also attended the second and the third performances and was called to the stage many more times. Just before the new year Rimsky-Korsakov and his wife left for Moscow, where they spent several days. They visited Mamontov's Opera, where they saw productions of *The Maid of Pskov* along with the prologue from *Vera Scheloga* and *Sadko*. At the Bolshoi Theatre they saw a performance of *Christmas Eve*. They also visited the Tretyakov Gallery, where Serov's portrait of Rimsky-Korsakov was on display. Rimsky-Korsakov reminisced later: "Our leisure time was filled with dinners, small parties organized by Mamontov, and visits to the Vrubels and Kruglikov, etc."

On 6 March 1899 Rimsky-Korsakov turned fifty-five. Yastrebtsev came for lunch to congratulate Rimsky-Korsakov, and in the evening the family held a big party. Lyadov, Glazunov, Zabela, Belyaev, Stasov, Belsky, and many others were there. There were also some young people, friends of his sons Andrey and Vladimir. Zabela and Chuprynnikov, a tenor from the Mariinsky Theatre, sang several duets. The former performed Marpha's aria from the last scene of *The Tsar's Bride* twice, as well as the romances *The Nymph* and *I Still Can Feel, My Dear Friend*, both of which Rimsky-Korsakov dedicated to her. This lovely party finished only about 4 a.m. The next day was the beginning of the second tour of the Moscow Private Opera in St. Petersburg. It lasted until 3 April. They put on *Sadko*, *The Maid of Pskov* with the prologue from *Vera Scheloga*, and *Mozart and Salieri*. Zabela and Chaliapin were again among the soloists.

On 8 April the Rimsky-Korsakov family held another musical evening. Chaliapin and Zabela were the distinguished guests. The party began rather late, about 11 p.m., and a considerable amount of music was performed. Chaliapin sang Rimsky-Korsakov's romance *Herald*. He also sang two of Rimsky-Korsakov's ariosos twice, *The Antar* and *The Prophet*, at Stasov's request. Then Chaliapin sang the Song of the Varangian Guest from *Sadko* and the song of Varlaam from *Boris Godunov*. Dinner began only at 2 a.m. Chaliapin, who was a brilliant storyteller, entertained the guests with anecdotes. He illustrated his stories with facial expressions and gestures and created scenes. For example, he acted out the following episode: a very old, nearly blind woman who knelt praying in the church and who confused spittle with a coin. She interrupted her praying, reached to it, and tried to pick it up; only then did she realize her mistake. It was worth seeing, as Chaliapin's face changed into the face of the elderly woman little by little as he expressed greed, disappointment, and disgust caused by her mistake. The other story was about his "knowledge" of English. Once when he was in a restaurant, he turned to his neighbors, some Englishmen, and made a brief speech consisting just of the imitation of the sounds and rhythm of the English language, which was, however, completely meaningless. The foreigners seemed to like Chaliapin's impressive figure, and they responded with a toast in his honor. Judging by the expressions on their faces, the toast was flattering, but Chaliapin did not understand a word, just as the Englishmen did not comprehend his speech.

The Tale of Tsar Saltan

When Zabela left for Moscow after her St. Petersburg tour, Lyadov, Glazunov, Rimsky-Korsakov, and Yastrebtsev saw her off. Yastrebtsev wrote in his memoirs: "Rimsky-Korsakov was in some strange mood. When Nadezhda Zabela asked him why he was in low spirits, he responded that he was not, but there were some reasons why he was very concerned and due to this a little absent-minded." Yastrebtsev asked himself whether Rimsky-Korsakov had been thinking of composing a new opera. The reasons Rimsky-Korsakov was so concerned remain unknown. He began composing a new opera soon. Already in February he had written down the first musical ideas for his new opera based on the plot of Pushkin's fairy tale *The Tale of Tsar Saltan*. The plot was suggested by Stasov. The year 1899 was the centenary of Pushkin's birth. Rimsky-Korsakov frequently met Belsky to discuss the plot of this new opera. Soon Belsky was absorbed in composing the libretto. They kept it a secret; no one knew about this, including Yastrebtsev.

Mikhail, Rimsky-Korsakov's eldest son, was twenty-five years old when he met Elena Rokkafuks, his future wife. They met for the first time in Latovka. In mid-May 1899 Mikhail and Elena were married in Elizabethgrad.[6] From the Rimsky-Korsakov family only his mother and Andrey attended the wedding. When they returned to St. Petersburg, the family gathered in Vetchasha. Rimsky-Korsakov had been completely absorbed during this time with the composition of *Tsar Saltan*.

Two friends of Andrey and Vladimir visited Vetchasha: Nikolay Richter, a young talented pianist and a student of Professor I. A. Borovka, and Stepan Mitusov, a true enthusiast of and later an expert on Russian music, especially the music of Rimsky-Korsakov. Mitusov was keen on art and literature. Yastrebtsev and the family of Belsky also visited the Rimsky-Korsakov family. Rimsky-Korsakov composed very quickly. Belsky was not always on time to catch up with the musical thoughts of the composer and sometimes was behind him with the libretto. When Belsky was too late again with the text of the libretto, Rimsky-Korsakov sent him a letter: "I was so seduced by a love episode that I couldn't help but compose the music as though on a 'customs bill.'[7] [...] I asked you to proofread and change my 'customs bill' according to your taste, but you should save the pattern, the consequences of thoughts and the measure. [...] You might become angry with me for this, [...] but truly, I'm too impatient to wait."

Rimsky-Korsakov composed *Tsar Saltan* very quickly. The whole opera was sketched during the summer and partially orchestrated. Rimsky-Korsakov used the tune of a lullaby that their favorite nanny used to sing to his children so many times. The composer reminisced later: "To commemorate Avdotya, our favorite nanny, who passed away a year ago, I chose the tune of her lullaby for the song of the nanny rocking the little Gvidon to sleep."

In September 1899 the Rimsky-Korsakov family returned to St. Petersburg from Vetchasha. Yastrebtsev visited Rimsky-Korsakov and brought a bust of Pushkin because of Pushkin's jubilee. Yastrebtsev wrote later: "When Rimsky-Korsakov thanked me for the present, he told a joke. It happened during an examination. When one of the female students was asked what 'Apollo' was, she responded confusingly that it was a myth; when the professor asked what myth she meant, she answered, after thinking for a while, 'The myth is a bust.'"

Owing to the student demonstrations of 1899, the environment at St. Petersburg University had become unsafe.[8] Andrey, who had finished his first year by that time, was advised to carry on with his studies abroad in order to be kept as far as possible from likely troubles. He chose Strasbourg University. Andrey sent a letter to his mother on his way to Berlin:

> My dear, dear Mama,
>
> We were together just recently and now we are so far away from each other. I think I didn't understand up until the very departure what it means to be so far from you. My heart is aching when I think that I won't see you and Papa for some months. But, please, don't think that I doubt or I hesitate if I should go or not. [...] When I crossed the border I also felt pain and sorrow, but certainly much less than when I parted from you. A strange, pitiful feeling captured me completely when the train crossed over a small river, which serves as the border. [...] No sooner had we crossed the border than German officers and soldiers with Wilhelm-type faces appeared. They all had shaved chins and turned-up moustaches. Their faces were ugly.

Rimsky-Korsakov responded to him in Strasbourg: "If you were sad when you were parting with us, we were also not joyful. We have been thinking about you all the time."

12

Travels and Triumphs, 1899–1901

*He was nearly buried with little wreaths and bouquets that were
thrown from the upper rows. No musician has been honored
with such a cordial and special reception, not at least in our St.
Petersburg.*

—Vasily Yastrebtsev, in his memoirs, on Rimsky-Korsakov
at the 1900 premiere of *The Tale of Tsar Saltan* in Moscow

In Moscow

In October 1899 Rimsky-Korsakov went to Moscow to supervise the production of his opera *The Tsar's Bride* at the Private Opera Theatre. He wrote to his wife from Moscow:

My dear Nadyusha,

[…] The opera has been rehearsed well; the selection of voices is wonderful; I am very pleased. You won't believe it but I was very glad to listen to the ensembles. […] Why am I so satisfied this time? Is it just my vanity? No, I am sure, nobody judges *The Tsar's Bride* correctly. They think it is the worst one of my operas, because I didn't follow the path of the "mighty handful." I think they make an unforgivable mistake. […] Believe me, the opera sounds very fresh. The music is not old-fashioned at all. You should certainly come and take Sonya with you. You shouldn't think about choosing dresses. Otherwise, who knows when she would have an opportunity to listen to it? Yesterday I had dinner with Kruglikov. Today I am visiting Vrubel's family.

Rimsky-Korsakov's wife and his daughter Sonya arrived in Moscow for the opening night of *The Tsar's Bride*. The performance was successful. Zabela sang the part of Marpha; Rostovtseva, a talented singer, the part of Loubasha;

Shevelev the part of Gryazny; and Sekar-Rozhansky the part of Lykov. The newspaper *Kouriere* (*Courier*) published the following review:

> The applause in honor of the composer started after the first act when Rimsky-Korsakov appeared on the stage. Everyone in the theatre in unison called him to the stage. He was presented with a wreath with the initials R.-K. from the Moscow Philharmonic Society under a storm of applause. Then the composer was called to the stage several times. Everything was repeated again after the second act when Rimsky-Korsakov was presented with a wreath from the performers. There were curtain calls after the third and fourth acts as well. The composer was deeply touched and thanked the audience as well as the performers.

Rimsky-Korsakov stayed for the second performance in Moscow, whereas his wife returned to St. Petersburg after the first one. She might have behaved this way since she did not like the opera. Maybe it was caused by her involuntary jealousy of Zabela, since her husband Nikolay admired her singing so much. Nadezhda criticized the opera relentlessly in her letter to her son, Andrey:

> Certainly it's good that everything is going well with his opera, but as for me I don't share this sympathy. I consider this opera much worse than *Sadko* and in general the worst among your father's operas. [...] I don't appreciate the return to old opera patterns like "Long Live the Tsar." I think those old forms are unsuitable for such dramatic stories because [they] prevent the development of scenes on the stage. [...] Even if those forms were to be used, then they should be defeated by perfect music, which can cause you to forgive the lack of movement, and this very thing is absent in his opera. In my opinion, the music of all those duets, trios, quartets, and sextets is trivial and [only] just good enough, though you can feel the touch of genius. [...] I don't see in this opera even one powerful or tremendous piece.

The other letter to Andrey revealed that his mother seemed to be the only one who did not appreciate the opera, which put her at odds with the general opinion. She wrote: "It goes without saying that I don't express my opinion to anybody else."

One can imagine that Rimsky-Korsakov was upset that his wife disliked the opera. He wrote to Andrey about *The Tsar's Bride*: "Despite the fact that I am sure of the good points of this opera, and taking into consideration that even the most intelligent and sincere admirers appreciated it greatly, I still ache a little because Mama is displeased with *The Tsar's Bride*."

Home Theatricals

The Rimsky-Korsakov family held a merry party on Christmas Day 1899. They put on two plays: *The Cock-and-Bull Story* by Scheglov and *The Bear* by Chekhov. The performers were Nadezhda, Sonya, Andrey (who came home from Strasbourg), Volodya, and Nadya, with their girlfriends, Richter, Mitusov (who was also in charge of makeup), and Vladimir Troitsky, a student at the university. Rimsky-Korsakov was also supposed to take part in the performance; however, when he found out that there would be guests, he backed out. His participation was only to open and close the curtains. After the performance, Volodya recited a poetic joke written by his father using the name of a critic.

Andrey had to leave for Strasbourg after the Christmas holiday. He wrote home to St. Petersburg: "How long and dull my way to Strasbourg was. How upsetting and routine my future life in Strasbourg seems to be." While Andrey was living in Germany, he became keen on art. Rimsky-Korsakov praised Andrey: "My darling Andreyushka, [...] among all the human activities, appreciate art and science most of all, as they are the best. This is my advice to you."

Rimsky-Korsakov spent the first days of the new year of 1900 in Moscow. By that time the Private Opera Theatre had been renamed the Association of the Solodovnikov Theatre. In the meantime, Mamontov had gone bankrupt and could not maintain the theatre group. His railway-construction business had lost money and caused him to go bankrupt. He was arrested but soon released and was offered the position of general director at the Bolshoi Theatre. However, Mamontov did not want to return to managing a theatre and turned down the offer.

Rimsky-Korsakov attended the nineteenth performance of *The Tsar's Bride* at the Solodovnikov Theatre, where Lykov performed a new aria for the first time. Rimsky-Korsakov composed the new one at the request of Sekar-Rozhansky, who sang this part. He wrote to Andrey, who was in Strasbourg: "The performance was full of ovations and curtain calls. There were also some wreaths. [...] After the performance I was presented with a greeting address from the board, then with a special dinner, in one word, an incredible binge." Olga Knipper, who attended that performance, wrote to Anton Chekhov in Yalta: "I was in the opera listening to *The Tsar's Bride* for the second time. What wonderful, subtle and elegant music! [...] Zabela acted and sang Marpha brilliantly. I was so touched in the last act that I cried."

Nadezhda wrote to her husband in Moscow:

> Dear Nika,
>
> Now it's about 11 p.m., and I just received your letter. Our neighbors brought it to me. The postman must be drinking alcohol during the holidays, as they put strangers' letters into our mailbox and deliver our mail to the neighbors. [...] On New Year's we didn't have any guests at all, as you know. And the next day we didn't even have time to have breakfast as they came to visit us, so that [...] Sonya and I finished our breakfast only at 4 p.m! [...] Yesterday Volodya went to a ball at the girls' gymnasium, so he returned home only about 5:30 in the morning and then stayed in bed till 2 p.m. today. He leads an awfully fast life! That is all the news. Goodbye. Kisses.

At that memorable ball, Volodya was enraptured by the lovely face of Katya Benois, a schoolgirl, daughter of Leon Benois, an architect.[1] They never met again, but Volodya kept in mind that bright short meeting for the rest of his life. At the end of his days, when he found out that she was still alive, his memory about their meeting was so strong that he even composed a poem about it entitled "Comet K. B."

Rimsky-Korsakov was exhausted again after his hard work on *Tsar Saltan*. He complained to Nadezhda Zabela:

> I'm extremely tired, but I'm afraid to take a break. It seems to me that if I decide to rest and not compose for some time, I will never be able to start composing again and it will be the end. Frankly speaking, I'm not afraid of the end itself. I'm very frightened at the very thought of being old, especially of being helplessly old. That's why I'm working so hard, which you might confuse [...] with lively energy and vitality. I'm just like a walker who keeps on moving and is afraid to sit down for a rest, because he knows perfectly well if he sits down he will never reach his destination.

Second Trip to Brussels

It seems that Rimsky-Korsakov followed his own advice. He began composing a new opera, choosing another drama of Mey about ancient Rome for his plot; he titled the new opera *Servilia*. Rimsky-Korsakov had to interrupt his composition because he left for Brussels, where he was invited again to conduct a concert of Russian music. After seeing her husband off, Nadezhda wrote to him: "Dear Nika, we are all thinking of you: where you are now, whether you're warm, how you speak to Germans and what your mood is. I wish you to be in a good mood and in high spirits, and then the concert will proceed smoothly. Yesterday when we returned home from the railway station, we drank tea together, then read. Stepan stayed with us."

As usual, Nadezhda worried about her husband and expected his telegram impatiently. She was afraid that her husband would be hungry during his trip. Certainly he was not hungry. Although he did not get out of the railway carriage when it stopped at the stations, there was a buffet car on the train where he could have meals. Nikolay sent a greeting card to his wife from Berlin: "I'm in the cafe Bauer and I'm bored to death,[2] as I have nothing to do. I rambled for about an hour and a half along empty Berlin streets and I still have about two and a half hours to wait for the train. […] I slept at night in the train. I ate chocolate and apples. I kiss you and the children. I hope it won't be so boring tomorrow in Brussels; at least it is supposed to be much better."

As soon as he arrived in Brussels, he wrote to his wife:

My dear, I'm in Brussels. […] The room was ready for me when I arrived. In the morning the director of Des Concerts populaires, whom I met last time, picked me up and we went to the rehearsal. The rehearsals are held again in the hall "La Grande Harmonie" and the concert itself will take place in the theatre. D'Aust and Zhilson, a composer, met me there. D'Aust introduced me to the orchestra and told them so much about me that I had to keep silent and only bow from time to time. After the rehearsal I had lunch with d'Aust and his son in some fashionable restaurant. Then I had a nap; then I walked idly for a little. I bought a soft hat for myself and now I'm sorry I have done it, as I have to fix it every minute. I wish I had bought a derby hat! Now, I'm about to go to the opera to listen to *L'Africaine*.

When Rimsky-Korsakov was abroad alone, he missed his family very much and used to kill time walking about the streets in different cities. He frequently sent letters to his wife. His next letter read:

> My darling, I can tell you that I'm bored and awfully bored. One and the same thought comes to my mind frequently as to whether I would be happier here if I were with you or Sonya. I think it wouldn't make any difference. It would be dull for you and dull for me, and my boredom plus your boredom wouldn't result in joy. I'd better be the one to get bored here. The thing is, I have absolutely nothing to do. Take today, for example: In the morning I visited Gilson.[3] I asked him to play the prelude from his opera *Demon* for me,[4] and he did. I can't say I enjoyed his music. I had to say, "It's very interesting," and other similar trivial phrases. He played his cantata for me and even presented me with its score. He is so kind, and he is a real admirer of Russian music. [...]
>
> Gilson has the score of the opera [*sic*; tone poem] *Don Quixote* by R. Strauss, and we studied it together a little. It's an awful cacophony that just proves Strauss is wretched. I became so irritated that I tried with all my might to express my great disgust and show my contempt for such music. Gilson seemed to agree with me. I was at his house for about an hour and a half, and then he and I went to d'Aust, who was expecting me. We had lunch all together at the restaurant. Then d'Aust took me to the Musée d'Art Moderne. We visited it briefly. There were many paintings there, and as usual among them one could find good ones. It was nice. Then I said good-bye to d'Aust, who was really very kind, and then I didn't know what to do to occupy myself. I returned to the hotel, idled a little in my room, and then went out and walked a little. I bought two shirts for my tailcoat, six collars, and three pairs of sleeves. Then again I had nothing to do. Now I'm writing a letter to you. Then I'll go downstairs to have dinner, and then again I'll have nothing to do. I'll try composing, but I think it won't work out. (My room is too gloomy.) Then I'll go for a walk again. I think I'll drink beer in various small restaurants. I don't feel like going to the Opéra. Today they have *Hamlet* by Ambroise Thomas, and it's absolutely uninteresting. You are surprised that I'm not reading. But frankly speaking, I don't want to. I don't know why. Sometimes I go downstairs to read *Le Figaro* or the *Independent Belgium* or something like that, and I enjoy reading the *New Times*. (I really enjoy it, as it is something dear, something like ours.) I look forward to the time when I'll have rehearsals every morning, and therefore I'll be truly busy for two and a half hours.

I haven't decided yet what I'm going to do tomorrow after the rehearsal. I think I'll visit the Museum of "old" Art. I'm having dinner with d'Aust on Thursday. This nasty R. Strauss conducted his *Don Quixote* in Paris, and *Le Figaro* published serious articles about this event. I think if he were to be introduced to me, I wouldn't give him my hand.

Some days later Rimsky-Korsakov sent another letter to his wife: "Certainly, I've got used a little to my loneliness here and to the local routine, and nonetheless, I think of my departure with great delight. During all my stay here I have not been able to do anything. I've read Zola. The beginning of his novel is extremely boring. [...] Today I'm having dinner with Gubert, a professor and composer. Then I'm going to listen to *Cendrillon*." Rimsky-Korsakov described this opera by Massenet as flippant but interesting and harmonically musical.

While Rimsky-Korsakov was in Brussels, the Kharkov Opera group of Tsereteli performed *The Tsar's Bride* in St. Petersburg. The performance enjoyed great success, and Nadezhda sent a telegram to her husband: "I'm happy about the success of your opera." He was especially glad to receive such a telegram from his wife, who previously did not seem to like this opera very much.

The repertoire of the concerts in Brussels included the music of Glazunov for the ballet *Raymonda*. Rimsky-Korsakov did his best to encourage d'Aust and the other Brussels musicians to like the music. He wrote to his daughter Sonya: "To achieve this, during the rehearsal I praised the music aloud while conducting, and I turned to the listeners from time to time and tapped my head, and winked at them. It seems to have worked." Rimsky-Korsakov wrote home that Glinka's music was almost unknown to Brussels musicians and that they confused his compositions with Italian music; that they thought Borodin to be the director of the New Russian School; that Rimsky-Korsakov himself was still in the naval service, as, according to their opinion, all Russian composers were supposed to be either chemists, sailors, or engineers. To entertain the family, Rimsky-Korsakov sent the following letter concerning his impressions about Brussels written in a style mocking Old Russian:

My beloved offspring: Sophia, Andrey, Vladimir, and Nadezhda,

I am dispatching my inviolable paternal blessings to you, and I wish you to abide in robust health and prosperity. I am also bowing to your revered aunt Sophia and your uncle Semyon, and I am wishing prosperity and happiness to them. [Some more bows and wishes to different relatives were included.] I have been in this remote barbarian land, Belgium, for a long time, and I have been missing you very much. There is only one thing that I enjoy here: the thought that I only have to stay here for two more days. The people here are mischievous and drive along the roads in the city at high speed, so a pedestrian should be very careful if he does not want to be run over. The streets are filled with newspaper boys shouting at the top of their lungs. There is a myriad of idle people on the streets. People here drink beer a lot and enter their chambers wearing their coats, and they also do not remove their hats since there are no holy icons in the chambers. And dogs draw carts here and bark a lot. There is awful disorder here, and they do not respect the king at all. There are only a few mailboxes on the streets, and in my remote corner there aren't any at all. There is only a post office in my neighborhood. The post office building is vast, and people enter it without taking off their hats; it is even permitted to smoke inside. During the rehearsals, which are the mother of any experience, as the Latin proverb says, they chat and produce much noise. They play fiddles well but they do not play the pipes called oboes well, and their trombones are not extendable but have valves, which makes the sound produced weaker. Nevertheless, they play with zeal and after playing my suite clapped their hands. Herr Marshot plays the lead violin. The last name of the chief director, i.e., general manager, is Berendey [Bérendés].[5] Though he usually talks a lot of nonsense, he is a nice person. And local music composers write music very badly and imitate Strauss and d'Indy, and because of this I tell them off a lot. I'm looking forward to the long day when I get on the train. As soon as I get on the train, I will go straight to Peter at full speed, where I hope to embrace you, all my children.

You are forever in my good graces,

Your Father,

16 March 1900. The city of Brussels.

The concert of Russian music was held on 18 March 1900 in the Théâtre de la Monnaie. Rimsky-Korsakov chose for the concert the overture to *Ruslan and Lyudmila* by Glinka, his own *Scheherazade* and main theme of *Sadko*,[6] the interlude from the opera *Oresteia* by Taneyev, and the *Polovetsky March* from Borodin's opera *Prince Igor*. Rimsky-Korsakov arrived in St. Petersburg on 20 March 1900. He spent the evening of the next day at the Mariinsky Theatre, where he listened to the Berlioz Requiem. Several days later Rimsky-Korsakov attended his opera *The Tsar's Bride*, performed by Tsereteli's group. Rimsky-Korsakov could not imagine anybody else singing the part of Marpha but Zabela. After the performance, he wrote to her:

> Insarova (who acted as Marpha) is very pretty, and she acts and sings in the last scene perfectly; [...] But in terms of beauty of voice and the art of acting, nobody can be compared to you. She is far below you. I can't forget your A-flat and C-flat, and how perfect they are in your performance. In any case, she doesn't have that very "mezzo voice" at all, which you possess and which is only your own. Well, what else can I add? You know how I love your voice and your singing, and after you, I'm certain no Marpha can be satisfactory.

Since the composer was in Brussels on his birthday, they decided to celebrate it on 22 March in St. Petersburg. All of his close friends, as usual, gathered in his house on that day. Unfortunately, Blumenfeld failed to attend. Because of this, *Tsar Saltan* was not performed, since Rimsky-Korsakov refused to play the piano for it himself. *May Night* was staged in Frankfurt am Main in April 1900. Andrey came to attend the performance from Strasbourg. After the performance he wrote to his parents that most of the German performers did not understand the humor and poetry of Gogol's tale and the music of this opera.

Strasbourg and Switzerland

The summer was approaching. The Rimsky-Korsakov family decided to spend it abroad to be closer to their son Andrey, who was still studying at Strasbourg University. They decided to stay for some time in Strasbourg. The family traveled there through Berlin and Cologne, then by ship along the Rhine River to Mainz, and then at last to Strasbourg. First they settled down at the Villa Victory in Strasbourg, and then they moved to the Villa Peterstal in the mountains of the Black Forest, where Andrey visited them on weekends. They all went together to Allerheiligen in a carriage, an interesting place nearby, where they visited the remains of an ancient monastery, a beautiful gorge, and a waterfall. By the middle of July Andrey's studies were completed, and the whole family went to Switzerland. On the way they visited the Rhine falls. Rimsky-Korsakov signed a special guest book and included a musical phrase from his opera *Tsar Saltan*. They spent almost a week in Lucerne and from there left for Vitznau, on Lake Lucerne on the slope of the Rigi Kulm mountain. They stayed there for a relatively long period of time. Rimsky-Korsakov wrote to his son Mikhail, who remained in St. Petersburg with his own family: "Mama, Andrey, Sonya, and I hiked to Vitzenauerstock: we climbed for about two and a half hours. I didn't get very tired despite the steep slope." They also visited Lausanne, Geneva, and Chamonix Valley, where they were able to enjoy the view of Mont Blanc and walk in its foothills.

Servilia

Rimsky-Korsakov had already been thinking about a new opera, *Servilia*, for a long time. He began making first drafts in 1900 and wrote the libretto by himself. During the family trip, he kept on composing this opera despite the fact that he did not have a piano at the places where they stayed, nor any opportunity to play the completed pieces. As was his custom, he kept his work on the new opera secret.

By 1 September 1900 all except Andrey had returned to St. Petersburg. Mikhail and his wife and son met them at the railway station. Rimsky-Korsakov described his trip to Switzerland in a letter to Kruglikov after their return home: "Instead, I walked much of the time: climbed at Rigi Kulm, Vitzenauerstock, and Mer de Glace, and did not work properly. Now I will be occupied with my usual 'winter' long, drawn-out proceedings, that is, I'm starting my work at the Conservatory tomorrow and making preparations for the Russian Symphony Concerts."

The same autumn the Moscow Private Opera began rehearsals of *The Tale of Tsar Saltan*. Rimsky-Korsakov arrived in Moscow on 12 October and stayed at the Loskutnaya Hotel, whose general manager, Sergey Belanovsky, was a friend and a true admirer of Rimsky-Korsakov's music. The composer began to attend the rehearsals of his opera immediately after his arrival.

He wrote to his wife: "I can't say anything exactly about the hotel yet. It seems to be expensive. My room is small: you can't put another bed into it. But it costs 2 rubles 25 kopeks (on the third floor). There is an elevator there. I am thinking of looking at other rooms tomorrow. Maybe I will change my own room and find something suitable for you." The next letter described the hotel:

The Loskutnaya Hotel is a very old house that was renovated to meet modern requirements. There is electric light, an elevator, the toilets are just perfect, but the rooms are not so good. Mine, at least, is not, for sure. The windows are very old. They have arranged for the bells to call only male servants; so if you need a chambermaid, you should just ring once instead of a set number of times, then a man comes and you should ask him to call a chambermaid. Luckily, they do all this without delay. If you want to have your clothes cleaned, you shouldn't put them out in the evening; instead, you should give them to a footman in the morning. Coffee here is also not any good. I'm looking forward to your letter. How are you getting on? I hope you're all right. Inform me when you are planning to come.

His wife responded: "If this hotel is so expensive, why don't you look for another, cheaper one? I don't mind coming a little earlier to listen not only to *Saltan*, but to something else as well."

The rehearsals proceeded smoothly. Rimsky-Korsakov was pleased, though he criticized his own opera. He wrote to his wife: "My dear Nadyusha, yesterday we completed all the pieces of *Saltan*, and rehearsed the last scene well. […] I noticed that with my getting old I've changed my view of the opera. Now the most attractive part of the opera for me is the singing, not the philosophy, which is always too reasonable. Somehow I know you wouldn't agree with me. When the Saltan and the Tsarina start the duet, I understand that it should be longer, that it's not long enough and I'm sorry it's too short." His wife contradicted him:

My dear, you are not right about *Saltan*. You're always insulting this opera. Well, it's true; you haven't said anything new in this opera and remained loyal to your old musical patterns. It reminds one of *Christmas Eve*, *Mlada*, and a small part of *The Snow Maiden*. However, first of all, you can borrow from yourself; every composer practices this. Secondly, *Saltan* has beautiful and expressive music. You composed it as skillfully as all your other mature compositions. In general it produces the effect of a lovely humorous tale, and that was your main objective. Some days ago I played the whole of *Saltan*. Taking into consideration all I've mentioned above, I beg you not to insult this opera and, what is even more important, not to repeat your critical words and comparisons to anyone else. It can be very harmful to this composition. You're often your own worst enemy. Never say anything bad about yourself—your friends will say it soon enough. Please, remember this genius phrase of Prosper Mérimée.[7]

Rimsky-Korsakov considered the music to be the first priority in any opera and was certain that all other aspects should be subservient to it. He wrote to his wife that Lentovsky, the producer of *The Tale of Tsar Saltan*, wanted to use a mechanical bumblebee to fly to Tsar Saltan and a mechanical toy squirrel to eat the nuts. Rimsky-Korsakov strongly objected. He said, "Firstly, it's difficult to arrange. Secondly, any mechanical device can be broken easily. The mechanical bumblebee might catch on something and get stuck, and then the audience would just laugh. And finally, the toys will attract all the attention: everyone will follow their flight and movement. I've insisted that children should act as the squirrel and the bumblebee. I think it would be nice and won't distract one from the music."

Rimsky-Korsakov did not like being far from his family for a long time, but the circumstances were such that he could not count on returning to St. Petersburg immediately after the opening night of *The Tale of Tsar Saltan*. There were two performances in a row, on Saturday and Sunday. The composer wrote to his wife: "I have to stay in Moscow on Sunday. There will be a special dinner with the opera group after the second performance, and the next day I will give my word to Sekar-Rozhansky to have dinner with him, so I will take a night train on Monday." Rimsky-Korsakov thought his wife would come to Moscow much earlier, but it did not happen. He went on in his letter: "It's a pity you're not coming today. I'm getting bored here with all this fuss and I'm missing you. On the other hand, my constant visits to rehearsals and the theatre, together with the absence of interesting performances, would not help make our stay in Moscow enjoyable. I'm expecting you to come on Friday by express train. I will meet you at the station."

The next letter was the last one the composer sent to his wife before her arrival:

> My darling Nadyusha,
>
> You will receive this letter on 19 October. So I congratulate you on your birthday and kiss you heartily. I'm writing my letter at 1 at night. I've just come back after *The Tsar's Bride*. […] In accordance with tradition, the board presented me with a beautiful wreath. I had to bow after each act. […] Thank you for your

comments about *Saltan* and your advice, which I'm certain to follow. In general, I agree with your opinion about *Saltan*; however, you must agree that in *Saltan* I didn't reach the high level that I did in the last scene of *The Tsar's Bride*, which forever will remain among my best compositions; and at the same time *The Tsar's Bride* doesn't repeat anything from my earlier works. That is why I love this opera. So, any criticism about this very opera—any "but," "yet," and so on—makes me very upset. Moreover, *The Tsar's Bride* represents a new and abrupt change in the singing parts. Hence, it's a move ahead, not backward. If this turn doesn't cause the art of opera to develop further then it is bound to sink in a swamp, where it's got stuck despite all my talented attempts to be realistic, which the art might try out only to some extent.[…] I had dinner with Kruglikov today. Kiss the children for me. Do, please, come to Moscow. I embrace you. Your N. R.-K.

Moscow Triumph: *The Tale of Tsar Saltan*

Rimsky-Korsakov's wife, their eldest daughter, and their sons Mikhail and Volodya, along with Belsky and Yastrebtsev, arrived in Moscow to attend the premiere of *The Tale of Tsar Saltan*. The dress rehearsal was held on the eve of opening night, at which time "the whole of the musical society of Moscow was present and the room was filled," according to the newspaper *Today's News*. Yastrebtsev wrote in his memoirs about that rehearsal: "Sergey Rachmaninov sat right behind me with two ladies (his old friends) and chattered the whole time. He was very worried about some key he had lost or left somewhere. His constant talking prevented me from listening to the music." Yastrebtsev described the first performance of the opera as follows:

> After the prelude Rimsky-Korsakov was called to the stage three times with an orchestral flourish and the thunderous applause of the public, who stood up when the composer appeared. He received large laurels from the Society of Russian Music Admirers. After the first act, Rimsky-Korsakov was called to the stage four times; after the second, six. A large silver lyre was engraved "From the performers of the Private Opera grateful for trust," and a lovely gilded wreath in the shape of the letter "S,"[8] with flowers in the shape of a lyre, was engraved with the inscription: "To the Glory of Russian Music and the Happiness of the Moscow Private Opera from the grateful Board." The wreath was decorated with a beautiful white silk handkerchief. There was an embroidered colored

picture on the handkerchief that depicted one of the scenes from the opera and was embroidered with lines from the libretto: "The swan flapped her wings, flew over the waters, and landed on the shore at the bushes. She shook her wings, roused herself, and turned into a beautiful Princess." He was nearly buried with little wreaths and bouquets that were thrown from the upper rows. No musician has been honored with such a cordial and special reception, not at least in our St. Petersburg. I repeat: it was something tremendously powerful, something monumental. After the first scene of the third act, Rimsky-Korsakov was called to the stage once, after the second scene of the same act he was called twice, after the first scene of the fourth act, twice, and when the opera was over, seven times. (All in all it totaled twenty-five times!)

Ippolitov-Ivanov, a conductor, reminisced that "the performance was a continuous triumph for Rimsky-Korsakov, with an endless list of pieces of evidence justifying by Muscovites' strengthened love of him." The second performance enjoyed a similar success, and the composer was called to the stage twenty-six times.

The Moscow newspapers wrote: "It was another new triumph for the Russian operatic art and our talented national composer. The first performance was just a great triumph for the composer, who was greeted with storms of ovations. It goes without saying that all tickets for all announced performances have been sold already." The *Peterburgsky listok* (*St. Petersburg Leaflet*) also published a review: "The Moscow newspapers wrote unanimously about the great success of Rimsky-Korsakov's new opera, which has beautiful melodies, powerful flights of fancy, and bright colors."

The part of the Swan in his opera was sung by Zabela, to Rimsky-Korsakov's great pleasure. The scenery and the costumes were based on the sketches by Vrubel. In addition, Vrubel painted a wonderful portrait of his wife, Zabela, in the costume of the Swan Princess.[9] Rimsky-Korsakov wrote to Zabela that she should take care of her voice and not work too much: "I don't want the voice I love so much to be spoiled or exhausted, especially from singing my compositions. I would only blame myself."

Servilia was not yet completed when Yevgény Petrovsky, a music critic, offered his libretto *Prince Ivan* to Rimsky-Korsakov, based on the Russian fairy tales. Rimsky-Korsakov became interested in the plot, although he thought the libretto itself needed much editing. In mid-November Petrovsky paid his first visit to Rimsky-Korsakov's house. He shared his impressions of the visit in a letter to N. Findeisen:

> I wasn't kept waiting. Rimsky-Korsakov received me as soon as I came and I was taken by his charm. […] I was struck and delighted by the fact that during our long conversation I felt so comfortable, so easy, and all of this was only because of his manner. If you think that this person might have become inflated to a rather large extent by the admiration of others' loyalty, maybe even by flattery, then for his manner to remain so simple and to make you feel so comfortable seems to be "something" special and innate like a talent.

The same letter told about the libretto he offered to Rimsky-Korsakov. He thought that Rimsky-Korsakov's views were a little old-fashioned and commented: "To make the comparison clearer, I would call my opera project 'the forest.' N. A. wishes me to make an orchard from it with linen paths and surrounded by a hedge." They parted with the agreement that they both would think about how to improve the libretto.

Soon Petrovsky wrote to Rimsky-Korsakov: "Just the idea that my work might serve You later on somehow encourages me to work harder." Petrovsky edited the plot twice, and both times Rimsky-Korsakov did not like it. Petrovsky was upset and decided to terminate his collaboration with Rimsky-Korsakov. Many people suggested plots for new operas to Rimsky-Korsakov. In particular, when Yastrebtsev and Belsky were the guests of the composer, Yastrebtsev named some specific works that he considered suitable for new operas; among them he listed *Fyodor Ioannovich* by A. Tolstoy, *Vasilysa Melenteva* by Ostrovsky, and *Servilia* by Mey. Ystrebtsev did not have the least idea that Rimsky-Korsakov had nearly completed his opera *Servilia* by that time. After listening to all of Yastrebtsev's suggestions, Rimsky-Korsakov said, "When I tell you what exactly I'm composing, you will be very surprised."

The date of 19 December 1900 marked thirty-five years since Rimsky-Korsakov had begun his work as a composer. However, various special concerts and performances devoted to this anniversary were held earlier in November. The first celebration in his honor took place on 25 November in St. Petersburg during the third Russian Symphony Concert in the Hall of the Assembly of the Nobility. The reason Belyaev, the manager of the Russian Symphony Concerts, scheduled a banquet in honor of Rimsky-Korsakov so early was that he was unable to organize an additional concert in December. The first part of the concert included the ballad *The Voevoda* by Tchaikovsky,[10] the main theme from *Sadko*, and *The Procession of the Princes* from *Mlada*; the latter was played twice at the request of the audience. Rimsky-Korsakov conducted the concert. After *Sadko* was played, Belyaev came up on the stage and delivered a speech about the significance of Rimsky-Korsakov for Russian art. The next speaker was Stasov, who, as the newspaper *Rossiya* (*Russia*) described it, "made a heartfelt, sincere statement full of emotion, which delighted the public greatly." Stasov drew a parallel with *Sadko*, saying that like Sadko, Rimsky-Korsakov was a sailor who had undertaken a long voyage; like Sadko had captured a beautiful princess (i.e., Russia) with his talent; and at last Rimsky-Korsakov, like Sadko, had his own troops, but in this case his troops were made up of his outstanding students. People presented wreaths to Rimsky-Korsakov again and again under continuous orchestral flourishes.

The concert of the Russian Musical Society was scheduled for 2 December 1900. Zabela was invited to sing Marpha's aria from *The Tsar's Bride* at it. Rimsky-Korsakov wrote to her: "Honestly, I can't understand what you might be afraid of in your planned trip to St. Petersburg. If I had the right I would forbid you to feel frightened. By the way, I can assert this right on the grounds of being the composer of this aria. Hence, I have this right, since I have the grounds, and I have these grounds because I understand how my own work can be performed." Zabela arrived in St. Petersburg and sang. After the concert the Rimsky-Korsakovs were invited to have dinner with the Vrubels. Ekaterina Ge, a sister of Zabela who was also there, made the following entry in her diary: "Vrubel proposed a toast to the first Russian musician. He was looking at Lyadov, but toasted Rimsky-Korsakov instead. Then [...] again he looked at Lyadov, and proposed a toast to the home in which the talent of Rimsky-Korsakov had been developed. Again, everyone thought it was Lyadov, but it turned out to be a toast to Nadezhda Rimskaya-Korsakova. It was fun!"

There were eight more concerts scheduled to celebrate Rimsky-Korsakov's anniversary—six in December 1900 and two in January 1901. In addition, Rimsky-Korsakov himself had to substitute for Napravnik, the conductor in St. Petersburg, and for Safonov, the conductor in Moscow, who became sick. When Yastrebtsev visited Rimsky-Korsakov, he found him in low spirits. Rimsky-Korsakov was annoyed with all these celebrations, which seemed to be endless and could even be compared to a chronic illness. The Moscow Private

Opera informed Rimsky-Korsakov about their giving two performances to honor his anniversary: the operas *Tsar Saltan* on 19 December and *Sadko* on 20 December. They also told him that the whole group wanted to congratulate him. The Moscow Bolshoi Theatre also scheduled a festival performance in honor of Rimsky-Korsakov on 19 December. They were to perform *The Snow Maiden*.

Rimsky-Korsakov complained to Yastrebtsev:

> All of a sudden the Association of Music Teachers has decided to hold a festival in honor of my thirty-five years in the composition business and has sent out invitations all over Russia and elected me the first honorable member of this Association from the time it was founded. It's much too much. I can't bear all of this. I will certainly become sick from all this fuss. It goes beyond my strength.

"Maybe I should really follow the advice of Laroche and go to the operetta on 19 December," he added, laughing: "Indeed, it would be even a kind of joke!"

On Saturday, 16 December, the fourth concert of the Russian Musical Society was held in the Great Hall of the St. Petersburg Conservatory. Rimsky-Korsakov conducted his suite from *The Tale of Tsar Saltan*. As soon as the music stopped, there were many great ovations. A. Gerke, a member of the board of the Russian Musical Society, delivered an address of welcome, and then he read congratulatory telegrams from Grand Duchess Alexandra Iosifovna, Grand Duke Konstantin Konstantinovich, the Moscow branch of the Russian Musical Society, and many others received from all corners of the country.

On 17 December the Symphony Orchestra of Sheremetev held a concert in the Hall of Kononov. The first part of the concert was made up only of Rimsky-Korsakov's compositions. Although there was a severe frost on that day, with the temperature falling below -30° C [-22° F], the hall was packed. Rimsky-Korsakov was called to the stage many times during the concert and presented with laurels decorated with the roman numerals "XXXV." That evening there was a meeting of the Association of Music Teachers devoted to Rimsky-Korsakov's anniversary. The meeting was held in the Peter School Hall. Yastrebtsev described it in detail:

> So many admirers of Rimsky-Korsakov's talent gathered there that many people had to stand, since there were no vacant seats. The guest of honor entered the room at about 8 and was greeted with his "Glory" sounding triumphantly. While

the music was being played, the audience stood up, including the Grand Duke Sergey Mikhailovich, who attended the meeting and who was the patron of the Association. Rimsky-Korsakov was very pale and looked anxious. Next to him his wife walked with N. Findeisen on her arm and carried a beautiful bouquet of white roses. The composer was greeted by a number of delegations, twenty in all. They congratulated Rimsky-Korsakov in the following order:

First of all Glyasser, Deputy Chief of the Association of Music Teachers, made a statement full of emotion in which he announced to the audience that Rimsky-Korsakov had been elected an honorable member of the Association. Then Mr. P. I. Lelyanov, Chief Executive of the city, read an address of welcome from the St. Petersburg City Assembly; […] Mr. Arensky from the Chapel; Mr. Findeisen from the editorial board of the newspaper the *Russkaya muzikalnaya gazeta* [*Russian Musical Gazette*]; Count Sheremetev from his orchestra with a chorus; Bessel from the St. Petersburg Philharmonic Society, the management of the Public Symphony Concert, and the Association of Musical Publishers; Mr. Y. Kurdyumov from the music critics of the St. Petersburg press; Mr. G. Kazachenko from the Chorus of the Russian Musical Society; students from the Group of Amateur Choir Singers and the Chorus of Students of Technical Colleges; Mr. I. Glyasser from the Musical Courses; Mr. Krivoshein from the Musical Society of Dannemann and Krivosheev; Mr. Rangoff from the Musical Society of Rangoff; Professor P. Weinberg from the Writer's Association; Mr. E. P. Weinberg from the architects; Scholar Lunacharsky from the circle of Polonsky and in the name of all admirers of Rimsky-Korsakov. Almost every delegation presented him with a wreath. After each greeting the symphony orchestra of Count Sheremetev played a fanfare, composed by Rimsky-Korsakov.

When this part of the festival was over, the guest of honor and his wife took seats in the front row. Nadezhda sat between her husband and Grand Duke. The Chief of the Association, Senator Markovich sat next to the composer. After the concert, Rimsky-Korsakov was called to the stage and greeted excitedly. A special dinner in honor of the composer crowned the celebration. It was held at the Hotel de France. There were many people there, about eighty. […] There were many toasts to Rimsky-Korsakov. […] Glazunov made a toast to "Padre Rome" [*Rimsky* is the Russian name for Rome] and apologized for his lack of words; "Our dear Teacher failed to teach us speaking, but he taught us composing. The poet E. Solomirsky recited his poem devoted to Rimsky-Korsakov. The dinner ended at about two in the morning. The guest of honor finished it with the following words: "Even the best composition has its final chord."[...] When I was approaching my house, it seemed to be getting warmer; the sky was clear; a few clouds could be seen; and a crimson moon on the wane hanging on the skyline called to mind the beginning of the eighth scene from.

The next issue of the *Russian Musical Gazette* was devoted entirely to Rimsky-Korsakov. There were many articles about him and his music, and a poem was included by A. Kalinovsky, which was read by Lunacharsky during his address of greeting. Stasov wrote to his sister, Varvara Komarova: "On Saturday evening there were ovations, four wreaths, statements of thanks, one rose to one's feet, words of praise. On Sunday morning in the other hall there were ovations, wreaths, statements of thanks, one rose to one's feet, words of praise." Rimsky-Korsakov became dispirited!

The next day, on 18 December 1900, Rimsky-Korsakov left for Moscow. Before his departure, he had the following letter published in the newspaper *New Times*: "Due to my departure for Moscow and my lack of opportunity to thank in person all of the organizations of St. Petersburg and other cities as well as individuals that honored me with their greetings on the occasion of my thirty-fifth year anniversary as a composer, I would like to express my sincere and profound gratitude for their doing me the honor."

Rimsky-Korsakov left for Moscow alone. He stayed again at the Loskutnaya Hotel. As soon as he had settled down, he sent a greeting card to his wife notifying her that he had arrived safely, that it was very cold in Moscow, and that the sledges were moving with difficulty there. On the evening of 19 December he attended the Private Opera, where they performed *Sadko* in honor of his anniversary. The next day, he sent the following letter to his wife:

Dear Nadyusha,

   I'll write you just a brief note since I'm short of time. Yesterday the festival was organized well: I liked it very much that they just mentioned my anniversary in the posters and during the performance; the only address read was from the Private Opera. The whole group was on the stage, and the orchestra played a flourish during which little wreaths and flowers were showered from above onto the stage. I was presented in person with three wreaths and a huge bouquet of lilies of the valley. The theatre was overcrowded. The Highest Personage did not show up, I'm pleased to say. I was called to the stage at each intermission. After the performance, a special dinner was held at the Bolshoi. Fortunately, only close colleagues were invited to it.

Vrubel designed the address of greetings presented by the Private Opera. Vrubel depicted an ancient psaltery player who bore a close resemblance to the composer, whose music in its essence is based on folk melodies. Upon his return home, Rimsky-Korsakov hung the address in his study.[11] Rimsky-Korsakov apologized to the Bolshoi Theatre for his inability to attend *The Snow Maiden*, which was performed on the same evening as *Sadko* on 19 December 1900. However, despite his sincere apologies, the board of the Moscow Imperial Theatres felt insulted, and afterward relations with the board became cooler. In her turn, Nadezhda Rimsky-Korsakov celebrated this day in her own way in St. Petersburg. She wrote to her husband: "We celebrated the anniversary of your First Symphony on 19 December in the following way: we played it with Richter. I thought this symphony could be played in concerts from time to time. It is lovely, especially its first three movements. In my opinion, the finale seems to be not as perfect as the first [three] movements. [...] A huge pile of telegrams and letters is waiting for you."

During the next few days Rimsky-Korsakov was occupied with rehearsals for the concert, which he had to conduct instead of Safonov, who was ill. In addition, on 20 December he went again to the Private Opera to see *Tsar Saltan*. Rimsky-Korsakov wrote to his eldest daughter: "I was sitting with Cui in the box of the dress circle. They called me after each scene, and after the second act the chorus and the performers remained on the stage and (as they did in the first performance) applauded and waved olive branches. Moreover, they presented me with laurels."

The concert that Rimsky-Korsakov conducted was held on 23 December. During the concert, there was another celebration in his honor. Rimsky-Korsakov was presented with two more addresses of greeting: one from the professors of the Moscow Conservatory and the other from the regular participants at the concerts of the Russian Musical Society, with signatures of more than a thousand people. Russian Records published remarks by I. Lipayev: "Rimsky-Korsakov celebrated the thirty-fifth anniversary of his creative work with Muscovites. Recently they have begun to treat him as a close friend or a dear relative [...]. No wonder that the celebration managed to be very warm, sincere and tender." Rimsky-Korsakov was very touched by their admiration for his composition of operas and in his turn sent a letter of thanks to Russian Records for their publication, where he expressed his sincere gratitude to Muscovites for their cordial reception and those two unforgettable special evenings held in his honor.

Meanwhile, in St. Petersburg, Rimsky-Korsakov's family members, including Andrey, who had come home for the Christmas holidays, were busy with preparations for the Christmas family performance. They held rehearsals and designed scenery. Nadezhda wrote about this to her husband:

> We decided to have the performance on the morning of 25 December. It will be more convenient for you and Andrey. [...] I'm getting sad already that he has to leave so soon. Yet he is lucky to study abroad, not at our university. Here again they are preparing to struggle against the expulsion of thirty students. Those students are going to be expelled for taking part in protests against the play *The Son of Israel* [it was anti-Semitic]. Isn't it outrageous? The poor youth will suffer again. I'm afraid our Volodya would be engaged in these actions.

At home Rimsky-Korsakov found letters of greeting and telegrams from Astrakhan and Warsaw, Vladikavkas and Kazan, Kishinev and Kiev, Nizhny Novgorod and Odessa, Rostov-on-Don, Saratov, Tiflis, Kharkov, and Yaroslavl. In response to these greetings Rimsky-Korsakov published another grateful letter in the *New Times* in which he named all of the cities that had sent him greetings.

On the first day of the Christmas holidays many people came to Rimsky-Korsakov's home to see the performance. The program included the one-act comedy *The Burning Letters* by P. Gnedich, where the main character is a sailor, which might be one of the main reasons it had been chosen; the comedy *Good Manners* by V. Bilibin; and the satire *A Rash Turk*, or *Would You Like to Be a Grandson?* by Kozma Prutkov, in which a writer and a musician are made fun of. On 1 January 1901 Yastrebtsev visited the Rimsky-Korsakov family and brought a new issue of *Shut* (*The Jester*) with him, which had an anonymous poem published in honor of Nikolay. Later in January there was another festival in honor of Rimsky-Korsakov held by the St. Petersburg Conservatory. The student orchestra played his First Symphony, followed by a special dinner with professors and teachers of the Conservatory. Also, the Association of Musical Meetings held a big concert consisting exclusively of Rimsky-Korsakov's vocal compositions. After the first part Rimsky-Korsakov was presented with a wreath, and he was called to the stage and greeted after each part of the three-part concert. It was the last concert in a long train of festival performances in honor of the anniversary.

Rimsky-Korsakov joked that he got used to being congratulated so much that he had become an expert in anniversary celebrations, and "now he could be easily hired to act [...] as an honorable guest of any kind: an honorable guest without speeches, an honorable guest with greetings and even with speeches, tears, and touching gestures." The board of Imperial Theatres of St. Petersburg was the only one that did not take part in celebrations, although in January they were rather busy with rehearsing *Sadko* at the Mariinsky Theatre.

Sadko opened at the Mariinsky on 26 January 1901. The theatre was packed despite the high price of tickets, higher than usual since it was a benefit performance for the orchestra. Rimsky-Korsakov relinquished his royalties for this performance in favor of the orchestra. That night the composer was called to the stage many times. (Yastrebtsev counted eight.) The performance was a gala night. The tsar's family (except for the Queen Mother) honored the performance with their attendance. Many outstanding figures of art and science were there as well. Although Tsar Nikolay II arrived at the theatre at 6 sharp, the performance was delayed for ten minutes at His Majesty's request because they hoped that Maria Fyodorovna, the Queen Mother, would arrive. *Sadko* was performed five times at the Mariinsky within a two-week period, to great success. The author was called to the stage many times at each performance; however, Rimsky-Korsakov said that these calls were quite cold. The most touching presents among those he received on the occasion of his anniversary were from his children. These were a group picture of all of his five children, which always stayed on his desk after that, and a photograph of his family house in Tikhvin, where he was born. The latter was a present from Yastrebtsev's family. Alina Yastrebtseva ordered the photo, and Yastrebtsev framed it and made an inscription of two lines of music from *The Snow Maiden* and *Sadko*. This photo was hung on the wall of his study and reminded him of his intention to visit the place again. Unfortunately, his busy life did not allow him to undertake this return trip.

13

"My Own Monastery—My Art," 1901–1902

My compositions are clever but they lack sincere, heartfelt feelings and passion; they are all like snow maidens.

— Vasily Yastrebtsev quoting Rimsky-Korsakov
in his memoirs

A lot of people gathered at the party devoted to Rimsky-Korsakov's birthday on 6 March 1901. They performed a great deal of music. Maria Insarova, a member of the Tsereteli opera group, and Mitrofan Chuprynnikov, an actor from the Mariinsky Theatre, took an active part in the evening. From then on musical evenings again became a frequent occurrence in Rimsky-Korsakov's home. The composer chose one of those evenings, 25 March 1901, to show off his new opera, *Servilia*, for the first time.

The day before he wrote to Yastrebtsev: "If you promise me to keep secret (i.e., not to tell anybody) some information, which I bet you'd like to know, then you could visit us tomorrow, on Sunday at 8:30 p.m. If you're not sure that you will be able not to tell anyone else, then you'd better not come. But if you don't come, you'll show lack of interest, and then you'll find out the information one day, but much later." His surprise was *Servilia*. The invited guests included the Vrubels, Glazunov, Belsky, Lyadov, Bessel, and the students Vladimir Troitsky and Nikolay Mironov, as well as Mikhail, the composer's eldest son. Zabela sang Servilia's aria and several of Rimsky-Korsakov's romances. When Yastrebtsev returned home late after midnight, he wrote in his memoirs: "So, Rimsky-Korsakov has nine operas." In mid-May 1901 *Servilia* was performed in Rimsky-Korsakov's home.

Krapachukha

The spring came and the composer's wife, Nadezhda managed to find a suitable summer house for the family in Krapachukha. At the end of May Nadezhda left for Krapachukha with her daughters and Volodya. Her husband saw them off at the Nikolayevsky railway station. The house was completely ready for the new inhabitants; they even found the table laid with fresh milk, cream, and clotted sour milk. Nikolay's son Volodya was the first to send a letter to his father:

> There is [...] a huge wonderful desk in your study. The arrangement of the rooms is well planned. The kitchen is so huge that I think that it might serve as a concert hall. In any case, I think you should give a concert exactly in this kitchen: the huge stove will be booked for distinguished guests who will have exclusive honorable warm seats. We all are in high spirits. Even Mama this time did not say that we'd better return on the same train. [...] Dear Papa, come as soon as possible. We embrace you and kiss you heartily. We are looking forward to your arrival here impatiently. Everyone assisted in composing this letter, but it was written by Volodya. 28 May 1901, between 11 and 12 p.m.

The composer's wife wrote another letter:

Dear Nika,

    [...] This summer house is very good, I would even call it elegant, and furnished luxuriously. The surroundings are picturesque, and, in my opinion, the orchard is large. I wish the river were wider. But even as it is, it is not bad. To my mind, there is only one essential shortcoming—bad water in the river. This water is a brown color and has a disgusting taste, and it's rather cold for swimming. In any case we need a filter to use it. When we can't purify it, we use milk for drinking instead of water. The milk here is very delicious. [...] Everything here shows that the landlady is fond of cleanliness and order. She shouldn't even be compared to that Maria, who keeps everything in a great mess. [...] There are plenty of lamps and splendid candlesticks, several beautiful clocks that work. [...] Goodbye. I kiss you heartily. How are you feeling? I hope you were not hurt yesterday while you were carrying our heavy suitcase? Your N.

Rimsky-Korsakov was detained by his business in St. Petersburg. He stayed in the city until 1 June. By the time of his arrival at Krapachukha, Rimsky-Korsakov had completed the orchestration of *Servilia*. He felt exhausted from all of his hard work on the opera, and he could not make himself undertake composing anything new. However, he had some second thoughts about two new projects: Homer's *Odyssey* and *The Legend of the Invisible City of Kitezh* (a folk tale), which Belsky had suggested to him. His wife, in a letter to her son Andrey in Strasbourg, warned him "not to mention this to anybody." If Rimsky-Korsakov did not compose, he called his state of mind idleness. He wrote to Yastrebtsev: "Krapachukha is a lovely place. Our summer house is wonderful. Nonetheless, I feel a craving to go abroad. I'd like to see truly picturesque scenery. I'm bored with Russia."

As usual, life changed his plans. He informed his son Andrey:

> Mama has begun playing the piano a lot. I'm training Volodya. Why should this stop? Mama plays a lot every day. She has already replayed all the sonatas of Beethoven, then all of the early etudes of Chopin. She plays the variations of Glazunov, and his sonatas; and the barcarolle of Lyadov, etc. [...] Volodya plays duets with Nadya. He still does it rather badly, but he will certainly get better at it. I teach him harmony and solfège. He plays the violin a great deal and with much enthusiasm.

Kashchey the Immortal

Rimsky-Korsakov doubted whether it was worth using Homer's story for an opera. *Kitezh* still seemed very obscure. At the end of June 1901 he decided to again try the libretto suggested by Petrovsky. Since he did not fancy the libretto itself, Rimsky-Korsakov only used the plot and wrote a new libretto himself in verse. His daughter Sophia assisted with the libretto, and Rimsky-Korsakov began making the first musical drafts of the new opera. Thus was born the new opera, titled *Kashchey the Immortal*. Sophia reminisced later: "When *Kashchey* was being composed, I helped my Papa to compose the libretto. It was like this; he would come up to me with his eyes shining and say, 'Sophia, could you come with me? Let's have a talk.' And we went to the nearest forest, and discussed the plot of the tale and developed the details." As usual, when Rimsky-Korsakov liked the plot, he composed pretty quickly. He decided to compose a short opera, consisting of only three scenes, to be played without intermission.

However, fate broke into their peaceful country life. Rimsky-Korsakov's family received a worrying telegram about the serious illness of Natasha, Mikhail's daughter. Mikhail, the composer's eldest son, was on business in Heidelberg at that time. He rushed to his wife and his sick daughter. The composer's wife also left for Kherson, where the little girl was staying with her mother. Rimsky-Korsakov sent a letter as soon as Nadezhda began her trip:

> Dear Nadya,
>
> [...] Now it's 11 p.m. You're supposed to be in Sinelnikovo or just about to leave it. I can imagine how tired and exhausted you are. It's good that you went by luxury class [train]. Our children and I are accompanying you in our thoughts. The house has become empty after your departure and the days seem endless. [...] Take care of yourself, my darling. Have a good rest after the trip. Your aim should be to be there and not to work hard around the house. I can imagine how poor Misha feels and how he is frightened and speeding along the foreign roads. He will be so exhausted when he arrives! Kiss him heartily for me. Bow to Lelya [Mikhail's wife] and try to comfort her. [...] I'm embracing you, my sweet.

Poor little Natasha never recovered from her serious illness. She died on 9 July. The composer's wife was already there, but Mikhail was still on his way to Kherson. Nadezhda sent a letter to Krapachukha:

> My heart is hurting and my soul is crying so much that I can barely write to you, dear Nika. I didn't have any strength to drop you even a single line yesterday. Yesterday we went through the apex of woes, through the most painful experience. Today we will have to go through all the ordeals again since Misha is arriving in the evening. It's frightening to even think of how he will cope with this. [...] There is one thought that tortures me and haunts me constantly: why didn't I convince Lelya and Natasha to stay with us in our summer house and [and why did I] allow them to undertake that difficult and long trip when Natasha was such a weak and fragile child? I will never forgive myself for this.

The next day Nadezhda sent another letter to her husband:

Dear Nika,

Misha arrived yesterday. Our meeting was awful. I was entrusted with the hardest duty: to meet him at the railway station and prepare him somehow for the news. Indeed, there was nobody else to carry out this task. Lelya was out of the question, [...] and I couldn't allow strangers indifferent to Misha to touch his heart at such a moment. I pulled myself together and went to the station. I felt as if I were forced to be a butcher who was going to execute his dearest one. On my way I was thinking of what I would say, how I would prepare him step by step, but all my plans failed. When I saw him, my anxiety was so high that I couldn't say a word. I felt suffocated; it was some kind of nervous fit. So Misha understood everything at once. He was shocked, he cried. His head was resting on my shoulder all the way. He said he didn't want to hear about any details and we kept silence all the way home. [...] Right now we're expecting a priest to come to bury Natasha. He was sent for. Now it's about 10 a.m. When this awful final act is over, I will talk to Misha about everything and I will insist on his going with Lelya somewhere as soon as possible, and it's better if they go abroad.

Rimsky-Korsakov responded:

We received your letter yesterday. We all read it with sorrow and pain. But this letter doesn't say a word about the state of health of each of you. It's ridiculous that you put the blame on yourself absolutely for nothing and you torture yourself. Who could predict this? It's always easier to say what should have been done, but when you are about to do something it's difficult to forecast everything. Sorrow is sorrow! But what can be done? Many people have had to go through it. We also went through it twice when we lost Slavchik and Masha. I'm still very worried about you and everyone else. [...] Certainly it would be good if Misha went on business abroad again with Lelya. Hard work and his business [sic] would comfort his aching heart better than anything else. Certainly you should give them as much money as they need for such a trip. [...] Take care of yourself. I think you're absolutely exhausted both morally and physically. I embrace you.

Despite all of these misfortunes, Rimsky-Korsakov kept on working on *Kashchey the Immortal.* He wrote to Glazunov that he had been composing a new opera based on a fancy plot, but he did not reveal the title: "I think I will have completed the whole draft or nearly the whole by the end of the summer since the ideas are developing rather quickly."

Yastrebtsev arrived at Krapachukha at the beginning of August. Rimsky-Korsakov hid his new work from Yastrebtsev and neither showed him his new opera nor told him a word about it. Instead, Nikolay complained that he had been composing too little during the summer and that he was dissatisfied with his own work. However, Yastrebtsev felt somehow that Rimsky-Korsakov was just pretending and suspected him of composing something huge. They played a lot of music for four hands and discussed various musical events and music itself. The composer thought that, although his compositions usually were successful, in general the public appreciated them much less than they might. He thought that his talent was likely lacking something. Yastrebtsev quoted Rimsky-Korsakov's own words in his memoirs: "I'm always able to express the feelings of my characters, whereas by identifying myself with them in my thoughts I don't feel anything. My compositions are clever but they lack sincere, heartfelt feelings and passion; they are all like snow maidens. It may be very good but not for the public, which remains indifferent to my music due to that very fact. Lyrics and Love are the highest power, beauty and poetry." The same summer he composed the prelude-cantata *From Homer*, Op. 60, for orchestra and female voices. He did not complete his new opera that summer and even thought that it might not be worthwhile to continue working on it.

Moscow

At the beginning of September 1901, Rimsky-Korsakov returned to St. Petersburg. In October he left for Moscow, where he stayed for several days. The Bolshoi staged *The Maid of Pskov* with the prologue to *Vera Scheloga*. As soon as he returned to St. Petersburg, he was occupied with supervising the rehearsals of *The Tsar's Bride*, which was to be performed in the Mariinsky Theatre. Opening night of *The Tsar's Bride* was 30 October 1901, and the opera enjoyed a great success. It was performed six times during the following two weeks. However, the season ticket holders remained rather cold to this opera. Rimsky-Korsakov's wife attended the opening night and shared her impressions with her son Andrey:

I remember what I told you after the first performance of *The Tsar's Bride* in the
Moscow Private Opera, and I believe I will repeat much of that now. [...] Nonetheless, it's just only one side of the story. [...] I didn't say at that time anything
about the strengths of this opera. There are plenty of them: many wonderfully
written recitatives, the highly dramatic fourth act, and, at last, perfect orchestration. [...] There we can see a rare interlacing of talent and great skillfulness. The
orchestra expresses truly and beautifully at the same time not only the state of
mind of the characters but to some extent the emotion in their hearts.

In mid-December Rimsky-Korsakov left for Moscow again. This time he
was accompanied by his wife; Andrey, who had returned from Strasbourg;
and Yastrebtsev. They all stayed at the Loskutnaya Hotel. The concert of the
Russian Musical Society was scheduled to be held on 15 December 1901.
Rimsky-Korsakov was to conduct it. The first part of the concert included the
third act of *Mlada*. The orchestral arrangement of *Night on Bald Mountain*
was also included.[1] Yastrebtsev made the following entry in his diary:

Before the concert, Rimsky-Korsakov came around just to ask for friendly advice
whether it would be appropriate to put on a white flannel shirt with a stiff collar
with a tailcoat. "I'm afraid I will make a scandal with such an outfit," he said. [...]
He seemed to be upset that I also wouldn't advise him about wearing anything
reasonable. Before going to the concert (it was about 7:20 p.m.) I visited Rimsky-
Korsakov. He had managed already to change the flannel shirt for a starched one
and was in high spirits.

And again Rimsky-Korsakov appeared on the stage with the sounds of an
orchestral flourish played three times, and again he was presented with a message
of greeting with seventy-seven signatures. After *Night on Bald Mountain* was
played, he was called to the stage many times.

Safonov invited Rimsky-Korsakov and all those who had arrived with him to
a special dinner after the concert. Yastrebtsev wrote in his memoirs that when
they left the Conservatory, crowds of young people were staring at Chaliapin
and Rimsky-Korsakov. Chaliapin was also among the guests who were invited
by Safonov. At the party, the time passed quickly owing to Chaliapin's presence
and his talent as a storyteller. He described vividly all the troubles he had met
on his way to the Bolshoi Theatre. The dinner was not over till about 4 a.m.

Rimsky-Korsakov's family spent the next two days sightseeing. They took a trip to Vorobyovy Gory (Sparrow Hills), visited the Kremlin, and listened to the ringing of the Moscow church bells. The family left for St. Petersburg by a night train.

During their travel together in the railway car compartment, Rimsky-Korsakov and Yastrebtsev had a long talk about life. Rimsky-Korsakov complained about his aging. He said that he had come to the conclusion that he had lived much of his life just because of his desire to contradict: when he was said to be known mainly as a composer of symphonic music, he undertook composing an opera; when he was said to be perfect as a composer of crowd scenes, he created operas where the soloists' parts were given special attention; when Laroche, a critic, criticized Musorgsky's *Boris Godunov*, he immediately undertook the reediting of the opera for it to be staged; when Stasov told Rimsky-Korsakov that the latter could not compose recitatives, he in response composed his *Mozart and Salieri* in no time. Rimsky-Korsakov summed up at the end of their conversation, "You cannot believe, but my realization of this fact disparages the character and significance of my talent in my own eyes."

The thirty-sixth anniversary of Rimsky-Korsakov's musical career was 19 December 1901. Yastrebtsev came to congratulate him and brought a basket of lilies of the valley for Rimsky-Korsakov and three roses for his wife. He did this following his mother, who used to send a basket of flowers to the Rimsky-Korsakov family on each anniversary of the day. After Alina Yastrebtseva died that year, her son carried on her custom.

Rimsky-Korsakov spent a lot of time giving serious thought to the development of art in general and music in particular. He still hoped to write his own treatise on the aesthetics of music. At the beginning of January 1902 Rimsky-Korsakov worked out the preliminary contents of such a treatise. At the end of this draft he wrote: "The art of the nineteenth century is developing staggeringly fast. Is it likely to proceed further? Aren't we approaching the end?" Rimsky-Korsakov assessed the future of his own compositions very pessimistically. He thought they would not survive after his death. Yastrebtsev recorded the composer's thoughts:

> At first I think there may be some increase in interest in my personal reputation and my compositions. They might even publish some books about me, and then I'll be buried in eternal oblivion. [...] By the way, Telyakovsky told me recently,

"We intend to produce Your *Servilia* next year, and then I think we should wait for a while." "Otherwise," he added, "they might reprimand me. They say already that I produce only Your operas." So you can see that the near future of my compositions doesn't seem optimistic.

The Rimsky-Korsakovs celebrated his fifty-eighth birthday in 1902. They received numerous guests, among them his son Mikhail, Stasov, Glazunov, Lyadov, the Blumenfeld brothers, Sokolov, Belyaev, and Belsky. Some other students, including Mitusov with his fiancée, Troitsky, Mironov, and Dobrzhinsky,[2] a young talented artist, also attended. The party was very joyful, and a lot of music was performed. Yastrebtsev described it:

> During the special dinner, Nikolay Sokolov entertained the group with funny anecdotes. He also recited Pushkin's poems, mimicking the manner of a deacon and a church reader, then he recited a "Scottish Ballad" as if he were speaking English (he can't speak a word of English). Blumenfeld performed the talk of two cocks crowing to each other at a distance. All the guests enjoyed this and laughed very much. After the dinner, they composed and performed a one-act opera extempore. It was a parody on an Italian opera of the old days, mostly with an artificial tragedy and one death. [...] Stasov was delighted. After this impromptu event, Mitusov danced a "wild dance of a savage" with Glazunov's accompaniment, who also played it extempore. At the end of the party Blumenfeld played "The Farewell to Shrovetide," "The Dance of the Buffoons," and "The Hymn of the Berendeyans," and the final song was one devoted to Yarilo the Sun. We sang the last two things all together. Stasov and I were the first to leave the party, but it was already after 4 a.m. When we went downstairs, I made a remark that ages had passed since the Rimsky-Korsakov family had held such a lovely and joyful party.

Those days were marked by an unpleasant incident that strained the relations between Rimsky-Korsakov and Balakirev. During the intermission at one of the concerts in the Hall of the Assembly of the Nobility in St. Petersburg, Rimsky-Korsakov met Balakirev on the way to the performers' dressing room. The former came face to face with Balakirev and said, "How do you do, Aleekseevich!" The latter ignored his words and turned his face away haughtily. Rimsky-Korsakov did not expect such behavior. Those who witnessed the incident said later that Rimsky-Korsakov turned as white as a ghost and went to a smoking room, where he stayed for a long time trying to calm himself down. Rimsky-Korsakov never found out what had made Balakirev behave in this way. In any case, after that very moment all of their personal relations were finished forever. "That's the end!" Rimsky-Korsakov said to Yastrebtsev. "That's it. We don't know each other anymore."

Time passed, and the composer decided to reveal his secret. He played his *Kashchey the Immortal* to his friends. However, at first he showed only the score of the opera to Yastrebtsev. During their discussion Rimsky-Korsakov suddenly felt ill: it was difficult for him to breathe for a while, and he turned extremely pale. Although it lasted not more than a half a minute, it was a very bad sign. On the other hand, it was no wonder, as the health of the composer was certainly being undermined by all of his hard work. He attended the rehearsal of *Servilia*, which was being staged in the Mariinsky, and various concerts and performances, as well as official meetings. He also conducted classes at the Conservatory and continued to compose. Rimsky-Korsakov's life continued to be stressful, and he was smoking too much. All this certainly affected his health. The next day Rimsky-Korsakov played his *Kashchey* to Lyadov, Belsky, and others, excluding Stasov. The musical performance began late, about 11 p.m., since the composer had a prolonged rest beforehand. It helped him to appear sound and in high spirits before the gathered guests. The opera was played twice in a row, so the dinner did not start until 1:30 a.m. and the party was not over until about 3 a.m. The music of this new opera greatly impressed everyone who listened to it, especially Glazunov, who was delighted. At dinner he made a toast: "I'm drinking to the 'culprit' who slew Kashchey the Immortal, but who nevertheless deserves to be acquitted completely, since this very wicked deed gave birth to some great new music."

Rimsky-Korsakov sent the text of the libretto to Petrovsky for him to look through and give his opinion. The latter did not approve of the changes made by Rimsky-Korsakov and answered: "It is my pleasure to confirm that the changed text has all of the distinctive features of the character of Korsakov. In other words, now it is light, life-assured, joyful, and healthy in character, exactly the opposite of what was found in all the drafts I offered to You."

On 9 May 1902 Rimsky-Korsakov received guests on the occasion of his name day. The party was lively, and as usual there were a lot of young people among the guests. Glazunov played his own compositions. Then he and Lyadov played a piano four-hands arrangement of Richard Strauss's *Ein Heldenleben*.

All of a sudden they stopped playing, and Lyadov commented that he would prefer playing *Künstlerleben* by Johann Strauss Jr. to this other Strauss composition. Yastrebtsev wrote later in his memoirs: "When Belsky and I approached the Fontanka, the rising sun gilded the cross of the Church of the Trinity. It was already as light as at noon."

Pan Voevoda

Some days later when Yastrebtsev paid a visit to Rimsky-Korsakov, they had a serious discussion about domestic politics in Russia. Nikolay listened to the arguments for a while and then said, "For God's sake, stop arguing about this! It is irritating me greatly. Meanwhile, I'm hiding myself from the brutality of life in my own monastery—my art." (The conversation was recorded in this way by Yastrebtsev.) And, true to his word, Rimsky-Korsakov immersed himself in working on a new opera, the twelfth one—*Pan Voevoda*. The composer reminisced later:

> I have been preoccupied with thoughts of composing something on a Polish plot for a long time. On the one hand, some Polish tunes that I heard in my childhood from my Mama and that I used for composing my violin mazurka were haunting me. On the other hand, I was undoubtedly under Chopin's influence. [...] I have always been delighted with Polish national accents in Chopin's compositions, which I adore. I'd like to pay homage to my love of this feature in Chopin's music in terms of an opera composed on a Polish plot. I think I'm capable of composing something folklike, truly Polish.

It was 1899 when Rimsky-Korsakov discussed a plot of such an opera with Tyumenev for the first time, and at that time he asked the latter to draft the text of the libretto. But the composition of *Pan Voevoda* was postponed. Then, in 1902, Rimsky-Korsakov returned to the libretto and began to compose music for it.

Heidelberg

The Rimsky-Korsakov family decided to spend the summer of 1902 in Heidelberg. In addition to his studies in Strasbourg, Andrey studied during the summer term at Heidelberg University. Mikhail, Rimsky-Korsakov's eldest son, was also due to come there to conduct his scientific research. Nikolay and Nadezhda, with their daughter Nadya, were the first to leave for Heidelberg. They stayed there in a cottage called Orotava. Rimsky-Korsakov wrote from the cottage to his eldest daughter: "The view from my room is very pleasant. I can see a high hill covered with trees. Yesterday the evening was warm, and the sky was clear. We took a short trip to that hill in the darkness. From this elevation we managed to see the lights of the town spread below. The stars were shining brightly as well as the thoughts in our heads. We also saw Antares and Spica in the night sky."

Igor Stravinsky

Soon Rimsky-Korsakov's children—Mikhail with his wife, Sonya, and Volodya—joined their parents. Volodya met Igor Stravinsky again in Heidelberg. Stravinsky was an acquaintance (they had studied together at St. Petersburg University) and the son of Fyodor Stravinsky, a well-known Russian bass singer. They were living in the resort at Vildulgen, where Igor's father was receiving medical treatment. Although both Igor Stravinsky and Volodya were students at the law school, Igor had been composing music at the same time. He brought his first compositions to Orotava to show to Rimsky-Korsakov with the secret hope of becoming his student. The dreams of the young man were granted. Igor Stravinsky, destined to become a famous composer in the future, became not only a student of Rimsky-Korsakov but also a close friend of the family and a frequent guest of their household. He spent much time with the Rimsky-Korsakovs and was a regular participant at all the musical soirees held in their home.

Rimsky-Korsakov was working on his new opera, *Pan Voevoda*, in Heidelberg, and in addition he undertook reediting Dargomizhsky's opera *The Stone Guest*. Now, in his mature years as a composer, Rimsky-Korsakov had become somewhat dissatisfied with his previous orchestration of the opera, and he considered it his ethical duty to Dargomizhsky to reedit it. Rimsky-Korsakov sent a letter to Kruglikov:

> Dear, the best and the dearest Monsieur Krouglikoff,
>
> I've received your letter today and I'm writing my answer immediately with great pleasure. We arrived here about three weeks ago. Nad. Nik. and I with Nadya were the first,[3] then Misha with his wife and child came, and then Sonya and

Volodya joined us. Andrey met us since he is studying here in Heidelberg for the summer term. We've rented a cottage with a lovely orchard and have been living here all together. The place is just lovely. There are wonderful high hills covered with woods. The view is very thrilling. You can see a vast valley as far as to the Rhine, and when the weather is fine you can even see *das Vogesen-Gebirge* (*die Sehenswürdigkeite*) and Gart-Gebirge beyond the river. The orchard is full of various trees and climbing roses in bloom. Birds sing in the mornings and in the evenings; fireflies flash. We have a piano that is quite good. We've rented it as well as the furniture. We hired a cook, Frau Muller, who makes dishes "à la Russe" at our request. There are too many wild strawberries, currants, and cherries. In general we keep our Russian lifestyle, as if we were [living] at a country house somewhere in holy Russia, with the only exception; we get up much earlier, like Germans do.

In the same letter Rimsky-Korsakov shared his thoughts about his own music: "Did you notice that in each of my new compositions I try to make something new myself? [...] I don't want to be restrained by the limits set by Stasov, Cui, Balakirev, and others: Dargomizhsky means good recitatives; Musorgsky, scenes full of people; Korsakov, fantasy; Cui, great dramas; Borodin, powerful music; and so on and so forth!!! Should I keep to my own style or follow the others?"

Kruglikov was in Vichy, France, where he was receiving medical treatment. He responded from there:

I'm so happy today and the reason for my happiness is Your wonderful letter, my dear Nikolay. I adore such letters full of life, spirit, love of nature, and beauty. I adore You when You're in such high spirits. I'm happy to see that during all those recent years of Your industrious work, You are in such a good mood most of the time. However, I like You very much and [even] at other times, even when You have modulated into a dark "minor" [key] and have caused me to worry about You greatly and to have pity on You heartily; and these days everything is just great! [...] It's very hot here, about +34° [93° F] in the shade. But I'm not afraid of heat and bear it perfectly well. I even enjoy walking under the light of the French *yarilo*. [...] There is only one bad thing: I am not accustomed to walking much; my feet ache at nights. [...] I'm kissing the hand of Nadezhda. I'm embracing you heartily.

Yours, Kruglikov.

At the same time Bessel sent the score of *Kashchey the Immortal* to Heidelberg. Rimsky-Korsakov commented on this in his letter to Kruglikov:

> I'll tell you about myself. I'll be in the "major" [key] today. My next letter will be in the "minor" [key]. Like a joke: I don't eat porridge and *shchi*,[4] I have my *Kashchey*. In other words, I've received the score of the first act of my opera. I looked it through yesterday, and now I doubt whether I "put too much salt into *shchi* and porridge"? In feudal times they said that "too much salt will be on your back,"[5] and I think I might deserve it for what I've done. But, on the other hand, I have the right to spoil myself once in my life (I mean my dissonant harmonies).

"Unbearably Tired"

Rimsky-Korsakov was absorbed with working on his new opera and enjoyed this as usual, but he did not feel as well as Kruglikov had assumed. Kruglikov was a person with whom Rimsky-Korsakov could afford to share his thoughts and worries, and he complained to him:

> You won't believe how tired I feel. Unbearably! After my arrival in Heidelberg and settling down here, I began composing. I will reveal my secret to you; but for God's sake don't tell it to anybody else. I've begun composing a new opera in four acts.[6] […] And for about a week already I've been feeling so exhausted. Having worked for two hours, I feel no desire to keep working. Moreover, the work itself is going badly: I confuse notes, I can't group correctly the easiest musical piece at the first attempt; sometimes I can't decide on a musical interval without the piano. If any musical thought strikes my mind, I have to jot it down immediately; otherwise I won't remember it in a quarter of an hour. When I rewrite something, I can't remember two bars together definitely and I have to look at each note separately, and so on. […] In addition to my opera, I have spent quite a lot of time on "my cousin-nephew's upbringing," i.e., for the orchestration of *The Stone Guest*, which I have to get done. When I look back at my previous years, […] I think I didn't have any such exhaustion, just a normal, even pleasant tiredness after work, which left me completely as soon as I had a walk, or dinner, or tea, or something like that. […] This spring, after my *Kashchey*, when I was occupied with its orchestration and preparation for its publication, I began to feel seriously exhausted and an aversion for further work. Now I have a feeling that

I've never experienced before: an inability to work, which can't be overcome by short rests. The conclusion is obvious: aging is slowly creeping up on me unawares. And when you notice the signs, you are surprised when actually it is nothing to be surprised about. It's natural. And yet it's a little too early. [...] I'm trying now to have frequent rests, but it seems I have acquired a new bad habit—composing—and I'm bored if I don't do it.

Some days later Rimsky-Korsakov sent another letter to Kruglikov:

Two or three days passed and brilliant new ideas have crossed my mind. [...] I should keep up the pace, but I feel that soon weakness and torpor will fight me again. Don't think that I mope. Everything I told you in my previous letter is just the objective enumeration of facts. Yes, I become tired easily, but there is another thing that troubles me. It often occurs that I haven't rested enough but, all of a sudden, a new musical thought strikes me, then another one, and another, and so on. My tiredness disappears immediately and I'm ready to work again, but it results in even quicker exhaustion and aversion to work. My aversion is not to the musical content itself—that I always like—but to technique, writing, perhaps to music in general. I become absentminded and incapable of linking pieces that I thought of before or planning [new] musical pieces. If I decide to be idle a little, and again when I'm still not energetic enough to proceed further, a new unexplained and unexpected anxiety sweeps over me. And everything from the very beginning is "da capo" without end. In a word: it's "the same old story." And I'm a new victim of that "old story." Music is just like some hard-to-satisfy beautiful woman, and a composer is her weary lover who, being weak of will, yet keeps on spending nights with her. She would certainly send him away if he were completely unable, but he is. So she doesn't send him away, and he is still good enough for her. (I'm sorry for such a frivolous comparison.) [...] You might say it's never happened to me before. You might say that when good but unbidden thoughts cross one's mind, one shouldn't take care of them, but save them until one is at full capacity. This can't be done. My memory fails me. I have to work them out immediately, at least to some extent, write them down, take every advantage I can from them; otherwise I will forget them and be unable to do anything with them, and even if I manage to remember them later on and take advantage of them, it takes so much effort, and in any case they lose their attractiveness. I've experienced this already several times.

Kruglikov responded: "Your 'same old story' is very nice. It would be much worse for You and for us, Your admirers, if You had to confess openly that everything had disappeared and the 'story' had come to an end, and the music was over." Despite all of Rimsky-Korsakov's complaints about himself, *Pan Voevoda*, an opera in four acts, was nearly completed by the middle of August.

Switzerland

The Rimsky-Korsakov family left Heidelberg on 12 August 1902. They undertook a wonderful trip across Switzerland. First, the family spent several days in Meiringen.[7] They gathered again all together there and spent some days at the foot of the Matterhorn, from where they took a sensational trip to Görner Glacier, at the peak, by funicular. The view from the peak was tremendous: they were able to enjoy a magnificent view of the glaciers and snowy peaks of the Swiss Alps. Rimsky-Korsakov wrote to Bessel: "In Zermatt from the Görner, we saw a range of snowy peaks a short distance away, and we were lucky with a cloudless blue sky. I know Switzerland pretty well, but I've never seen anything more impressive than that view." Then they went to Lausanne, where they visited the famous Chillon Castle, among other sights. From there they headed to Geneva, then to Munich, where they visited the art gallery. Then they paid a visit to Dresden in order to look at the famous Madonna by Raphael in the local art gallery. They attended Wagner's opera *Götterdämmerung* at the Dresden Theatre. At last they reached Berlin, where Nadezhda and her sons Andrey and Volodya stayed to wait for Mikhail, who was supposed to come to Berlin on his way home; Rimsky-Korsakov went with his daughter back to St. Petersburg on 1 September. Rimsky-Korsakov wrote to his wife from St. Petersburg: "I'm constantly thinking of you and the boys walking alone in the Berlin streets. I dislike everything here except my apartment and my meals. What a dull and gray city! And the people are dull too!" Nadezhda responded from Berlin:

> My dear Nika,
> [...] We've decided to stay here till Friday; firstly, to listen to *Das Rheingold* and, secondly, because of Andrey. When I said that we were to leave on Wednesday, he became upset. We are wasting money here. We go to the theatre every day; only yesterday, we went to the Botanical Garden instead. We watched how they

feed the animals there; it was so amusing. Today we've visited the Reichstag in the morning, where I sat down on Bebel's chair.[8] The building itself is the vision of luxury.

On 1 October 1902 Rimsky-Korsakov attended the opening night of his opera *Servilia* at the Mariinsky Theatre. The performance proceeded smoothly. Rimsky-Korsakov was called to the stage many times (according to Yastrebtsev's records, fifteen times altogether). After the theatre Rimsky-Korsakov invited Blumenfeld, who had conducted *Servilia*, Belsky, Yastrebtsev, and Glazunov for dinner. The latter remarked as a joke that at last Rimsky-Korsakov justified his last name by creating an opera about Roman life. The critics viewed this new opera indifferently, to put it mildly. It had no success with the public, although it was performed seven times during a two-month period. The seventh performance was held in a half-empty theatre. The next day Yastrebtsev received a letter from Rimsky-Korsakov: "Dear Vasily! I thank you for the wreath, which beautified the ugly emptiness of the Mariinsky Theatre yesterday. It seems that the author has the full right to publish an announcement in the *New Times* outlined in black: "I sincerely regret to inform the honorable public of the death of my dear opera *Servilia*."[...] On the board's part, it would be ridiculous if they gave one more performance of *Servilia*." Indeed, the seventh performance was the last for that opera.

And yet, nothing could prevent Rimsky-Korsakov from composing again. He had already conceived a new opera, which he described to Yastrebtsev as the most mysterious one yet. Rimsky-Korsakov meant *The Legend of the Invisible City of Kitezh and the Maiden Fevronia*. Belsky wrote the libretto for this opera himself. At the same time, *Kashchey* was approved for staging at the Moscow Private Opera. At the beginning of December 1902 Rimsky-Korsakov left for Moscow. He sent letters to his wife from there:

My dear Nadya,

There were two rehearsals yesterday: one was in the morning, and the other in the evening. [...] I can't say I like my music very much. I think I put too much "salt" into dissonance. In my opinion, the best parts are those that don't present anything advanced, and which, according to Czech people, are a step back, namely the song with the sword, the duet of the Princess and the Prince (A major), and the arietta of the Prince (A-flat major). By the way, the decadent duet of Kashchey's wife and the Prince is not bad. All the rest needs getting accustomed to, since without familiarity one can reject it. Although I like the chorus ["Snowstorm"] on the one hand, I can't write in the same manner [again] as I did in *The Tsar's Bride*: it would be a shame. On the other hand, it is not worth repeating the manner in which *Kashchey* is composed, since I perceive it as false and full of lies. On the one hand, the Imperial Theatres have the financial means but lack the desire to stage and perform my operas; on the other hand, the Private Opera has the desire but a shortage of resources. I'd better give up composing operas, because I won't create a second *Snow Maiden*, and the theatres can stage whatever they want.

Nadezhda arrived in Moscow to attend the dress rehearsal of *Kashchey* and stayed for the opening night, 12 December 1902. The theatre was not completely full, although they called the composer to the stage several times and presented a wreath to him. She described the performance in her letter to Andrey:

As soon as the aria of Kashchey's wife with a sword was sung, the audience just burst into applause. The emotions ran so high that even I didn't expect ovations like this. The aria was repeated, and at the same moment the soloist was presented with a basket of flowers. It certainly spoiled the whole picture of the scene, and your father was so upset that he left the audience when the aria was sung again. But what could be done? It was such a spontaneous burst of delight that, frankly speaking, I was very pleased with it in any case. [...] In general I personally enjoyed *Kashchey* greatly. I consider it one of Father's best operas. I thought this before, and now I'm just fully convinced. [...] The opera produces a very strong impression. It's not just my opinion. A lot of musicians here are enraptured with *Kashchey*. Grechaninov just beamed with delight.[9] The composer Taneyev was extremely excited;[10] I've never seen him behave in this way before. He said, "This opera is a new word in music."

Rimsky-Korsakov's family left for St. Petersburg soon after the performance was over.

On New Year's Eve in 1903 Sonya, Volodya, and Nadya went to the theatre, while their parents stayed at home and entertained themselves by playing music for four hands on the piano. They played Strauss's *Till Eulenspiegel*, and

Rimsky-Korsakov made fun of this fact in his letter to Andrey: "They say that what you do on New Year's Eve you will do the whole of the following year. Should we play only Strauss for the whole year? [...] We celebrate New Year as usual all together, eating hazel hens, marmalade, nuts, etc., and toasting the health of all of our family members with champagne. Troitsky was with us as well."

Troitsky and Sonya had announced their engagement. The young members of the family decided to produce a New Year's family performance, and the first rehearsal was held on 2 January 1903. All were so engaged with the preparations and rehearsals that they completely forgot about Stasov's birthday, which was on the same day. Rimsky-Korsakov's wife wrote apologies to Stasov with explanations about how it had happened that nobody from the family had managed to come to the Public Library to congratulate him, as they usually did each year.[11] The performance took place at the Rimsky-Korsakov home on 5 January. They produced *The Sick* by Gauptman, and the *Lady's Nonsense* and the *Chance-Comer* by Scheglov. The performers were Sonya, Volodya, Nadya, Troitsky, his sister Olga, Mitusov, Richter, and some other friends of the family. The audience consisted of thirty-five guests, including Alexander Purgold, Nadezhda's eldest brother. He was over seventy already, and he brought his grandchildren Sasha and Olya de la Foss with him. The special party did not wind down until 1 a.m.

Staying Apart

Meanwhile, Andrey's studies at Strasbourg University were approaching their end. He was expected to take the examination to confirm his doctor of philosophy degree in the near future. Nadezhda went to Heidelberg to be as close as possible to her son. Coincidentally, Mikhail was pursuing his scientific research in Gleisberg; his family also lived there with him. While Nadezhda was on her way, her husband sent her his first letter: "My dear, after seeing you off, I went to the Conservatory. [...] In the evening all the children were at Stepan's home. I think often of you and follow your way in my head. The children also think of you often. [...] I came home earlier than the children did. Now it's 9:30 a.m. and they are all still in bed. Take care of yourself, my sweetie."

Nadezhda wrote her first letter to her husband also while she was traveling: "Dear Nika, I'm sorry for such bad handwriting, as I'm writing in the [railway] carriage. Sweet Germany! I have such nice feelings every time I cross the border. The business class here is so good that I confused it with luxury class. The bright light is especially pleasant after the candle ends in our trains."

Upon her arrival in Berlin, Nadezhda wrote again: "My dear Nika, I stayed in the Berliner Hof. I think it is reasonable not to spend two nights in a row in the train. I think you'd approve of my decision. [...] I traveled in luxury on the German railways: velvety sofas, cleanliness, bright lights, and in addition, I was all alone in a compartment for six. [...] This time tomorrow I'll already be in Heidelberg."

Rimsky-Korsakov received a telegram from his wife and became confused. He wrote in his letter:

Dear Nadyusha,

Today at 2 at night I received your telegram reading as follows: "Gesund blibe grüsse."[12] Everyone was in bed already, and I had to research two awfully big dictionaries of Pavlovsky and Makarov in order to understand that "blibe" derives from the verb "bleiben" and it means that you've stayed in Berlin, which pleased me. I believe your word "gesund" but not completely. Thank God nothing bad happened on your way, but I'm sure your exhaustion is on the verge of sickness. We are looking forward to receiving your telegram from Heidelberg. [...] Take care of yourself; if need be undertake some treatment.

(The German word "blibe" was misspelled; it should have been "bleibe," which means "to stay.")

Rimsky-Korsakov received a second telegram from Heidelberg on 18 January. Yet Rimsky-Korsakov still worried about his wife and was awaiting a letter from her impatiently. Mikhail and his wife, Elena, met Nadezhda at the railway station, and they walked to their home, which was a rented apartment not far from the station. When they reached home, Goga, Mikhail's eighteen-month-old son, was in bed. Goga later became close friends with his grandmother. Nadezhda wrote to her husband:

I appreciate the local way of life very much. I don't need to register my passport anywhere; they don't have any building caretakers; the landlord, who lives in the same building, sweeps the stairs himself; the servants bring the coal and everything carries on in such a simple way. What would it be if we also got rid of caretakers? [...] I had a minor incident in the Berliner Hof. I was cheated. I haven't got used to German banknotes yet, and I confused 10 German marks for 5 marks when I paid the bill at the hotel. I gave 11 marks instead of 6 marks to the receptionist and he didn't say anything to me. It doesn't do the hotel honor to benefit from foreigners' confusion. I was in such a hurry that I didn't have time to check the bill. It turned out that they included charges for heating, even though I didn't have any and the room was extremely cold. We shouldn't stay at this hotel anymore.

Nadezhda settled down in Heidelberg, not in Strasbourg, just because she thought her presence there would distract Andrey from his preparations for his important examination. Needless to say, she was dying to see him. The next letter she wrote from Strasbourg:

Dear Nika,

Yesterday I went to Strasbourg without saying anything to Andrey beforehand. I thought that even if it might happen that Andrey was not at home, the landlord would let me in and I would wait for him inside. [...] I went to his house and rang the bell, but in vain. Nobody opened the door. I sat down on the stairs and began waiting. It was after noon. I counted on Andrey's quick return, but time was passing and he was still somewhere else. I had let the carriage go and didn't know what to do next. After waiting for him for an hour and a half on the stairs, I became hungry and tired and decided to try finding the Hotel Union by myself to have a rest there. And what a coincidence that I should meet Andrey in the street. Andrey was walking with a stranger. He was so astonished to see me that he even got frightened that he might have seen a ghost. Besides, my slim figure struck him. He found that I had changed a lot. We were both absolutely happy to see each other. We went back to his apartment, where he looked after me and we chatted the whole evening. I was supposed to catch a 5 train, but we forgot about it completely and talked until midnight. Then Andrey saw me off to the Hotel Union, where I was offered a lovely room for the night. [...] Andrey's apartment is nice. There are only two rooms, but they are spacious and furnished nicely. They are very clean and cozy, and I find them very attractive. Moreover, Zornstaden is a safe part of town, and a respectable one. There are many trees there, and a lot of orchards and parks near the houses. I think the air in spring must be marvelous there. By the way, it's evening now.

Mikhail also came to Strasbourg the next day, and they returned to Heidelberg together. After spending some time with the family of her eldest son, Nadezhda concluded that Elena, his wife, was too lazy to run the household smoothly. She wrote to her husband: "She virtually can't do anything without Misha. And he, in his turn, is busy with other things and extremely impractical. [...] I can just say, 'Poor Misha.' I'm so sorry for him." And another letter continued:

> Lelya is very kind to me.[13] She is generally very kindhearted. She possesses good traits of character, but I wish she had broader interests, that's why I wrote "poor Misha." He is a very intelligent man with broad interests in all spheres of life in addition to his specialty, and he is sociable. I think a wife like this with little interest in important matters of life cannot satisfy him completely. Nonetheless, he seems to be happy and pleased. Goga is a charming boy. [...] I should confess, I couldn't help laughing (although I was sorry about your waiting for my telegram until 2 a.m.) and reading about your research with the dictionaries. I imagined you with two heavy volumes late at night searching for the verb "bleiben."

Meanwhile, in St. Petersburg, Rimsky-Korsakov went to listen to the opera *Götterdämmerung*. He shared his sad thoughts with his wife:

> Wagner's advances [in music] are truly astonishing. Just think, he composed this in the beginning of the '60s. All my operatic music is a half century after his. I wonder if I should continue to compose in my own manner, against the mainstream. It might result in my obsolescence in the near future. Similar to the melodies of Donizetti and others, which we now consider to be like street-organ tunes, the next generation would perceive the songs of the Snow Maiden, Sadko, Marpha, and others funny and old-fashioned.

The next letter was his response to his wife's complaints: "My dear, I'm so sorry for you! You had to sit all alone for an hour and a half at the door of Andrey's apartment. Poor Mama! But I can imagine how you enjoyed your long talks with him later on. I'm glad you feel all right. [...] Tell Andrey that he shouldn't be afraid of his examination. I don't have any doubt that he will pass it successfully and I'm not afraid for him. Tell Misha and Lelya that they should fatten you [up]."

His wife sent him letters regularly describing her life abroad:

I'll tell you about my day. I get up after 9 and about 10 I drink cocoa without any cookies, just with some kind of crackers. Then I play with Goga; then I go to my room and stay there reading or writing letters. At 1 p.m. or about that, Misha comes. By this time I usually become hungry enough to eat. After lunch Misha leaves again, and I go for a walk if the weather is fine. About 5 I have tea with Lelya, then play with Goga again, read, or knit. About 8 I start helping with dinner. I undertake this duty voluntarily to help Lelya. She becomes tired by the evening and her back aches sometimes. My help with dinner consists only of boiling water or making tea, not cooking dishes. Sometimes we just warm something on the stove. After dinner conversation Misha brings his papers into the dining room and writes his articles for the dictionary. I read or do something about the house at this time. At 11 we usually go to our rooms. At midnight I blow out my candle. This way of life is certainly far more beneficial for one's health than ours. Sometimes Misha receives guests. [...] Yesterday I walked along the embankment up to the Alte Brücke [Old Bridge], crossed it and came back along the Neue Brücke [New Bridge]. The weather was wonderful: sunny and dry. By the way, today is the same. The view from the Alte Brücke is magnificent. I saw the castle for the first time, but it was foggy. It is very beautiful to walk along the embankment. I'm feeling well, and I think I don't need any consultations with doctors. Frankly speaking, I'm getting tired easily now from walking, but it might be firstly due to my lack of exercise, and secondly, alas! due to my aging.

To Nikolay's complaints his wife responded: "You said that nobody needs your operas when, meanwhile, the whole of Russia listens to them. Even if St. Petersburg, headed by the theatre board, is not very sympathetic to them, you can't say the same about Moscow as well as about the rest of Russia. I'm sure the Moscow Private Opera will be happy to produce your *Pan Voevoda* if you [will] allow them."

Andrey had been cramming for his examination and was full of anxiety. The examination itself was of great importance, and, moreover, Andrey was to take it in German. Nadezhda also worried about her son greatly. She shared her concern with her husband: "I'm still extremely worried about his exam. It will be such a relief when he passes it. I'm very afraid to disturb his studies, and so I refrain from going to Strasbourg." Yet it was too difficult for a loving mother to stay not far from her son and not see him. Nadezhda went to Strasbourg to visit doctors, as her husband had advised. She wrote from there:

> The Hotel Union has changed a little. The prices have risen in the restaurant. Now lunch costs 2.5 German marks and you can't get beer there, only wine. The cleanliness of the hotel is still perfect. I have a room on the upper floor and it is furnished just like brand-new. It is minimalistic: there is only a bed with an end table, a washbasin, a wardrobe, a table, and two wooden chairs. That's all it has. The furniture, the walls, and the bed set just shine with cleanliness. It's beautiful. I like it very much. I visited the doctor today. […] It was absolutely unnecessary to go there. I wasted time and money, and it was just unpleasant. After the doctor, Andrey and I went to the restaurant, where I had lunch. Then we went to Andrey's home. I'm still with him and writing a letter to you in his room. At first I wanted to go back to Heidelberg today, but I decided to postpone my departure until tomorrow morning. Andrey is studying in the same room where I'm writing my letter, but we do not talk.

While Nadezhda was away, Sonya was in charge of the family apartment. Nikolay wrote to his wife: "You can't even imagine how nice and caring she has been to me during your absence. She takes care of me with such devotion. […] I embrace you. I miss you greatly." He continued in his next letter:

> You wrote that you became so anxious to see me. I've written to you already that I missed you very much during the first days of your absence. The main feeling was worries about your trip: how you were traveling, what if something bad happened to you on the way, and so on. Then, after I received your first letters, this changed to a feeling of joy for you: that you were safe and sound, that you saw our children, that they were happy to see you and you were happy. And now, when all emotions have become more or less stable, the main desire is for you to return soon. I wish you were here with me and the other children. I can't get used to your absence. I wish for those two or three weeks to pass as soon as possible. We have been keeping a quiet life, although we go to the theatre fairly often. We don't have many visitors these days: Vladimir is our regular customer, and yesterday the Balambergies paid a visit. By the way, Volodya and Nadya had great fun yesterday. They went to Mitusov's wedding, which took place at last, and the reception was in Gatchina!!!! Not in Moscow. They went to

Left: Anatoly Lyadov, Alexander Glazunov, and Rimsky-Korsakov in 1905.

Bottom: Left to right: Igor Stravinsky, Nikolay Rimsky-Korsakov, his daughter Nadezhda, Maximilian Steinberg, and Ekaterina Gavrilovna Nossenko (later Ekaterina Stravinskaya after marriage to Igor) in the living room of Rimsky-Korsakov's apartment.

Left: Left to right: Nikolay Rimsky-Korsakov, his wife, Nadezhda, son Andrey, and daughter Nadezhda during breakfast in the dining room, 1906.

Bottom: Nikolay Rimsky-Korsakov and Semyon Kruglikov in Rimsky-Korsakov's apartment, 1907.

Right: Igor Stravinsky, who studied privately with Rimsky-Korsakov, about 1907.

Bottom: Nikolay Rimsky-Korsakov in the living room of his St. Petersburg apartment, 1907.

Left: Rimsky-Korsakov and Vasily Vasilyevich Yastrebtsev in Loubensk, 1907.

Bottom: Nikolay Rimsky-Korsakov in the study of his St. Petersburg apartment with Anatoly Lyadov. The last photograph of Rimsky-Korsakov, taken April 1908.

The 1912 monument on Nikolay Rimsky-Korsakov's tomb in the Tikhvin Cemetery, St. Petersburg. The designer was Nikolay Rerich, and the sculptor was Andrioletti.

Fragments from Rimsky-Korsakov's letters to his wife, Nadezhda. Nikolaev, 7 and 14 June 1881.

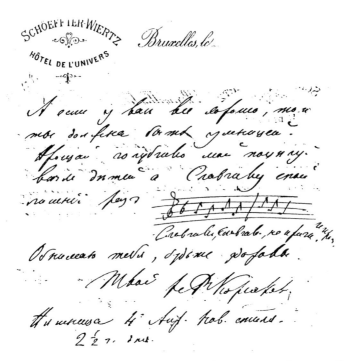

Fragment from a letter of Rimsky-Korsakov to his wife concerning their son Slava's health and crying. Brussels, 4 April 1890.

Rimsky-Korsakov's musical letter to his son Andrey about preparing vegetables for a meal. Vetchasha, summer of 1898.

Rimsky-Korsakov's musical letter to Vladimir Belsky about his visit and the first part of the composer's next opera. Vetchasha, summer of 1898.

Rimsky-Korsakov's musical letter to Yastrebtsev, about his own youth. Venice, summer of 1906.

Valentin Serov's portrait of Nikolay
Rimsky-Korsakov for posters
publicizing his concerts in Paris,
March 1908.

the reception, then visited the family of Putyatin, and they came back only at 1 at night.[14]

Nadezhda had been enjoying her stay in Heidelberg and went on to describe the local events in her letters:

We have a carnival today. The show is new and interesting for me. About 2 p.m. the procession was passing our house. It was huge and consisted of a lot of carriages. For example, there was a carriage with a monument to the Handschuhsheim Parliament, which has ceased to exist owing to the merger of the two cities: Handschuhsheim and Heidelberg. The other carriage was buzzing loudly (in fact there were several carriages joined together), which represented an electric railway and was meant to protest against the awful noise that it produced. One carriage was decorated with green branches and flowers and filled with little children all dressed up. I don't know what it was supposed to symbolize, but it was very cute. We watched the procession from our balcony. It is a little colder today, although it's sunny and cloudless. The carriages were supposed to proceed along all the main streets, make a circle, and return to the Brückenstrasse, at the beginning of which they were to disperse. Misha and I decided to walk to the Hauptstrasse to see what was going on there. There were crowds of mummers, noise, laughter, confetti, blows made in jest with sticks carried by all the mummers. Because of the crowds of people in the streets, horse-drawn cars didn't operate during the carnival, and carriages moved slowly. Misha had to go back to his business, and I walked alone for a while and was about to go home when I got the brilliant idea of hiring a carriage and riding along the Hauptstrasse all together. Lelya dreamed of watching the carnival, and Annushka [the nanny] did as well. I went to the railway station, took a carriage, and picked everyone up, including Goga, and we headed to Hauptstrasse. As soon as we reached the bridge, two maskers disguised as clowns hung onto the back of our carriage. We sprinkled some confetti in the Hauptstrasse and they did the same in return; the clowns hung on and off and pretended to hit us with their sticks, I also received some blows. As we moved very slowly, we were able to watch the maskers, the plays, and the different scenes closely. Goga was also sprinkled with confetti, but he behaved bravely. He watched everything with astonishment and sat quietly. There was so much noise: music, sounds of trumpets, screams, jocular battles; different maskers jumped on the back of our carriage. And can you imagine,

Goga didn't become frightened at all! He is so brave! He surprised me.—Well, I'd better finish up. It's difficult to put everything in one letter. Good-bye. I'm kissing you and the children.

The day of Andrey's examination was fast approaching, and the parents' worries were growing. The composer wrote that he would be thinking the whole day only of Andrey and would be with him in his thoughts during the examination. Nadezhda went to Strasbourg, where she met with Mironov, who also arrived there to support Andrey. Nadezhda was very pleased to see him, since she was extremely worried about Andrey and would be able to wait in his company for the result and not be all alone. Meanwhile, in St. Petersburg, they all stayed awake expecting a telegram from Strasbourg with the results of Andrey's examination. At last, at 3 p.m., the telegram arrived announcing that the doctorate degree was confirmed. In the morning the father sent a telegram to his son: "With a calm heart but impatiently I'm looking forward to seeing you."

In her turn, Nadezhda immediately sent a letter to her husband describing the event:

My dear Nika,

Thank God! All worries are left behind and Andrey and I are happy. […] I'm so glad that Mironov has arrived here. He was actually a great help to me and to Andrey as well. Mironov is very kind and really likes Andrey very much. He saw Andrey off to the university and came back to me. The examination began at 3:30 and finished at 6 p.m. The results were announced at 6:15. First Mironov and I stayed at Andrey's apartment, and then we went to the university in the hope of seeing Andrey during the breaks. But we didn't succeed. Then we went to the restaurant next to the university and sat there till 6 p.m. Mironov drank something, but I couldn't eat or drink, I just waited. Yesterday I didn't eat at all till 8 p.m. By 6 we were at the university. We met Andrey, who was still expecting the results, but he was happy. In a quarter of an hour Andrey came up to us and told us the decision of the faculty. Several of Andrey's friends and acquaintances were also at the university supporting Andrey and awaiting the results. I got acquainted with one of them. It was very kind of him to hire a carriage for us, as it was raining hard and Andrey was wearing a tailcoat and silk hat.[15] We went home first and then to the restaurant to celebrate all together: Andrey, Mironov, and I. And today Andrey is giving a party for his friends on the occasion of his doctoral degree. He will certainly serve a couple of bottles of champagne. Unfortunately, I will have to stay alone during his party. Andrey is absolutely happy, especially with the fact that he will come back to St. Petersburg soon and for an indefinite time. Sweet Andrushonok! He worried greatly and even has lost some weight.[…] I can't find more paper in Andrey's apartment, so I have to finish. I'm kissing you and embracing you. See you soon.

N. R. K.

The letter had an attachment. It was a greeting card from Andrey on he had written: "To Papa. Beat the drum and the tambourine! Andrey is a Doctor of Philosophy!!!"

Certainly his mother was happy to share these important moments of her son's life with him. She was a support for him during his difficulties. In his turn, Andrey was also happy, since he liked his mother very much. They had to stay in Strasbourg a little longer than they had expected. Andrey needed time to pack all of his belongings (he had too many books) and to pay his last visits to friends and acquaintances in Strasbourg. His father wrote to them impatiently: "Come, come, 100,000,000,000 more times come!" Nadezhda was afraid that they had spent too much money, but her husband reassured her: "Your expenses neither surprise nor upset me. It makes me happy! We received 640 rubles for two performances of *The Tsar's Bride*. What are all your costs after this? What nonsense!"

While Andrey and his mother were busy with packing things, Mikhail's family left Heidelberg for France. He was transferred to the Russian Biological Research Centre, located at Villefranche-sur-Mer near Nice. It was well-known in Russian and European scientific circles at that time. Nadezhda and Andrey returned to St. Petersburg just two weeks before Rimsky-Korsakov's birthday. On the morning of 6 March Rimsky-Korsakov received a basket of hyacinths and a rosebush from Yastrebtsev. In the evening the birthday honoree received his guests, including Igor Stravinsky. As usual, the party was crowded. Yastrebtsev wrote in his diary about that evening:

Blumenfeld played many of his compositions and also some of Chopin, Liszt, and Schumann. Stravinsky played his lovely and witty musical jokes. It seems Igor Stravinsky is undoubtedly talented. We had tea, ate fruit and grapes, then a special dinner.[…] At dinner Stasov, as the oldest among the guests, toasted

Nikolay's health, adding to the "youngest one," meaning a newborn. Rimsky-Korsakov responded wittily that as a newborn baby he was supposed only to say "Wah-wah"; nevertheless, he would allow himself to cheer his dear guests who honored him with their presence. Besides, the young people sang the "Hymn of the Berendeyans" from *The Snow Maiden* in honor of Rimsky-Korsakov ["Greetings to the Dearest, the Wisest, the Greatest Berendey"].

They also toasted the engaged couple: Sophia Rimsky-Korsakov and Vladimir Troitsky.

14

The Last Russian Music

He [Glazunov] is the last among us currently composing Russian music, i.e., new Russian music will cease to exist after him! It's awful!

—Rimsky-Korsakov to Vladimir Stasov,
during a dinner at Glazunov's home

The Legend of the Invisible City of Kitezh and the Maiden Fevronia

In the spring of 1903 Rimsky-Korsakov began composing a new opera, *The Legend of the Invisible City of Kitezh and the Maiden Fevronia*, which he had first conceived much earlier. He wrote to his son Mikhail, who was at Villefranche: "I'm beginning to work on *The Invisible City of Kitezh*. I have made some drafts already and soon I'll start writing the first scene. [...] On the advice of Spengler I take iodine regularly, I don't drink wine at all and feel well."[1] This time Rimsky-Korsakov did not keep secret the fact that he was composing. He even suggested to Yastrebtsev that he visit him to get an idea about the plot. Yastrebtsev even thought that the composer was afraid he would not have enough time to complete the opera.

Rimsky-Korsakov's family decided to spend the coming summer season in Krapachukha, where they had been before. Andrey was staying with them at the time, and he and his mother were the first to move to the summer house. Nikolay and his son Volodya, who was taking examinations at the university, stayed in St. Petersburg. Nadezhda sent her first letter to her husband from Krapachukha:

My dear Nika,

It's very nice here. Now it's the best time of the season: the green leaves are of that beautiful color that they will lose soon and won't regain; the air is full of the fragrance of different plants; the birds are singing all day long; and at last it's completely quiet because the other summer residents haven't moved in yet. [...]

Yesterday we found the first lily of the valley. We are going to have millions of poppies. Won't they give rise again to one more beautiful composition like *Kashchey*? Andrey is always playing your *Snow Maiden*. Its music suits the surroundings so perfectly. It's better to say even that music and nature are united.

When they had lived at that house in the summer of 1901, there were a lot of red poppies that bloomed unbelievably beautifully. This carpet of poppies caused musical associations with the scenes that occurred in the kingdom of Kashchey's wife. Rimsky-Korsakov responded: "I'm glad that *The Snow Maiden* enlivens you and suits the time and the place well." The composer arrived at the summer house on 20 May. Andrey met him and told him the latest news: he had another grandchild, a baby girl named Vera, born to Mikhail and his wife.

Rimsky-Korsakov again felt exhausted from the past winter season. He wrote to his eldest son: "When I was just planning to go to Krapachukha, I thought I would rest completely for at least the first several days. But now that I am here, how can I fulfill my plan? I cannot just sit on my hands all day long, but to be reading all day long is also impossible for me, and I cannot idle around the whole day; therefore, I have to start working, at least in the mornings. I write down some pieces that I have kept in my head from the second act of *Kitezh*." In addition, Rimsky-Korsakov had been working on the orchestration of *Pan Voevoda*, and on such days he laid the composition of *Kitezh* aside. Preparing his *Pan Voevoda* for publication, Rimsky-Korsakov asked Lyadov to undertake the first proofreading of the opera. The latter did it thoroughly. Now it was time to undertake the second proofreading, and Rimsky-Korsakov composed his request in verse. When the corrections were made, he sent another letter of thanks to Lyadov, again in verse.

Rimsky-Korsakov felt so tired that he even wondered whether he should have undertaken something else instead of *Kitezh*. In his next letter to Mikhail he reported: "Mother and the children go to pick mushrooms. [...] I live a routine life and go for a walk occasionally. I have completed *Pan Voevoda* in terms of score and orchestration and now I am making some changes and improvements to it. I still can't take up *Kitezh*: I don't feel like it." Yastrebtsev's arrival at Krapachukha was like a kind of entertainment for Rimsky-Korsakov. Yastrebtsev found out about *Pan Voevoda* only after he arrived there. It was a great surprise for him. During the visit Yastrebtsev took some photos of

Rimsky-Korsakov in the orchard and at the house. As usual, he made a new entry in his memoirs:

> Rimsky-Korsakov seems to miss St. Petersburg, with its good orchestra, this summer, so he is inclined to dream of autumn with some delight. He has reread *On the Eve and Fathers and Sons* by Turgenev and is excited about them. [...] I had tea and a quick supper, as I was in a hurry. I wanted to catch the 11 a.m. train and it was 10:20 already. Despite the rain, I went out. Had I not been given Andrey's raincoat ("impromocable" for people leaving),[2] I would have been drenched. All the members of Rimsky-Korsakov's family were very kind and hospitable.

The composer's exhaustion, which had been steadily increasing during his years of hard creative work, was not an easy thing to get rid of with just the help of a brief rest. As a result, the composition of *Kitezh* was proceeding slowly and with great difficulty, which annoyed the composer. To make things even worse, his two friends Belsky and Yastrebtsev, who were composing the libretto of the opera, began to give advice and recommendations concerning the musical part of *Kitezh*. Rimsky-Korsakov wrote to Belsky:

> In general, the composition is progressing roughly and slowly. If it goes on like this, I will hardly ever complete this opera, especially when you demand that it meet requirements that are so difficult to attain and, which I am not able to satisfy. For example, your "would you like to show breathless excitement in the last scene"? It is easy to say (but hard to do). There are many words in the language, and good ones. Have you tried to show it with music? Eventually I will manage to compose good music, but let somebody else compose your breathless excitement with some other music, and I will see who will be able to do it. It is just easy to say (but hard to do). "Music that causes listeners to cry, or music that causes listeners to feel mystery or horror, or something like this." And how are you supposed to do it? Or where does such music exist? Tears of the listeners are just [caused by] their poor nerves, and mysterious horror is just put on. [...] Yastrebtsev spent two days in Krapachukha and frightened me to death with his ideas that "*Kitezh* must certainly be of some especially high quality." [...] When everyone makes such demands, the only thing that comes to my mind is, wouldn't it be better for me to give up this composition in order not to fail? It seems that even if I am

not in my dotage, I appear to have become a child to some extent and to obey grown-ups. You said that recitatives are poor things, and now when I have to compose a recitative this opinion of yours will haunt me and I'd better not [try to] do it at all. You wish I would enlarge the orchestra, I obey: I will do it. You would like me to write for a reed: here it is, I will compose a part for a reed and even for a piccolo, although, in my opinion they are unsuitable for the music of this opera. There is only one thing that goes beyond my capacity: I cannot produce graceful wordiness. It might just kill me, and I'd like to live [some] more yet.

His next letter was an apologetic one. Rimsky-Korsakov asked forgiveness for being rude: "I became awfully irritated and irritated without any reason.[...] My mature years have brought with them such things as shortness of temper, weak memory, frequent complete absentmindedness, or, better, 'occurrence of odd thoughts' and the other 'benefits' of the age of sixty."

Rimsky-Korsakov wrote to Yastrebtsev soon after: "I'm developing my opera cautiously, as you've frightened me; nonetheless, I'm still developing it." Indeed, by the time he was to move back to the city, the opera was nearly complete. At the end of October 1903 the Mariinsky Theatre produced *The Maid of Pskov*, this time with the prologue to *Vera Sheloga*. Thirty years had passed since it had been staged at this theatre for the first time. The first performance was for an orchestra benefit, so the ticket prices were very high. Rimsky-Korsakov paid 80 rubles for tickets to the box in the dress circle. Nevertheless, the theatre was packed, owing mostly to Chaliapin, who played the part of Ivan the Terrible. Rimsky-Korsakov received three wreaths, including one from Chaliapin with the inscription: "In memory of the serf Ivan." Rimsky-Korsakov decided to give his author's royalties to the orchestra.

Death of Mitrovan Belyaev

Belyaev celebrated his birthday on 23 November 1903. Many guests, including Rimsky-Korsakov, attended the event. Soon after the party Belyaev was sent to the hospital. He had been feeling ill for some time, and the doctors found that he needed surgery urgently, as they had diagnosed an open stomach ulcer. Rimsky-Korsakov visited him twice. He jotted down on of a draft of the opera *Kitezh*: "Today I saw Belyaev for the last time. 25 December." Belyaev died on 28 December 1903.

A Russian Symphony Concert was held in February 1904. Rimsky-Korsakov composed a short prelude for it, *At the Tomb*, in memory of Belyaev, and the whole concert was to commemorate this outstanding person who had done so much for Russian music. Rimsky-Korsakov included the sound of a mournful bell in his prelude like the one he used to hear in Tikhvin when he was a child.

The composer wrote in his memoirs:

> Providing his family first with an essential fortune, Belyaev, in his deathbed will, left all the rest to develop musical activities and divided the capital into several parts: Russian Symphony Concerts, publishing houses, funds for the Glinka Prize, funds to hold competitions in composing chamber music, and funds to support needy musicians. There were also some other minor provisions. He designated Glazunov, Lyadov, and me to manage all of these assets, with the duty of nominating our assistants. The assets were so large that for all the concerts, publishing, prizes, etc., we were supposed to spend not the capital itself but only the interest, and the capital itself was to grow over time. Thus, owing to Belyaev and his utter devotion to musical art, a new, unique, and unprecedented institution that provides Russian music with publishing houses, concerts, and prizes was set up.[3]

A Typical Day in the Composer's Life

The Rimsky-Korsakovs' family life kept up its pace. On a typical day, the composer woke up early, and at 9 he had breakfast. Without waiting for anybody else to wake, he made coffee for himself. He was addicted to good coffee and he used to joke frequently: "Thank you, Lord, for creating this wonderful drink!" Usually breakfast consisted of coffee with cream and fresh hot rolls with butter and honey. The favorite of the family, a red setter named Rex, always accompanied the head of the family. Each time the composer was about to leave the dining room, he instructed the pet, "Would you like to go out?" and he obeyed. On the way to his study, Rimsky-Korsakov passed the living room, where he usually stopped for a while at the piano to play a chord in the key he needed. As soon as he was in his study—the Holy of Holies of his creative work—he immersed himself completely in work. His desk became gradually piled up with musical notations. Rimsky-Korsakov believed that a composer should not wait for inspiration to be granted but should cause it to come by his own tirelessly industrious work. If it happened that the composer was not demanded by Apollo to pay for its sacred contribution, then, in any case, he would find many things to keep him busy, such as orchestration of pieces or polishing what had been created already but was still in its original chaotic state.

Fortunately, inspiration made it its duty to visit Rimsky-Korsakov regularly without asking for his permission, and frequently it occurred in odd hours when he was not working. When that happened, a stranger seeing him at such a time might think him odd. For instance, in the Black Forest Rimsky-Korsakov happened to be at a table of a hotel with some stiff English ladies and gentlemen when his gaze suddenly went blank. He became preoccupied with his musical thoughts; he began whistling and waving with his right hand as if conducting an orchestra. The English people were puzzled, and the family members sitting next to him looked at each other and tried to bring him back carefully to reality. The same thing often happened at home. Once Rimsky-Korsakov came back home after being tired from his work at the Conservatory and asked to have dinner served. The family sat at the table and waited for him. Five minutes passed, then ten, then fifteen....One by one the children knocked at the bathroom door and said that everything was ready, but they received no response. At last Sonya summoned up her courage enough to enter the bathroom and found her father standing next to the washbasin with the familiar blank look and conducting with his soapy hands.

Rimsky-Korsakov composed at a fast pace. From time to time he came into the living room to play over a composition. During these holy hours of hard work and inspiration, all of the family members tried to keep quiet; however, they had to bother him sometimes with urgent things. It is peculiar that he had the unique ability to distract himself from any external hindrances rather quickly and restore his inspiration immediately. When he lived in the apartment next to the bell tower of Our Lady of Vladimir Church, even the chiming bells, which were right above his window, did not prevent him from composing his music. Moreover, in the last apartment they rented, a woman who gave piano and singing lessons lived one floor above his study. It got on Nikolay's nerves, but he got used to working even under such unfavorable conditions.

Rimsky-Korsakov usually put his desk into complete order at noon; he put all of his papers in the drawers of an old bureau that he had inherited from Tikhvin and joined his family for lunch. After lunch he usually went to the Conservatory, coming back by 5 or 6 p.m. Rimsky-Korsakov's family often received guests at dinner. The family was especially glad if such a guest was Kruglikov, who would travel to St. Petersburg from Moscow. If they did not have guests for dinner, Rimsky-Korsakov allowed himself to doze for fifteen or twenty minutes and always asked to be woken up in case he fell asleep and was late for his evening work. His evening work was usually of a technical character, such as rewriting neatly what he had composed in the morning, proofreading, writing letters, and so on. He used to work until midnight or sometimes even later. It is difficult to understand how Rimsky-Korsakov managed to compose when he was constantly surrounded by a large family and, in addition, all of his children were taking music lessons. If Sonya decided not to have her singing lesson, in order to keep the house quiet the result was always the same: Rimsky-Korsakov would come out of his study and ask, "Sonyushka, why don't you sing?"

Although the composer reserved the evening hours for technical work, it was not always possible. In the evening he often went to the theatre, a concert, or a musical evening, or received guests at home. Sometimes during the day he managed either to attend rehearsals of operas or concerts or conducted them himself, or he participated in different meetings. The parties at his home usually ended late at night, and sometimes they began only after the evening performances. So Rimsky-Korsakov went to bed late but he always got up rather early, irrespective of how late he went to bed. Moreover, he worked every day, even if it was a state or local holiday. Rimsky-Korsakov was constantly engaged in various activities. The proof of this can be found in his dated manuscripts. Therefore, it was difficult for him to devote much time to his own creative work while he was in the city. As a result, when he went out of town in the summer to a country house. he was usually completely absorbed with composing his own music.

When Rimsky-Korsakov was about sixty years old, he became more and more concerned about the fate of Russian music. Once, during a dinner after a recital at Glazunov's home, when everyone was enjoying the party and in high spirits, Rimsky-Korsakov, who was sitting next to Stasov, turned to him and unexpectedly said the following: "Do you know what is torturing me secretly, haunting me persistently in my thoughts among all those special dinners, toasts, and speeches? Can you think? I'll tell you today." Then he pointed to Glazunov and continued, "He is the last among us currently composing Russian music, i.e., new Russian music will cease to exist after him! It's awful!"

The participation of young people in the musical evenings held in Rimsky-Korsakov's home enlivened them and brought in fresh blood. Yastrebtsev described one such evening:

> Richter played the piano. Then Zabela sang arias and romances. After dinner young Stravinsky played his comical songs, and Richter sang a famous and at the same time utterly meaningless gypsy song, "Raspasha," and even danced the "cakewalk," to the horror of Rimsky-Korsakov's wife, Nadezhda. Mitusov and Stravinsky helped Richter by showing him their own way of performing that dance and mimicking him. In general the party was lively and merry today, and it was very interesting.

Despite the fact that Rimsky-Korsakov was occupied with so many different activities, he continued composing the music for *Kitezh*. The major part was already completed. Rimsky-Korsakov wrote to Petrovsky: "I think that *Kitezh* will be not unfashionable, but a modern and even an advanced opera [for its time]. Moreover, it will still possess valuable musical elements such as melody, musical forms [structure], harmony, counterpoint, and . . . consequently beauty." In the same letter, he made a note: "After Wagner's time, the West should post an announcement: 'Beauty in music is lost. If you have any information or are able to find and deliver [some], contact the authorities and you may be eligible for a cash reward.'"

Sixty Years Old

On his sixtieth birthday Rimsky-Korsakov made a resolution to keep up his own diary. The first entry appeared on the same day: "I spent the morning well since I managed to orchestrate about seven pages." He meant the fourth act of *Kitezh*. In the evening there was a special dinner with many guests. In his diary the composer continued: "At dinner, when champagne was poured, the singing started in the living room. It turned out that Igor [Stravinsky] had composed a chorus of greeting in my honor. The chorus is not bad. The soloists were Sonya, Nadya, Ossovsky, Stepan, Lapshin, and Volodya." Those present demanded that the chorus be repeated again. That same evening a vocal quartet consisting of Mitusov, Lapshin, Ossovsky, and the composer himself sang a comic song written by Borodin and dedicated to his wife, "The Serenade of Four

Admirers," which used to be performed at the Purgold household. Although Rimsky-Korsakov's new opera was not yet finished, he played the first act of *Kitezh* to his friends. Ossovsky wrote to the composer later: "You again have created a unique and distinguished landmark! It not only points in the direction of the development of Your genius but will leave its mark on the history of operatic music itself and on music in general."

The spring of 1904 came, and Rimsky-Korsakov's family moved into another country house. This time they rented it again at Vetchasha. The composer was lucky to be able to take a vacation in May before the examinations began at the Conservatory. To make this possible, he made Glazunov responsible for giving the examinations. Rimsky-Korsakov was happy that at least this spring would be spent it in the country. He did not have the opportunity to watch as the first leaves appeared on the trees and the flowers blossomed in the city. He arrived at Vetchasha on 4 May, and the next day he sent a greeting card to Kruglikov in which he repeated the words of Fevronia: "Day and night there is sweet singing and exulting in all voices." The surroundings were perfect for the work needed to complete *Kitezh*. As Belsky said, "The erection of the city of Kitezh was proceeding at a fantastic speed." In July Belsky received several greeting cards from Rimsky-Korsakov that included musical notes:

> I will finish tomorrow or in a day.
> 8 July 1904. Vetchasha

Then in the next:

> I've finished
> 9 July 1904. Vetchasha

Again in two more days:

> I've not finished yet
> 11 July 1904. Vetchasha

And in another three days:

> It seems I've finished although not completely.
> 14 July 1904. Vetchasha

At around the same time Rimsky-Korsakov wrote to Kruglikov about *Kitezh*: "I've completed everything in draft form. Now I can allow myself to stop, and I think Glazunov won't refuse to undertake the orchestration of my opera." Another happy event that took place in July in Vetchasha: the composer's eldest daughter gave birth to a baby girl named Irina.[4] Rimsky-Korsakov worked hard until the end of July and was pleased that nobody came to disturb him. In August the family received their first guest, Igor Stravinsky, who stayed for some weeks to continue his studies on orchestration with Rimsky-Korsakov. Kruglikov was next. He spent three days with Rimsky-Korsakov's family, and the composer played his new opera through for him. It seemed that Kruglikov's departure was always accompanied by bad weather. This time he again had to borrow the same raincoat so as to not to get wet on his way to the Plussa railway station. He soon sent a letter on his way to Moscow:

> Dearest and the most wonderful Nikolay! You are like a breath of fresh air. I arrived safe and sound in your "impromocable" at Plussa. My best regards to you, my dearest friends. I got so many joyful impressions during those three days. My kindest, I will write to you from Moscow about *Kitezh*. I told You so little about it. But I am always like this. First I should fully absorb the music, but even now I admire Your miracle with my mouth agape. I embrace You so hard, as I love You.

On the day of Kruglikov's departure Yastrebtsev came to Vetchasha. The next day he wrote in his memoirs: "I took some photographs of Vetchasha while all were away (they went to pick mushrooms). Rimsky-Korsakov played the second act of *Kitezh*, it's just a paragon of beauty! I cried. […] After tea, Nadezhda and Igor Stravinsky played the Fifth Symphony of Glazunov (and not very well)." Yastrebtsev took some photographs of Rimsky-Korsakov in the Vetchasha garden and sitting at his desk in the room that served as his study, where Rimsky-Korsakov had been composing his *Kitezh*. Soon after the guests hurried home, he wrote in his memoirs: "On the day of my departure, the weather was fine. The youngsters were playing croquet in front of the house when my carriage arrived. […] At 4:15, I started on my way. Everyone gathered to say good-bye to me. Rimsky-Korsakov was the last to say some warm words of farewell. What a kindhearted man he is!"

Dreams of Loubensk

On 7 September 1904 Rimsky-Korsakov returned to St. Petersburg while his wife stayed in Vetchasha. She wrote to her husband:

> My dear, there is something wrong with nature. Today is 12 September, and it's still +10° [50° F] at night, and during the day there are swarms of mosquitoes; grasshoppers chirp; the wind is warm, there is a blue sky above us, and the yellow trees under this ultramarine cloudless sky are especially beautiful. In such circumstances I just can't leave Vetchasha. It's a pity that you, Sonya, and Nadya are not with us enjoying these wonderful days. [...] We've taken a lovely trip today as our farewell. I've been intrigued by the hill located not far from Polos. Today we've decided to reach it. We went along the Great Bridge on the way to Polos.[5] Though all the roads are dry now, this particular one is flooded with water, and it covers a substantial area. We barely managed to cross it using those thin birch saplings and found ourselves in a place where there was only dirty water around, no roads, only moss and tussocks. We wanted to turn back, but our desire to reach that hill forced us to move ahead. So we jumped from one tussock to another. Sometimes we fell through the moss into the water; it splashed up and poured into our boots, so our feet got wet. But at last we reached dry land and achieved our goal. The view that opened up at the top of the hill was so rewarding that we were not sorry about having endured the awfully unpleasant crossing. You can see wide open spaces in all directions from there: many settlements, estates, two lakes, forests, endless fields and valleys, everything just as if it were on a map. We didn't want to cross that swamp again on our way back, and so we took the other road in the direction of Kotorsk and returned home along a fine dry road.
>
> Do you know that Bukharov is up to his ears in debt to such an extent that they are selling Loubensk. I'm terribly sorry for them. That's as dramatic as Chekhov's *The Cherry Orchard*.[6] I wish I could be that Lopakhin. I would certainly not cut down the orchard and build cottages, except only an additional one for Misha. Sonya could live with us. Loubensk is perfectly located. The view from there is wonderful. And it's possible to use the lake to keep our own horses. The estate itself is just about 8700 acres. But the price is excessive considering that most of it is cut down. They'd like to have 120,000 rubles! I'm sure nobody will buy it at that price. [...] Besides, they might sell us a lot. Then I wish we

could buy an estate with a little piece of land. I'm going to visit Mrs. Bukharova in a few days to say good-bye, and then I will have an opportunity to speak to her about Loubensk.[7] [...] Andrey and I read in the newspaper that you have become a tenured professor. I don't congratulate you about this, as I think this title is meaningless. [...] Volodya plays the violin regularly. Yesterday I played some sonatas of Beethoven and Schumann with him. Why doesn't Nadya write to me? I'd like her to tell me herself how she finds her new college, if she likes it or not, if she is wishing to apply for the Higher College for Women again.[8]

The story about the promotion of Rimsky-Korsakov to the rank of distinguished professor is somewhat complicated. Rimsky-Korsakov himself first learned about this from the newspapers, and only later on, when he was at the Conservatory, did he receive the official document confirming the rank. Yastrebtsev, who visited him on that very day, recorded the composer as saying: "The title seems to sound great. But does it bear any significance? No, absolutely not. Today you are a tenured professor and tomorrow if someone might not appreciate you, they would deprive you of it. They are capable of doing this since we're all hired under the terms of a contract of service!" When Yastrebtsev asked the composer to show him that supposedly impressive document, Rimsky-Korsakov refused with the following words: "Oh, now, it doesn't matter. You will see it in any case one day after my departure, and I'm not sure right now where I put it."

Rimsky-Korsakov did not write to his wife for three days, and she became worried. Her letter reads:

My darling,

Why haven't you written to me for several days already? Maybe you are angry with me for my long stay here? Since Nadya's arrival, I have had some concern about your staying alone in our home. I would come sooner, but when I think of the hateful Petersburg, when I imagine how stuffy and disgusting it is now—stone walls are the only things you can look at there—and on the contrary everything is so beautiful here—open spaces and lovely air—I do not want to move back into the city again. The boys are happy to survive the winter here. They hunt rabbits every day. Do you think it is wrong that Volodya has been missing his classes at the Conservatory? Do they proceed regularly? [...] The autumn is so exceptionally beautiful this year that I expect people will stay longer in the country. […] The orchard has changed drastically. Today while I was walking along the linden alley, I noticed suddenly that many of the lindens next to the pond have lost their leaves and are completely bare; the pond itself is covered with leaves, and the path to it as well. Leaves fall down rustling with just the gentlest breath of wind. However, there are still plenty of leaves on the trees, and they are marvelous. It is curious that some apple trees have lost all of their leaves already and those that still have apples are green. Poplars are also still green, and the lilac bushes are becoming yellow, and the ash-trees are lovely in their yellowish and pale green attire. […] The dream about buying the estate is still occupying my mind. It is certainly silly, as it is impossible for it to be fulfilled. It is very late now. Everyone has been in bed for a long time. I am winding up. I am kissing you. Your N.

P.S. Why didn't you come here for a weekend? You could have done so. It could have been such fun. Though you like your dusty, stuffy, dirty Petersburg, which I can't stand.

Rimsky-Korsakov could not come for the weekend, since he was very busy at the Conservatory. He wrote to his wife:

My dear, […] Certainly our home is empty without you and I miss you all, but I'm just absorbed in different activities: I'm working on the orchestration of scene 2 from the third act [*Kitezh*]; I attend the Conservatory; I visit Sonya regularly. […] I am not bored at all, I mean the days are not dragging on, or that I spend them tediously, but I certainly long to see you all and to be with you. […] I am absolutely healthy. I drink beer just a little, something between half to three-fourths of a glass a day. I don't think it is much, and so it is not harmful for me. Well, I will promise, I will try to take Borjomi mineral water too. I am not going to take iodine right now, as I had enough during the summer. […] I think your dreams of buying Vetchasha or Loubensk are just vain dreams; it would cost a fortune, and we do not have it. […] I forgot to tell you, Belsky and Ossovsky visited me on Saturday evening. Sonya and Igor also came around, and I played the second act and the first scene from the third. Do not become angry with me for my playing it for them when you are not here. You have been staying in Vetchasha too long, and I suddenly had a great desire to play it. They liked it very much.

Kruglikov was still impressed by his trip to Vetchasha and the music of *Kitezh* he had heard there. He wrote to Rimsky-Korsakov:

> What I have heard stuck inside me.[...] It is good, it is very good, my dear friend. It is certainly R.-Korsakov, undoubtedly recognizable R.-Korsakov. One can realize immediately that it is R.-Korsakov. But here, in your great *Kitezh* you are the same, although quite different at the same time. You are always like this.[...] I felt very comfortable in your household. My first days [back] in Moscow I spent constantly talking with my relatives about you and your family, your good-heartedness and that lovely, bright, and healthy atmosphere that reigns in your family, which seems to be friendly, close, and free at the same time.

At last Nadezhda decided to return to the city. She sent a letter to her husband: "My dear, I've received all of your letters and I'm kissing you for them. I did not hear from you for three days and I became very sad. We are starting to pack tomorrow. We are to dispatch our things on 24 September, and we ourselves leave the next day." Nadezhda was so touched with the beauty of nature that autumn that she became very sentimental and even wrote a poem about their preparation for the departure.

At the beginning of October 1904 the opening night of *Pan Voevoda*, produced by Tsereteli, was held in the Grand Hall of the Conservatory. The first performances of almost all of Rimsky-Korsakov's operas were successful. The composer was called to the stage many times. However, he thought that this opera would not remain in the repertoire of the theatre for very long. Even while he was working on *Pan Voevoda*, he wrote to Tyumenev: "*Voevoda* seems as insipid and average (I'm speaking about the music) as *Servilia* (I don't mean mediocre)." He considered it to have been a mistake on his part to deal with non-Russian plots, and that he was in his element when he composed on Russian fairy tales and legends. Indeed, the new opera survived only for a few performances. The same thing happened a year later in Moscow when the Bolshoi Theatre produced *Pan Voevoda*. Even though Rachmaninov conducted the opera perfectly, it did not help. Findeisen commented on this in the *Russian Musical Gazette*:

> A bad musician cannot produce a great opera, just as a distinguished composer cannot create a bad or mediocre one. He will always be protected from the latter

by inborn artistic intuition and technical mastery. N. A. Rimsky-Korsakov belongs exactly to such exclusively talented geniuses, who are fortunate. He is often reproached, especially recently, for composing too much and for producing the score of a new opera almost every year, that he is using up too much of his creative resources. This rebuke will seem unreasonable if you consider the predestination of such a creative individual who produces [works of] art. It is ridiculous to demand that the latter produce only masterpieces. A composer composes under the pressure of creative thoughts irrespective of their value and their quality, and he cannot suppress them, in the same way that a singing bird cannot stop singing just because of some extremely reasonable theories of a zoologist.

Andrey wrote later that these two operas, *Servilia* and *Pan Voevoda*, were like an intermezzo in the middle of his father's composition of more significant works.

By the end of the October the opera *The Legend of the Invisible City of Kitezh and the Maiden Fevronia* was completed. Rimsky-Korsakov complained to Kruglikov: "I've become very tired from writing my own music and from my own orchestration of it. The latter is about to make me sick, as it is proceeding too smoothly. When it is not challenging, music gets uninteresting to me, and it seems so to others as well."

Rimsky-Korsakov went to Moscow for four days, where the Private Opera had been preparing for the production of *Servilia*. He attended the rehearsals, and on the day of the opening night he visited Taneyev. During the evening he left for St. Petersburg without waiting for the end of the performance. Soon afterward Rimsky-Korsakov played the second and the third acts of his *Kitezh* to Lyadov, Ossovsky, Yastrebtsev, and Belsky at his home.

Musical Wednesdays

On 1 January 1905 Rimsky-Korsakov played the first scene of the fourth act of *Kitezh*. On that day Belsky suggested that they should produce musical *jours fixes*—musical parties at Rimsky-Korsakov's home. They agreed on odd-date Wednesdays, so the musical evenings were to be held twice a month, and nobody was supposed to get official notification of such parties. Knowing in advance about this day, everybody who liked to could come. In this way, the musical program for these evenings was to be chosen spontaneously. On 5

January Rimsky-Korsakov played the fourth act of his new opera to his friends. Yastrebtsev recorded: "What inimitable poetry! What purity and eternal light! (I cried.) [...] I should say we all are excited about *Kitezh*."

The next day Yastrebtsev sent a letter to Rimsky-Korsakov:

> You remember, dearest friend, most respected Rimsky-Korsakov, the demands I made for You about the music of the opera you were composing at that time. I should [tell You] now that all my ambitious dreams about this composition have been realized. Well, once I was utterly excited by *The Snow Maiden*, *The Maid of Pskov*, *Mlada*, *Sadko*, *The Tsar Saltan*, and *Kashchey*; now I am completely captured by Your *Kitezh*, which is absolutely incomparable, fully idealistic, and tremendous. Indeed, "You have managed to unlock the secrets of nature and reveal Your enormous talent." I would like to thank You once more for the ecstasy I experienced yesterday while I was listening to Your *Legend*, the work of a genius. I am still under that impression. Amen!

Many guests were hosted at the "musical Wednesdays." On Wednesday, 9 February 1905, the program for the musical evening was as follows: Richter played music by Stravinsky and Glazunov. Zabela performed compositions by Glazunov and Rimsky-Korsakov, and Glazunov accompanied her on the piano. After this Wednesday, Yastrebtsev wrote in his memoirs: "Belsky's and my *fixes* are flourishing extensively, though they have brought unwanted fruits: *Kitezh* was forgotten completely!" However, he had nothing to be worried about. The next "musical Wednesday" was marked by the performance of the first and the second acts of *Kitezh*. On 27 February Yastrebtsev sent another letter to Rimsky-Korsakov:

> Dear Nikolay!
> Yesterday, while I was listening to *Boris Godunov*, it brought back memories to me of my mother, who adored this opera, and recalled Your operas—the greatest miracle You have created—*The City of Kitezh*, and so strong were the feelings that I had a great desire to kneel before You. Do not become angry with me for this struggle of mine, especially since today is Absolution Sunday. Right at this moment Your *Kitezh* is before me. While looking through it by myself I cried tears of joy. Please do not think that I have become as mad as Vakula—nothing of the kind. I just wished to express in words at least a little of that

feeling I had deep in my heart under the influence of Your new inspirational "Gospel."[…] I can imagine how angry at me you will become after reading my letter. But what should I do? It is You who are to be blamed: You should not have composed such music.

Rimsky-Korsakov responded: "You are talking nonsense, my dear V. V.," and added, "It seems I borrowed this phrase from Gogol."

On 6 March it was the composer's birthday. The family expected to receive guests, and Rimsky-Korsakov sent out invitations; he wrote one for Lyadov in verse. Kruglikov sent a congratulatory letter for the birthday:

With these loving words I congratulate You on your birthday. I also congratulate all of Your relatives, and myself, and our Russian music, and all those who serve it faithfully. This is a special occasion to celebrate. We have Rimsky-Korsakov— the dearest, wonderful, innocent, and great man, who should be loved heartily and appreciated for everything he has done and is doing, for his being as he is. Let everything in Your life be great, let all troubles pass You by.

However, the Rimsky-Korsakovs failed to escape troubles. All of a sudden their son Andrey was taken seriously ill. The illness was very grave—rheumatic fever and inflammation of the heart. His condition was critical: high fever, hallucinations, and the effects on his heart. The whole family was alarmed. Meanwhile, the situation at the Conservatory was darkening.

Upheaval at the Conservatory

The end of 1904 marked the renewal of the student demonstrations at St. Petersburg University. Soon afterward the tragic events of 9 January 1905 took place.[9] The young people in the Conservatory could not stand aside; they began to organize group meetings. The situation was worsened by the fact that one of the Conservatory students, Manets, boasted that he had taken part in the suppression of that demonstration. The only professor who expressed his outrage against the behavior of that student was Rimsky-Korsakov. Rimsky-Korsakov was certainly concerned about current events and even asked people not to mention this topic when talking to him, as it would make him extremely upset. The newspaper *Nashi dni* (*Nowadays*) published an appeal from Moscow musicians, which stated: "When there is neither freedom of belief nor freedom of speech nor freedom of the press, when any current creative public under-takings meet only obstacles, the creative work of artists is relinquished as well....Russia must, at last, take the path of crucial reforms." The appeal was signed by Grechaninov, Taneyev, Rachmaninov, Chaliapin, and Kruglikov, among others. Having read this, Rimsky-Korsakov sent a letter to the same newspaper: "I sympathize with all my heart with the Appeal of the Moscow musicians and composers published in issue no. 37 of *Nowadays* and I would like to add the signature of a Petersburg musician via this respected newspaper. N. Rimsky-Korsakov."

The events that followed and Rimsky-Korsakov's part in them are described briefly but clearly in the composer's autobiography:

> The board and the arts council called emergency meetings. I was nominated to an ad hoc committee to carry out negotiations with the rioting students. The board proposed various measures: expelling the rebels, allocating police officers in the Conservatory, closing the Conservatory. I had to defend the rights of the students. The heated arguments and disagreements between the members of the committee were increasing. The conservative part of the professors and the board of the St. Petersburg Branch of the Russian Musical Society, the supervisory body of the Conservatory, started to look at me as if I had been the leader of the revolutionary movement of the students. [...] I published an open letter in the newspaper *Rus'* [*Russia*] in which I reproached the board for not understanding the students, and that confirmed the uselessness of the existence of the board of the St. Petersburg Branch and the need for the Conservatory to be independent. Bernhard, the head of the Conservatory, called for an investigation and denun-ciation of my letter at the council meeting. He was strongly opposed, and he put an end to the meeting. Then a significant part of the professors, I among them, sent Bernhard an official letter asking him to resign from the Conservatory.[10] The result of this was the following: the Conservatory was shut down; more than one hundred students were expelled; Bernhard left; and I was discharged by the board of the Russian Musical Society in accordance with a writ issued by Grand Duke Konstantin. Moreover, when the board decided this issue, they did not inform the arts council, the members of which were mainly the professors of the Conservatory. After being dismissed in this way, I published a letter con-cerning these matters in the newspaper *Rus'* [*Russia*], and in the same letter I

relinquished my position as an honorable member of the Petersburg Branch of the Russian Musical Society.

Then something unpredictable happened. I began to receive letters and statements from various organizations and individuals that both belonged to and did not belong to the musical community of Moscow and Petersburg, and other cities and towns, in which they expressed their sympathy for me and bridled at the board of the Russian Musical Society. I received representatives of different organizations and corporations, as well as private persons who made similar claims. All of the newspapers published articles investigating my case. The directors were being dragged into the mire, and they felt awful. […] All of this was crowned with the decision of the students to hold a performance of my opera *Kashchey* and a concert of my music at the Komissarzhevskaya Theatre.

They chose this opera on purpose. The plot of *Kashchey* paralleled the mood of the student movement, since the oppressive atmosphere of the *Kashchey* regime was identified with the current tsar's regime, and the collapse of this regime at the end of the opera was perceived as desirable freedom from the yoke of autocracy. The opera was rehearsed by the students of the Conservatory and performed with Glazunov as conductor on 27 March in the Komissarzhevskaya Theatre. Rimsky-Korsakov's autobiography continues: "As soon as they finished the opera, something outrageous happened. I was called to the stage, and they started to read addresses to me from various organizations and societies and made passionate speeches. Then somebody upstairs cried out, 'Down with the autocracy!' There was a hullabaloo after each address or speech." According to Yastrebtsev's memoirs, "Rimsky-Korsakov squirmed and said, bowing to the orchestra and the public, 'Thank you ladies and gentlemen, thank you ever so much. Believe me, I do not deserve it.'"

The composer describes the events that followed in his autobiography:

The police ordered the iron curtain to be dropped to stop any further proceedings. The concert [i.e., performance] part of the event was canceled. Such overblown exaggeration of my deserts and of my supposedly incredible bravery as a citizen can be explained only by the anxiety of all Russian society, which chose this way, i.e., addressing me, to express aloud their burning indignation at the government. I was a scapegoat. As it was obvious to me, I did not feel any need to satisfy my self-esteem. I just waited for it all to come to an end. However, it dragged on for two months. I was myself in an unbearable and awkward situation. The police banned the playing of my compositions in Petersburg. Some provincial authorities followed the capital and issued a similar ban. Due to this, the third Symphony Concert was also suppressed, since the program included the overture to *The Maid of Pskov*. By summer the enforcement of the ban gradually became weaker, and provincial orchestras began including my compositions in their repertoires. Since I was in fashion again, many of my compositions were played. Only in the provinces did the zealous local authorities continue to consider them revolutionary.

After the performance of *Kashchey*, the newspaper *Slovo* (*The Word*) published an article by Ossovsky describing the events in the theatre. It was crowned with the following phrase: "The main idea of all the speeches was the glory and honor of the great man of art and citizen now and forevermore; shame on those who dare to stand against him."

Yastrebtsev wrote in his memoirs at the time: "Thus, our Conservatory found itself separated from the man whose name is our pride, and one who is recognized and respected throughout Europe." The newspaper *Russia* published an open letter to the board of the Russian Musical Society signed by ninety Moscow musicians:

> Dear Sirs!
>
> Though now you have glorified your [own] names with the fame of Herostratus, you were earlier indifferent to the chronicles of the history of art. You dared to "discharge" N. A. Rimsky-Korsakov from the faculty of the Conservatory. […] But you should remember, it does not matter how many times you strike his name off your bureaucratic lists and registers; this name will forever illuminate the whole of Russia as well as the world. […] Shame is not on him whom you "dismissed," but on you, who, being madly blind, ventured to raise your hand against the pride and fame of our national art—a great artist and spotless citizen.

Rimsky-Korsakov himself received numerous letters of sympathy from both distinguished and ordinary people. He received one letter from a group of peasants of six villages of the Yriev district of Vladimir province:

> To the discharged professor Rimsky-Korsakov. We learned about the injustice done to You from the newspaper. We have not heard your name before due to

our ignorance, and frankly speaking, we do not know You at all, and You, in your turn, do not know us, but in any case we are writing to You to express our feelings toward You. We have realized that you have suffered because of being true and because you did not want to obey the unlawful orders of the authorities and did not want to act together with the police. You behaved correctly. We, the peasants, offer You our sympathy over the incident that happened to You.

It was very touching that Rimsky-Korsakov found enclosed 2 rubles 17 kopeks, which they had collected for the sake of the victim. Although the sum was small, Rimsky-Korsakov contributed it to the assistance for the peasants of Tula province, who had suffered from famine. Overall Rimsky-Korsakov received forty-six telegrams with expressions of sympathy from private persons and organizations. The only two who did not react at all were Balakirev and Cui. Stasov was outraged and wrote to Cui: "What a huge difference there is between Cui, a composer of lyrics and love compositions, and Cui, a participant in real life! The whole of Russia is crowning Rimsky-Korsakov with laurels, [...] all are flying to him with their hearts and gratitude...well, Balakirev has turned into a dry old stick a long time ago. But you! What about you? What is this? Shame and disgrace on you!!!!"

At the beginning of April 1905 the opera singers Kastorsky and Labinsky gave a concert in Voronezh. When they began singing some of the romances of Rimsky-Korsakov, someone in the audience cried out, "All rise!" And the audience continued listening to his compositions standing up. At the end of the concert the public was so excited that they carried the performers in their arms with cries of "Long live Rimsky-Korsakov!" Loud ovations were repeated in the street. Rimsky-Korsakov thanked all of the people who had expressed their sympathy to him via the newspaper *Russia*. To demonstrate against the actions taken by the board of the Russian Musical Society, Glazunov and Lyadov left the Conservatory. Some of the professors followed their example. Studies at the Conservatory were discontinued. However, Rimsky-Korsakov and several other professors kept on teaching their Conservatory students at home. One of the last things that he received during this period was an invitation from New York on 1 May to teach the theory of composition there. "I certainly won't go," Rimsky-Korsakov said, although the terms would have been quite beneficial for him.

15

"Live and Love Living," 1905–1906

Music itself is entering a new and confusing phase of development (Strauss, d'Indy, Debussy, etc.). And I, like many of us, am a figure of a different, past period. Isn't it time to look back and sum up everything instead of trying to join them with something alien?

—Rimsky-Korsakov to Nadezhda Rimsky-Korsakov,
30 June 1905

Alexander Siloti, a pianist and conductor, a student of Nikolay Rubinstein,[1] Liszt, and Tchaikovsky, and the organizer of the Russian Symphony Concerts, suggested that Glazunov, Lyadov, and Rimsky-Korsakov, all of whom had resigned from the Conservatory, set up their own Higher Music College. They produced a charter for the proposed college, but events prevented their plans from being fulfilled. They had to obtain a license from the governor-general, who, in his turn, decided that if the director of this new establishment of higher education was to be Rimsky-Korsakov, it would attract "young people promoting ideas alien to the existing government order." The officials suggested that instead they should open a school rather than a college of higher education. The governor-general requested that the board of the Imperial Russian Musical Society give their opinion about this issue. However, in their official response to the governor-general, the board did not state its opinion. It avoided offering any judgment, saying that the matter was beyond its competence. The organizers of the proposed Higher Music College understood perfectly that the board of the Russian Musical Society would not support their plan. Siloti, however, insisted on keeping on with their efforts. Rimsky-Korsakov wrote to him: "We wanted to open the Higher Music College, and we are allowed to set up only a school. [...] We are not permitted to establish what we wish. Then, let it be." Soon they all gave up on the idea.

Kruglikov was extremely concerned about the events at the St. Petersburg Conservatory, and he wrote to the composer:

> I'm beside myself all this time, unsettled and I cannot understand anything. It seems to me that they will soon try to prove that 2 × 2 = 5. It's complete chaos, nonsense and gibberish! [...] Some Klimenkos dared to judge and whom! What the hell! After this, I suppose nothing will surprise me! They are just a group of dry, shabby mannequins, their articles and clauses [that] stink of mold, which are called by mistake justice and equity. Where is humanity? Where is their intelligence? At least some rudiments of understanding, and the ability to feel with their hearts? They are just stupid puppets! And you, certainly, should not stay among them! [...] you are at the center of attention now; most people look at you with excitement. And to hell with them! [...] The Imperial Russian Musical Society meant to ruin you, but it turns out they have ruined themselves completely and irrevocably and glorified you. They are miserable, stupid creatures! [...] I have lost my balance. My nerves are spoiled. I do not want to do simple things. All ordinary things seem disgusting. I am embracing you doubly tight. All the best, invaluable, wonderful Nikolay. Always yours, Kruglikov.

At Vetchasha

Since Rimsky-Korsakov was free from giving lessons at the Conservatory, he left for Vetchasha on 3 May 1905. Yastrebtsev wrote to him: "I can imagine how nice it is now in Vetchasha, how inspiring and subtle the song of the spring forest is. How wonderful the fresh lilies of the valley are!" Unfortunately, Rimsky-Korsakov had to return to St. Petersburg in only a week since his son Andrey, who had seemed to be much better, became ill again. Two weeks later, Andrey became better and his family on the advice of doctors decided to send Andrey to Nauheim, Germany, for treatment. At the beginning of June, on the very same day, from the very same railway station—Warsaw station—the family set off in opposite directions; the composer's wife, Nadezhda, and their son Andrey left for the resort, and Rimsky-Korsakov and his daughter Nadya left for Vetchasha. On her way to Germany, Nadezhda wrote to her husband: "Dear Nika, we are already in Germany. At last, we have got rid of the awful Russian train. Sweltering heat and lack of air—did not allow us to sleep there." They stayed at a hotel in Berlin, from which Nadezhda sent another letter to her husband:

Having reached this destination I have become sure that in Russia one should travel in luxury class if one does not want to be overwhelmed by exhaustion. And we, poor ones, were unlucky to get an especially bad carriage; it was old, dirty, and stuffy, the seats were too short, so that Andrey could not stretch himself out fully, the lavatory looked like a pigsty. [...] After being so tortured by the trip so far, we were happy to find the hotel impeccably tidy, airy, though the rooms are a little small but with wonderful beds and nice bathrooms. [...] I forced Andrey to move as little as possible; so we use the lift to go up and down to the restaurant. Andrey is in high spirits and lively. [...] Berlin seems to be very lively. Petersburg is just a village, full of rubbish. I am kissing you and embracing you tightly. N. R.-K.

P.S. No, Petersburg is not even a village, it's just a corpse.

In response to the telegram received from Berlin that they had reached it safe and sound, Rimsky-Korsakov sent the following letter:

My dear Mama and Andreyka,

I hope that Andrey's exhaustion, which is just natural after the trip, will not lead to complications. [...] We went swimming for the first time yesterday. The water is warm, about +18–19° C [64–66° F]. There is much fresh greenery, many flowers, and many wild strawberry flowers. The birds are singing, but there are no nightingales. However, today, early in the morning, about 6 all of a sudden a nightingale trilled. Frogs in the puddles also sing as loudly as they can. [...] Frankly speaking, if Maria had been lost somewhere,[2] Vetchasha would be just a paradise on earth. I cannot even hear anything about Maria without being annoyed: the bathhouse is falling apart, the windows cannot be closed, and the lace curtains are all in knots, milk is sour, and so on. Volodya has mended the electric bell. He had been working on it for two days. The bell either rang without stopping or did not produce any sound at all. He and Nady had to work at it several times; at last they achieved success. [...] Dear Nadya, you should also take the advice of the doctors in Nauheim and maybe have some treatment yourself.

In two days he wrote again:

I'm happy that your trip is over and you're safe and sound. [...] I decided to write down my memoirs because music does not seem to come to my mind and I do not feel like composing anything. [...] I will try to work on my memoirs. When

I reread them, they seem to be of interest to others. [...] Take care, my dear. Andreyushka, get well and gain strength! All kisses to you. Hugs.

Your N.

Upon their arrival in Nauheim, Nadezhda and Andrey at first stayed at a hotel, but it turned out to be quite expensive. They hurried to find some cheaper accommodation and ended up renting suitable rooms at the villa Sans-Souci. Nadezhda reported to her husband:

Dear Nika,

We've just moved into the villa. We are rather exhausted. Although we went by luxury class yesterday, we were the only two in the compartment. [...] In my opinion, Andrey has gained some strength. He used the staircase today and he moves around a lot. Certainly, I was the only one who was looking for a new place to stay. [...] We sent a telegram yesterday, but it was very difficult to convince them to take it. They do not know the place Plussa—there is no such station in their books. I'm afraid you have been worried.

The next letter that Nadezhda sent her husband was about Andrey's visit to a Dr. Yankovsky, who recommended baths and a treatment regimen. She wrote:

We are glad that there is no common lounge for tea. We all have coffee in our own rooms, or on the balcony or in the garden. It is as if we are at home. The property owner considers us as if we were milk cows, and she is certainly milking us for all she can. She even charges 30 pfennigs for boiling water for tea. She says directly, "The season is very short, only four months; I should get as much profit as I can." [...] The park is wonderful here, although we have seen only a little of it. We went for a walk for the first time with Andrey.

Nadezhda did not receive any letters from her husband for some time and became worried. In turn, Nikolay wrote to his wife: "Doesn't our post office know Nauheim, as Germans don't know Plussa? I put on the envelope—to Germany. Maybe our postmen don't know where Germany is? I'm healthy, take iodine and swim."

Rimsky-Korsakov did not care that the trip to Nauheim was costing a fortune. He wrote: "I beg you to enjoy the luxury this time as much as possible,

since this luxury will bring about conveniences that are so necessary for you."
He wrote nearly the same thing in his next letter:

> For God's sake, do not feel sorry if you spend a lot of money to buy everything
> you need to make your stay there comfortable and enjoyable. [...] Our life is
> quiet and routine here. The weather is wonderful. There is no rain and it's hot.
> The sky is cloudless usually and even if there are some clouds, they are light and
> cumulus. The water is +22° C [72° F], so swimming does not refresh us at all,
> though we swim twice a day. [...] We have coffee, breakfast, lunch, dinner, and
> supper in the orchard under the trees. We do not even carry the table away.
> Today Volodya fixed a bell on the tree.[3] [...] The strawberries have ripened. Today
> we bought some, but three days ago we went to pick the berries ourselves; by the
> way, it was I who found the places that are rich in wild strawberries. [...] I am busy
> with writing my memoirs, which I titled *My Musical Life*. In Vetchasha I managed
> to describe the 1880–81 and '82 years. I wish I could remember everything before
> 1892; after that I have entries in my diary again. Besides, I have nothing between
> 1865 and 1872. To remember all of the events that happened is very difficult and
> a huge job. [...] I embrace you and Andrey. Do the same to all the rest. Be healthy,
> calm, and patient. Write, write and once again—write!

It took a long time for the letters to reach their destinations, perhaps because
of the censorship that was strong at that time, so sometimes Nikolay received
four or five letters from his wife at one time. Nadezhda wrote: "The things that
are going on in Russia now are extremely interesting and of great importance.
It is ridiculous that one can learn about the true events only living abroad,
as the *Frankfurter Zeitung* has reported that all the Russian newspapers are
ordered to keep silent about things that are happening. They have posted the
latest news from Russia even in the streets and people stop to read it."

Rimsky-Korsakov advised his wife to take some treatment for herself.
However, Nadezhda responded to him negatively:

> I told you once already, I'm not going to take any treatment myself. I can cure
> myself only at home. I hate all these German resorts. I don't believe in their bene-
> ficial effect, at least for me personally, so I will never take any kind of treatment
> abroad. Moreover, I wrote to you already that I came here not to cure myself but
> only to look after Andrey, and under such circumstances my treatment is utterly

impossible. [...] I listen to the stories of patients here all the time with horror; they all come for several years in a row, several even for ten years already. Is it possible that Andrey will have to endure the same fate? Then we'd better not come to Nauheim. [...] I'm about to read Chekhov's "The Steppe" aloud to Andrey.[4] This story is perfect, one of his best. [...] I wonder if I will ever see Vetchasha again, or will my small poem, in which I said, "Farewell, Vetchasha, forever," turn out to be a prophetic one?

Nadezhda was thinking of going somewhere in Switzerland. Her husband supported her idea:

Anywhere is good in Switzerland. In addition, there are millions of places abroad that are good. You can go wherever you like. Vetchasha is still a very attractive country house for me and an uncommonly nice place. The orchard, the lake, wild strawberries, honey, a peaceful life—all this is wonderful, I just no longer like Russian people. They can be loved and felt sorry for, like hospital patients. You can wish them to get better soon, to be useful to them, but I can't say that it is pleasant to spend time with them or to keep company with them. It is the same as keeping company with patients in the hospital. I read newspapers and become outraged at people who barely try to use their brains. Yesterday, when Sonya told our nanny about the incident with the battleship *Prince Potemkin*,[5] her nanny said indifferently, "Certainly they were bribed. They would sell their own father for money." Or something like that.

You are reading the truth there, and we here can only think about what is going on in Russia right now, what horrible things are taking place to suppress and make us knuckle under; we are trying to interpret the hints published in the press. And that incident with the ship *Prince Potemkin* is a case, and an unusual case! And this is all the result of scuffles, whipping, shooting, and hanging. There will be even much more of this. [...] I tried to compose a romance; it didn't come and I gave up. I tried again to work on my textbook on orchestration, but it seems to be a hopeless effort.

Nadezhda worried that if Andrey's illness turned out to be an incurable one, then he would not have the chance to live a normal life and work for a living. Rimsky-Korsakov comforted her as best he could: "Take it easy, dear Nadya. When Andrey's treatment is over, then you will see what to do further. I'm embracing you and kissing you. You're so nice!"

Their eldest son, Mikhail, arrived at Vetchasha to stay for three days. Rimsky-Korsakov was happy. He wrote to Andrey that he was talking a lot to Mikhail and they had discussed the incident on the *Potemkin* for a considerable amount of time. "I didn't have enough time to talk over everything with Misha. He slept on the sofa in my study and we talked until 2 a.m. Indeed, we talked not only about politics, but also insects and music, in a word: about everything.[6] Certainly we talked a lot about you and Mama. We walked to a forest, gathered wild strawberries, and even played croquet. I also played one time." He also shared his opinion about current events in Russia with his son: "What is going on here in Russia! [...] I am myself again thinking about current events all day long and I can't do anything else. And what is the use of my thinking?"

Nikolay and Nadezhda Rimsky-Korsakov's thirty-third wedding anniversary was approaching. They managed to keep their deep mutual feelings throughout all those years and even wrote the same words to each other. She wrote:

> Dear Nika,
>
> You are supposed to get this greeting card on our wedding day. It is the first time we've been apart on this day. [...] I'm kissing you and embracing you tightly. How are you going to spend 30 June? Could you write to me about it? I will be thinking of you.
>
> Your N. R.-K.

The composer wrote to his wife:

> My dear friend,
>
> Maybe you will get this letter on our wedding day, which we will spend this time far away from each other. I'm embracing you tightly and kissing you, and on 30 June I will be thinking of you even more, although thoughts of you and Andrey are haunting me persistently. Take care of yourself, my heart.
>
> Your N. R. K.

And on 30 June Rimsky-Korsakov wrote:

> My dear Nadyusha,
>
> Today is 30 June—our day. You asked me to tell you how I would spend it. I spent it as usual. And it couldn't be different. The weather is bad. First it gave us

hope that the sun would appear and there would be breaks in the rain. By evening the wind died down and the sky became covered completely with clouds. And it is drizzling and drizzling now without stopping. Even so, we had dinner on the balcony, as it is rather warm in any case. We toasted your and Andrey's health and mine as well with Madeira wine. (Irina was also drinking, or I should say licking.) We got our mail before dinner. I received a greeting card from Andrey. Kiss him for it. And there was another one from Mikhail also with congratulations. At noon I worked on the analysis of *The Snow Maiden*. [...] I'm not developing my *Memoirs* now.[7] But I will deal with it again as soon as I finish with the analysis of the prologue to *The Snow Maiden*. It seems to me now is my time to undertake literary and musical business instead of composing music, in which I would not wish to create anything weak or of low quality. In any case, after ten years of hard work [since 1894] I should either cease or rest for a considerable period of time. Before I used to have rests, but for the last ten years I have not had any. Moreover, music itself is entering a new and confusing phase of development (Strauss, d'Indy, Debussy, etc.). And I, like many of us, am a figure of a different, past period. Isn't it time to look back and sum up everything instead of trying to join them with something alien?[8] [...] I'm embracing you tightly, my dearest. Be safe and sound. And how did you spend this day?

Memoirs: *My Musical Life*

Later Rimsky-Korsakov wrote to Yastrebtsev: "Unfortunately, I'm really not interesting this summer, as I'm not with the family. [...] I am certainly engaged in different activities, but not in composition or even orchestration of my old works. [...] I'm working on my *Memoirs*, the critique of *The Snow Maiden*, *Fundamentals of Orchestration*, and so on; I'm skipping from one to another and being idle as well." He seemed to be concerned that he was not composing music, and he shared his mood with his friends. Lyadov responded to a letter from the composer: "I've read between the lines in your letter that you are bored and seem to be dissatisfied with yourself. You are not composing? You should remember, dear friend, that all of your [musical] notes even of average value are priceless, so you should write and write. Everything you've done should be placed behind glass so as to be protected from dust and kept secure for the future." Rimsky-Korsakov wrote in an invitation to Belsky to visit Vetchasha: "I'm an absolutely uninteresting object at this time—I haven't composed a single note."

Sobering Thoughts

Stasov, who was eighty-one years old at the time, took the death of two young relatives who were very close to him hard. He complained to Rimsky-Korsakov: "What is waiting for me? The 'queue' is getting shorter and shorter! It's awful, awful, awful." Rimsky-Korsakov responded to Stasov's concern about death:

> I must tell you that I also think often of it, since it might claim one's life any minute. However, I see this matter in another way, and I think that if I reach the age of eighty I will not change my view that I peaked a long time ago. I am not afraid of death, although it is always a pity to be parted from life. Well, but death itself is a very beautiful thing. Only think, what can be more horrifying than eternal life? All others would have died and I would be living! It is just terrible! And if nobody dies and all live forever, then it will look like paradise on earth or the kingdom of heaven. Oh, God! It would be so boring. What is the use of living then? Not to be developing? To be at a standstill? Birth and development cannot be seen without death, and if it cannot be, then it should be like this. And it is just wonderful that there is no life after death; I believe that it does not exist. How would you feel if you saw from there how everything you had worked on and loved was perishing and being forgotten, and even if it were not perishing, then dispersing and vanishing into thin air. For example, I loved Glinka, and then there came a time when everyone forgot about him, and he became useless to them. What an utter justice death is, that is, absolute zero! No rewards, no revenge. That is the best deed of God's mercy. Well, while you are alive, you should live and love living. I love living and I don't wish to die, and I think that everything is arranged in the best way because as soon as I start to exercise my small brain to plan changes or think of them, nothing works out. So, I wish for you to live long and be healthy, and to go on with your business, and for much more of your work to be published. I am sorry for philosophizing. It is just nothing.

Nadezhda criticized Russia; nevertheless, everything abroad was alien to her as well. She wrote to her husband:

> About Nachkur, you've said that we should go where we'd like, but we'd like to go only to Vetchasha. We will go to any other place unwillingly and only to Vetchasha with joy. [...] You cannot even imagine how I get bored with this foreign, useless,

and repugnant crowd. I would give anything for the opportunity to flee from them and spend at least a few minutes with my dearest and beloved. I am feeling deep loathing for Germans. You talk about our peasants being uncivilized. Certainly, civilization is a good thing, but as with any other thing in our world, it has two sides: on the one hand, it is perfect; on the other hand, it is no good at all. What about the Russian peasant…I consider him not as a sick man, but as a dormant, virginal power. Due to this he is much more interesting than a German one, as ours seem like a challenging riddle. This is the first time I have lived in a German resort, and I can say that they have aimed not at helping the sick, but at stuffing German pockets. Germans wish to prove that if they build a "Badehaus" [bathhouse], allocate parks, and place folding screens on balconies, they will provide sheer comfort for the sick, and the latter must be grateful for this and pack Germans' pockets with money and not dare to complain. Indeed, there is no comfort at all for the sick. It is impossible to find the healthy food that is recommended by the doctors, real peace and quiet are absent from any of the villas, and the air is as polluted as if you lived in the city, but you're supposed to breathe fresh air. And so on and so forth. Well, that is enough about resorts, which I cannot stand. You wrote that you do not feel like composing. I hope you will. You need a good rest. And that you are going on working on your *Memoirs* is very good and must be interesting.

When Andrey had only a few baths left to take, he suffered a sudden relapse of his rheumatism. Andrey was taking baths from a spring that was supposed to be the most beneficial and salubrious one. His temperature rose, and all of his baths had to be delayed for some time. The illness itself and the necessity to stay longer in Nauheim distressed everyone in the family. Rimsky-Korsakov kept on writing letters to his wife: "I'm longing to see you and Andrey as soon as possible here in Vetchasha. Everything is the same here. Sonya and Nadya are trimming blackcurrant bushes now. Volodya has gone hunting. We often cook what he bags. Today, for example, for dinner we had a teal and a great snipe that he had shot. The last two days were lovely: it was warm and the table has again been placed under the tree. […] Be healthy, my dears." The composer was alarmed at Andrey's condition. He wrote to his wife: "I beg you to write everything about Andrey. I can't say that we won't be extremely worried, but any even a slight indisposition can't help alarming us. I can imagine how worried you were when Andrey got a fever! You, at least, take care of yourself. You're so thin and exhausted. […] Write! Write!"

He was eager to learn about his son's condition as soon as possible and decided to send a telegram from Vetchasha to Nauheim. He was unpleasantly surprised when he got a refusal at the post office: "Look here! They did not accept it at the telegraph because it was written in a foreign language (!!!???!!!). Tomorrow I'll try sending it again along with a letter to the manager of the post office." Yet Rimsky-Korsakov failed in his attempt to send the telegram. The post office refused to take it, since they did not have either rates or a list of foreign cities. They had to stick to writing letters. A similar story happened to his wife in Nauheim when she tried to do the same. She wrote to her husband:

> The telegraph at the Bahnhof [train station] is just a short step away, so I decided to go there. Unfortunately, the obstinacy of the German clerk was unbreakable. Nothing could help—neither persuasion nor argument. I told him that I had sent a telegram to Plussa once from there and it was received by the addressee. It was useless. He was set in his ways: he can't send a telegram to a place that is not on his list, and that's it. We hesitated whether we should send a telegram at all, since time had passed and you might have received the letter already. Yet today I decided to try the main post office. I succeeded. They took it without any questions and even did not look it up in the list, but the family name confused the clerk. He reached a dead end. He asked and asked again what the family name was; although I told him clearly enough that it was a "doppelte Familienname" [double family name]. Oh, you can't imagine how I'm getting mad at those blockheads! In the pharmacy they still can't pronounce our name properly. Every time when they give you your medicine they pronounce your name, i.e., read it on the prescription. The last time a chemist read it in that way he could not help laughing himself, and I followed him. They seem to be literate, but they are little better than our servants.

This was not the end of the story about the telegram. Although written in German and sent from Nauheim, somehow or other it arrived in Vetchasha written in Russian! Life was proceeding quietly in Vetchasha.

On 15 July Rimsky-Korsakov sent his regular letter: "Today Volodya has shot eight young game birds and one mature one for his birthday dinner. The game turned out to be delicious. In the morning there was an accident: Arapka stole one of the birds and ate it.[9] It caused Nadya a great deal of displeasure, and she has been ignoring her dog all day. [...] I have been absorbed in writing my book on orchestration for two weeks in a row already. This time it seems to be proceeding well."

Yastrebtsev arrived in Vetchasha on 22 July and stayed there until 25 July. He came early in the morning when all were still in bed. He wrote about it later:

> The whole house was asleep. The morning was wonderful. I walked around the orchard and even took a photo from the alley in front of the balcony. Everything was as usual; they only have more flowers this time (gillyflowers, flowering tobacco, lobelias). At 8:30 Rimsky-Korsakov came out, and we smothered each other with kisses. […] After breakfast Rimsky-Korsakov sat working on his book on orchestration and almost completed the part for strings. After going for a walk he played his Homer prelude-cantata score. Then we walked again in the orchard. […] After dinner he got down to work again; then we went to the lake to "see the sun off." We admired the sky and clouds. Rimsky-Korsakov said that he had fallen in love with the sky and now he can understand why people think that God is there. We went to our rooms at 10:30. Rimsky-Korsakov was going to write some letters.

The next day Yastrebtsev took some more photographs of Vetchasha. His memoirs continue:

> After breakfast Rimsky-Korsakov and [his daughter] Nadezhda went to Loubensk to visit Bukharov. […] After dinner Rimsky-Korsakov did not work much. We walked along the Loubensk road. We went to watch the sunset. […] After tea Rimsky-Korsakov resumed his work, and I went to the lake. The evening was quiet, warm, and starlit. Later in the evening we all walked along the Zapesenskaya road. We went to our rooms at 11 p.m. Today we had breakfast and dinner outdoors, in the orchard in front of the balcony. […] This year Vetchasha gave shelter to three gray kittens; they not only climbed the trees but also sat on Nikolay's shoulders.

Yastrebtsev also described the next day of his visit: "I got up rather late, about 7:30. All were asleep except Irisha and her nanny. The morning was lovely. We had tea in the orchard. What a paradise! Rimsky-Korsakov was the first to come out at 8:45. He was in high spirits. He made coffee for himself and then he left to do some work. I looked through the fourth act of *Kitezh*. During a break in his work we went to the orchard." And then about the last day of his visit:

> At noon we ate cucumbers with honey. An old local man, Ilia Petrov, who sold them, was a little under the influence, and he assured Rimsky-Korsakov that his honey was the best in the empire! He sounded proud. By the way, his honey was really delicious. […] After dinner Rimsky-Korsakov played dance music for Irochka (the Krakovienne and the Waltz from *Faust* and *Freischütz*, and the chorus from *William Tell*). In the afternoon Rimsky-Korsakov, his daughter Nadezhda, and I went to watch the sunset. […] We sat on the porch and saw falling stars. […] Before my departure we all went together to the lake again. To the right there was an orange reflection of the moon in the water (ripples of light on the water).

Yastrebtsev left Vetchasha later that night.

Rimsky-Korsakov kept on writing letters to Nauheim: "Everything's the same here. Jam-making time is over. Today we went to gather mushrooms. […] I continue working on my *Fundamentals of Orchestration*, and it is developing at a fast pace." In the meantime, Andrey became much better, and Nadezhda wrote to her husband:

> Now that Andrey is all right, I can confess that I have experienced an awfully hard time. Though his temperature was not so high and when he was on his feet, I was constantly worried that his condition might worsen; that his temperature might rise, which was quite possible. I would certainly have had the same concern at home; but here, far from you, in a foreign country with an unfamiliar doctor, whom you do not trust completely, staying in furnished rooms where you don't feel comfortable, it was ten times worse. Thank God, these troubles are over.

After Andrey completed his course of treatment, they went to Eisenach, Germany, to spend some time there, as was required for the *Nachkur* (convalescence). Nadezhda described the town in her letter to her husband: "Eisenach is a lovely and interesting place. It is a town surrounded with woods on the mountains; one of them is the home of the famous town Wartburg, where the singing contest takes place and where Luther's room is.[10] Eisenach is the hometown of Bach. There is a monument to him, and they showed us the house where he was born."

Andrey and his mother took a trip to Wartburg, which they enjoyed. Nadezhda wrote again: "The castle and the surroundings are very picturesque. And inside the castle there is much to be seen. Because it is very wearisome to walk around and watch everything, Andrey did not see much. He took rests sitting in the yard of the castle from time to time." At last they could return to Russia. They traveled via Berlin as usual, and Nadezhda sent her last letter to her husband on her journey from there:

> Dear Nika,
>
> I'm writing my last letter to you since tomorrow it will be too late—we will come before you receive it. […] There is an awful fuss, crush, and crowds here in Berlin. There are so many horse-drawn trams, vehicles, and bicycles that my head is spinning, and it is frightening to cross the street. Andrey and I walked a lot, looked in shop windows, and bought plenty of different things. […] Andreyka feels well, he walked a lot. I'm kissing you. See you soon.

Fundamentals of Orchestration

Andrey and Nadezhda arrived at Vetchasha on 7 August. By this time Rimsky-Korsakov had completed his book *Fundamentals of Orchestration*. He was so absorbed with the events at the beginning of the year and under the influence of these impressions that he had attempted to compose a new opera about Stenka Razin.[11] At the end of August Rimsky-Korsakov began making sketches for his projected opera and even asked Belsky to write the libretto. He hurried Belsky and asked a lot of questions concerning the text. Rimsky-Korsakov rapidly became infatuated with his project and then suddenly lost interest in it. It is likely that the reality of this plot, with the severely cruel events that take place in some of the episodes (Rimsky-Korsakov could not stand abuse of any kind), proved to be too violent for his liking. On 10 September 1905 the Rimsky-Korsakov family returned to St. Petersburg. In the city he went on working on this opera for a short period of time and then gave up on the project completely. There are only a few drafts of some episodes left.

The Mariinsky Theatre decided to revive *The Snow Maiden*, and they began rehearsals. At the same time in Moscow, the Bolshoi Theatre was preparing

Pan Voevoda for staging. Rachmaninov was to be the conductor. He asked Rimsky-Korsakov to come to Moscow to help supervise the production. Rimsky-Korsakov arrived in Moscow on 23 September and stayed there for a week. He wrote to his wife from the Loskutnaya Hotel:

> Dear Nadya,
>
> I don't have a spare minute here to write a letter. There are serious disturbances in Moscow. The newspapers are not being published—the printers are on strike. There are crowds on Tverskoy and Strastnoy boulevards, they deliver speeches, they are broken up with whips. Two days ago, I witnessed myself a huge crowd marching and singing "Dubinushka,"[12] and Tverskaya Street was shut off by the Cossacks and gendarmes. I had to go around. On that day a police corporal was killed and a junior officer was beaten severely. Yesterday again there were crowds and shots were heard. Today bakers joined the strike. There was shooting at Filippov's bakery. They say the main city water pipe is endangered. [...] I'm longing to go home.

Pan Voevoda opened on 27 September. It was successful, but due to the riots everywhere there were only a few people in the audience. The next day Rimsky-Korsakov left for St. Petersburg. He caught a cold on his way home and arrived slightly unwell and had to stay at home for several days.

The scene he witnessed—a crowd singing "Dubinushka" in the Moscow streets—impressed Rimsky-Korsakov so much that he decided to orchestrate it. Yet Rimsky-Korsakov was not satisfied with the results. According to his own words, it turned out to be loud, of trifling merit, and devoid of interest. He made a new orchestration for it again the next year, but even so the song did not sound as good as he wished.

At the end of October 1905 Rimsky-Korsakov received a letter from Kruglikov, who was worried about him since the latter had not responded for a long time, in which Kruglikov begged the composer to at least drop him a few lines. Rimsky-Korsakov wrote to Kruglikov:

> I'm safe and sound, i.e., I was not attacked by hooligans, etc. [...] I haven't written to you for a long time because I do not have any time. Indeed, my thoughts are constantly occupied with something. Newspapers, rumors, shifting from hope to despair and so on. [...] There is a terrible anger in your Moscow. Petersburg

is more or less quiet now, but today there is another strike. Each day brings something unexpected. Scarcely had Kronstadt become peaceful than the Polish issue arose. But we are living in great times—the old order has been blown away forever.

The first revival of *The Snow Maiden* was held on 8 November and the second on 11 November 1905. They were both very successful, and the theatre was packed. The author was called to the stage ten times during the first performance and thirteen at the second one (by Yastrebtsev's count); several musical numbers were also repeated. The third performance of *The Snow Maiden* was for season ticket holders, and the theatre was full again. The opera was given eleven times that season. *The Snow Maiden* was followed by *Mozart and Salieri*. The Mariinsky Theatre scheduled the performance of *Mozart* on the same day along with the opera *Pagliacci* by Leoncavallo.

Rimsky-Korsakov was asked to organize a concert in support of the victims of the strikes. At the beginning of December 1905 the concert took place in the hall of Tenishevsky College. The returns totaled 1500 rubles.

Back to the Conservatory

In December the first meeting of the arts council of the Conservatory was held. This arts council had become independent from the Russian Musical Society. Glazunov was unanimously elected director of the Conservatory by secret ballot. There was only one vote against him, and it must have belonged to Glazunov himself. They also approved a request to Rimsky-Korsakov to return to a teaching position at the Conservatory. It was necessary to set up new relations between the Conservatory and the board of the Russian Musical Society. During the meeting of the board, Glazunov raised the question of Rimsky-Korsakov's dismissal about a year earlier and demanded an explanation. The board's response read: "The decision was necessitated because of the fatal convergence of circumstances to safeguard his reputation and his respected name, which had become a symbol for great and serious disorders taking place in the Conservatory at that time." Thus, after a nine-month break Rimsky-Korsakov was again among the professorial staff of the Conservatory, although until the end of that academic year he still gave his lessons at home.

Glazunov offered to celebrate Rimsky-Korsakov's anniversary of forty years of creative work with a concert consisting only of his own compositions on 19 December 1905. However, Rimsky-Korsakov asked him not to organize such a concert, owing to the current circumstances: "At this very moment, when such awful things are taking place in Moscow, different demonstrations and other horrors, it will be hard for me to bear it if anything 'unrelated to music' might happen on that day." Rimsky-Korsakov had another reason to be very concerned about events in Moscow. It was reported that the building belonging to the Romanovs, where Kruglikov rented an apartment, was fired upon. He wrote to Kruglikov asking him to send some news about himself and his family. Kruglikov responded: "All of my family members and I are safe. Bullets aimed at the Romanov house, in which we rent an apartment, missed us. Only one random bullet flew into our rooms, yet it wounded no one except two window panes since we were all hiding in the interior rooms during the fusillade. That attack by gunfire happened on 14 December. In general, despite the happy ending, the accident was unpleasant and resulted in many having frayed nerves."

On 19 December 1905, the day of Rimsky-Korsakov's anniversary, the whole family attended the noon dress rehearsal of *Mozart and Salieri* at the Mariinsky Theatre. Then the composer gave lessons to his Conservatory students and to Igor Stravinsky as well. During lunch he received greeting telegrams, and in the evening he went to a meeting concerning Belyaev's will.

At the beginning of 1906 a lively musical evening was held in the Rimsky-Korsakov household. Thirty-five people, including Stasov, were gathered there. The program consisted of the opera *Marriage*, on the plot of Gogol, composed by Musorgsky, and *The Avaricious Knight*, composed by Rachmaninov and based on Pushkin's drama. Chaliapin took the main part in the performance of Rachmaninov's opera. The accompanists were Felix Blumenfeld and Nadezhda, the composer's wife. Igor Stravinsky introduced his fiancée to those present at that party. It was the first visit for Maximilian Steinberg, a gifted student of Nikolay, to the Rimsky-Korsakov family.

On 11 January 1906 the Rimsky-Korsakovs attended Igor Stravinsky's wedding. However, in the evening they received some guests themselves. The composer told Yastrebtsev about his intention to leave the Conservatory. At the beginning of February a monument to Glinka was erected the Theatre Square in St. Petersburg. Shestakova could not be present at the ceremony. She had died two weeks earlier at the age of ninety.

One pleasant event that occurred at the beginning of the year was the decision made by the Mariinsky Theatre to produce *The Legend of the Invisible City of Kitezh and the Maiden Fevronia*. In its turn, the Bolshoi Theatre in Moscow began rehearsals of *Sadko*.

On 15 February the Rimsky-Korsakov family again received guests. Many people came, and most of them were young: Richter, Mironov, Gilyanov, Steinberg, and Guriy Stravinsky. During the evening, while Rimsky-Korsakov was talking to Yastrebtsev about the lullaby "Hush, Baby, Hush," composed by Tchaikovsky and dedicated to his wife, Nadezhda, he said: "The saddest thing about all of this is that they will not compose music like this anymore, they seem to have lost the art of writing music like this. And it was such a beautiful thing!" Rimsky-Korsakov thought of using the plot of Byron's play *Heaven and Earth* for a new opera and he began making drafts of some pieces. Rimsky-Korsakov wondered if the idea was worth working on and said to Yastrebtsev, laughing, "By the way, how would you suggest I should dress them if they were all naked at the time? Yet the plot is great."

The party on 6 March 1906 for the composer's sixty-second birthday was crowded. He received many flowers. There were more than thirty people, and a great deal of music was performed. Zabela and Blumenfeld sang. Felix Blumenfeld and Glazunov played piano pieces for four hands. "The Serenade of Four Admirers" was sung three times in a row with the participation of the composer. The dinner did not start until 2 a.m. They drank the honoree's health, and Blumenfeld proposed an amusing toast for Rimsky-Korsakov: "Ladies and gentlemen, today I have become convinced that Rimsky-Korsakov, like Mendelssohn, is not free from sentimentality in arranging for electricity in his house; deep in his heart he became sorry for paraffin."

Most of the guests left after dinner, but the young people stayed and went on having fun. Richter mimicked Isadora Duncan, sweeping around the living room imitating her dances. Then he mimicked Feliia Litvin,[13] a singer at the Mariinsky Theatre. Mitusov sang kekyok in the manner of French cabaret songs; Blumenfeld accompanied him on the piano. The party did not break up until 4 a.m.

Yastrebtsev went on a business trip to the estate of Count Mussin-Pushkin, located in the area of the Kerzhensk Forests. He brought spice cakes from Kitezh back to Rimsky-Korsakov and said, "He was proud of being the first who had honored the Volga region by filling it with the sounds of *The Legend of the Invisible City of Kitezh and the Maiden Fevronia."* He also boasted that, when docking, his ship stopped at a place called Gorodets, and that he managed to hear the bells of Kitezh. It was said that Yastrebtsev had planned a trip to Tikhvin and hoped that Rimsky-Korsakov would join him to visit his birthplace. Rimsky-Korsakov commented:

> You know, the last time I was in Tikhvin was to attend the funeral of my father, who passed away on 19 March 1862. Since then I have never gone back there. I can imagine how everything has changed. I wonder if they have kept the old names of the parts of the town: Romanihka, Vypolzov, and others. Have the paths on the top of the monastery wall where I used to run in my childhood survived? Does the grave of my Papa still exist? Or have all of those things disappeared in Tikhvin?[14]

The troubles at the Conservatory did not cease after its independence was obtained. At the regular meeting of the Arts Council, differences of opinion arose between some professors and Rimsky-Korsakov, Glazunov, and some other members of the Council. This disagreement made Rimsky-Korsakov want to leave the Conservatory. Glazunov was greatly concerned and wrote to his former teacher: "I have always been sure that You should spread musical education in Russia.[…] How can I allow myself to release You, and how can I leave my post, taking into account that I was the one who was nominated by You? The students will forgive me my 'illness' rather than Your resignation. Do not permit the Conservatory to be belittled and allow Sacchetti and Puzyrevsky to triumph." Rimsky-Korsakov commented on this event in his memoirs, *My Musical Life*: "Having pity on my dear Sasha [Glazunov] and also my numerous students, I decided to postpone my resignation until the autumn. Glazunov had good intentions, and I was sorry to spoil his plans."

Yastrebtsev discussed current events with Rimsky-Korsakov and later recorded: "All this political mess made him worried to death. He even lost interest in music to some extent. The Conservatory, with all its petty quarrels, has grown wearisome to him as well. He is thinking of leaving it completely. Meanwhile he is dreaming of fleeing abroad, the sooner the better, to escape all of this fuss and disorder."

On 3 May 1906 Nadezhda and Andrey left again for Nauheim in order for Andrey to take another course of baths. Rimsky-Korsakov was busy with the examinations at the Conservatory; Volodya, who had passed his finals at the law school of the university, and Nadya remained in St. Petersburg. It was decided that the family would be united in Riva del Garda, Italy, at the end of May. Nadezhda sent a letter to her husband on her way from Berlin to Nauheim:

> Dear Nika,
>
> In Berlin my thoughts are in a whirl caused by its crowds, noise, and crush. There are so many visitors that all the hotels are overbooked. We hardly managed to get two rooms and they were extremely expensive. It cost 19 DM for both of us. [...] In the evening we had a walk in the Tiergarten and saw the monument to Wagner. [...] There are beautiful plants in the Tiergarten: plenty of flowering trees, wonderful azaleas, and the rhododendrons are in bloom. The lilacs have shed their blossoms already. They sell lilies of the valley in the streets, but they are already too wide open; I think they are the last ones. [...] We certainly felt tired after the trip, but much less so than we did last year.

On their arrival at Nauheim, Nadezhda sent another letter to her husband: "My dear Nika, Contrary to our expectations, the further we moved from Berlin, the colder it became. Here in Nauheim we are shivering with freezing cold. [...] It seems to be colder indoors than outdoors. Andrey is sitting in his coat and I'm in my shawl. [...] Since Andrey moves about like a healthy person now, we have visited a lot of places. The objects that seemed very far away last year turned out to be very close." Her next letter read:

> Andrey and I undertook a long trip to Sonnenberg. The road there goes through a forest. We heard a cuckoo, breathed some wonderful air, and enjoyed a lovely view. I'm very glad that we have experienced the spring here. Last year we didn't even smell it. This time there is a true spring, and we are in a springlike mood. Some trees have little young leaves, and all the bushes and trees are in bloom. The yellow acacias are lovely here with their hanging clusters of flowers. And you are in stuffy Petersburg. Come to us, it is better here. What about Volodya's exams?

Rimsky-Korsakov responded: "My dear, Volodya passed two exams today: civil law and international law. He did quite well in the latter." And his next letter read:

Volodya is taking the last exam on Tuesday, and I have to bother about his liability for military service. He should immediately choose a regiment, register with it and forward a petition (to the Highest Name [the tsar]!). The regiment will impose a medical examination on the spot. If the doctors find something wrong he will have to take a second one [examination] but at the central council. That one can be postponed until autumn. Meanwhile, after the examination at the regiment, he can go wherever he wants until October. [...] I will ask Dr. Neiman for Volodya to be rejected as unfit somehow, if it is impossible in the regiment. [...] Glazunov said that if he fails to obtain the status of a public organization for the Conservatory, he will leave it himself. He is trying to get rid of the disgusting board of directors of the Russian Musical Society in this way.

Surprisingly, Nadezhda changed her mind and decided to take some medical treatment. She reported to her husband: "My dear Nika, You should be happy. They've succeeded in persuading me. I'm also drinking water and taking baths. What you are writing about the events in the Conservatory is so outrageous that I think you shouldn't remain there even for a little while. Do not give a damn and leave saying that you can't stay in such an institution."

Her husband went on reporting the news from home:

Dear Nadya,

Volodya met the commander of the Chasseur regiment yesterday. He was kind enough to register him as a candidate. [...] Volodya can be free until autumn and only then will he meet him again to submit the official application and [have the] medical examination. [...] The officer noticed that Volodya has a very narrow chest and there is hope that he will be released completely.[15] [...] We decided to travel via Vienna. [...] We think we will go from Vienna straight to Riva through Innsbruck. It's a pity you are not here. And I'm bored with Peter. Volodya's liability worried me. So far it is over at least for the moment. Now we are going to pack things, and I think I will feel well only [when I am] in the [railway] carriage.

P.S. Volodya left with Rex for Plussa. It is a pity we have to say good-bye to Rex. Recently he began walking back and forth on his hind legs and turned around on command. Don't think that nobody spoiled him without you. He was fed regularly and received enough treats.

On 24 May Rimsky-Korsakov, Volodya, and Nadya went to Vienna by train. Yastrebtsev, who saw them off, recorded that Rimsky-Korsakov was in high spirits and said: "Contrary to previous days when I was afraid to forget anything through my senile habits and constantly got irritated with something, I'm cheerful and jolly again today."

16

The Last Opera:
The Golden Cockerel

Sometimes I become a little sad, but I do not complain. It's better to stop at the right time than experience a failure.

—Rimsky-Korsakov to Semyon Kruglikov, 1906

Nadezhda wrote to her husband in Vienna: "It's so good that you're moving closer to us, my dear Nika. I'm dying to know about your trip and when exactly you're to be in Riva. [...] Today we walked across Frauenwald and gathered a whole bunch of buttercups."

In turn, Rimsky-Korsakov wrote to Nauheim:

Dear Nadya,

Now we are in Vienna. When we left Petersburg the weather was good. We were seen off by Mironov and Yastrebtsev, and certainly Misha and Belsky. We slept enough on the train. [...] Yesterday evening the weather was dull though warm and without rain, so it was pleasant to walk around the city. First we went to the Grand Hotel on the advice of Mironov and Belsky, but it turned out to be overbooked. Then they recommended to us the Hotel Metropol, where we are staying now. We have two rooms: one of them is very large for me and Volodya, and the other—a little one—is for Nadya. It costs a lot: sixteen crowns for both rooms [1 crown = 40 kopeks]. On the other hand, we are in the center of the city; the hotel is wonderful and fairly clean. We were very tired after the trip and didn't have enough strength to go round the city looking for cheaper accommodations. We had a late dinner at a cheap restaurant. [...] We went to bed early enough, about 10 p.m., and today we woke up at 8 a.m. During morning coffee we were glad to learn from the newspapers that *Die Meistersinger von Nürnberg* will be performed tomorrow, on Sunday. We immediately hurried to buy tickets and were lucky to get three in the stalls. We wandered around the city all morning, then had lunch in some restaurant, and after lunch went shopping. I bought an umbrella for myself (I promise not to lose it this time), six collars, and three pairs of cuffs. [...] On Tuesday they are giving *Das Rheingold*, and we are tempted to stay here till Wednesday morning. We are planning to make our way to Riva like this: we are going to have two breaks, one in Salzburg and the other in Innsbruck; both are to be short, just for a night.

Another of Rimsky-Korsakov's letters was also sent from Vienna:

My dear Nadya,
    We've just came back after watching *Das Rheingold*. We liked it less than *Die Meistersinger von Nürnberg*, although it went very well. [...] Tomorrow at 10 we are leaving for Salzburg, where we are going to spend two days. [...] Today was not a very lucky day for us since it rained all day long. We meant to go to the cemetery but didn't make it. The only thing we did was go shopping. Volodya and I bought straw hats "to be worn to one side." Volodya bought rubber boots after reading the telegram from Andrey. Nadya hesitated to buy anything and left only with a parasol. The traffic is heavy in Vienna. Electric trams are passing by our hotel, back and forth, howling up and down the chromatic scale. We used trams a lot for our trips. We went to the theatre and back also on them. Take care of yourselves, my dears. We embrace you. I wish we could see each other sooner. Your N. R.-K

Then he sent a brief note from Salzburg: "My dear, we are in Salzburg already. It is raining. If the weather doesn't change, we will have to flee from here. [...] I wish we could meet sooner. Volodya and Nadya are all right." And again Rimsky-Korsakov wrote to his wife: "I'm craving for Riva, for getting letters from you, for seeing you as soon as possible." Volodya, Nadya and their father were supposed to arrive in Riva ahead of Nadezhda and Andrey, so she sent her letter to Riva:

Now I'm looking forward to hearing from you from Riva. Andrey has become half Italian. He can even write letters in Italian. There are only three baths left to take. Then he will have taken twenty-three baths in total. [...] My baths will amount to twenty; that is also enough I think though I haven't asked the doctor. In any case we are not going to stay any additional days here for my baths. We are getting sick and tired of this Nauheim. Andrey is dreaming of fleeing from here. [...] What is going on in our Russia! Nothing has changed. The government makes no move to be conciliatory. Today we read in the *Frankfurter Zeitung* about the massacre carried out by the authorities in Belostok. It is just horrible! One hundred and fifty houses were destroyed, fifty-three people were killed. The Chornaya Sotnya [Black Hundreds] pulled poor Jewish people out of train carriages and murdered them with the assistance of [military] officers.[1] The Duma is in a state of high chaos and turmoil. They sent their representatives for investigation on the spot. According to the *Frankfurter Zeitung*, the government wanted to cause general distress by those massacres and to dismiss the Duma and suppress any movement toward liberty. All this is so outrageous that one can only give way to despair. What an unhappy country it is! It will never have any kind of order.

On the next day, after their arrival in Riva, Rimsky-Korsakov wrote to his wife:

My dear Nadya,

We arrived in Riva yesterday at 7:30 p.m. We've settled down in the Hotel du Lac and we've bargained full board at a price of 7 crowns for each. We have two neighboring rooms facing the garden. The rooms are simple with painted floors and ordinary furnishings. There are no fleas at all, and the bedsheets are clean. The hotel belongs to Germans, and it has a quiet, large, and pretty garden adjoining a lake. There are plane trees, cypresses, palms, magnolias that are about to bloom, and others in the garden. Yuccas flower beautifully, and the jasmine is still in bloom; the first roses have opened. The evening was lovely and warm. Fireflies are flying in the garden and "Vetchasha" frogs are trilling. The night was starlit, and you can see Spica and Antares. The morning was wonderful, and the noon is lovely today. It is rather hot, and the birds are singing in the garden. The view over the lake is marvelous. The lake looks blue and is surrounded by high, steep mountains and cliffs and covered with blue mist. You can see snowy mountaintops. The hotel is a little remote from the town, although not very far. This is a small Italian town. After coffee we went downtown to the post office to send a telegram to you, and we also received letters from you, Andrey, Sonya, and Misha and picked up the newspapers. [...] It's so good that you decided to take treatment in Nauheim and you feel its beneficial effect. [...] We spent three nights in Salzburg. The first day was rainy. And we had to shelter ourselves from the rain either under the arches or in the cafes. Yet we succeeded in visiting Mozart's house, Hohensalzburg Castle, and Mönchsberg. The next day the weather was better, but it was cloudy and a little cool. We took a carriage and went to Königsee and to the salt mines. Volodya was the only one who went inside the salt mines. By the way, he was in one group with some princess of Saxon-Meining. At the very beginning of my way inside, I too felt as if it was very difficult for me to breathe; Nadya forced me to go out, and she herself stayed [outside] with me. Generally she and Volodya are taking good care of me, and I seem to behave myself well.

The next day, after walking in the town and listening to the glockenspiel in a bell tower playing "Là ci darem la mano," we set off. The road to Innsbruck is very beautiful, and we traveled along the banks of the Salzach River and between snowy mountains. We arrived in Innsbruck at 10 p.m. and spent a night in the Hotel zum goldenen Sohn, walked around the town, and witnessed a church procession on the occasion of some church holiday, I suppose Whitsunday. We took the 12 train (it is the same one that you will take to go from Munich). The route [Brennerbahn] also lies between snowy mountains and is very pretty. As soon as we began going down [after the Brenner station] it got much warmer and the sky became clearer. In Mori we made a change to a narrow-gauge railway (it is similar to the one that connects Lugano and Como). Again it was a long way going up and then coming down again to Riva. They all speak Italian here except at our hotel.

Our rooms are located in a remote wing of the building, and we are the only ones here. There are two vacant rooms next to ours that might serve you when you arrive. [...] In addition, we are going to inquire about other options. For example, our landlord has a villa that he lets out, and I plan to have a look at it. This villa is fully furnished and has all of the kitchen cutlery and dishes, but a cook must be hired. I think Riva is the most beautiful place on the lake. Farther away the banks are much lower. [...] What an Italian our Andrey is! I've written to you already that Volodya is our guide and cashier and Nadya is our auditor; I think I am like a king.

I embrace you and Andreyka—an Italian. Take care,

Your N. R.-K.

At last Andrey's course of treatment was over, and the doctor was pleased with the results. He said that there was no need for Andrey to come to

Nauheim. Nadezhda was so happy that she wrote a little poem titled "Nauheim." She sent a greeting card to her husband: "They have a holiday tomorrow. A new spa is to open tomorrow, and they are expecting the duke to come for the occasion. All the streets are decorated, and there will be fireworks. Good-bye. I embrace you, Nadya and Volodya."

Rimsky-Korsakov sent his greeting card two days prior to his wife's arrival: "My dear, you are leaving tomorrow and we'll see you soon." On the day of their arrival, 23 June, Nadya and Volodya along with their father prepared a surprise for Andrey and their mother: they met them at the Mori station. Nadezhda wrote to her eldest daughter, Sophia: "The meeting was a pleasant surprise for us. […] We boarded the train and paid little attention to the very scenic views and we talked without pause and never got tired of it."

The week passed and Nadezhda sent another letter to her daughter:

> We have a piano, which is located in Nadya's room. There are few people here, and everything is done in a free and easy manner. So we can play music, especially taking into account that we occupy a separate part of the building. Under our rooms there is a dining hall where people gather only at lunch and dinnertime. If not for that dull table d'hôte, which is also very uncomfortable, we might feel absolutely free. The garden is huge (like the one in Vetchasha but not in terms of plants), a little wild, and with untidy paths. The view over the lake is wonderful, but you can see it only from the garden; unfortunately, you can't see it from the rooms. […] The most pleasant thing is a lake boat trip. […] Walks on foot are not very pleasant here because there is a strong wind from the lake every day and it blows up clouds of superfine white dust into the air. Riva is a small Italian town and a little dirty, like most Italian towns. […] With the acquisition of a piano we are living here as if we were at home.

Completing the *Memoirs*

Rimsky-Korsakov kept on developing his *Memoirs* and orchestrating some pieces of music, but he did not compose anything new. He wrote to Kruglikov:

> It has been about two and a half weeks since we arrived in Riva. […] We occupy a separate wing of the Hotel du Lac; therefore, we are living apart, and we have even obtained a piano. We leased it from some maestro De Gregory, who is the

composer of an opera and a mass, and he is a friend of Boito,[2] etc., etc., etc., who has retired here and is living by leasing and tuning instruments. Well, we didn't see the maestro himself, since he is away. His son substituted for him, and he leased us the piano. The son is a priest, also in retirement, and he looks quite old. […] What about my composing….It seems that it's time to put a full stop to it, at least for huge compositions. I predicted that it would be like this while I was composing *Kitezh*, and now I'm becoming more and more convinced of this. Sometimes I become a little sad, but I do not complain. It's better to stop at the right time than experience a failure. And I have certain thoughts concerning art. I think I, like all of us, am a figure of the end of the nineteenth century and of the period from the liberation of the peasants to the fall of the monarchy. As now, with the changes in the political life in Russia, a new term is about to begin. It will be either a golden age or the decay of art, and the latter is more likely. In the West this decay has started already, and one might see the first signs of its approach in Russia. As you know, during times of regression, geniuses still keep on working as if from inertia, that force which was produced during the golden age. However, they differ from us; they are not like us—men of the '60s, '70s, '80s, and '90s, and even not like Glazunov. They are far younger. […] Such kinds of men provide me with some plans and opera plots (quite good ones); even so, I don't have any desire to think of them or try them. I have another job; I don't remember if I've mentioned it to you or not: I began working on my book *Memoirs of My Musical Life* a long time ago, and I'm developing it at present. It will be my "oeuvre posthume." […] I'm not having a fit of spleen at all. Having in mind the poem of Fet:

> My dear, I like the stars
>
> And I don't mind feeling sad,

I allow myself to feel sad no more than is permitted in that poem. You must agree the sadness is not desperate. At nights I look at the stars while sitting beside the lake. What a wonderful blue lake! The garden here is beautiful, but you have seen it. Sailing is miraculous on our lake. […]

P.S. Oh, dear! What is going on in Russia?

The composer shared his thoughts with Kruglikov:

Certainly, everything will be for the better; nonetheless, we are living in troubling times of change. To my mind the dismissal of the Duma will bring nothing but suppression for the first time, and then I predict it will be something else, though the chronic status of that something makes one utterly exhausted. From my point of view, it would have been better if it had happened at some other time, when we weren't here, so we can live in peace and quiet, but right away I become ashamed thinking of this. It goes without saying that now, during this disaster, and then in the future disorder I will try to continue my creative work and realize all my potential, but my potential is diminishing gradually as my strength ebbs away slowly but surely. Generally speaking, I'm not inclined to whining and disappointments, but I feel that there is something wrong. The younger generation is joyful and hopeful, and the old one can only be joyful looking at them and in no way at themselves.

The family lived in Riva for more than a month and then set off on a tour of Italy. They visited Milan, Genoa, Pisa, Florence, Bologna, and Venice. Rimsky-Korsakov wrote to M. Steinberg from Florence: "I'm a convinced skeptic; therefore, the situation in Russia is extremely bad, in my opinion. We don't possess consent, unity; everything is going on without any coordination—the result is that we are not successful. We can all reproach and blame each other, but we can't do anything reasonable. [...] How much blood was shed! Either way I'm sure that an artist's life must be devoted to creative and constructive labor and that that is his moral obligation."

They reached Venice by 14 August. Rimsky-Korsakov wrote to Yastrebtsev from there: "I'm in the miraculous city of Venice. The city is utterly fabulous." Rimsky-Korsakov jotted down some musical notes on the notepaper of the Hotel de Rome & Suisse and accompanied them with the following words:

> My dear friend Vasily!
> > "When I was young
> > And my years were green,"
> i.e., during the years 1860–1861 I composed this romance, and my friend Skrydlov (now *ammiraglio* [admiral]) sang it. The romance was about Venice. Now that I'm here I have a strong desire to refresh this nonsense in my memory and send it to you. 17 Aug. 1906

The words of the romance were very simple. Rimsky-Korsakov sent a letter to Kruglikov as well:

How many works of art and relics of the past have we seen! No country has more of them than Italy. Finally, I'm tired of art galleries, churches, and so on. By the way, I notice that there are too many repetitions of one and the same. [...] Art nestled next to the church, riches, despotism, intrigues, and vanity. Will it be cooped up next to the freedom, equity, and brotherhood that we are striving for? And we are rushing to it in a bad way: via murders, robberies, lies, and hostility. Revolutionary parties are not cognizant of each other. Nothing works out, and even if something is gained, the price is too high. And it [all] seems to be prolonged.

They returned to Riva on 22 August, and there Rimsky-Korsakov ended his book and wrote down the last words:

The chronicle of my musical life has come to an end. It is chaotic, uneven in presentation, written in a poor style, often too dry, but it contains only the naked truth, and that is why it will be of interest to others. On my return to Petersburg I might fulfill my long-desired wish to keep a diary. Will it last for a long time? Who knows?

    Riva sul lago di Garda

    22 August by old style, 1906.

    N. R.-Korsakov.

It seems that the composer had some grounds for thinking about how much time he had left. During their trip to Italy he experienced his first asthma attacks. They ended fairly quickly, but they were to remain unpleasant memories.

Before his departure from Riva he wrote to Yastrebtsev again: "What wonderful weather it was there! What a lovely lake! The mountains are so beautiful!" They traveled back to Russia via Germany and Austria. Rimsky-Korsakov sent one more letter to Kruglikov from Munich. He began it with a musical line—four bars from Azucena's part in Verdi's opera *Il trovatore*—and included the following lines:

> "We are back in dear Riva
> We were determined to rest there.
> We meant to stay only five days
> However, we spent two weeks there."

These are the bare facts. Indeed, the trip around Italy was a little tiring, and we longed to come back to Riva. The weather was so wonderful; the lake was so blue, and the mountains were so beautiful that we didn't want to leave. [...] In Venice I lost my cigar case and my health. The former was stolen, the latter happened due to drafts. The former was gone forever, the latter has returned.

After Munich they went to Vienna and then to St. Petersburg. They arrived on 2 September, and the next day Nikolay and Nadezhda attended a musical evening held at Stasov's home, where they listened to Chaliapin, who sang a great deal and with much inspiration. Nikolay's ordinary life with the lessons at the Conservatory and different meetings there resumed. Once when Yastrebtsev paid a visit to Rimsky-Korsakov, the latter showed him a manuscript of his book from a distance and said, smiling, "There is something in it about you too. You will read it only after my departure. Till then, even my wife, Nadezhda, won't be allowed to read it. Now I am thinking of starting my diary."

Rimsky-Korsakov's musical *jours fixes* were renewed. The first was held on 27 September 1906. That evening Nikolay Richter played many pieces on the piano. The Public House produced *Sadko* with the troupe of the Russian Opera Partnership of M. Kirikov and M. Zimmermann. Yastrebtsev, who attended the performance, wrote: "There were many people in the theatre, and it seems, all of the existing critics in Petersburg [were there too]. Rimsky-Korsakov was called to the stage [...] all in all twelve times." Rimsky-Korsakov was presented with a wreath from the troupe with the inscription "Glory to N. A. Rimsky-Korsakov, a Great Russian Man of Art. Russian Private Opera. Public House."

Loss of Vladimir Stasov

The next day, on the name days of Nadezhda and Sophia, several guests came to visit them. Stasov was the last to arrive. Yastrebtsev wrote: "He entered when I was saying good-bye. I had time only to shake his hand, and it was our last handshake. I didn't see him alive anymore." Stasov suffered a second stroke. Talking to Yastrebtsev, Rimsky-Korsakov said: "The second stroke happened to be much stronger. They say that he has begun speaking [again], but the fact that he has stopped being indignant at his illness as he was last year is a bad sign in my opinion. Do you know what? [...] It turned out that

Vladimir inquired persistently whether I visited him or not. And when he was told 'yes,' he calmed down."

Stasov died on 10 October 1906. The funeral took place on 13 October at the Tikhvin cemetery of the Alexander Nevsky Lavra. Yastrebtsev wrote: "Almost all of the existing aristocracy, intelligentsia, and art world was there." The mourning wreath from the Rimsky-Korsakov family read: "To our Best Friend."[3]

There was another "musical Wednesday" on 11 October 1906, and a lot of visitors attended. A considerable amount of music was performed. At the beginning of the evening Berson, a singer, and the composer's daughters Nadya and Sophia sang the trio *Dragonflies* of Rimsky-Korsakov twice, and Zabela sang three romances of Steinberg. After tea, Zabela sang Stasov's favorite romance composed by Rimsky-Korsakov, *The Sea Is Not Sparkling*, to commemorate Stasov. Then she performed *The Nymph*. There were many more of Rimsky-Korsakov's romances sung that evening as well. At the end Rimsky-Korsakov together with his two daughters sang a Neapolitan song, *Funiculì, funiculà*, which they had heard in Riva and Florence, to entertain those present. It was repeated twice.

The Golden Cockerel

Despite the fact that Rimsky-Korsakov assured everyone that he was not inspired to compose any music, inspiration visited him when he least expected it. On 15 October 1906 he made an entry in his pocket diary that was nothing but the first musical phrases of his new opera. It was a cock crowing: "Cock-a-doodle-doo, reign lying on your side." He had decided to compose the opera *The Golden Cockerel* based on the plot of Pushkin's fairy tale. He wrote to Belsky that he would like to meet him and discuss the possibility of their working together on the libretto for his new opera. Thus, on 2 October 1906 the first discussion between the composer and the librettist for the new opera took place. After one of the regular "musical Wednesdays" Yastrebtsev wrote: "By the way, it seems to me that Rimsky-Korsakov is composing a symphonic poem." Yastrebtsev was mistaken. It was not a poem but Rimsky-Korsakov's fifteenth opera.

On 24 October 1906 the Bolshoi Theatre put on the opening night of *Sadko* in Moscow. Rimsky-Korsakov did not attend either the rehearsals or the opening night. The second performance of *Sadko* was held for the benefit of the chorus of the Bolshoi Theatre. The composer found this out later and immediately sent a telegram saying that he would contribute his royalties for this performance to the chorus as well. Concurrently the Zimin Theatre in Moscow produced *The Tale of Tsar Saltan*. At almost the same time, a concert was held in St. Petersburg in memory of Stasov. It began with the symphonic prelude *In Remembrance of Stasov*, composed by Glazunov. The concert included compositions of Balakirev, Glazunov, Lyadov, Musorgsky, Rimsky-Korsakov, and Tchaikovsky.

The musical evening that took place on 26 November 1906 in Rimsky-Korsakov's home was memorable. Chaliapin was the hero of the night. The party was not over until 4:30 a.m. Yastrebtsev noted: "We thought that Chaliapin would let us down. At last, about 11 p.m., we heard the bell, and the hero of the occasion came in. The music began. Fyodor sang 'all of the parts': bass, baritone, tenor, and soprano." With the accompaniment of Blumenfeld, Chaliapin performed the first scene of the first act and a part of the second one of *The Stone Guest*, in which he sang both male and female parts. Then he sang the whole of *Mozart and Salieri*, both the parts of bass and tenor, and the Musorgsky romance *Gathering Mushrooms*.

Yastrebtsev's notes continued: "When Chaliapin was about to leave, he tried to persuade Rimsky-Korsakov to write an opera on the plot of *Oedipus Rex*. This did not happen, since Rimsky-Korsakov was absorbed in working on *The Golden Cockerel*." Yastrebtsev's memoirs state: "Rimsky-Korsakov seemed to be happy that he was composing again, despite the fact that there are millions of things that prevent him from being able to fully concentrate." He was distracted by lessons at the Conservatory, concerts, and the rehearsals of *Kitezh* that had begun at the Mariinsky Theatre. Therefore, the composition of his new opera proceeded irregularly. He sent greeting cards to Belsky sometimes with the words "Cock-a-doodle-, cock-a-doodle-doo, nothing comes to my mind," or "Cock-a-doodle-, cock-a-doodle-doo! Developing a musical line." Rimsky-Korsakov said to Yastrebtsev that now he was again afraid of his death since it could happen when he was composing: He added, "It might happen that one would die and wouldn't finish what one had conceived. It would be awfully stupid and a pity."

On 17 January 1907, on another "musical Wednesday," many people gathered in Rimsky-Korsakov's home. A lot of music was played both before and after tea. During tea the host entertained his guests with anecdotes. Yastrebtsev wrote: "One was about a cab driver who was taking Rimsky-Korsakov to the Conservatory, another about a French envoy. When the cabman was asked if he knew to whom that monument was (they were passing the monument to Glinka), the man said in the affirmative, "Yes, to Prince Kholmsky who laid down his life for the tsar." A student of Rimsky-Korsakov, Garcia-Mancilia, an Argentinean envoy, retold his conversation with Bonnar, a French envoy. Yastrebtsev continues in his memoirs retelling Rimsky-Korsakov's story:

> Bonnar said that he was a great admirer of Rimsky-Korsakov and liked his music, although he considered it a little out of fashion. When Garcia-Mancilia contradicted him, saying the opposite, that Rimsky-Korsakov had kept up with the times all his life and could be even called a bold pioneer in music, the former began to assure him with absolute seriousness that Garcia was mistaken and that he might have confused Rimsky-Korsakov with someone else, since Bonnar knew for sure that Rimsky-Korsakov had died about sixty years ago (!).

On the occasion of the twenty-fifth anniversary of Glazunov's creative work that was to take place that year, Rimsky-Korsakov undertook the organization of the festival concert to celebrate the jubilee. Having laid aside his work on *The Golden Cockerel*, Rimsky-Korsakov composed *Zdravitsa* [*The Grace-Song*] for symphony orchestra for the silver jubilee of Glazunov's activities as a composer. The festival celebration lasted two days. A symphony concert was held in honor of Glazunov in the Hall of the Assembly of the Nobility on 27 January 1907. Rimsky-Korsakov conducted the First Symphony of the honoree. Then, to the strains of *The Greetings*, composed by Lyadov, Glazunov mounted the platform, and the festival addresses commenced. There were more than forty deputations giving jubilant greetings and presentations of wreaths. The hero of the day descended to the stage during the sounds of Rimsky-Korsakov's *The Grace-Song*. After the concert there was a banquet (by subscription) that was held at the St. Petersburg Liberal Economic Society Club. Rimsky-Korsakov chaired the dinner, which lasted until early morning. The next day a celebration in Glazunov's honor was held at the Mariinsky Theatre. The program was devoted to Glazunov's ballets. The theatre was packed, he was given outstanding ovations and gifts, and he delivered a brief speech of thanks.

From the end of January until the beginning of February 1907 Rimsky-Korsakov was very busy with rehearsals for *The Legend of the Invisible City of Kitezh and the Maiden Fevronia* at the Mariinsky Theatre. The opening night of *Kitezh* took place on 7 February 1907. The design of the decor was carried out by A. Vasnetsov. The costumes were created by Korovin. The stage director was B. Shkafer, and the conductor was Blumenfeld. The part of Grishka Kuterma was sung by I. V. Ershov, who remains the unsurpassed performer of this extremely complicated part. The part of Fevronia was performed by M. N. Kuznetsova-Benois.[4] Yastrebtsev, who attended the opening night, wrote in his memoirs: "Starting with the first act, the audience called for the author persistently, but he did not appear. Rimsky-Korsakov was called to the stage nine times [...] and he received two wreaths: one from us [the Belskys, N. Tcherepnin,[5] Count Timofeyev, the Bulichs, I. Lapshin, and ten others] with the inscription "To the Genius Singer of the Invisible City," and the other with a lovely sash with silk embroidery from the Stravinsky couple and others." Ershov was also presented with flowers, a wreath, and a gift.

The Legend of the Invisible City of Kitezh and the Maiden Fevronia was performed several more times before the end of the season. The reviews praised the mastery of the author but not the opera itself. V. Kolomitsev, a critic, published a review in the newspaper *Russia*: "This music is as pellucid as rock crystal and very beautiful to the ear. It is almost all made of fascinating details and subtle patterns that are painted in a masterly way and there in bright colors. [...] Deprived of bright flashes and strong emotional moments, lacking in animation and even sincere religious passion, the music seems to be cold and rational despite all of his genius." Issue no. 7 of the *Russian Musical Gazette* said that Rimsky-Korsakov's new opera "was such an outstanding work of art in the Russian operatic literature that reviews of the newspaper records would be too narrow to give an account of all the impressions that the new opera had left."

The "musical Wednesday" of 21 February 1907 began very late, since the guests arrived only after Rimsky-Korsakov had come home from attending the Russian Quartet Evening. This time Kuznetsov and his wife, Zabela, and some others were there. The program of the party included some romances of Igor Stravinsky. The next week the Rimsky-Korsakov family organized a quartet evening at their home. The quartet consisted of Volodya (violin), N. Sheinin (a friend of Volodya, violin), M. Steinberg (viola), and Andrey (violoncello). They played Borodin's Quartet. Sometime later there was another quartet-party at Rimsky-Korsakov's home, where the same quartet played compositions by Borodin, Haydn, Tcherepnin, and Beethoven.

Rimsky-Korsakov's birthday was approaching. Owing to some sad events, it passed quietly and was surrounded with sorrow. The day before his birthday, Rimsky-Korsakov attended the funeral of V. Tolstoy, a professor at the Conservatory. Maria, one of Nadezhda's sisters, died on 6 March 1907. On 7 March 1907 he had to attend the funeral of Bessel. Then, on 8 March 1907, there was a memorial service in honor of Maria. However, Rimsky-Korsakov received many flowers on his birthday, and during the evening Lyadov and Glazunov came around to congratulate him.

About the same time Sergey Diaghilev began arranging for the Russian Symphony Concerts to be held in Paris, and he counted on Rimsky-Korsakov's participation. The composer, although sympathetic to the idea of promoting Russian music in the West and supportive of these efforts, declined to go to Paris himself. Diaghilev was upset with his refusal and Rimsky-Korsakov's desire to remain at home. He wrote to the composer:

> I do not give up my hope for Your participation in the Paris concerts. With all the numerous difficulties that this business deals with, it is impossible to work without the thought of the support of our beloved and dear teacher. Think of how much Your refusal will sadden us and even more of the damage it will do to the good cause for which You have expressed your sympathy. I beg You to grant our request. The journey will not be hard for You since, I promise, we will surround you with care, and we will be honored to be of service to You. Your acceptance would be a great favor for us and help us as much as anybody could.

This letter hit its target. Rimsky-Korsakov visited Diaghilev and, finding him not at home, left his visiting card, on which he had written: "If we should go then let's go, said a parrot as it was being pulled out of its cage by a cat."

Rimsky-Korsakov was still working on *The Golden Cockerel* when the *St. Petersburg Gazette* [*Peterburgskaya gazeta*] published an article in which the author stated that Rimsky-Korsakov was composing an opera called *Ilia from the City of Murom* and had asked P. I. Vainberg to write the libretto, but the latter had turned down the offer because of illness. *The Russian Musical Gazette* was right to label that article as nonsense and informed the readers that Rimsky-Korsakov was composing the opera *The Golden Cockerel*. Thus, everyone became aware that he was composing this new opera. The work on the opera itself proceeded unevenly. On 8 April 1907 Rimsky-Korsakov wrote to Belsky: "Cock-a-doodle-doo, I can't bring it to an end." Soon after Rimsky-Korsakov played the first act of *The Golden Cockerel* to his friends. After the performance, Yastrebtsev wrote: "Rimsky-Korsakov said when we happened at last to be alone, 'Well, dear friend. What do you think? Should I continue?' 'Certainly, you should,' I answered. At that moment Igor [Stravinsky] entered and our conversation stopped abruptly."

Ivan Bilibin was a true admirer of Rimsky-Korsakov's music. When he made the illustrations for the edition of *The Tale of Tsar Saltan* by Pushkin, he wrote for the illustration on the cover of the book: "This work I dedicated to the Russian composer Rimsky-Korsakov." In April 1907 Bilibin presented a copy of this book to Rimsky-Korsakov, and from then it always stayed on one of the end tables in the living room of Rimsky-Korsakov's home.

It was becoming harder for Rimsky-Korsakov to stay in control of his many activities related to Belayev's foundation, so he decided to quit his work as a trustee. Lyadov commented on this in his letter to his cousin: "Korsakov took part in the meeting for the last time yesterday. On leaving for home, he kissed everyone and thanked them for their 'pleasant company.' I became sad! Life forces you to resign and bury everything. Having been close to Belayev, Korsakov has torn himself away and buried the past. The end! 'Everything comes to an end!' as Hans Christian Andersen used to say."

Another Trip to Paris

On 28 April 1907 the Rimsky-Korsakov family, including Andrey, Volodya, and Nadya, set off on their journey to Paris. They went by train. On 1 May 1907 they settled down in the Grand Hotel and the next day attended a rehearsal. Nadezhda wrote to her son Mikhail: "The rehearsals are held in different and unsuitable rooms. For example, today the rehearsal was in the lobby of the Théâtre du Châtelet, where the orchestra filled the room completely. We had to sit behind the double basses. The orchestra reads the notes perfectly well and pays great attention to the work. Every time Papa is greeted with loud cheers."

The first of five Russian Historical Concerts contained the suite from *Christmas Eve*, conducted by the composer. Nadezhda wrote again to her son:

"The first concert took place yesterday. The theatre was packed, and it was a great success. They received father well; he was called to the stage three times after the suite." The program of the second concert included the prelude and two songs of Lel from *The Snow Maiden* and "Night on Mt. Triglav" from *Mlada*. They were also performed with Rimsky-Korsakov as the conductor. The third concert contained the suite from *The Tale of Tsar Saltan*. The fifth included the introduction and the scene in the underwater kingdom from *Sadko*, which crowned the program. These compositions of Rimsky-Korsakov were conducted by Arthur Nikisch.

During their stay in Paris, the Rimsky-Korsakovs led a very busy but enjoyable life. They saw the opera *Salome*, composed by Richard Strauss and conducted by its composer, at the Théâtre du Châtelet. Nadezhda did not like the opera at all and commented on it in her letter to her daughter: "It is such a disgusting thing that you won't find another one like it in the world." They spent one evening at Scriabin's home, where the host played his *Poem of Ecstasy*. They went to the Opéra-Comique, where they listened to Claude Debussy's *Pelléas et Mélisande*. Upon listening to this opera, Rimsky-Korsakov said to Diaghilev, "Don't force me to listen to horrors of that kind; otherwise I will end up loving them!" On 14 May Rimsky-Korsakov attended a reception held by Camille Saint-Saëns in the Salle Pleyel. Although Rimsky-Korsakov stayed in Paris for more than three weeks, he did not visit the Russian community or attend the reception given by Grand Prince Pavel, to which he had been invited and where Chaliapin sang his romance *The Prophet* after A. Pushkin. "Well, but I was at Camille Saint-Saëns's in April 1907, and I, Colonne, and others autographed a lot [of things]," Rimsky-Korsakov said to Yastrebtsev upon his arrival in St. Petersburg. They returned home on 24 May, and Yastrebtsev paid a visit three days later. He wrote:

> We talked about Paris and the Russian Concerts. […] I congratulated Rimsky-Korsakov on his huge success. Indeed, Rimsky-Korsakov said he and Chaliapin were the tops. […] In addition to that, he added that Saint-Saëns, Burgh d'Cudre, and others do not appreciate the music of Richard Strauss at all, whom they call "a haughty calf." Rimsky-Korsakov commented, "Thus, we Russian composers were just some kind of Mozarts compared to R. Strauss, Debussy, and Dukas." […] He became acquainted with Richard Strauss at Colonne's home. But they barely spoke to each other. Rimsky-Korsakov shared

his opinion: "We had nothing to say. They say that after listening to the first act of *Ruslan*, the first act of *Prince Igor*, and the suite from the *Christmas Eve*, Strauss stated, 'All this is good but, unfortunately, we are not children anymore.'"

After some time the *Russian Musical Gazette* published an article about the Russian Concerts in Paris, which said: "The composer, conducting some of his own compositions, was the hero of the concerts, and received the loudest and most thunderous ovations. *Night on the Mt. Triglav* and the third act of *Saltan* enjoyed a certain success. [...] It turned into a triumph for Rimsky-Korsakov in Paris rather than one for the Russian Historical Concerts."

Loubensk

Spring was in full swing, and it was time to go to the countryside. The Rimsky-Korsakov family leased a house at Loubensk, on the estate of Bukharov, for the summer of 1907. In the 1860s the village of Loubensk and the vast land with its settlements belonged to Major-General Nikolay Bukharov. In the 1880s his son, Dmitriy Bukharov, inherited all of his properties. In the 1890s these lands were taken over by his widow, Alexandra Bukharova, and their children, Zoia and Boris. By 1907 Bukharova had sold almost all of the land to her peasants. She held only the title to the estate itself, which occupied 27.5 acres. Approximately half of the area was a fruit orchard, mainly apple trees. In addition, she was the owner of about 25 acres of tilled and hay lands.

This charming small country seat was located only about half a mile from Vetchasha and a hundred feet above it, so it had a beautiful view from the main building over Lake Pesno and the forest on the skyline. In front of the main house there was a huge central flowerbed with flowering tobacco and splendid red, white, and pink Chinese peonies. Rimsky-Korsakov's dream of purchasing a small country seat had finally become a reality. Bukharova, despite having sold some of the land, needed 6,000 rubles more to pay off the mortgage, so she made a decision to sell the country seat and the adjoining land. The sale price she asked for the house and the land was 30,000 rubles. The Rimsky-Korsakov family could only just afford to buy it.

Later Yastrebtsev wrote in his memoirs:

> After dinner, when I was sitting with Nikolay in the living room, I asked him
> how much he was making per year. I found out that it was approximately
> 12,000–14,000 rubles (3,000 rubles from the Mariinsky Theatre, 2,000 rubles
> from the Bolshoi Theatre in Moscow; he received about 2,000–2,500 rubles
> from the provinces. Moreover, he received funds of 1,500 from the tsar, and
> 2,000, the salary for a distinguished professor, and in addition, royalties for his
> works). Furthermore, I also found out that he had saved about 30,000 rubles
> during his lifetime.

We should take into consideration that all this money was made by the
composer himself; neither Rimsky-Korsakov nor his wife Nadezhda had inherited anything. Having moved to Loubensk, the Rimsky-Korsakov family
negotiated with the owner on the purchase of the country seat. At the same
time, they started to work on the documents for purchase. In the middle of
June Rimsky-Korsakov wrote to his son Mikhail:

> We all admire Loubensk and keep talking about what we are going to do and
> how we are going to decorate it when it belongs to us. It is not ours yet. […] I
> am feeling a little concerned that the deposit has not yet been put down. Your
> mother and siblings are making household plans while I am only listening with
> excitement. Indeed, it is so pleasant to have something of your own. We will
> never have to think of a summer house anymore. What country house that we
> could lease could compare with one's own house?

The writing of *The Golden Cockerel* was undertaken very quickly, since
Rimsky-Korsakov was afraid that he would not be able to finish it in his lifetime. Later his son Andrey wrote in his book about his father: "N. A. could
not foresee his death. Still, he had a feeling about the end, as is always the
case in a sensitive personality. From his first heart attacks, this feeling never
left him. Maybe that is why he was in such a rush to write *The Golden Cockerel*
and finish it by the end of the summer of 1907?"

Rimsky-Korsakov had been corresponding frequently with Belsky on
different corrections and the editing of the libretto. Belsky was not always
happy about the composer's remarks, but he always followed his advice. "Your

whim, Your order—it is the law for me," Belsky wrote to Rimsky-Korsakov, quoting the line from the text of *The Golden Cockerel*, when he sent him the next verses for the libretto.

Glazunov spent the summer of 1907 in England, where he was awarded doctorates in music from Oxford and Cambridge Universities. He wrote to Rimsky-Korsakov asking him how he would react if he was also awarded a doctorate from one of these universities. The composer wrote back to him:

> I would like to decline a doctorate from Oxford and/or Cambridge University. First, I do not think that any kind of award is acceptable for composers and for me in particular (maybe it is my eccentricity, but let it be this way); second, I have no intention of going to England. Having stated this second reason, please keep me away from this offer; but please give them my thanks for their intention to honor me.

The Rimsky-Korsakov family enjoyed their stay in Loubensk very much. The writing of *The Golden Cockerel* proceeded smoothly. The composer wrote to Belsky at the end of June 1907:

> The second act is nearly finished (of course, as a draft). Wild strawberries, jasmine, peonies...
>
> Sincerely yours, N. R.-K.

That summer Rimsky-Korsakov had some correspondence with Diaghilev. The latter wanted to stage his opera *Sadko* in Paris at the Opéra. He asked the composer's permission to make some changes, since the French did not want to listen to opera from 8 p.m. to midnight and were ready to leave the theatre by 11 p.m. The composer was concerned because he did not want to agree with Diaghilev's changes to the opera. Diaghilev tried to convince the composer, but Rimsky-Korsakov responded rudely:

> You have made a plan of action before asking me for any advice and a plan you are not going to give up on. [...] Personally, I am interested in art, and I am indifferent to the French taste; on the contrary, I want them to appreciate me as I am and not adjusted to their taste and customs. [...] If the weak French audience in evening dresses cannot stand *Sadko*, it makes no sense to stage it there.

It ended up that the opera was staged in a shortened version. Only the first four acts are given in the program. Each act had to be complete without editing. Moreover, the music director of the Paris Opéra-Comique, Albert Carré, decided to stage *The Snow Maiden* and asked for permission to make some changes. He suggested giving Lel's part to a male mezzo-soprano, because the French didn't like cross-dressing. Rimsky-Korsakov refused.

Not everything was smooth at home either. The composer wrote to his son on 9 August:

> You cannot even imagine how worried I always am about something: the housing problem (there is a need to look for a new place, but later), the purchase of Loubensk, and Volodya's coming compulsory military service. […] all these undecided questions bother me a lot. Even more, I am becoming a hypochondriac and more timid than before. So the writing of *The Golden Cockerel* is an escape for me, so I can distract myself and forget my concerns for a while.

Soon after Yastrebtsev came to Loubensk with Andrey. They arrived in the evening of 28 August. "We finished talking at 1 a.m.," Vasily wrote in his memoirs. "Personally, I didn't go to bed 'til after 2 a.m. I was sleeping in the composer's study. […] I could see the white stone fence and acacia trees. There on the desk was the manuscript of *The Golden Cockerel*, which, with the author's permission, I was allowed to look at before going to sleep."

The next morning Yastrebtsev woke up before 8 a.m.:

> At 8:45 the sun came out and Rimsky-Korsakov as well. We went to the dining room. We had coffee. […] The garden was astonishing: lots of beautiful alleys, wonderful old oaks, next to the house a huge, majestic ash tree, bushes of white acacia, lilacs, sweet peas, Indian cress, pansies, in front of the pond a huge flowerbed of tobacco plants, a birch-tree allée and, what I like the most, a lime-tree allée (not far away, to the left of the house). The allée has become known as "my allée" since. Everything was incredibly beautiful. […] At 10:30 Rimsky-Korsakov started to continue working on *The Golden Cockerel*. Only twenty-six bars were left to be finished. Meanwhile, Andrey and I went to the garden, where I noticed two little cannons that had belonged to the former owner of the house. […] At noon we set up the breakfast. Soon (twenty minutes after noon or so) Rimsky-Korsakov appeared, having just finished his *Cockerel*. We rewarded him by clapping. The

only person who refused to clap was his three-year-old granddaughter Irina, the adorable daughter of Troitsky. When we explained everything to her, she joined in with us in great joy. Right after breakfast Rimsky-Korsakov performed twice (the first time for me and the second for the others) all three acts of *The Golden Cockerel.* The music was surprisingly interesting and unique.

After dinner Rimsky-Korsakov's wife sang all of Rimsky-Korsakov's five "naval" romances. Yastrebtsev talked a lot to the composer about *The Golden Cockerel,* and before going to bed he looked through the manuscript of the score and he wrote down the comments made by Rimsky-Korsakov about the sounds of nature. "A swarm of midges hum in F major, a bee hums in B major, a beetle in D, a bumblebee in C or C-sharp major."

The next morning was chilly but sunny. Andrey took a picture of his father with Yastrebtsev in the middle of the lilac allée and next to the birch tree on the driveway, behind the mansion's gate. That day Rimsky-Korsakov played the second act of his new opera.

Yastrebtsev wrote:

> Before dinner Nikolay and I sat behind the gate (in front of the entrance to the mansion) and admired the celestial distance. The composer told me that he would like to visit Tikhvin one more time, where he had not been since his childhood. […] Having come back to the house, we ate plums and apples from the garden. Having noticed how Rimsky-Korsakov was scrutinizing the plums, I made a little joke: "As you haven't been trying hard, Nikolay, you will never be a real landowner, and, according to your opinion, I will never be a theoretician."— "Well," he said, "that is how it is, because you are not a theoretician but a dreamer in the sphere of harmony."

After dinner we walked again in the garden. Coming back home, passing "Korsakov's" ash tree, the composer said: "Pay attention to this wonderful tree, it is positively prophetic. Its leaves don't turn yellow, but as soon as it feels the coming frost all of its leaves fall off immediately."

The train was leaving at 6:30 p.m. Because of that, we had dinner earlier, at 4 p.m. Rimsky-Korsakov joined the dinner while his wife was walking about the room. The composer was very grateful to me for coming to visit him. Saying good-bye, I embraced the composer and his son.

On 31 August Rimsky-Korsakov's wife wrote to their eldest son: "Father finished *The Golden Cockerel* three days ago. He orchestrated the third act unbelievably quickly. [...] Father is feeling quite well, although I am worried about his eyes. He has dark circles [around his eyes] and his eyes are not in good condition."

17

Final Days,
September 1907–
June 1908

*But should I compose being old? Isn't it better for me to do something
else, something more productive?*

—Rimsky-Korsakov in his diary, 28 November 1907

Rimsky-Korsakov spent the first days of September 1907 in St. Petersburg.
During this time, he kept very busy: he attended the performance of *Kitezh* at
the Mariinsky Theatre, and negotiated the final terms and conditions for the
purchase of his dacha in Loubensk with Bukharova, who visited him. Upon
returning to Loubensk, he became occupied with the orchestration of *The
Golden Cockerel*. Nikolay's wife had a bad cold, so they had to stay in Loubensk
until 19 September 1907. On 23 September 1907 Yastrebtsev visited the
Rimsky-Korsakov family and he wrote: "Rimsky-Korsakov looked tired, a little
pale, and his face seemed to be sharpened. Before and after tea Maximilian
Steinberg played the second and the third acts of *The Golden Cockerel*. Rimsky-
Korsakov commented on his 'music of the mist' from the second act and said
that it was his 'bribe for decadence.'"

Soon after his return to St. Petersburg Rimsky-Korsakov completed the
piano transcription of *The Golden Cockerel* and even composed a short orchestral
piece, *The Neapolitan Song*, based on the Italian folk tune "Funiculì, funiculà."

The problem of Volodya's military service was resolved happily. Since he was
"narrow-chested," and thanks to the assistance of Cui, Volodya was assigned
to serve as a draftsman in one of the departments of the military engineering
office. To be accepted in that position, Volodya had to take some examinations,
one of which involved making sketches. He succeeded in passing his exams.
This meant that he could live at home and needed to put on his military
uniform only to go to his work. Cui wrote to the composer: "My dear friends!

I'm very glad that everything ended well with Volodya's service. I'm very pleased if I made some contribution as well."

In October 1907, when Yastrebtsev happened to be in Rimsky-Korsakov's home, Andrey arrived from Loubensk late at night with a huge bag stuffed with many different things. Yastrebtsev wrote:

> We all surrounded him, and even Rimsky-Korsakov was watching with pleasure and some curiosity while the things were being unpacked. Standing at the doorway and saying good-bye, I was inspired to make witticisms and said in a deeply serious way, "I think Turgenev was right when he distinguished fathers from sons so sharply. Take this case. What do we see? The father brought *The Golden Cockerel* from Loubensk, whereas his son only brought some ordinary chickens and cauliflowers from the same estate." Everyone burst out laughing.

On the last day of October 1907 the Rimsky-Korsakov family started hosting their at-home functions again. The guests were Zabela, the Stravinsky brothers, Gilyanov, Steinberg, Berson, Ossovsky, and Belsky. The musical part of the evening consisted of compositions by Stravinsky, Steinberg, and Rimsky-Korsakov. The Rimsky-Korsakovs renewed their home quartet evenings as well.

In November 1907 Rimsky-Korsakov received a letter informing him that he had been named as a corresponding member of the Academy of Fine Arts of Paris. Cui wrote to him, "Of all the institutions of art and science, this one is certainly the most honorable. There are only six corresponding members in the department of music. Of Russian composers, there are Rubinstein, Tchaikovsky, and me. [...] You are the fourth."

The Diary

In March 1904 Rimsky-Korsakov began to keep his diary, but it had only a few entries. The reason he did not make further entries before 22 August 1906 is obvious: he was completely occupied with writing his *Memoirs*. But what prevented him from keeping his diary later? There is no obvious answer. The fact that he was absorbed in composing *The Golden Cockerel* does not explain it completely. While Rimsky-Korsakov was working on his *Memoirs*, he was composing as well. Maybe it can be explained by the fact that he became unwell after *The Golden Cockerel* was completed. In any case, on 28 November 1907, after a long break, Rimsky-Korsakov made another entry:

> Yesterday, during the rehearsal for Siloti's concert, we tried out my *Neapolitan Song*. Glazunov, Belsky, Ossovsky, Yastrebtsev, Siloti, Steinberg, Nadya, and Lyadov were there. The piece was played twice. The piece turned out to be of little value. The best part that it contained was the tune of the very song itself. The variations, short developments, and little coda are in vain, and their composition is technically unremarkable. The orchestration failed. The timpani playing a three-note tune as a coda sounded obscure. Generally, there was no effect at all. It made me sad. I will throw the piece away. But should I compose being old? Isn't it better for me to do something else, something more productive? I can't just read without producing anything. I could get bored to death. To compose when one is bored is a sin. I'll try keeping a diary or writing down the events I'm witnessing. Maybe it will fill my life up to some extent.

The next day Rimsky-Korsakov made one more minor entry, and then the diary came to an abrupt end.

On 30 November 1907 the twelfth and the last performance of *The Legend of the Invisible City of Kitezh and the Maiden Fevronia* was given at the Mariinsky Theatre. Yastrebtsev, who attended the performance, wrote: "The theatre was packed. The success was considerable despite the bad performance. The composer was called to the stage twice after the second act, twice after the third, and three times when the opera was over. All in all he was called to the stage seven times."

Seventeen people, including the Rimsky-Korsakov family, were present at the "musical Wednesday" on 5 December 1907. Tcherepnin and Steinberg played a four-hand arrangement of the suite from Tcherepnin's ballet *Armida's Pavilion*. Berson sang a number of romances, and Steinberg played some pieces from *The Golden Cockerel*, including the scene with the parrot. For this scene Rimsky-Korsakov used a melody of a children's song that he had heard in his childhood in Tikhvin. His mother had a parrot that had been taught to sing this very song, and little Nika accompanied it on the piano. So his mother's parrot became immortalized in the character of the parrot that belonged to Tsar Dodon. The next *jour fixe* contained much music as well. They played compositions by Steinberg, Medtner,[1] and Rachmaninov. Yastrebtsev wrote: "When I arrived,

Rimsky-Korsakov was still resting. When he came in, he seemed to have a sour, tired look (he was even shivering a little), and only later on did this clear up."

Ill-Health

Right before Christmas Kruglikov came to St. Petersburg and visited Rimsky-Korsakov twice. During one of his visits Volodya took a photograph of his father with Kruglikov next to the piano in the living room. On the first day of Christmas, when Yastrebtsev came to visit the Rimsky-Korsakov family, he found the Stravinsky brothers there with their mother and Steinberg. Yastrebtsev wrote in his memoirs: "Rimsky-Korsakov did not look too bad. However, when Mrs. Stravinsky asked him about his health he answered, "I managed to get sick. I have some kind of choking in the mornings. And again I'm taking 'lily of the valley.'" Rimsky-Korsakov became sick with bronchitis, and his coughing was followed by choking. He experienced shortness of breath, which prevented him moving about quickly and made him feel weary, keeping him from working hard. All this weighed heavily on his mind and made him short-tempered. In spite of his ill health, he refused to see a doctor. At the end of December Rimsky-Korsakov wrote to Belsky: "I have to stay indoors these days since I've caught a cold and I have got bronchitis a little, and it has become aggravated with substantial heavy breathing, to which I am inclined in general." N. Malko, a conductor who once attended Rimsky-Korsakov's classes in the Conservatory, remembered later an incident that happened that year: "Once during the class N. A. felt ill, left his seat at the piano, and sat down on a little wicker sofa; he supported his head with his arm and waited for the attack to pass. We were at a loss. M. Gnessin rushed to open the window. Somebody decided to comfort him and said, 'Nikolay, that is just nerves.' N. A. was clearly outraged. 'That's nerves, that's nerves! What are nerves? It's simply the first sign.'"

In November 1907 the Rimsky-Korsakov family had a telephone installed. It was a new and amusing thing for them at the time. Yastrebtsev was among the first to call. However, its use started with some misunderstanding: Rimsky-Korsakov confused Yastrebtsev with Siloti. On 1 January 1908 Rimsky-Korsakov used the telephone to congratulate Yastrebtsev on New Year's Day and his name day. Yastrebtsev wrote in his memoirs: "Speaking about the telephone, Rimsky-Korsakov said, laughing, 'Isn't the telephone something enigmatic and even mysterious? We are now at a distance of four versts, but we are speaking to each other.'" During the first days of January Rimsky-Korsakov began to go out again, although he worked little and filled his time with reading. In particular he read *The Darkness*, by Leonid Andreyev.[2] "This is some kind of completely disgusting thing," he said to Yastrebtsev. "It just stinks and nothing more. After him I'm reading Chekhov with even greater pleasure than before. I'm getting to appreciate the latter more and more."

The American dancer Isadora Duncan became very popular at that time in Russia. Rimsky-Korsakov did not see her performances, but he commented on them:

> I believe she is graceful enough and a perfect mime. etc., but what I personally don't like about her is that she applies and fastens her art to musical works that are so dear to me and that do not need her accompaniment at all and whose composers do not count on such interpretation of their works. I would be very upset if I found out that Miss Duncan was dancing and explaining with mimicry my *Scheherazade*, *Antar*, or my *Russian Easter Festival Overture*. [...] Moreover, mimicry is not an independent kind of art and can only accompany words or singing, and when it is bound to music it just damages the latter by drawing attention away from it.

Rimsky-Korsakov got a little better, and on 9 January a regular "musical Wednesday" was held again. This time twenty-seven guests gathered, including Bukharova with her daughter; Artsybushev, a student of the composer; and Siloti, Zabela, and others. Blumenfeld played the prelude, "Wedding Procession," and second act of *The Golden Cockerel*. Zabela sang some romances by Spendiarov, Steinberg, and Rachmaninov. Then Rimsky-Korsakov's wife sang two arias from *Samson et Dalila*, the opera by Saint-Saëns, with the piano accompaniment of Richter. Then Berson performed an aria of Scarlatti; a romance of Kossa, a German composer; and two romances of Richard Strauss. The latter received a mock ceremony made up by Guriy Stravinsky. Yastrebtsev described it: "The amusing procession appeared from the study; they were carrying cushions, on top of which a lot of stuff was displayed: a stuffed fox, a silver foot, an inkpot, a paperweight, pens, and so on and so forth. All were laughing a lot." To crown the party, Zabela devoted her singing to Rimsky-Korsakov's romance *The Nymph*. The repertoire of the next "musical

Wednesday" was made up of romances by Gnessin, Steinberg, Spendiarov, and Rimsky-Korsakov performed by Zabela. Also some romances of Tchaikovsky and Stravinsky were sung by Nadya, and some other pieces of Tchaikovsky, Borodin, and Rimsky-Korsakov were performed by Guriy Stravinsky on the piano.

The Public House produced Rimsky-Korsakov's opera *The Tale of Tsar Saltan*. The performance took place on 5 February. It was quite successful, and during the performance the author was called to the stage five times. In the middle of February 1908 *Kitezh* was staged at the Bolshoi Theatre in Moscow. This time Rimsky-Korsakov did not go to Moscow, so he attended neither the rehearsals nor the opening night. He worried about the results and was expecting a letter from Kruglikov with news about it. The latter attended the opening night and wrote to Nikolay:

> After 15 February, i.e., the first Moscow performance of *Kitezh*, I love it even more (if it's possible) than after my first acquaintance with it in the Mariinsky Theatre. In terms of the music it appeared to be more refined and transparent, and at the same time bolder. […] I enjoyed it to the fullest extent and soaked up a substantial dose of beauty and incomparable poetry. The last scene touched me so that I was simply riveted to my chair and I could not get enough of it. You can't even imagine how annoyed I was when the curtain was lowered. I wished to listen and listen, and then all of a sudden I had to get up and go away and awaken from my marvelous dreams. My dear friend, don't feel vexed with the pastiche of Mikhailov's production. […] The music did not suffer from this, and it made its way. And the best men of Moscow knelt before it. I'm absolutely honest and [not] deceiving you. I would be happy if my news could smooth out the wrinkles on your face.

Kruglikov also sent a letter to N. V. Salina, who performed the part of Fevronia:

> For me *Kitezh* is poetry, it's a new world. I've become intoxicated by *Kitezh*, its naive motionlessness, its being far removed from common operatic conventions, from what the general public have become used to seeing at the theatre, to what they applaud and scream "encore" at with one accord. This is Pechyersky revived in music,[3] its "Forest" and schismatic hermitages.[4] This is an icon painting with sounds. Some peculiar mysticism adorns the music in its harmonic and orchestral painting. It carries me away to an inaccessible height of gentle feelings.

Rimsky-Korsakov responded to Kruglikov and described his state of health:

> My cold, chronic cough, and other minor things have gone. But I feel something else; something different has been disturbing me since this winter. This very something has been developing for a long time. On the one hand, I breathe heavily, pant for no reason; on the other hand, I experience fits of rather shallow, short breath: I can breathe only one-third deep and cannot breathe fully, which makes me despondent. The causes are sclerosis and the weakening of my heart's activity. I'm taking medicine and trying to be in the condition of a healthy man. I also feel some kind of exhaustion of my head, distraction, and even insanity. I'm tired of proofreading.

At the time Rimsky-Korsakov was editing *The Golden Cockerel* for publication, and *The Snow Maiden* and *Boris Godunov* for the staging of these two operas in Paris.

A very pleasant event happened in February: Rimsky-Korsakov's daughter Nadya and Maximilian Steinberg announced their engagement. It was a pity that the joyful event coincided with a sorrowful one. Akhsharumov died at the age of seventy-nine. Yastrebtsev visited Rimsky-Korsakov on the day of the funeral and was glad to find him fairly well despite his mighty tiredness. Yastrebtsev recorded: "Rimsky-Korsakov said that recently an awfully eloquent student came around and offered to make him either an honorable member or a cofounder of some newly formed society of art and philosophy with an extremely broad scope. Speaking all of this, the student was spouting out citations of different philosophers, scholars and poets." Rimsky-Korsakov declined the honor, saying that he was too old and would be philosophically too illiterate for such a society.

Censorship Troubles

The Bolshoi Theatre in Moscow approved the staging of *The Golden Cockerel*, but it had to go through censorship first. That was when the trouble began. On 27 February 1908 Rimsky-Korsakov spoke on the telephone to Yastrebtsev, who recorded the conversation:

> The drama censors had crossed out plenty of things in the *Cockerel*. At first, he had received the libretto back without any changes, then (probably owing to

somebody's complaint) on the following day it was demanded back for reexamination. The result the second time was that the prologue, the epilogue, and many of Pushkin's words were crossed through, e.g., "King, lie on your side," "We are expecting an attack from the South, oops, the troops are approaching from the East," and so on. Meanwhile they left in some more controversial things. "What fools! I'm almost certain they do not know the fairy tale of Pushkin well."

On the same day another "musical Wednesday" party was held; it began at 8:30 p.m. and lasted until the early hours—3 a.m. Steinberg played his First Symphony, and N. Richter played a great number of pieces for the piano. As Yastrebtsev wrote: "By the end of the evening the youngsters began fooling around. Nikolay Ivanovich Richter mimicked Litvin, a singer, acting the part of Isolde in the scene where she throws herself into the arms of Tristan. He was so good at imitating her that we all split our sides with laughter.[5] [...] The next Wednesday is to be postponed, so, as Rimsky-Korsakov said, 'This Wednesday will be on Thursday.'"

Meanwhile, Rimsky-Korsakov's birthday was approaching. On the evening of 6 March his friends and relatives gathered to congratulate him on turning sixty-four. Among them were Lyadov and Glazunov, the Stravinsky brothers, Belsky, Lapshin, Mikhail and his wife, and Artsybushev. Yastrebtsev described the evening:

> Rimsky-Korsakov received a great many flowers. The living room and especially his study resembled the scenery from the fourth act of *Kitezh*. [...] During the tea, Rimsky-Korsakov lowered his voice so others would not hear and told me that his heart was getting weaker, that all this shortness of breath and short sighs speak louder than words, and that his body was prematurely aging. "Do you know" he continued, "my heart was absolutely healthy when I was young. I could swim round the ship two or three times. In the '80s I was able to swim no more than 3–4 *sazhens*. And at the beginning of the '90s I had to give up swimming completely. Almost at the same time, my sclerosis began to worsen. As you can see," he concluded, "everything is going on naturally and approaching one and the same end."

During the same party Lyadov told Rimsky-Korsakov that the latter was a kind of a "fossilized ichthyosaurus" compared to other modern men of art:

"Now we have just some sand and pieces of broken crockery. You will not see huge mountains and gigantic landscapes anywhere anymore."

Two days later Rimsky-Korsakov attended the third Russian Symphony Concert. Yastrebtsev wrote: "He was very serious and greeted me in a rather official manner. It turned out that in the morning Rimsky-Korsakov had an attack of heavy breathing, and this may have made him upset." Nonetheless, after the concert a lot of people went to Rimsky-Korsakov's home to celebrate his birthday once more. All in all, there were about thirty people. Vera Scriabina, the wife of Scriabin, who had just taken part in the symphony concert, was among the guests. At the party in Rimsky-Korsakov's home she played three etudes of her husband; Zabela sang the part of Tsarina Shemakhanskaya from the second act of *The Golden Cockerel*. Yastrebtsev described the party:

This evening was very lively and we laughed a lot. The Stravinsky brothers created a complete story consisting only of family names of singers, composers, and conductors. At first Rimsky-Korsakov was shocked at this nonsense but then he got involved and added some lines with Lyadov to the excitement of the guests, who were fooling around. [...] There were many toasts, as usual. This time, as soon as champagne was served, Blumenfeld stood up and proposed a toast to the health of the bride and the groom, i.e., to Maximilian and Nadezhda junior. Then we made a toast to Rimsky-Korsakov (he made a circle holding his glass and thanked everyone in person), to Rimsky-Korsakov's wife, and in turn to Lyadov, Blumenfeld, and Glazunov (who was absent), Steinberg, Vitol, and some others. There were two humorous toasts: one was proposed by N. I. Richter in very pretentious French (the youths begged him to do this), and the other one by Mitusov, who said that only here, in the family of Rimsky-Korsakov and owing to Rimsky-Korsakov in particular, only here did he "comb" his soul and did he long for such a "combing" to reach his full satisfaction. We all split our sides with laughter listening to those two toasts. We stayed at the Rimsky-Korsakovs' from 11:45 p.m. to 4:30 a.m. And Lyadov stayed even longer. As Steinberg and I were heading to the Island, the church bells called for the early service.

This happy, crowded party at Rimsky-Korsakov's home turned out to be the last large one.

Diaghilev had been preparing the next Russian Season in Paris, and since he could not imagine his concerts without Rimsky-Korsakov, he ordered a new portrait of him for the poster for the concerts. V. A. Serov was entrusted with the task. The artist came to Rimsky-Korsakov's house in the middle of March 1908 and created the portrait in charcoal very quickly, in just two sittings. This portrait became well-known later on. One of Rimsky-Korsakov's relatives noticed that the portrait resembled an icon. Serov responded, "Well, it should be like that. Let the French idolize him."

At the same time, the Opéra-Comique was preparing *The Snow Maiden* to be staged. In order to produce it as faithfully and as well as possible, since the French might try to distort it, Tcherepnin was sent to Paris at the composer's behest to conduct the opera. Tcherepnin wrote to Rimsky-Korsakov from Paris that all of his suggestions were treated as if they were the composer's own and were adopted without question. Nonetheless, Rimsky-Korsakov was horrified with the different "idiocies," as he called them, that the French tried to introduce into the production of the opera. Although Rerikh made beautiful sketches of the decor at the request of Princess M. K. Tenisheva, they were not used. Tcherepnin wrote to Nikolay:

> Among the sets I saw only that for the prologue, and there was one outrageous idiocy that was canceled after my prolonged negotiations. The thing is that after the scene where Frost talks to Spring, right when the chorus is singing behind the stage [...] and before it appears on the stage. the picture of a winter landscape (by the way, it is nice) all of a sudden is replaced with a *plein été* where the back curtain represents a Hungarian valley in full bloom with leafy bushes on the slopes of high mountains covered with a blue mist (it is from the last part of *Raymonda*), and exactly against this background the Berendeyans with their sledges barge into this beautiful scene. Don't you think it would be "charming"?! [...] Then I should mention that the closest advisor of Carais [the conductor]—his "ma foi," the evil genius of this production, is an old lady in a tremendous hat who is a maître de ballet by profession. Due to her, during the first stage rehearsal there were dances everywhere. I even hesitated to say whether it is a ballet called *The Snow Maiden*, and I think it will take enormous effort to exterminate this ugly loathsomeness. While I am here I will be safeguarding *The Snow Maiden* like an Alsatian dog.

Rimsky-Korsakov thanked Tcherepnin for taking such a special interest in his opera: "Stand up for native music in general and *The Snow Maiden* in particular."

In hopes of eliminating censorship requirements, Rimsky-Korsakov and Belsky asked V. A. Telyakovsky, who had served as the director of the Imperial Theatres in St. Petersburg since 1901, for help. Vladimir Telyakovsky admitted that the censors had overdone it when they banned Pushkin's verses. He discussed the matter with A. V. Belgard, the head of the press department, and the latter agreed to make some concessions and weaken the censorship requirements. Since this concerned only the libretto, Belsky altered the text a little and met with Belgard in person on the advice of Telyakovsky. Not long thereafter Belgard reported to Telyakovsky that all the changes that Belsky had made, with the exception of six lines, had been approved by the drama censors. Rimsky-Korsakov wrote to Boris Jurgenson, the publisher: "Reverting to the censorship issue, I am certain we should not change anything either in the score or in the libretto. The piano part and the score should be saved in their original form forever, and the libretto deserves the same. In the old novel of Paul de Kock the mother demanded that her daughter always use the word *topinamour* [artichoke] instead of *amour*, so we can adopt this technique for the stage as well."

Bilibin drew a wonderful picture for the program cover of that production. Although Rimsky-Korsakov felt tired, he was thinking about which plot to select for his next opera. He wrote to Belsky, who had earlier suggested the plot of *Heaven and Earth* by Byron:

> I need something plain, clear, and definite in terms of drama. Demonic personalities are not for me. Nihilism, great arrogance, and the like do not please me. […] I'd prefer something Russian, from folklore, but not necessarily; it might be something other than folklore, a tale like *Mozart and Salieri*, for example. I need rest and entertainment rather than destruction of worlds and rebellion against God. In addition, I don't think our art is capable of this. Literature can do it: it doesn't mind being a habitual liar.

Serious Illness

Rimsky-Korsakov tried to be cheerful; he attended opera performances, received guests—his friends, the youngsters, and others—and paid visits himself. Nevertheless, in the early morning of 11 April 1908 he suffered a serious asthma attack. Drs. Spengler and Borodylin were sent for immediately. Shortly afterward Rimsky-Korsakov felt a little better. The doctors diagnosed an attack of angina pectoris, or cardiac asthma, as they called it at that time. Not long before, Rimsky-Korsakov had become acquainted with Dr. Lazarev, who said that Nikolay's ashy complexion and chest distension while he was talking were bad signs and that the composer needed a complete rest. In her turn, Nadezhda complained that her husband had not been taking care of himself recently: he climbed stairs to the third, fourth, and even fifth floors in order to visit his friends, and he still went to bed very late. Rimsky-Korsakov asked her to send for Lyadov. The latter arrived and found the composer in his study lying on the couch in his robe. After the visit, Lyadov wrote to Korsakevich:

> The asthma attack has passed, yet he is very weak. Korsakov was very glad to see me; he thanked me and remembered my playing to him. I was afraid I would burst into tears, so I made myself out to be as composed as possible, which sobered me up. […] I think things are very bad. I'm so sorry for him! I felt so close to him and all his family. I have lived a huge part of my life with him and his family, and all those stupid misunderstandings were just bubbles produced by our stupid life.

Glazunov could not visit Rimsky-Korsakov due to his own illness. The next day he sent a letter to Rimsky-Korsakov and got the following response: "At this very moment I feel better, though my head is still not very good. The most awful thing is that this ugly attack that has occurred will inevitably happen again sooner or later and more than once. I obviously have to live with this for the rest of my life. Yet at present everything is all right."

Rimsky-Korsakov felt much better for the next few days, although he was very feeble. His friends visited him; Lyadov came daily. He wrote to Korsakevich: "This illness is of the kind that today you are all right and tomorrow [you] 'rest with the angels.' He was very pleased when I praised him for his *Golden Cockerel*. He thanked me, 'for me that is a great present for the holiday.'" (Easter was approaching.)

Yastrebtsev was also a frequent visitor. Nadezhda told him that he had a very beneficial effect on her husband and that Rimsky-Korsakov seemed to feel better in his presence. Yastrebtsev responded that Rimsky-Korsakov should know that he loved him sincerely with all his heart. On the evening of 15 April Yastrebtsev came to visit the family. Richter and Steinberg were there too. After dinner they all moved to the living room, where Richter played the second act of *The Golden Cockerel*. Vasily wrote:

> About 7:45 Rimsky-Korsakov seemed to feel like going to bed, and without saying a word he got up from the sofa quietly and headed to the study. Walking around the living room, I noticed that first he went to the window, paused there for a while, and then walked slowly to the sofa. (The study was in darkness.) He was already lying down when I came to say good-bye. His last words were, "You're welcome, my dear friend."[...] When I was about to leave, I closed the door to the study gingerly at the request of Rimsky-Korsakov's wife, and at this moment I suddenly felt such sorrow and horror. The lullaby melody from *The Golden Cockerel* kept running through my head for a long time and made me sick at heart.

A new acute asthma attack was not long in coming. It happened at dawn on 16 April. Rimsky-Korsakov's pain subsided only after an injection of morphine. He was told to have a complete rest. All visitors were banned, and Rimsky-Korsakov was told to abandon his favorite coffee and cigarettes. All this made Rimsky-Korsakov miserable. He did not leave his bedroom: he either lay in bed or sat in the armchair next to the bed dressed in his robe. Every day Lyadov and Glazunov came to Rimsky-Korsakov's home to inquire about his health; Cui also called. Yastrebtsev telephoned twice a day to find out about his condition. The newspapers *Slovo* (*The Word*) and *Rech'* (*Speech*) published information about Rimsky-Korsakov's illness. The sad news reached Kruglikov as well. The composer's wife wrote to him on 21 April:

> Unfortunately, the newspapers tell the truth. Indeed, Rimsky-Korsakov is seriously ill with cardiac asthma. He has experienced two utterly acute and painful asthmatic attacks. The first one took place during Holy Week. If after that he had taken care of himself and had had peace and quiet then in all likelihood the second one would not have happened at all, or at least not so soon. However, N. A. has been used to being so active and involved in everything that it was utterly impossible, in spite of all our efforts to force him to stay in bed and not receive visitors. As a result, on Wednesday night, during Easter week, there was another attack, after which he was much weaker. This time the doctors (there was a conference of three specialists) entirely forbade him to move, to do anything, or to receive any visitors. He obeyed their instructions. Today is the sixth day since

he last left his room. He lies in bed or sits in his armchair doing nothing. He has stopped smoking, drinking coffee, and eating meat. [...] The family are lavishing [their] care upon him and trying to do their best. Today we all are in high spirits because he is feeling better. But we are so anxious about the future. How can we manage to eliminate all negative effects, avoid any worries and agitation, which might cause the recurrence of more attacks?

Being concerned over Nikolay's illness, Igor Stravinsky, who was at Ustiluga (the Stravinsky estate), sent a letter to the family:

Dear Volodya and Andrey,

    I cannot say what weight sits heavy on my heart, how it bleeds. I think of my darling, beloved Rimsky-Korsakov every minute. I wish I could be next to him, know each tiny detail! And it takes such an unbelievably long time for letters to arrive. I've received your telegram. I beg you for only one thing—write to me. My dears, if you only knew how wretched I am. Write me as though you were writing to your brother, since Rimsky-Korsakov is very dear to me. You know that. I learned about N. A.'s illness from the newspapers and sent you a telegram immediately. [...] Thank your Mama for sending me a card. I am finishing my letter, for gloomy thoughts are not worth sending; you have enough of them without mine.

    Yours,

    Igor.

Little by little Rimsky-Korsakov was getting better. He could not be idle, so he begged the doctors to give him permission to look over the score of *The Golden Cockerel*; later he began working on his *Fundamentals of Orchestration*. At last guests were allowed to see the sick man, but only one visitor a day. Glazunov was the first to be received; the second was Lyadov, and the third, Yastrebtsev. The number of visitors gradually increased; Rimsky-Korsakov had only been moving around his house so far. However, the main concern that was so dangerous for the composer's health was about to happen. Despite the fact that the changes in the libretto of *The Golden Cockerel* appeared to have been approved, S. K. Gershelmann, Moscow's governor-general, was strongly against producing the opera even in its altered version. He sent a secret letter to A. V. Belgard in which he stated that he found the libretto improper and undesirable for staging, especially at the Imperial Theatres: "Although some phrases have been weakened in the censored copy, [...] all in all the meaning of the libretto, containing only a hundred verses from Pushkin's fairy tale, remains the same; it is insulting and scoffs at the tsar's dignity." Gershelmann cited several instances from the libretto in the same letter. In response to the letter, Belgard sent a telegram in code to Gershelmann: "Kindly withdraw the opera *The Golden Cockerel* from the repertoire by your order." Rimsky-Korsakov still was not aware of this development.

On 2 May Yastrebtsev visited him and wrote in his memoirs:

> We talked about the fact that Rimsky-Korsakov was feeling perfect that day, [and] that he had not felt so well for ages. In the morning he spent much of the time in his study working on his "orchestration." [...] Today Rimsky-Korsakov has been wearing his jacket already. He walked around the rooms; he peeped out behind the door of the dining room when I entered the hall; and he stayed in the living room for a long time. [...] Today I left at the very moment that the Rimsky-Korsakov family was about to have dinner and Vladimir Rimsky-Korsakov had come home after his [military] service. It was the first time I had seen him in uniform, and I thought he seemed extremely tall.

Move to Loubensk

At Rimsky-Korsakov's request, and since everyone assumed it would be beneficial for him, it was decided to take him to Loubensk as soon as possible. "I might not walk [...] farther than to the nearest bench there, though. How boring and unpleasant that is!" Rimsky-Korsakov said to Yastrebtsev. On the same day Nadezhda wrote to Kruglikov: "N. A. is much better. He walks around all the rooms, though very slowly; he carries on with his projects; he again began working on his textbook on orchestration. His coughing is over, and his heart is working a little better."

Among pleasant events, two premieres were held in theatres in Paris: the Opéra held *Boris Godunov* with Rimsky-Korsakov's orchestration on 6 May, and the Opéra-Comique presented *The Snow Maiden* on 7 May. Blumenfeld, who was in Paris at the time, wrote to the composer: "This is history that we are witnessing today! Two theatres in Paris are holding two Russian operas in the same week!" On 8 May 1908 Nikolay Konstantinovich von Boole, director of the Moscow department of the Imperial Theatres, wrote to Rimsky-Korsakov that *The Golden Cockerel* was not to be included in the repertoire of the coming season, which made the composer upset. The next day was Nikolay's name day, and many friends came to congratulate him. He could not receive most of the visitors because of his exhaustion. The hero of the day received a lot of flowers and was very pleased. He used to say that "a true man of art can't help cherishing flowers, admiring their beauty and delighting in their aroma."

The family had been preparing for the move to Loubensk. Andrey and Vladimir were dealing with some repair work in the main house on the estate. They were having the rooms covered with new wallpaper, the furniture reupholstered, and new curtains and portieres hung up. Mikhail, the eldest son, had rented a summer house not far from Loubensk in Utkina Muza, and Rimsky-Korsakov was happy about that. The move was scheduled for 21 May. Yastrebtsev as usual was a frequent guest at Rimsky-Korsakov's home, and he visited him on the eve of his departure. When he arrived, Rimsky-Korsakov had just gone to bed, so he went to Volodya's room.

Yastrebtsev wrote in his memoirs: "We talked about what had happened that day.... Shortly before my arrival Servigor [the doctor] had paid a visit and taught them how to give injections. He found Nikolay's condition pretty satisfactory but still recommended a complete rest. They might stay in Loubensk for the winter as well, since it will be utterly impossible, according to Volodya, to protect his father from unwanted worries, from various rehearsals that he is interested in, and exciting visits in the city." His memoirs continue:

> The next day at 8:30 sharp in the morning I was at the Warsaw Railway station. […] Rex was sitting between Rimsky-Korsakov and me in the lounge there. Rex was his favorite dog, whom he kept on a chain leash and cuddled during our conversation. When I mentioned the fact that I prefer bronze dogs to live ones, Rimsky-Korsakov contradicted me: "But what a wonderful heart living dogs have! That heart is the very thing which bronze dogs have a lack of." And he lovingly petted Rex, as it was wagging its tail. However, it was time to go to the train. This time God favored Nikolay. First, the coach (first class, no. 126) where he was to ride was placed right in front of the entrance. Second, by coincidence, a general with panache was going to ride in the same coach, so a plank covered with red cloth was placed between the platform and the carriage door; thus, Rimsky-Korsakov was spared not only excessive walking but also the necessity

to climb the stairs into the carriage. As one can see, generals may be useful sometimes! [...] On the whole, Rimsky-Korsakov was in high spirits. However, yesterday, after looking through Leonid Andreyev's "Seven Hanged Men," he had to take bromide before going to bed, since this story had made him upset and irritated at the same time. At 9 a.m. sharp the train set off. Before I got off the coach we kissed each other heartily four times. Gilyanov turned up. I asked Rimsky-Korsakov to let me know how his journey to Loubensk was, and he certainly promised to do so. Rimsky-Korsakov persistently invited me to Loubensk any time, and especially to the wedding.

It was decided that the wedding of Nadezhda, his youngest daughter, to Maximilian would be on 4 June 1908 in Loubensk, where the whole of Rimsky-Korsakov's family would be staying. Andrey, who came back to St. Petersburg, told Yastrebtsev that Rimsky-Korsakov had arrived in Loubensk safe and sound, but during the first night he had experienced another asthmatic attack, though not a very serious one. Yet even after that he had either to lie down or sit in an armchair for a whole week. By 31 May 1908 Rimsky-Korsakov felt somewhat better. He could walk around his room, and, seizing any good-weather opportunity, he sat on an armchair on the balcony. His wife decided to arrange for a doctor to look after Nikolay's health for the summer. But he objected to this mightily. Nadezhda sent a letter to her son, Volodya, who had gone back to St. Petersburg: "I talked about the doctor. Papa said that I should do as I was told, that it is an unnecessary luxury, and the last [thing was] that the young doctor was not reliable. When I raised the same issue for the second time, Papa said that I should abandon that idea and he didn't feel like discussing it anymore."

On 2 June 1908 Rimsky-Korsakov wrote to Kruglikov in what would be the composer's last letter to him:

> At present I'm feeling a little better. I go out not only on the balcony but also to the park; I move very slowly and just a little. The third attack put sad thoughts into my head that despite the treatment and precautions it turns out that I am not safeguarded against these hateful attacks at all. But what can be done! I have begun working. I will try to further my long-conceived textbook or notes on orchestration. I'm glad that you like the "Golden Cockerel." [...] In a day there will be Nadya's wedding, very plain, in a country style. The season is nice—lilacs, acacias, apple trees in bloom—but the weather is very changeable.

Nadezhda and Maximilian's wedding ceremony took place not far from Loubensk, in the parish church in Kritsy on N. N. Tiran's estate, to which the local inhabitants of Loubensk and Vetchasha belonged. Rimsky-Korsakov did not feel too bad, but he did not go to the ceremony and instead stayed at home with his daughter Sophia. Local peasant girls met the newlyweds at the gate of the estate. Rimsky-Korsakov was on the doorstep of the dacha and sprinkled them with oats in accordance with the custom at the time.

The next day Rimsky-Korsakov sent a letter to I. Kobylin's shop in which he asked them to send him "two dozen [sheets] of writing paper with blue lines and necessarily of the best quality. The kind of paper on which ink does not run and bleed through as sometimes happens with such paper." On the same day Rimsky-Korsakov received a letter from Telyakovsky in which he reported that things were not going well with *The Golden Cockerel*: "The Moscow governor-general is against producing this opera and has submitted his opinion to the censorship committee; therefore, I think they will reject it in St. Petersburg as well." In addition, he received a letter from Paris. Rimsky-Korsakov might not have worried so much about the letter; nonetheless, it too left an unpleasant feeling in its turn. The letter said that the Society of Musical Writers in Paris did not want to accept Rimsky-Korsakov as their member, and therefore they were unwilling to pay for the royalties for the production *The Snow Maiden* in Paris.

The emotional experience caused by the failure to produce *The Golden Cockerel* resulted in another asthma attack, though not a very bad one. The next day, 6 June, Rimsky-Korsakov continued his work on his textbook on orchestration and seemed to be calmer. He wrote a letter to Jurgenson in which he described the sad fate of *The Golden Cockerel* and asked whether he could try to promote the production of *The Golden Cockerel* in Paris with the assistance of Michel-Dimitri Calvocoressi, a French musicologist and advocate of Russian music.[6] (Recently some pieces from the opera had been successfully performed at a concert in Paris.) This letter was the last one that Rimsky-Korsakov wrote.

Last Days

Rimsky-Korsakov spent his last days surrounded by all of the members of his family. Mikhail, who was about to go away on business, arrived in Loubensk as well. Being frightened by the attack that had occurred on the night of 6 June, everyone tried to follow each of Nikolay's steps, actions, and movements. Rimsky-Korsakov was very happy about the arrival of his eldest son and talked to him a great deal. On 7 June 1908 Rimsky-Korsakov worked again for a long time and finished the conclusion to his textbook. (This manuscript has the last date written down by the author.) During the day he walked a lot in the garden and counted how many times he went down to the garden from the balcony. He walked very slowly, and when he went up the stairs to the balcony he rested for fifteen seconds on each step.

Later the composer's son Andrey reminisced:

> It was a lovely day in June. The Loubensk garden park was full of scents. The spring, delayed by the cold weather in May, asserted itself after the third quarter of May. Hundreds of apple trees, valleys of violet and white lilacs, bushes of sweet-scented Chinese peonies, berry bushes, acacias, and fresh green leaves of centenarian oaks and birches turned the damp air of the park into a kind of heavy, rich atmosphere, like a hothouse or a forcing frame. There were huge, beautiful bouquets of flowers in each room and on the balcony. The ocean of large apple trees covered with pink-and-white flowers like milk produced a unique effect. [There were more than a thousand apple trees in the Loubensk garden.] The apple trees were edged with violet pathways of lilacs. N. A. admired all of this paradise with its symphony of colors and fragrances from the balcony. During the second part of the day N. A. put on his jacket and his usual headgear—a blue cap—took his walking stick, and stepped down a few stairs very slowly to the garden, and at the same slow pace he walked around all his favorite places accompanied by Mikhail Rimsky-Korsakov. [The next day the servants at the Loubensk dacha would say he had said farewell to everything.]

Then Rimsky-Korsakov sat on the bench behind the estate gate for a long time enjoying the colors of the sunset that were so dear to his heart. After tea the composer played the piano a little without sitting down. Then he retired to his bedroom. Andrey's reminiscences continued:

> By nighttime the air was threatening a storm. Heavy, stuffy air filled the rooms. It was difficult to fall asleep even though all the windows were open. The white night was tormented and filled with restless, painful presentiments. At some

minutes past 2 we heard hurried steps and a knock on the door. In a moment my brother and I were in Papa's room. He was sitting in the armchair next to the bed, breathing heavily with short sighs and demanding a morphine injection. N. N. was heating water for his feet. [...] It took just a few minutes to boil the syringes thoroughly and to give orders to send a horseman to bring the doctor. My brother and I gave him two injections: one of morphine and the other one of camphor. But contrary to our hopes, the desired effect did not occur. At this time we heard a short but severe thunderclap followed by the noise of a summer downpour. A few minutes of dreadful agonizing anxiety.... All of his sudden short rapid sighs were replaced by a long. torturous exhalation; N. A.'s gaze became fixed, and one thought was engraved on the minds of those around him: death.... Only an hour or even more later I burst into tears while I was writing a telegram to Glazunov, and the words were dancing before my eyes: "Today, this night, after another attack, Rimsky-Korsakov was gone for good."

When the doctor arrived, everything came to an end. He simply issued the death certificate. Vladimir Rimsky-Korsakov also remembered his father's demise: "I remember Papa's face, how it was changing when his life was leaving, and later as he was lying attired and surrounded with bouquets of lilacs in the large hall of the Loubensk house."

Dr. Krogius was brought to Loubensk in order to embalm Nikolay. On 10 June 1908 his body was transported to St. Petersburg, to the church of the Conservatory. The next day the burial service took place. (Nikolay Smiryagin, a priest, officiated at the service.) The funeral procession for his mass headed to the cemetery of the Novodevichy Convent,[7] where the remains of the great composer were buried. Glazunov delivered a speech at the grave of his teacher and friend: "We are deprived of a man the like of whom never existed in this world before and will probably never come again. Rimsky-Korsakov was a great genius with a keen intellect and a big heart. He was always striving for lofty ideals."

Many articles appeared in the St. Petersburg newspapers giving detailed information about Rimsky-Korsakov's last days, and about his death and funeral. Kruglikov was informed immediately about Nikolay's end and in turn passed on the news to most of the publishers and editors of the Moscow newspapers.

Epilogue

On the ninth day after Nikolay's death, the funeral service was held in the church of the Novodevichy Convent. Afterward Glazunov wrote to Kruglikov: "From the churchyard I made straight for the home of the deceased. I think Nadezhda has taken the family grief much harder than the other members. She has a stark look." Rimsky-Korsakov's death left a mark of sadness and suffering on her face that remained there for the rest of her life. Her endless care of her children, even though they were already married, could not suppress that hard feeling of irreparable loss.

Four years later the plain wooden cross at Nikolay's tomb was replaced with a wonderful headstone in the shape of an ancient Novgorod cross. It was paid for by his wife. Andrioletti, a sculptor chosen by Rerich, cut the gravestone from white marble. Rimsky-Korsakov was thought to have originated from the Novgorod region because at that time Tikhvin was part of it. First Nadezhda wanted to find an original ancient Novgorod cross and even went to Novgorod, accompanied by her son Vladimir, to buy one. However, such a cross turned out to be too plain, unprepossessing, and small. Then, with the assistance of Mitusov, she wrote to Rerich, one of his relatives, with the request that he design a tombstone in an old Novgorod style. Rerich was an admirer of Rimsky-Korsakov's music and undertook the project gladly. He designed a beautiful cross on which he portrayed Jesus and the Saints. The cross was placed at the top of the hill and surrounded with marble flagstones, with an inscription in Slavic ligature carved along them: "Rimsky-Korsakov. 6 March 1844–8 June 1908."

As Vladimir Rimsky-Korsakov reminisced:

> Rerich watched the erection of the cross in person and was very concerned to make the memorial look old. The flagstones were placed unevenly on purpose. There were cracks put in some places, and gaps were left between the flagstones in order to allow earth to be placed there and grass to grow. Rerich polished all the marble with oil so it would not be too white and seem older and darkened by time. Indeed, he produced a cross monument that doesn't exist anywhere else.

The hill symbolized the top of a burial mound and was sown with grass and edged with flowers the whole summer. Blue lobelias were placed there in the form of a wreath, which made the whole composition look livelier. (Blue was Nikolay's favorite color.)

A year after his father's death, Vladimir married Olga Gilyanovskaya, a sister of his friend Mikhail Gilyanovsky and a frequent guest of the Rimsky-Korsakov family. Vladimir and his wife lived apart from his mother, so that Nadezhda lived in her apartment with only her son Andrey. However, in 1914 Andrey married Julia Veisberg, a former Conservatory student of the composer, and gave up living with his mother.

During the hard years after the 1917 Revolution Nadezhda had to abandon her apartment. Later it was occupied by strangers and turned into a communal apartment. She moved in with Andrey but was destined to live there only a little while. She refused to be inoculated for a second time during an epidemic of smallpox, fell sick with the disease, and in May 1919 died from that awful illness. First she was buried at the same Novodevichy cemetery as her husband, but far from Rimsky-Korsakov's tomb. In 1927 they succeeded in placing her remains under the same monument with a cross in a small underground crypt similar to her husband's.

Nadezhda was a loving wife and faithful companion of Nikolay, and his assistant in all of his musical activities. Andrey wrote: "If the total amount of the legacy bequeathed to us by Rimsky-Korsakov seems so improbably enormous, then time and again we should remember with great gratitude his partner, who created the conditions that allowed him to spread his wings so widely and to give life to his poetic creations."

Soon after Rimsky-Korsakov's death Nadezhda began sorting out his papers, and as early as 1909 the first edition of *My Musical Life* was published under her editorship. She was the first person to promote the idea of establishing a museum devoted to Rimsky-Korsakov.

Three memorable places have become his museums to date: the house in Tikhvin, where he was born; the St. Petersburg apartment, in which he spent his last fifteen uniquely creative years, and the estate in Loubensk, where he died, which is united into one museum with the neighboring one at Vetchasha. Yet the best monument to Rimsky-Korsakov is his music.

Notes

Chapter 1: Beginnings

1. Tikhvin is a small town located 200 kilometers (124 miles) south of St. Petersburg. The first mention of Tikhvin is in 1383. In 1560, the Monastery of Dormition of the Mother of God was built on the left bank of Tikhvinka River by order of Tsar Ivan the Terrible. The monastery hosts the famous icon of the Tikhvin Mother of God, which attracts many pilgrims each year.

2. This and the following dates in this book (unless otherwise stated) are given in the Old Style. Although the Gregorian calendar replaced the Julian in much of Europe beginning in 1582, Russia and other Orthodox countries did not adopt the New Style until the twentieth century. In Russia the Gregorian calendar was adopted after the act of 24 January 1918 signed by Vladimir Lenin. In the nineteenth century, the gap between calendars is twelve days and in the twentieth century, the difference is thirteen days. Orthodox churches all over the world still use the Julian calendar for their rites.

3. Kronstadt is a Russian town and port, located 30 kilometers (19 miles) west of St. Petersburg near the head of the Gulf of Finland. It was built by Peter the Great in 1703 as a naval base and fortress to defend the larger city. The town is famous for the Naval Cathedral of Saint Nicholas, built by order of Nicholas II between 1903 and 1913 in the Russian late Neo-Byzantine style.

4. This was the November Uprising, also known as the Cadet Revolution or the Polish-Russian War of 1830–1831, which followed years of rising tensions in Poland after its 1815 partition among Russia, Prussia, and Austria. The uprising, initiated by a group of Warsaw cadets and eventually involving hundreds of thousands of troops, was ultimately crushed, and Poland's autonomy was extinguished until after World War I.

5. Étienne Nicolas Méhul (1763–1817) was a French composer. Considered one of the most notable opera composers of his time in France, his greatest success was *Joseph* (1807). Luigi Cherubini (1760–1842) was an Italian composer who spent most of his working life in Paris. His most significant compositions include operas and sacred music, and he influenced Beethoven's *Fidelio*. Alexey Nikolayevich Verstovsky (1799–1862) was a Russian composer. After first composing light operettas in the opera-vaudeville style, he turned to serious operas, writing six, of which the most successful was *Askold's Tomb* (1835), the first Russian opera staged in the United States.

6. Zhitomir is a small city in the northwest part of Ukraine. The first mention of Zhitomir dates from 1240.

7. *Gostiny dvor* is a term for an indoor market. The name translates as "Guest Court" or "Merchant Yard." Such structures were built in every large Russian town during the first decades of the nineteenth century, are fine examples of neoclassical architecture. One of the finest examples is Great Gostiny Dvor, designed by French architect Jean-Baptiste Vallin de la Mothe, on Nevsky Prospect in St. Petersburg. It is the first shopping center in the city and also one of the first shopping arcades in the world.

8. The Amur, which means "big river," forms the border between the Russian Far East and China.

9. Vasilyevsky Island is the biggest island in the Neva River delta in St. Petersburg. Its famous buildings include the Kunstkamera museum, the Old Saint Petersburg Stock Exchange and Rostral Columns, St. Petersburg State University, the St. Petersburg Academy of Science, and the St. Petersburg Academy of Art. Two bridges connect the island to the center of the city.

10. Chudovo is a town in Russia's Novgorod province, located on the highway connecting Moscow and St. Petersburg.

11. At that time there were two theatres opposite each other: the Bolshoi Theatre (it was later reconstructed and became the Conservatory) and the Theatre-Circus (the theatre was later destroyed by fire; the Mariinsky Theatre was built in its place).

12. Rimsky-Korsakov is referring to Friedrich von Flotow (1812–1883), a German composer active mainly in France and best known for his operas *Martha* (1847) and *Alessandro Stradella* (1844).

13. There are several rules for writing "You" and "you" in the Russian language. The one used in this book refers to writing "You" as a polite way of addressing friends and acquaintances and/or in personal correspondence with officials. Another example of writing "You" can be found in official documents when addressing an individual. But in letters between close relatives or between two persons who know each other well, "you" is used.

14. *Robert le diable* (1831) is a five-act opera by Giacomo Meyerbeer with a libretto written by Eugène Scribe and Casimir Delavigne. It was strongly influenced by the operas of Spontini and by Rossini's *Guillaume Tell*. *Mosè in Egitto* (1822) is a three-act opera written by Gioachino Rossini to a libretto by Andrea Leone Tottola and is based on Francesco Ringhieri's play *L'Osiride* (1760). *I puritani* (1835), in three acts, is the last opera by Vincenzo Bellini. Its libretto by Count Carlo Pepoli is based on *Têtes rondes et cavaliers*, by Jacques-François Ancelot and Joseph Xavier Saintine, which some sources suggest is based on Sir Walter Scott's novel *Old Mortality*. *Norma* (1831) is a tragic opera in two acts by Vincenzo Bellini with a libretto by Felice Romani.

15. *Lucrezia Borgia* (1833) is an opera with a prologue and two acts by Gaetano Donizetti to a libretto by Felice Romani, based on the play *Lucrèce Borgia* by Victor Hugo.

16. *La vestale* is an opera in three acts by Gaspare Spontini (1774–1851) with a libretto by Étienne de Jouy, completed in 1805 and first performed in 1807.

17. *Fenella, ou La muette de Portici* (*The Mute Girl of Portici*), originally called *Masaniello, la muette de Portici*, is a grand opera in five acts by Daniel Auber, with a libretto by Germain Delavigne revised by Eugène Scribe. The opera was first performed at the Salle Le Peletier of the Paris Opéra on 29 February 1828. *Askold's Tomb*, or *Askold's Grave*, was the most successful of Alexey Verstovsky's six operas. It was influenced by Weber's *Der Freischütz*. First performed in 1835 (a year before Glinka's *A Life for the Tsar*), *Askold's Tomb* became the most popular Russian opera of the nineteenth century. It had about two hundred performances in St. Petersburg and four hundred in Moscow just in its first twenty-five years. *The Mermaid* (*Russalka*, 1856) is an opera in four acts by the Russian composer Alexander Sergeyevich Dargomizhsky, based on a story by Pushkin.

18. *Le corsaire* is a ballet in three acts, with a libretto by Jules-Henri Vernoy de Saint-Georges and music by Adolphe Adam. The first performance of the ballet took place at the Théâtre Impérial de l'Opéra in Paris on 23 January 1856.

19. Goulard's extract is a solution of lead acetate and lead oxide that was used as an astringent during the eighteenth, nineteenth, and early twentieth centuries. It was named after its inventor, French surgeon Thomas Goulard.

20. Cesare Pugni (1802–1870) was an Italian composer of ballet music, a pianist, and a violinist. Pugni is most noted for the ballets he composed for Her Majesty's Theatre in London (1843–1850). In 1851 he became ballet composer of the St. Petersburg Imperial Theatres and the Court of His Imperial Majesty in St. Petersburg (1850–1870). Pugni is perhaps the most prolific ballet composer of all time, having supposedly contributed parts or all of the music to over 300 ballets. The ballet *Elerz e Zulmida* (1826) was the first wholly by him. From 1831 to 1834 he also wrote five operas and some orchestral music.

21. The krakovienne is a Polish dance that originated in Krakow. The mazurka is a lively Polish folk dance in triple meter, from the Mazovian region of Poland. The mazurka rhythm shifts emphasis to the weak beats of the bar.

22. The *Kamarinskaya* was composed by Glinka in 1848. It influenced Mily Balakirev, Alexander Borodin, and Nikolay Rimsky-Korsakov. Pyotr Ilyich Tchaikovsky supposedly called it the acorn from which the oak of later Russian symphonic music grew.

23. Nikolay Rimsky-Korsakov meant that he would like to purchase either some musical scores or staff paper on which he could write some music.

24. An overture to the opera *Iphigénie en Aulide* by Christoph Willibald von Gluck (1714–1787).

25. "In Flat Dales" is a Russian folk song written in 1810, purportedly (the authorship is disputed) by Alexander Merzlyakov (1778–1830), a Russian poet and a professor at Moscow University.

26. Maslenitsa (Pancake Week) is the week before Lent begins in the Orthodox Church, usually in February or March.

27. The Mariinsky Theatre is a historic opera and ballet theatre in St. Petersburg, where many stage masterpieces by Tchaikovsky, Musorgsky, and Rimsky-Korsakov were premiered. The original theatre, used by the Russian opera troupe in the 1850s, was the Theatre-Circus, which burned to the ground in 1859. Tsar Alexander II ordered it to be rebuilt. When it reopened in 1860 it was renamed the Mariinsky in honor of Empress Maria Alexandrovna.

28. Helsingborg is a city in Sweden in the Oresund region in north-west Scania, and is Sweden's closest point to Denmark. The Danish city Helsingborg is clearly visible on the other side of the Oresund about 4 kilometers (2.5 miles) to the west.

29. An aiguillette (from the French word for "small needle") is a braided cord frequently worn as a decoration on military uniforms (usually hanging from the shoulder) and sometimes formal academic dress, typically indicating a certain rank or honor.

30. Vladimir Vasilyevich Stasov (1824–1906) was a Russian art historian and critic. The son of the architect Vasily Petrovich Stasov (1769–1848), he graduated from the Imperial School of Jurisprudence in 1843 and joined the Imperial Public Library in 1845. He studied in Italy from 1851 to 1854, and after his return to Russia he rejoined the library and was admitted to the Imperial Academy of the Arts in 1859. He was a mentor to the group of composers known as "The Five." Although Stasov was not a creative artist himself, he encouraged a great amount of creativity in others and was the source of inspiration for operas that included Rimsky-Korsakov's *Sadko*, Borodin's *Prince Igor*, Musorgsky's *Khovanschina*, and Tchaikovsky's *Tempest* and *Manfred*. The *Tempest* was dedicated to Stasov. His writings and criticism cover the whole artistic spectrum: architecture, history, painting, and sculpture, in addition to music. (*Sobranie sochineniy V. V. Stasova*: 1847–1886, St. Petersburg, 1894, and *Vladimir Vasilevich Stasov. Selected Essays on Music*, Barrie and Rockliff, The Cresset Press, London, 1968.)

31. A government apartment refers to an apartment paid to reward naval, military, and/or governmental services. Voin was granted a government apartment for his naval services, while Nikolay was given one for his services at the Chapel.

32. Eli Parish (1808–1849) was an English harpist and composer who developed many innovative harp techniques. He changed his name to Elias Parish Alvars. From the early 1830s he lived mainly in Vienna, although he gave concerts in Germany in 1830 and Italy in 1833.

Chapter 2: The Sailor

1. *Almaz* means "diamond" in Russian.

2. The *sazhen* is a measure of length used in the nineteenth century. One *sazhen* equals seven feet, eight and one-eighth inches.

3. We think that Rimsky-Korsakov's mother is referring to the portrait of Saint Nikolay, the patron saint of sailors, merchants, archers, thieves, children, and students in Russia and elsewhere.

4. The port of Tilbury is located on the River Thames at Tilbury in Essex, not far from London.

5. Alexander Ivanovich Herzen (1812–1870) was a Russian writer and philosopher known for his promotion of socialism. His most important works include the novel *Who Is to Blame?* and the memoir *My Past and Thoughts*. One of Russia's largest universities, the Herzen State Pedagogical University in St. Petersburg, was named after him.

6. The Crystal Palace, built in 1851, no longer exists; it was burned down in 1936.

7. *Ruy Blas*, an opera written and composed by William Howard Glover (1819–1875), an English composer, conductor, and music critic, was first produced on 24 October 1861 at Covent Garden.

8. Anton Rubinstein's Symphony No. 2, *Ocean*, has seven movements, the result of many revisions over twenty-nine years. The original symphony, written in 1851, had four movements.

9. Nikolay Nikolayevich Lodyzhensky (1843–1916) was a composer and a diplomat born in St. Petersburg. His family was related to the Russian composer Alexander Dargomizhsky. In 1866 he joined The Five, led by Mily Balakirev. In 1873 he published his Six Romances for voice and piano. Rimsky-Korsakov and Stasov liked his early compositions, but criticism of his later works led him to stop composing and pursue a career as a diplomat.

10. The Free Music School, which existed from 1862 to 1917, was organized by Mily Balakirev and Gavriil Yakimovich Lomakin to teach singing, organize concerts, and encourage interest in the music of the New Russian School. The Free Music School was funded by ticket sales, annual dues from permanent supporters, entrance fees, donations, and subsidies. From 1871 to 1900 the School received free space for classes and use of the Duma Hall for concerts. The directors of the School were Balakirev and Lomakin (1862–1868), Balakirev (1868–1873), Rimsky-Korsakov (1874–1881), Balakirev again (1881–1908), and Sergei Mikhailovich Lyapunov (1908–1917). Subjects included solfeggio, solo and choral singing, music theory, and violin lessons. The concert program determined the educational content; choir practice and rehearsals took up most of the time. The Free Music School reached its peak of activity under Lomakin's directorship.

11. Korsinka was a nickname for Rimsky-Korsakov. His friends used to address him by that name in their letters.

12. Much of the music from that orchestral piece was transferred wholesale to Rimsky-Korsakov's opera *Sadko*.

13. Alexander Nikolayevich Serov (1820–1871) was a composer, music critic, and champion of Richard Wagner. He was the father of the famous painter Valentin Serov. His works include three operas, *Judith*, *Rogneda*, and *The Power of the Fiend*, all of which premiered at the Mariinsky Theatre and went on to great success. His operas influenced later composers: Musorgsky with his crowd scenes, Tchaikovsky with his dances, and Borodin with his folk-like choruses.

14. Tver is a city in Russia's Tver Oblast, north of Moscow. Founded in 1135, it was formerly the capital of a powerful medieval state in the Russian Empire.

15. Pargolovo used to be a favorite holiday resort for the St. Petersburg intelligentsia. Countess Sophia Bobrinskaya's summer cottage there welcomed Pushkin; the critic Stasov spent his vacation in the village of Starozhilovka, where he was visited by the composers Glazunov and Rimsky-Korsakov, the painter Vasily Vereshchagin, the singer Fyodor Chaliapin, and others. Nikolay and Nadezhda Rimsky-Korsakov were married in Pargolovo, at the Church of Sts. Peter and Paul, on 30 June 1872.

Chapter 3: Falling in Love

1. Matuta is one of the characters from Rimsky-Korsakov's opera *The Maid of Pskov*.

2. "Children" refers to Musorgsky's song cycle *Detskaya* (*The Nursery*).

3. Rimsky-Korsakov was a severe critic of his own music, so he often used the adjective "bad" to describe compositions of his that, in his opinion, suffered from imperfections and needed further development. Olga and Nanny are two characters in *The Maid of Pskov*; the author meant the pieces he had composed for their parts.

4. Vyborg is a town in Leningrad Oblast, Russia, located 130 kilometers (81 miles) northwest of St. Petersburg. The town was originally a fortress built by Swedes in 1293 on a small island.

5. Pheophil Matveyevich Tolstoy (1809–1881) was a music critic and composer. He composed romances and the opera *Il birichino di Parigi*, which was staged in Naples in 1832 and in St. Petersburg in 1849. Later Tolstoy concentrated more on music criticism. From 1850 he worked for the newspapers *Severnaya pchela* (*The Northern Bee*), *Golos* (*The Voice*), *Moskovskie vedomosty* (*The Moscow Bulletin*), and the *Journal de St.-Pétersbourg*.

6. *Sorochinskaya yarmarka* (Sorochintsy Fair) is a comic opera in three acts composed by Modest Musorgsky between 1874 and 1880 in St. Petersburg, based on the plot of this tale.

7. Sonechka was the nickname for Nadezhda Purgold's eldest sister, Sophia.

8. The Vetche was an assembly of citizens in ancient Russia.

9. In the Russian language, the middle name of a child is always derived from his or her father's first name. In archaic Russian, a male child's name would be rendered in the possessive case; for example, if the father's name was Andrey, the middle name

would be Andreyev. In modern Russian, this has been modified, and nowadays an adjectival form is used, so that the name instead would be Andreyevich. It seems that the archaic form was still used in those days for church records.

10. Later on, Semeyon Akhsharumov married Sophia Purgold.

11. Lake Lugano (Italian: Lago di Lugano or Ceresio) lies on the border between Switzerland and Italy.

12. Nikolay Pavlovich Molas was the brother of Mikhail Pavlovich Molas. The latter was a rear admiral who fell in combat on the battleship *Petropavlovsk* in 1904.

13. The author's account of this event is not entirely clear. In 13 February 1873, Tchaikovsky writes from Moscow in a letter to his brother Modest: "When I was in Petersburg, I played the finale one evening, and the whole company was so excited that, in their delight, they nearly tore me to pieces, and Mme. Korsakova begged in tears to arrange the music for four hands. Oh well, let her do it!" In a letter to his publisher, Vasily Bessel, he wrote: "Regarding the symphony, I believe it would be best if Mme. Korsakova took it upon herself to make the arrangement. With the exception of Laroche, apart from me, I cannot think of anyone else who could do it so well." Later Nadezhda withdrew from the task and Tchaikovsky made an arrangement himself, sending it to Bessel on 25 May with the suggestion that Mme. Korsakova should review it and, if necessary, make corrections.

14. Apollon Nikolayevitch Maikov (1821–1897) and Nikolay Grekov (1810–1866) were Russian poets.

15. Osip Afanas'yevich Petrov (1806–1878) was a famous bass singer of that time at the Mariinsky Theatre. He sang the part of Ivan the Terrible in Rimsky-Korsakov's *The Maid of Pskov*.

16. Eduard Frantsevich Napravnik (1839–1916) was a Czech opera conductor and minor composer. He became organist at the Mariinsky Theatre and assistant conductor in 1863, second conductor in 1867, and chief conductor in 1869, a position he held until his death. He conducted the first performances of many operas, including *Boris Godunov* by Musorgsky, five by Rimsky-Korsakov, and five by Tchaikovsky.

17. Herman Augustovich Laroche (1845–1904) was a well-known critic of Rimsky-Korsakov's and Tchaikovsky's music. He began writing music at the age of five. After graduating from the St. Petersburg Conservatory in 1866, he worked as a professor of music history and theory at the Moscow Conservatory (1867–1870 and 1883–1886) and the St. Petersburg Conservatory (1872–1875 and 1879).

18. *Tucha* is Russian for "cloud."

19. Mishka, Misha, and Mishkin are nicknames for the proper name Mikhail. Nadushonok is a diminutive nickname of Nadya.

20. This address to Nadezhda Nikolayevna as "Madam Admiral" was the natural outgrowth of the nickname by which her husband was known to Stasov.

21. The Great Hall of the Assembly of the Nobility in St. Petersburg now hosts the Shostakovich St. Petersburg Academic Philharmonia. The building was constructed in 1834–1839. It was originally designed to host the organization of the local administration, along with charitable events, concerts, and balls. In the second half of the nineteenth century the building became recognized as a center of musical culture in St. Petersburg and attracted Russian and foreign composers and musicians, including Hector Berlioz, Franz Liszt, Gustav Mahler, and Richard Wagner.

Chapter 4: A Busy Musical Life, 1874–1881

1. Vasily Vasilyevich Bessel (1843–1907) was a Russian music publisher. He studied violin, viola, and music theory at the St. Petersburg Conservatory. He co-founded the publishing house V. Bessel and Co. in 1869 and a print shop in 1871 in St. Petersburg, which published works by Russian composers including Balakirev, Borodin, Cui, Dargomizhsky, Musorgsky, Rimsky-Korsakov, Rubinstein, and Tchaikovsky. He was also a writer.

2. Gregorio Allegri (1585–1652) was an Italian composer and and singer of the Roman school. His *Miserere*, a setting of Psalm 51, brought him fame and was admired by Mozart and other composers.

3. Sonya is a nickname for Sophia.

4. Terti Ivanovich Philipov was a collector of Russian folk songs and the chair of the Council on Songs, under the aegis of the Russian Geographical Society.

5. Uncle "Oh!" was the brother of the composer's wife's father, Nikolay Purgold.

6. Sonka is a nickname for Sophia.

7. Mishuk is a nickname for Misha.

8. Nadyushart is a nickname for Rimsky-Korsakov's wife.

9. Dr. K. A. Rauchfuss was a famous pediatrician. There is a renowned children's hospital named after him in St. Petersburg. The hospital received its first patients on 25 May 1905 and is still in existence. The Children's Hospital was built in a series of separate buildings to prevent the spread of infectious diseases.

10. Ilia Fedorovich Tyumenev (1855–1927) was Rimsky-Korsakov's student in composition and theory and later his librettist for his operas *Pan Voevoda* and *The Tsar's Bride*.

11. Andryushka is a nickname for Andrey.

12. *Khovanschina* means "During the Times of Prince Khovansky." The fantasy referred to is Rimsky-Korsakov's *Fantasy on Serbian Themes*.

13. By "The Hymn" the composer probably means the tsarist national anthem, "God Save the Tsar."

14. Pavel Ivanovich Blaramberg (1841–1907) was a self-taught Russian composer of songs and stage works, a writer, and a professor at the Moscow Philharmonic

School (from 1878) and at the Moscow Philharmonic Society's Music and Drama School (1886–1898). He helped Balakirev to establish the Free School of Music in 1862. As a composer he was not much appreciated by other musicians and composers. Rimsky-Korsakov did not like his music and Cui described his music as "dry." Fyodor Dmitriyevich Gridnin was a publisher of a musical journal and the manager of the concerts of D. M. Leyonova.

15. Rimsky-Korsakov means Stasov; Bach was his nickname.

16. A *kalach* is a kind of fancy bread roll.

17. The sixteenth-century Arkhangelsky Sobor (Cathedral of the Archangel) stands on Cathedral Square in Moscow's Kremlin. It was commissioned by Ivan the Great (1440–1505) and constructed between 1505 and 1508 under the supervision of an Italian architect, Aleviz Fryazin Noviy. The new edifice was built over the site of an earlier cathedral dating from 1333.

18. Nadezhda is referring to Fyodor Mikhailovich Dostoevsky (1821–1881).

19. Ilya Yefimovich Repin (1844–1930) was a Russian painter and sculptor of the Peredvizhniki artistic school. Khamovniki and Plyuschikha are remote districts of Moscow.

20. Prechistinka and Molchanovka are parts of Moscow.

21. Nikolay Andreyevich added to the name of his little daughter, Sophia, the ending "scha," which means "huge" Sophia.

22. This nanny was hired when Sonya was born and had been living with the family ever since. She brought up all of the rest of the children. An illiterate former serf born somewhere in the Vyatsky region, she was loved by everyone in the family and lived with them until her death twenty-three years later. Nikolay Andreyvich remembered that once the nanny was walking through the rooms with a baby in her arms and singing her own lullaby. On noticing that the baby had fallen asleep, she whispered, "Madam, open the bed, he has fallen asleep," and kept on singing.

23. A *pannochka* is an unmarried daughter of a landlord (*pan*). The same names were used in the Ukraine, where the events related in a story by Gogol took place.

Chapter 5: *The Snow Maiden*, September 1881–June 1884

1. Rimsky-Korsakov's opera *The Snow Maiden* was based on Alexander Nikolayevich Ostrovsky's (1823–1886) play of the same name, written in 1873. One of Ostrovsky's plays is the 1859 drama *Groza* (*The Storm* or *The Thunderstorm*). Janáček, Rimsky-Korsakov, and Tchaikovsky drew upon Ostrovsky's work. Tchaikovsky wrote an overture called *The Storm* at the end of his studies under Anton Rubinstein. Ostrovsky was friendly with many musicians. He founded an Artists' Circle in Moscow with Nikolay Rubinstein in 1865.

2. They were the main characters of the tale and also became the main characters of the opera.

3. Berendey is a kindly fairy-tale character, an inhabitant of the forest. The name of the tsar in Ostrovsky's fairy tale was Berendey.

4. *Yarilo* means "sun" in Old Russian.

5. A *verst* is an old Russian measure of distance equivalent to 3,500 feet or 0.6 miles (1.06 kilometers). Luga is about thirty versts from Stelevo.

6. *Zakaznitsa* means "a woman who gives orders." *Podberezyevskaya* means "under the birch trees." *Volchinets* means "a place where there are a lot of wolves."

7. Podberezie stems from "under the birches," Kopytets from the word for hoof, Dremyach from the word for drowsiness, and Khvoshnya from the word for horsetail.

8. Being very old, Maria used a stick for walking, and Balakirev called it her third leg.

9. Saint Alexander Nevsky Lavra is the monastery in St. Petersburg named for Alexander Nevsky. It was founded by Peter the Great in 1710. One of the cemeteries is the Tikhvin Cemetery, where many famous people were buried, including Cui, Glazunov, Glinka, Musorgsky, Rimsky-Korsakov, Tchaikovsky, and Stasov.

10. The Baltic Railway Station still exists in St. Petersburg.

11. The Battle of Shipka took place during the Russo-Turkish War of 1877–1878.

12. Kharkiv, or Kharkov, is the second-largest city in the Ukraine. It was founded in 1654.

13. The Nebolsins had been friends of Rimsky-Korsakov since his first visit to Nikolayev.

14. Rimsky-Korsakov is referring to the writer Ivan Sergeyevich Turgenev (1818–1883). His best-known play, *A Month in the Country*, was written in 1850 and later influenced Chekhov. His most famous novel is *Fathers and Sons* (1862).

15. Khlestakov is the leading character in Gogol's *The Inspector-General* (Revizor, 1836), a satire on life in provincial Russia.

16. Arthur Nikisch (1855–1922) was a Hungarian conductor and teacher.

17. Franz Liszt was the honorary head of the organization Der Allgemeine Deutsche Musikverein.

18. Baba Yaga is a witch in Russian folk tales.

19. Rimsky-Korsakov had heard this bird's song before and used it in the music of the prologue to *The Snow Maiden*.

20. *Biryulki* (*Spillikins*) is a musical cycle for piano written by Lyadov.

21. There is a memorial plaque on the wall of the hotel with the names of famous people who stayed there. Rimsky-Korsakov's name is among them.

22. This pianist was Felix Mikhailovich Blumenfeld.

23. Nikolay Fyodorovich Sazonov (1843–1902) was a famous actor. In 1863, Sazonov joined the troupe of the Alexandrinsky Theatre in St. Petersburg. He was a

remarkable actor and performed twenty-five parts in Ostrovsky's plays. Pelageya Antonovna Strepetova (1850–1903) was a well-known actress. She was invited to play at the Alexandrinsky Theatre in 1881. One of her best roles was Katerina in Ostrovsky's drama *Groza* (*The Storm*).

24. Chatyr-Dag is a mountain range in Crimea. In the Crimean Tatar language *çatır* means tent and *dağ* means mountain. Alushta is a resort town on the Black Sea in Crimea. The Aluston fortress was founded in the sixth century by Emperor Justinian I to serve as a defensive citadel.

Chapter 6: Transitions and Travels

1. The Nobility's Assembly Rooms in Moscow were built in the first half of the eighteenth century. The building belonged to the Moscow governor-general Vasily Dolgorukov-Krymsky, and it was was later purchased by the Moscow Assembly of the Nobility. The whole of aristocratic Moscow would gather there for dazzling balls. Lev Tolstoy described this building in *War and Peace*, and Pushkin's description of a ball held in the Assembly Rooms is included in his poem *Yevgeny Onegin*. Several notable concerts were given there by Liszt, Rachmaninov, Rimsky-Korsakov, and Tchaikovsky.

2. The Iversky Gate of the Kremlin, also known as the Resurrection Gate (or Iberian Gate), is the only remaining gate of the Kitay-gorod in Moscow. Kitay-gorod, settled in the eleventh century, is one of the oldest parts of Moscow. Although the name can be translated as "Chinatown," it is probably derived from *kita* (wattle) and refers to the wall that surrounded this early Kremlin suburb.

3. *Rasstegai* is a meat or fish pie. Evstafi Stepanovich Azeyev was a teacher of choral singing; Stepan Alekseyevich Smirnov was the conductor of the Chapel choir.

4. According to the Russian Orthodox Church tradition, a name given to a child has to be the name of a saint, each of whom has an official holiday in the Church calendar. That day is also celebrated as something like a second birthday, and in fact, one's name day is traditionally of greater importance than one's actual birthday. In direct translation from Russian, this is the "Day of your Angel," since the saint for whom you were named is supposed to protect you throughout your lifetime. Many Russians, even those who do not have a strong connection to the Orthodox Church, continue with this practice and celebrate their name days.

5. Admiral Nikolay Ivanovich Kaznakov (1834–1906) was an acquaintance of Rimsky-Korsakov from Nikolaev.

6. The Armory Palace is located inside the Kremlin walls. It dates back to the fourteenth century. It was a storehouse for state treasures until 1813. Now it is a museum.

7. Archpriest Dmitriy Vasilyevich Razumovsky was a prominent historian of Orthodox Church singing and a professor of Church singing at the Moscow Conservatory.

8. The Trinity–St. Sergius Lavra is located in Sergiev Pasad, 74 kilometers (46 miles) northeast of Moscow.

9. Old Peterhof, a suburb of St. Petersburg, is about 29 kilometers (18 miles) from the city and the location of Peter the Great's Summer Palace, often regarded as the Russian Versailles.

10. Gatchina is a suburb of St. Petersburg.

11. A reference to Adelina Patti (1843–1919), the famed Italian soprano. She performed in major European and American cities, from Moscow and St. Petersburg to London, Paris, New York, and San Francisco.

12. Nikolay Mikhaylovich Potulov (1810–1873) was an amateur musicologist and composer who in 1873 published his *Handbook for the Practical Study of the Ancient Chant of the Orthodox Russian Church* as well as numerous harmonizations of the common (Obikhod) chants used in the Russian Orthodox Church, which are rendered in simple four-part harmony for men's chorus.

13. From 1721 to 1917, the Holy Synod, comprising a council of eleven bishops, was the highest governing authority of the Russian Orthodox Church.

14. Dimitry Bortniansky was director of the Imperial Court Chapel at the time of Alexander I (r. 1801–1825).

Chapter 7: Completing the Work of Others, 1884–1889

1. Mikhail Fabianovich Gnessin (1883–1957) was a Russian composer and teacher. In 1901, he entered the St. Petersburg Conservatory, where he studied under Rimsky-Korsakov, Glazunov, and Lyadov. He was expelled from the Conservatory for taking part in a student strike during the Revolution of 1905, but was readmitted the following year. Later he taught at the Gnessin State Institute in Moscow, where Khachaturian was one of his pupils. He mainly composed music based on Jewish themes.

2. Sergei Mikhailovich Lyapunov (1859–1924) was a Russian composer and pianist. He studied composition with Taneyev and graduated from the Moscow Conservatory with a gold medal in 1883. In 1885 he moved to St. Petersburg, where he became director of the Free Music School until 1908 and a professor at the St. Petersburg Conservatory from 1910 to 1923. He composed in the style of Chopin, Schumann, Mendelssohn, Balakirev, and Liszt. Along with Balakirev and Lyadov, he was commissioned by the Imperial Geographical Society to collect Russian folk songs. He served as assistant director of the Imperial Chapel from 1891 to 1902. Lyapunov died in Paris in 1924.

3. *Rimsky* means Roman in Russian, hence Stasov's nickname for him—Rimlyanin, a man from Rome.

4. Today Simbirsk is the city of Ulyanovsk, renamed by the Soviet communists to honor Lenin, whose real name was Vladimir Ulyanov. Tsaritsyn got its name in the

sixteenth century, but it was renamed Stalingrad in 1925 in honor of Josef Stalin; in 1961, after Stalin's death, the communists gave the city its current name—Volgograd.

5. Today Tiflis is the city of Tbilisi, the capital of Georgia. Tiflis (in Russian) was the name of the city until 1936.

6. The author's comments that "Belyaev was 'absolutely uninterested in the timber trade, and on leaving the business he received a rather large share of the capital'" seem somewhat misleading: Richard Beattie Davis, in the *New Grove Dictionary of Music and Musicians*, states that Belyaev joined the timber business at the age of fifteen. In addition, an article by M. Montagu-Nathan (*Musical Quarterly* 4, no. 3 [1918]: 454) states that upon "leaving school, he went straight into his father's business, and at thirty years of age was taking a prominent part in its management." Also, "only after his first attempts at music publication (of Glazunov's First Symphony) did he abandon the timber business. He turned the concern into a company, reverting to the position of shareholder, and in June 1885 opened a music publishing house in Leipzig" (again according to Montagu-Nathan).—*Eds.*

7. Glazunov was responsible for creating and orchestrating the overture from the main themes in the opera *Prince Igor* and his memory of Borodin playing it on the piano. Glazunov also used a few scraps of the overture completed by Borodin, but he said later that he had to compose much of the overture himself (*Russkaya muzikalnaya gazeta*, 1986).

8. Church readers in the Russian Orthodox Church are members of the lesser clergy responsible for chanting prayers during services. "Paskha Krasnaya" (Beautiful Easter) is one of the traditional hymns (*stithira*) sung during the paschal midnight service (matins) in the Orthodox Church.

9. *Paskha* is a rich mixture of sweetened curds, butter, and raisins eaten at Easter, traditionally after having been blessed by a priest.

10. Stepan Gedeonov studied at the Faculty of History and Philology at the University of St. Petersburg from 1833 to 1835. In 1850, he was appointed as assistant for a Russian archaeological commission in Rome. In 1863, he returned to Russia and was appointed the first director of the Hermitage Museum—a position he held until his death in 1878. While still acting as director of the Hermitage, in 1867 Gedeonov was appointed director of the Imperial Theatres. In 1870 he wrote a scenario for a fantastic ballet entitled *Princess Mlada*. The music for this ballet was to be written by Alexander Serov, with choreography by Marius Petipa. Serov's death in 1871, however, caused Gedeonov to change his original plan, and his scenario was eventually transformed into a libretto for an opera-ballet, with music to be written by Minkus and with musical scenes by Borodin, Cui, Musorgsky, and Rimsky-Korsakov—each of whom was to contribute an act. However, this fantastic opera-ballet was never performed in this form.

11. This schedule of eating would have been considered light and healthy by Russian standards of the day, since upper-class Russians would have been used to a more substantial breakfast and a fourth meal later in the evening.

12. Édouard Juda Colonne (1838–1910) was a French conductor and violinist and founder of the Concerts Colonne. He helped popularize compositions by Berlioz, Tchaikovsky, and Wagner.

13. The reference is to the well-known painting *The Ninth Wave* (1850) by the Russian painter Ivan Aivazovsky.

Chapter 8: Recognition, 1888–1891

1. May was the last name of the principal of the school where Misha studied.

2. Chichikov and Plyushkin are characters in Gogol's novel *Myórtvyjye dúshi* (*Dead Souls*), first published in 1842.

3. He was a son of A. I. Krakay, a well-known artist and architect of that time.

4. A gymnasium was a kind of secondary school or high school in tsarist Russia.

5. D'Aust was a Belgian musician and manager of the society Concerts Populaires.

6. Herrings from the shop that belonged to Glazunov (not a musician) were considered at that time in St. Petersburg to be the most delicious.

7. Suzdal is an ancient Russian city, not far from Moscow, that is famous for its great number of churches and church paintings.

8. St. Panteleimon is believed to help those who are sick.

9. The English Palace (in New Peterhof) was built by order of Catherine the Great in 1781–1789. It is no longer in existence, as it was destroyed in the Second World War.

10. Andrey Petrovich Rimsky-Korsakov, Rimsky-Korsakov's father.

11. *Pietät* means "piety" in English.

12. Nevsky Prospect was and still is the main street in the center of St. Petersburg.

13. A gonfalon, or gonfanon, is a flag or banner used in a religious procession in Christian churches. They are usually made of canvas and silk and are painted with Jesus Christ, the Virgin Mary, and saints.

Chapter 9: "I Fell Out of Love with Music," 1891–1892

1. After the loss of his mother, this was how the composer addressed his wife.

2. *Author's Note:* More than a century has passed since that time, but the tombstone is still in good order today; the marble has only darkened slightly.

3. "God's spark" is a direct translation; it means to be talented or gifted. Rimsky-Korsakov transformed the Russian idiom "God's gift," which can be compared to the English-language idiom "to be kissed by God."

4. Eduard Hanslick (1825–1904) was a well-known Viennese music critic, a fierce opponent of Wagner, and a strong admirer of Brahms. His most famous work is *Vom*

Musikalisch-Schönen (On the Beautiful in Music). George Henry Lewes (1817–1878) was an English philosopher and literary and theatre critic.

5. Émile Hennequin (1858–1888) was a French art and literary critic and the author of *La critique scientifique* (1888). Baruch Spinoza (1632–1677) was a Dutch philosopher. Herbert Spencer (1820–1903) was an English philosopher.

6. Alfons Erlicki (1846–1902) was a Polish physician, neurologist, and psychiatrist. From 1880 he worked at the Military Medicine Academy in St. Petersburg.

7. Vasily Ilich Safonov (1852–1918) was a pianist, conductor, and professor who was appointed director of the Moscow Conservatory in 1889. He established popular concerts in Moscow and later conducted frequently in New York and London. Tchaikovsky dedicated No. 5, "Méditation," of his Eighteen Pieces, Op. 72 (1893), to Safonov.

8. Gennady Petrovich Kondratyev (1834–1905) was a bass-baritone solo singer who in 1872 became director of the Mariinsky Theatre. He staged the first performance of *The Snow Maiden* in 1882.

9. The Russian Moguchaya Kuchka (Mighty Handful) was also called the Russian Five or the Mighty Five, was made up of a group of five composers—Balakirev, Borodin, Cui, Musorgsky, and Rimsky-Korsakov—who around 1865 united their efforts to create a national school of Russian music. The group's Russian name was coined in a newspaper article by Stasov in 1867. [By 1872, the members of the group were beginning to show their individuality and starting to go their own ways. They were also becoming more independent of Balakirev. —*Eds.*]

10. The private school of Stoyunina was established in 1881. Stoyunin, Stoyunina's husband, was a well-known teacher; he was the inspector of the school as well as a teacher of Russian, philology, and history.

11. Poprischin is the main character in Gogol's novel *Diary of a Madman*.

Chapter 10: Return to Musical Life

1. To welcome someone by presenting them with a loaf of bread and some salt (which in old Russia was traditionally sprinkled on the bread before eating) is an old Russian custom that shows respect for the person to whom it is given.

2. Yet Rimsky-Korsakov continued to write on the aesthetics of music. Some other drafts dated later were found among his papers after he died.

3. One of the family members was Vasily Tatishchev (1686–1750), a statesman, ethnographer, and author of the first full-scale history of Russia.

4. Vasily Andreyevich Zhukovsky (1783–1852), a famous Russian poet, also translated works by Byron, Goethe, Homer, and Schiller.

5. The new building was erected in front of the Mariinsky Theatre. Earlier this space had been occupied by the Bolshoi Theatre, which was built to the design of the

architect Thomas de Thomon. The theatre was rebuilt in 1805. On New Year's night in 1811 it burned down. Then it was rebuilt again, then renovated, and at last in 1891 demolished. The new building was designed by V. V. Nicolas. The special ceremony for the opening of the building took place on 12 November 1896. The day before, Yastrebtsev wrote: "Tomorrow is the opening of a new Conservatory building. However, R.-K. does not remember where all his medals are. Moreover, he doesn't know how, and in what order, and how many he should attach to his tailcoat."

6. Sergey Konstantinovich Bulich (1859–1921) was a Russian linguist and music historian. Bulich was born in St. Petersburg but studied at Kazan University. He worked primarily in the field of Russian and Slavic linguistics. He was a professor of Russian language at the Higher College for Women from 1891 and later was appointed as a director of the College (in 1910). (Rimsky-Korsakov's daughter Nadya studied there.) In addition to his immense works on linguistics, Bulich wrote reviews of several music books and also articles on music and musicians, publishing them in the periodicals *Rus'* and *Vestnik Evropi*.

7. The theatre of Solodovnikov was a private opera theatre established in 1885 by Savva Mamontov. It was located in Moscow in a building on Bolshaya Dmitrovskaya Street, known as the "Solodovnikov Theatre." It was built in 1894–1895 by the Russian merchant Gavrila Solodovnikov (1826–1901).

8. Apollinary Mikhaylovich Vasnetsov (1856–1933) was a Russian artist. He carried out the design of the décor for Rimsky-Korsakov's opera *The Snow Maiden*, which was staged by Mamontov's theater in St. Petersburg in 1898. Stasov was very impressed by Vasnetsov's decorations and said that he "had never seen anything like this before." Mikhail Aleksandrovich Vrubel (1856–1910) was a Russian painter who participated in the décor for Rimsky-Korsakov's operas *Sadko* and *Tsar Saltan*. Valentin Alexandrovich Serov (1865–1911) was a Russian portrait painter who painted Rimsky-Korsakov's portrait in 1898. Isaac Ilyich Levitan (1860–1900) was a Russian landscape painter. Konstantin Alekseyevich Korovin (1861–1939) was a Russian impressionist painter. Mikhail Vasilyevich Nesterov (1862–1942) was a Russian painter who mainly worked in the style of religious symbolism. Vasily Dmitrievich Polenov (1844–1927) was a Russian landscape painter.

9. Abramtsevo is an estate located north of Moscow, not far from the Trinity–St. Sergius Lavra. It was an intellectual and artistic center that played a significant role in the development of Russian culture in the nineteenth century. The estate was purchased by Savva Mamontov in 1870.

Chapter 11: From *Mozart and Salieri* to *Tsar Saltan*, 1897–1899

1. Apollon Nikolayevich Maikov (1821–1897) was a Russian poet. Maikov's poems were the inspiration for songs by Tchaikovsky and Rimsky-Korsakov.

Rimsky-Korsakov wrote several songs based on the poems by Maikov, including Octave, *What Am I Dreaming About*, *Nymph*, *The Singer*, and *Quiet Is the Blue Sea*.

2. It was included in the complete set of Rimsky-Korsakov's works published in 1970.

3. Nadezhda Ivanovna Zabela-Vrubel (1868–1913) was a Russian operatic soprano. She graduated from the St. Petersburg Conservatory in 1891 and made her debut in 1893 with the I. Setov operatic troupe in Kiev. She married the Russian artist Mikhail Vrubel in 1896. From 1897 to 1904 Zabela-Vrubel was a principal soprano in Savva Mamontov's Private Russian Opera, and from 1904 to 1911 she was a soloist at the Mariinsky Theatre in St. Petersburg. Her beautiful voice was an inspiration for Rimsky-Korsakov. She sang roles in several of his operas, including Volkhova in *Sadko*, Swan Princess in *The Tale of Tsar Saltan*, Snegurochka in *The Snow Maiden*, Marpha in *The Tsar's Bride*, Princess in *Kashchey the Immortal*, and Fevronia in *Kitezh*.

4. A *saklya* is a Caucasian mountain hut.

5. Vladimir Rimsky-Korsakov is referring to Ivan Alexandrovich Goncharov (1812–1891), a Russian novelist best known as the author of the novel *Oblomov* (1859).

6. Elizabethgrad, a city in Ukraine, was founded as a fortress in 1754 and was named after Saint Elizabeth. It is now Kirovograd, as it was renamed in 1939.

7. Once Rimsky-Korsakov told Belsky that, in general, one could compose on any text, even on a customs bill, since the composer considered his own text of the libretto to be very bad and compared it to a customs bill.

8. The Russian student demonstrations of February 1899 refer to the events that began with a celebration of the eightieth anniversary of St. Petersburg State University on 8 February. There were several confrontations between the police and the students who were celebrating the anniversary, some of which were very violent and resulted in the arrest of more than fifty students. Later the demonstrations spread to the Moscow University and Technological Institute and many other locations in both St. Petersburg and Moscow. More than twenty-five thousand students may have participated in the demonstrations.

Chapter 12: Travels and Triumphs, 1899–1901

1. The Benois family was active in the artistic life of nineteenth- and early twentieth-century Russia. Louis Jules Benois came to Russia after the French Revolution. His son Nicholas was an architect in the early nineteenth century. Nicholas had several children, including Leon Benois, who followed his father's profession; Alexandre Benois was a painter and designer for the theatre and collaborated with Stravinsky on *Petrushka* and with Diaghilev for the Ballets Russes.

2. Bauer was a famous Berlin café at the time that the Rimsky-Korsakov family used to visit when they were in Germany.

3. Rimsky-Korsakov is referring to Paul Gilson (1865–1942), a Belgian musician and composer.

4. *Le démon* (1890) is a dramatic cantata by Paul Gilson in two acts for soloists, choir, and orchestra based on a text by Mikhail Lermontov.

5. Rimsky-Korsakov is making a joke to his children that the director, Bérendés, has a similar name to the character King Berendey in his opera *The Snow Maiden*.

6. It is not clear whether the main theme from the early orchestral tone poem *Sadko* or that from the opera *Sadko* was included in this concert. The composer borrowed music from the tone poem for use in the opera.

7. Nadezhda Rimsky-Korsakov is quoting Prosper Mérimée (1803–1870), the French dramatist, historian, and short story writer best known for his novella *Carmen* (the basis of Bizet's opera), who, in one of his love letters to Jenny Dacquin, had attributed this piece of advice to an "old diplomat" friend. In 1874 Dacquin published these letters anonymously as *Lettres à une inconnue* (Letters to an Unknown Woman), revealing her identity only in 1892.

8. The first letter in the titles of the operas *Saltan*, *Sadko*, and *Snow Maiden*.

9. This painting is now displayed in the Tretyakov Gallery in Moscow.

10. *The Voevoda* (1891) is a symphonic ballad by Tchaikovsky after Mickiewicz. The first performance was in Moscow on 4 November 1891. The term *voevoda* refers to a military commander and governor of a province in old Russia.

11. The text of this address can still be seen in the study at the Rimsky-Korsakov House-Museum in St. Petersburg.

Chapter 13: "My Own Monastery—My Art," 1901–1902

1. *Night on Bald Mountain*, by Modest Musorgsky, was completed on 23 June 1867.

2. Viktor Antonovich Dobrzhinsky became a volunteer for the Russian Army in 1914 and was killed in World War I.

3. "Nad. Nik." refers to Nadezhda Nikolaevna, the composer's wife.

4. *Shchi* is a kind of Russian soup usually prepared with sauerkraut.

5. The saying is: If there is too little salt in food, it's all right, and it can be served, but if there is too much, you'll have too much on your back. In other words, it's better for something to be underdone than overdone. "You'll have too much on your back" means being beaten with a stick.

6. The composer was working on *Pan Voevoda*.

7. Meiringen is a town in Switzerland, famous for the Reichenbach Falls.

8. Nadezhda is referring to Ferdinand August Bebel (1840–1913), a German socialist. In 1869 he and Wilhelm Liebknecht founded the Social Democratic Workers' Party of Germany.

9. Alexander Tikhonovich Grechaninov (1864–1956), a student of Tchaikovsky and later of Rimsky-Korsakov, was a Russian composer. He wrote three operas and also church music. He immigrated to the United States in 1939 and died in New York at the age of 92.

10. Nadezhda Rimsky-Korsakov is referring to Sergey Ivanovich Taneyev (1856–1915), a Russian composer, pianist, and teacher of composition. Taneyev studied at the Moscow Conservatory under Tchaikovsky and Nikolay Rubinstein. He wrote his opera *Oresteia* in 1894. Taneyev was an eminent teacher; among his students were Rachmaninov, Scriabin, and Grechaninov. Taneyev was the soloist in the Moscow premiere of Tchaikovsky's First Piano Concerto in 1875. Tchaikovsky was impressed by Taneyev's performance and later asked Taneyev to be the soloist in the Russian premiere of his Second Piano Concerto. After Tchaikovsky's death, Taneyev also completed and premiered Tchaikovsky's Third Piano Concerto. Tchaikovsky dedicated his symphonic poem *Francesca da Rimini* to Taneyev.

11. In 1872 Stasov became director of the art division of the National Public Library of Russia in St. Petersburg. It is now known as the State Public Saltykov-Shchedrin Library, and is the oldest public library in Russia.

12. "Gesund blibe [*sic*] grüsse" is written in German. It means "stay healthy, greetings."

13. Lelya is a nickname for Elena.

14. The maiden name of Mitusov's mother was Golenischeva-Kutuzova. She was a former singer who had graduated from the St. Petersburg Conservatory with high honors. Mitusov was the last name of her first husband. Her second husband was Count Pavel Arsenevich Putyatin.

15. It was customary at that time in German universities to be dressed in a tailcoat to defend a doctoral dissertation.

Chapter 14: The Last Russian Music

1. Alexander Eduardovich Spengler was the family doctor of the Glazunovs; later he became a regular physician of the Rimsky-Korsakov family.

2. "Impromocable" is a made-up word meaning "not getting wet," taken from the Russian word *promok* ("get wet") and the French prefix *im-* ("not").

3. It turned out to be only short-lived. Under the Soviet regime, after the Revolution in 1917, all this capital was confiscated. The publishing house of Belyaev, in St. Petersburg, ceased to exist, and the publishing house in Leipzig was merged with another German enterprise.

4. Irina Vladimirovna Troitskaya (Golovkina after her marriage), a granddaughter of Rimsky-Korsakov, is the author of the novel *Pobezhdennye* (*The Defeated*), about the dramatic fate of the nobility after the Soviet Revolution; the novel was written in 1963 but not published until 1992. Its original title was *Swan Song*.

5. The Great Bridge was just a piece of marshland covered with birch saplings or small tree trunks for people and carriages to pass over. Local people named it the Great Bridge.

6. Ermolay Alekseyvich Lopakhin is one of the main characters in *The Cherry Orchard*. He bought the orchard in order to cut down most of the trees so as to build houses there for profit. The play, written by Anton Pavlovich Chekhov (1860–1904), was first performed in 1904.

7. A. V. Bukharova was the owner of the Loubensk estate.

8. Nadya studied at the Higher College for Women until she was expelled from it for her participation in the 1905 student demonstrations. She went on to study at Lesgaft High College, which is now the P. F. Lesgaft National State University of physical culture, sport, and health located in St. Petersburg.

9. On 9 January 1905, the police fired at a peaceful demonstration held at the Winter Palace in St. Petersburg; many demonstrators were killed.

10. A. B. Bernhard was director of the St. Petersburg Conservatory at the time of the 1905 Revolution.

Chapter 15: "Live and Love Living," 1905–1906

1. Alexander Ilyich Siloti (also Ziloti, 1864–1945) was a Russian pianist and conductor. Nikolay Grigoryevich Rubinstein (1835–1881) was a Russian pianist, conductor, and composer. He was the younger brother of Anton Rubinstein and a close friend of Pyotr Ilyich Tchaikovsky. He served as director of the Moscow Conservatory from 1866 until he died in 1881 in Paris.

2. Presumably the owner of the country estate.

3. Presumably the bell was used to summon the servants.

4. "Step" (The Steppe) is a short story by Anton Chekhov that was published in 1888 in Russia.

5. The battleship *Prince Potemkin* was a pre-dreadnought battleship (Bronenosets design) of the Imperial Russian Navy's Black Sea fleet, commissioned in 1903 with a crew of 800. The ship was made famous by a rebellion of the crew against their oppressive officers in June during the 1905 Russian Revolution. It later came to be viewed as the first action of the Russian Revolution of 1917 and was the basis of Sergey Eisenstein's silent film *Battleship Potemkin* (1925).

6. Mikhail Rimsky-Korsakov was an entomologist by profession.

7. *Letopis' moey muzikal'noy zhizni* (*My Musical Life*).

8. By "them" Rimsky-Korsakov means "modern" composers.

9. Arapka was the dog belonging to the Rimsky-Korsakovs' daughter Nadya.

10. While taking refuge at Wartburg Castle in 1521, Martin Luther completed a translation of the New Testament from Greek to German.

11. Stepan (better known as Stenka) Razin was a leader of un uprising against the nobility and the tsar's regime in the southern parts of Russia in 1670.

12. "Dubinushka" ("Cudgel") is an old work song. The words are after a poem by B. Bogdanov (1865), and the music is a Russian traditional tune. "Dubinushka," the oaken cudgel, symbolizes a struggle against injustice and mistreatment.

13. Feliia Vasilevna Litvin (real name: Françoise-Jeanne Schütz, 1861–1936), sometimes written as Felia Litvinne, was a dramatic soprano born in Russia into a family of French and German origin. She performed in major opera theatres around the world, singing in French, German, Italian, and Russian. As an outstanding Wagnerian singer, her roles included Isolde in *Tristan and Isolde*, Kundry in *Parsifal*, and Brünnhilde in the *Ring* cycle.

14. His father's grave still existed when Rimsky-Korsakov asked this question. But during the Soviet period it was demolished along with the other tombs located on the grounds of the Tikhvin Monastery of the Assumption.

15. A "narrow chest" indicated that the person was suffering from tuberculosis or some other serious ailment—Eds.

Chapter 16: The Last Opera: *The Golden Cockerel*

1. The Chornaya Sotnya or Chernosotentsy (Black Hundreds) was a nationalist movement in Russia (1905–1917) supportive of monarchism, and their main ideologies were Orthodoxy, autocracy, and nationality. The first meeting of the party known as "Russkoye sobraniye" (Russian Assembly) was held in St. Petersburg in October 1900.

2. Rimsky-Korsakov is referring to Arrigo Boito (1842–1918), the Italian composer, poet, and librettist most famous for his opera *Mefistofele* and for his librettos to Giuseppe Verdi's *Otello* and *Falstaff*.

3. In accordance with the Russian tradition of that time, funeral wreaths had ribbons with words written on them indicating for whom the wreaths were intended (e.g., "To My Beloved Husband") and from whom they were presented (e.g., "from his mournful wife"), or just a family name (e.g., "from the Rimsky-Korsakovs").

4. Maria Nikolayevna was a daughter of Nikolay Dmitrievich Kuznetsov, the painter of a famous portrait of P. I. Tchaikovsky. She took the double last name when she married Albert Nikolayevich-Benois, also an artist.

5. Nikolay Nikolayevich Tcherepnin (1873–1945) was a Russian composer, pianist, and conductor. He was born in St. Petersburg and studied under Rimsky-Korsakov at the St. Petersburg Conservatory.

Chapter 17: Final Days, September 1907–June 1908

1. Nikolay Karlovich Medtner (1880–1951) was a Russian composer and pianist.

2. *The Dark* (original title *T'ma*) was a novella written in 1907 by Leonid Niko-laievich Andreyev (1871–1919), a Russian dramatist, novelist, and short story writer.

3. The Pskovo-Pechyersky Lavra is a monastery situated not far from Pskov, an old Russian city. The monastery was founded in 1392.

4. Schismatic sects in Russia have existed since the seventeenth century. A hermitage is a small and secluded monastery.

5. Feliia Vasilyevna Litvin was a large soprano with a beautiful voice.

6. Michel-Dimitri Calvocoressi (1877–1944) was born in France of Greek parents. A multilingual writer, translator, and music critic, he wrote several books on music and composers, including three on Modest Musorgsky. He was an advisor to Sergey Diaghilev and a strong advocate of Russian music.

7. The cemetery of the Novodevichy (The New Maiden) Convent is a historic cemetery in the southwest part of St. Petersburg.

Index